STATUTORY PRIORITIES IN CORPORATE INSOLVENCY LAW

Markets and the Law

Series Editor:
Geraint Howells
Lancaster University, UK

Markets and the Law is concerned with the way the law interacts with the market through regulation, self-regulation and the impact of private law regimes. It looks at the impact of regional and international organizations (e.g. EC and WTO) and many of the works adopt a comparative approach and/or appeal to an international audience. Examples of subjects covered include trade laws, intellectual property, sales law, insurance, consumer law, banking, financial markets, labour law, environmental law and social regulation affecting the market as well as competition law. The series includes texts covering a broad area, monographs on focused issues, and collections of essays dealing with particular themes.

Other titles in the series

The Future of Consumer Credit Regulation
Creative Approaches to Emerging Problems
Edited by Michelle Kelly-Louw, James P. Nehf, and Peter Rott
ISBN 978-0-7546-7417-7

Electronic Commerce and International Private Law
A Study of Electronic Consumer Contracts
Lorna E. Gillies
ISBN 978-0-7546-4855-0

Human Rights in the Market Place
The Exploitation of Rights Protection by Economic Actors
Christopher Harding, Uta Kohl and Naomi Salmon
ISBN 978-0-7546-4694-5

For more information on this series, visit www.ashgate.com

Statutory Priorities in Corporate Insolvency Law

An Analysis of Preferred Creditor Status

CHRISTOPHER F. SYMES
Flinders University, Australia

ASHGATE

Published by
Ashgate Publishing Limited
Wey Court East
Union Road
Farnham
Surrey, GU9 7PT
England

Ashgate Publishing Company
Suite 420
101 Cherry Street
Burlington
VT 05401-4405
USA

www.ashgate.com

British Library Cataloguing in Publication Data
Symes, Christopher F.
Statutory priorities in corporate insolvency law : an analysis of preferred creditor status. - (Markets and the law)
1. Priorities of claims and liens - Australia 2. Bankruptcy - Australia
I. Title
346.9'4077

Library of Congress Cataloging-in-Publication Data
Symes, Christopher F., 1957-
Statutory priorities in corporate insolvency law : an analysis of preferred creditor status / by Christopher F. Symes.
p. cm. -- (Markets and the law)
Includes bibliographical references and index.
ISBN 978-0-7546-7519-8 (hardback) 1. Bankruptcy--Australia. 2. Corporation law--Australia. 3. Debtor and creditor--Australia. I. Title.
KU964.S964 2008
346.9407'8--dc22

2008030026

ISBN 978-0-7546-7519-8

Mixed Sources
Product group from well-managed forests and other controlled sources
www.fsc.org Cert no. SGS-COC-2482
© 1996 Forest Stewardship Council
FSC

Printed and bound in Great Britain by
TJ International Ltd, Padstow, Cornwall

Contents

Table of Cases

Re A and N Thermo Products Ltd [1963] 1 WLR 1341
Re ABC Coupler and Engineering Co Ltd (No 3) [1970] 1 All ER 650
Re Allders Department Stores Ltd (in admin) [2005] EWHC 172 (Ch)
Amni Pty Ltd v Williams [1981] 2 NSWLR 138
Re Anglo-Austrian Printing and Publishing Union; Brabourne v Same [1895] 2 Ch 89
Re Anglo-French Cooperative Society Ltd (1894) 50 LT 754
In the matter of Ansett Australia Ltd and Mentha [2001] FCA 1806
In the matter of Ansett Australia Ltd and Mentha [2002] FCA 2 (7 January 2002)
ASIC v Krecichwost [2007] NSWSC 1458
Re Association of Land Financiers (1881) 16 Ch D 373
Audley v Halsey (1628) Cro Car 148, 79 ER 731
Re Audrey Hall Cotton Spinning Company (1868) LR 6 Eq 245
Australian Liquor, Hospitality and Miscellaneous Workers Union v Terranora Country Club Pty Ltd (1996) 19 ACSR 687

Re Bank of Hindustan, China and Japan; Ex parte Smith (1867) LR 3 Ch App 125
Re Barleycorn Enterprises Ltd Mathias and Davies (A Firm) v Dunn [1970] 1 Ch 465
Re Beni-Felkai Mining Co Ltd [1934] 1 Ch 406
Re Berkeley Applegate (Investment Consultants) Ltd (in liq) [1989] 1 Ch 32
Re Blazer Fire Lighter Ltd [1895] 1 Ch 402
Re Bonham ex parte Postmaster General (1879) 10 Ch D 595
A Bonyton Ltd Hoffmann v A Bonyton Ltd [1910] 1 Ch 519
BP Refinery (Westernport) v Shire of Hastings (1978) 52 ALJR 20
Brace v Calder [1895] 2 QB 253
Brassey v Dawson (1734) 2 Stor 978, 93 ER 980
Re Buena Vista Motors Pty Ltd (1971) ACLC 40-019

Canada Panamericana De Bienes Y Servicios S A v Northern Badger Oil and Gas Ltd (1991) 5 WWR 557
Re Carpentaria Trading Pty Ltd [1982] Qd R 394
Re Carton (1923) 39 TLR 194
Re Celtic Extraction (1999) 2 BCLC 555
Re Cimaglia (1985, BC SD Fla) 50 BR 9
Re Circuit Developments Ltd ex parte Mortimer (1981) 2 NZLR 243

Commissioner of Taxation v Barnes (1975) 133 CLR 483
Commissioner of Taxation v Card (1963) 109 CLR 177
Re Commonwealth Agricultural Service Engineers Ltd [1928] SASR 342
Con-Stan Industries of Australia Pty Ltd v Norwich Winterthur Insurance (Australia) Ltd (1986) 160 CLR 226
Crawford v Greater Pacific General Insurance Co Ltd [1983] VR 299
Crest Insurance Co of Australia v Rosser (1985) 10 ACLR 109

Re Dant and Russel 853 F 2d 700 (9th Cir 1988)
Re S Davis and Company, Ltd [1945] 1 Ch 402
Re Deangelis Tangibles, Inc (1999, BC MD Pa) 238 BR 96
Delaney v Staples [1992] 1 All ER 944
Re Denton Sub-divisions Pty Ltd (in liq) and the Companies Act (1968) 89 WN (Pt 1) (NSW) 231
Deputy Commissioner of Taxation v Applied Design Development Pty Ltd (in liq) [2002] FCA 205
Deputy Commissioner of Taxation v Dexcam Australia Pty Ltd (in liq) [2003] FCFCA 148
Deputy Commissioner of Taxation v Stranger (1934) 50 CLR *468*
Re Dominion of Canada Plumbago Company (1884) 27 Ch D 33
Re Downer Enterprises Ltd [1974] 1 WLR 1460
Dry Docks Corporation (1888) 39 Ch D 306

Re E&L Constructions Pty Ltd (in liq) (1981) 28 SASR 154
Re Elsinghorst Bros Co (1995, BC WD NY) 180 BR 52
Re Esbon Grain Co (1985, BC DC Kan) 55 BR 308
Re Esplanade Theatre [1929] VLR 237
Exchange Bank of Canada v Reg (1886) 11 App Cas 157

FAI Workers Compensation (NSW) Ltd v Philkor Builders Pty Ltd (1996) 20 ACSR 592
Re Falcon Sportswear Pty Ltd, Hart v Barnes (1983) 1 ACLC 690
Farepak Foods and Gifts Ltd v Revenue and Customs [2006] EWHC 3272
Re Farmer Furniture Pty Ltd (1998) 16 ACLC 1110
Fisher v Maddern [2002] NSWCA 28
Re Flour and Grain Exchange Ltd ex parte Rix [1934] SASR 386
Food Controller v Cork [1923] AC 647
Re L E Force and W J Wilde v Thos Clark and Sons (Qld) Pty Ltd (1982) 1 ACLC 320
Re Foster Clark Ltd's Indenture Trusts, Loveland and others v Horscroft (1966) 1 WLR 125

Re Galaxy Media Pty Ltd (in liq) (2002) 20 ACLC 73
Re General Rolling Stock Company (Chapmans case) (1866) LR 1 Eq 346

Re Glynconwg Colliery Company Ltd [1926] 1 Ch 951
Green v Giljohann (1995) 17 ACSR 518
Griffiths v Secretary of State for Social Services [1974] 1 QB 468

Re Hawkins (1992, BC DC Idaho) 144 BR 481
Re Henley and Co (1878) 9 Ch D 469
Re Heritage Village Church and Missionary Fellowship (1991, BC DC SC) 137 BR 888
Re Home Investment Society (1880) 14 Ch D 167
Hopley-Dodd v Highfield Motors (Derby) [1969] ITR 289

Re The International Cable Company (1892) 8 TLR 307
International Harvester Export Co v International Harvester Australia Ltd (1982) 1 ACLC 580
Re International Marine Hydropathic Company (1885) 28 Ch D 470
Re International Smelting Company Ltd (1887) 13 VLR 236
Re Introduction Ltd (No 2) [1969] 1 WLR 1359
Irving v Construction Industry Long Service Leave Board (1997) 15 ACLC 95

Jackson and National Aboriginal Islander Skills Development Association Inc NSW IRComm 118 (24 April 2003)
James Miller Holdings Ltd v J D Graham (1978) 3 ACLR 604
John Plunkett Consolidated Pty Ltd (in liq) (No 3) and the Companies Act (1979) 4 ACLR 209, CLC 40-545

Re Kayford Ltd [1975] 1 WLR 279
Re Keep, McPherson Ltd (1931) 48 NSW (WN) 180
Korda, in the matter of Stockford Ltd (subject to Deed of Company Arrangement) [2004] FCA 1682
Krasner v McMath [2005] EWCA (Civ) 1072 ('Ferrotech')
Re Kratzmann Holdings Pty Ltd (in liq) (1982) 1 ACLC 320
Re Kyra Nominees Pty Ltd (1980) CLC 40-659

Leicester Club and County Racecourse Co Ex parte Cannon (1885) 30 Ch D 629
Re Leyland DAF Ltd, Re Ferranti International plc (1994) 4 All ER 300
Re Linda Marie Ltd (in liq) [1989] BCLC 46
Ling v American Express International [2003] NSW CTTT 249 (10 March 2003)
Re Lofthouse Riverside Nursing Care Pty Ltd (subject to Deed of Company Arrangement) (2004) 22 ACLC 215
Re London Metallurgical Company [1895] 1 Ch 758
Re Longo (1992, BC DC Md) 144 BR 305
Love v The Image Centre Pty Ltd (1991) 30 ILR 442
Re Lundy Granite Co Ex parte Heavan (1871) 6 Ch App 462

Re Mack Trucks (Britain) Ltd [1967] 1 WLR 780
Madrid Bank v Pelley (1869) LR 7 Eq 442
Re Massey Re Freehold Land and Brickmaking Company (1870) LR 9 Eq 367
Re Mailrite Pty Ltd (1985) 3 ACLC 528
Re Mawcon Ltd [1969] 1 WLR 78
McEvoy v Incat Tasmania Pty Ltd [2003] FCA 810 (1 August 2003)
Re Mesco Properties Ltd [1980] 1 All ER 117
Re The Metropolitan Bank Ltd (in liq) (1900) 25 VLR 697
Re Millingen's Ltd [1934] SASR 72
Re Mineral Resources Ltd [1999] 1 All ER 746
Mirror Group Newspapers plc v Kevin Maxwell and Ian Maxwell and the personal representative of Robert Maxwell (deceased) [1998] BCC 324, 1 BCLC 638
Morepine Pty Ltd v Crush Pacific Industries Pty Ltd (1996) 14 ACLC 898
K D Morris and Sons Pty Ltd v Bank of Queensland Ltd (1980) ACLC 34,292

Re National Arms and Ammunition Company (1885) 28 Ch D 474
Re New York Exchange Co [1983] 1 Ch 371
Re Nicholls Pty Ltd (1982) 1 ACLC 408
Nicoll v Cutts [1985] BCLC 322
Re Nolton Business Centres Ltd [1996] BCC 500
Re North Yorkshire Iron Company (1878) 7 Ch D 661
Northern United Furniture, IUOW v Furniture Makers (NZ) Ltd (in rec) (1989) 4 NZCLC 65,158

Re Oak Pits Colliery Co (1882) 21 Ch D 322
Re Office Co Furniture Pty Ltd [1999] QSC 63
Re Oriental Bank Corporation (1884) 28 Ch D 643
Re Oriental Hotels Co; Perry v Oriental Hotels Co (1871) LR 12 Eq 126

Re Pacific Coast Syndicate Ltd [1913] 2 Ch 26
Re Parkin Elevators (1916) 31 DLR 123
Ex parte Pavex Constructions and Others (1979) Qd R 318
Payne v Commissioner of Taxation Nos NG 461 of 1995, NG 239 of 1995 Fed No 347/96
Peacock v The New Zealand Performance and Entertainment Workers' Union (1990) 5 NZCLC 66,557
Re Peregrine Investments Holdings Ltd and Ors [1998] 3 HKC 1.
Perry v Aboriginal Legal Service Ltd [1997] Unreported Equity Division Supreme Court of NSW Number BC 900007618, 9 December 1997
Re W T and M E Peterie Pty Ltd (in liq) and the Companies Act [1979] 1 NSWLR 708
Re Peterson Ltd [1931] Q St R 134
Powdrill v Watson, Re Leyland DAF Ltd, Re Ferranti International plc [1995] 2 All ER 65

Re Pullins of Newcastle Pty Ltd (1966) 85 WN NSW 16

Quik Bake Products Ltd (in rec) v The New Zealand Baking Trade Employees Industrial Union of Workers (1990) 5 NZCLC 66,701

Reid v The Explosives Company Ltd (1887) 19 QBD 264
Re River Village Assocs (1993, BC ED Pa) 161 BR 127
Rolfe v Canadian Timber and Saw Mills Ltd (1906) 12 BCR 363
Russell v AGC (Advances) Ltd (1987) 12 ACLR 79

Salomon v Salomon and Co Ltd [1897] AC 22
Re Sew Hoy and Sons Ltd (in rec) (1991) 5 NZCLC 67, 009
SGIO (Queensland) v Rees (Liquidator of KD Morris and Sons Pty Ltd) 1979 CLC 40-586
Shirlaw v Taylor (1991) 9 ACLC 1235
Re Silkstone and Dodworth Coal and Iron Company (1881) 17 Ch D 158
Re Silver Valley Mines (1882) 21 Ch D 381
Sipad Holdings DDOP v Popovic (1996) 14 ACLC 307
Smith and Judge v Deputy Commissioner of Taxation 78 ATC 4561
Re Smith-Douglass Inc 856 F 2d 12 (4th Cir 1988)
Re South Kensington Co-operative Stores (1881) 17 Ch D 161
Re Standard Rubber and Leatherboard Co (1913) VLR 236
Stein v Saywell (1969) 121 CLR 529

Taylor v Scoular (1987) 3 NZCLC 99,963
Re W J Taylor and Sons (1931) 8 ABC 88
Re Terra Distrib Inc (1992, BC DC Idaho) 148 BR 598
Thomas v Lionitev Co (1881) 17 Ch D 250
Re Transcontinental Townsite Co; Plainview Farming Co Case (1915) 25 DLR 597
Trent and Humber Ship-Building Company, Baileys and Leetham's Case (1869) LR 8 Eq 94
Trevor Ivory Ltd v Anderson [1992] 2 NZLR 517

Re Universal Distributing Co Ltd (in liq) (1933) 48 CLR 171

Re VIP Insurances Ltd (in liq) [1978] 2 NSWLR 297

Walker and Sherman v Andrew (2002) 20 ACLC 1476
Re Wanzer Ltd (1891) 1 Ch 305
Re Watson, Kipling and Co (1883) 23 Ch D 500
Re Wearmouth Crown Glass Company (1882) 19 Ch D 640
Re H J Webb and Co [1922] 2 Ch D 369
Re Wenborn and Co [1905] 1 Ch 413

Re West Hartlepool Iron Company (1875) 34 LT (NS) 568
Re West London Commercial Bank (1888) 38 Ch D 364
Wheeler v Philip Morris Ltd (1988) 32 IR 323; (1988) 97 ALR 282
Whitton v ACN 003 26 886 Pty Ltd (Controller Apptd) (in liq) (1996) 14 ACLC 1799
Williams v Natural Life Health Food Ltd and Mistlin [1998] 1 WLR 830

Zilka v Westpac Banking Corporation [2002] NSW CTTT 527 (20 September 2002)

Table of Statutes and Other Instruments

Australia Commonwealth

Aboriginal Councils and Associations Act 1976
Australian Constitution
  s109
Bankruptcy Act 1914
Bankruptcy Act 1924
  s84(1)
Bankruptcy Act 1966
  s109
Companies Code
  s441
Corporate Law Reform Act 1992
Corporations Law (see Corporations Act)
Corporations Law Amendment (Employee Entitlements) Act 2000
Corporations Act 2001
  s9
  s95A
  s140(1)
  s433(3)
  s443A
  s443B
  s443BA
  s443D
  s466(2)
  s475(8)
  s477(1)(a)
  s485
  s539(6)
  s548
  s555
  s556(1)(a), (b), (c), (d), (da), (db), (dc), (dd), (de), (df)
  s556(1A), (1B), (1C)
  s556(2)
  s559
  s560
  s561

s563
s588FA
s588FE
s600F(1), (2)
Part 5.3A
Crown Debts (Priority) Act 1981
s3
s4
Environmental Protection (Impact of Proposals) Act 1974
s3
Income Tax Assessment Act 1915
Income Tax Assessment Act 1936
s218
s221
s221F
s221G
s221YU
s221P (1), (2), (3)
s221YHDC
s221YHG
s221YHJ
s221YHZD
s221YU
s222AOB
s222APB
Income Tax Assessment Act 1966
s17
Insolvency (Tax Priorities) Legislation Amendment Act 1993
Sales Tax Assessment Act 1930
s36
Taxation Administration Act 1953
s8Y
s12–35
s255–5
s255–40
Taxation Debts (Abolition of Crown Priority) 1980
Tax (Interest on Overpayments and Early Payments) Act 1983
Trade Practices Act 1974
s51AE
Workplace Relations Act 1996
s170CM

New South Wales

Absent Debtors Act 1840
Administration of Justice Act 1840
An Act for Giving Relief to Insolvent Persons and Providing for the Due Collection Administration and Distribution of Insolvent Estates within the Colony of New South Wales and for the Prevention of Frauds affecting same 1841 5 Vict No 17
s42
An Act for the Administration of Justice in New South Wales and Van Diemens Land 1823 4 Geo IV c 96
s22
An Act for facilitating the Winding up of Joint Stock Companies unable to meet their Pecuniary Engagements 1847 11 Vict No 10 (*Winding up Act*)
s10
Bankruptcy Act 1887 51 Vict No 19
Companies Act 1874
Companies Act 1899
Companies Act 1936
s296
s297(1)
Companies Act 1961
s196
s217
s281(1)
s292(1)
Companies (NSW) Code 1981
s441
Environment Offences and Penalties Act 1989
Fair Trading Act 1987
Funeral Funds Act 1979
s3
Funeral Funds Amendment Act 2003
Travel Agents Act 1986
Workmen's Compensation Act 1926

Victoria

Companies (Trading) Act 1864
s101
s127
Companies Act 1915
s197

s208
Companies Act 1938
s262
Companies Act 1958
s216
Companies Act 1961
s196
s217
Companies (Vic) Code 1981
Companies Wages Act 1885
s3
Environment Protection Act 1970
s4
s62
s65A
Fair Trading Act 1999
Funerals (Pre-Paid Money) Act 1993
Judicature Act 1883
s9
Mining Companies Act 1871
Travel Agents Act 1986

Queensland

An Act for the Better Administration of Justice in the District of Moreton Bay 1857
s20
Companies Act 1863
Companies Act 1931
s272
s273
s274
Companies Act 1961
s196
s217
s292(1)
Companies (Qld) Code 1981
Environment Protection Act 1994
Fair Trading Act 1989
Insolvency Act 1874
s143
Travel Agents Act 1988

South Australia

Western Australia

Companies Act 1893
s154
Companies Act 1943
s269
s271
Companies Act 1961
s292(1)
Companies (WA) Code 1981
Fair Trading Act 1987
Joint Stock Companies Ordinance 1858
Travel Agents Act 1985
Uniform Companies Act 1961

Tasmania

Bankruptcy Act 1870
s31
Companies Act 1869
Companies Act 1895
s29
Companies Act 1920
s198
s208
s209
Companies Act 1959
s227(2)
Companies (Tas) Code 1981
Environmental Management and Pollution Control Act 1994
Fair Trading Act 1990
Income Tax Act 1894
Joint Stock Companies Act 1859
Travel Agents Act 1987

United Kingdom

An Act Against Such Persons as do Make Bankrupts 1542 34 and 35 Henry VIII c 4
An Act to amend the Laws Relating to Bankrupts 1825 6 Geo 4 c 16
s48
An Act for the more speedy and effectual Recovery of Debts due to His Majesty, His Heirs and Successors, in right of the Crown of the United Kingdom of

Canada

s39
s60
s77
s130
Environmental Protection Act Ontario RSO 1990 c E-19
s154
Environmental Protection and Enhancement Act Alberta SA 1992 c E-13.3
s176
Fisheries Act RSC 1985 c F-14
s42
Wage Earner Protection Program Bill 2005 Bill C-55
Weed Control Act RSA 1980 c W-6
s27

Malaysia

Companies Act 1965
s292

New Zealand

Bankruptcy Act 1867
s217
Companies Act 1955
s308(1), (2)
Fisheries Act 1983
Lay-by Sales Act 1971
s10(1)
s11(1)
Motor Vehicle Dealers Act 1975
Radiocommunications Act 1989

Singapore

Companies Act 1967
s328

Sweden

Formansrattslagen 1970 9790

United States

Bankruptcy Code 11 USC 507
    chapters 7, 11
Bankruptcy Reform Act 1978 11 USC 101–1330
    s507
Comprehensive Environmental Response Compensation and Liability Act 1980

Preface

This book examines preferential debts derived from specific legislative provisions applying to corporate insolvency and has a particular focus on Australia. These legislative provisions, called statutory priorities, enhance the likelihood that certain identified and otherwise unsecured creditors will receive at least part payment of the debts owed to them by the insolvent company. In order to understand the concept of preferential treatment, the book employs doctrinal, theoretical and historical analysis of who it is that enjoys preferred creditor status.

Preferential debts militate against the fundamental principle of *pari passu* (equal) distribution to the detriment of ordinary unsecured creditors. Therefore, persuasive justification must exist to prefer these 'priority' creditors over other creditors and contributories and so this justification is explored.

Although not secured creditors, priority creditors are entitled to a statutory right of payment and, traditionally, the major categories of priorities include the administrative expenses of the insolvency, employees' claims for wages and other entitlements, and government claims for taxes and debts. Potential new categories for priority status by legislation could include environmental clean-up costs, international creditors, tort claimants, consumers and other miscellaneous and most likely non-consensual creditors. The book examines the justification for favourable statutory treatment of the historical, present and potential priority creditors of companies in countries with a common law tradition.

As corporate insolvency law has been and is influenced by international developments and so parts of the book are comparative, drawing upon the content and scholarship relating to similar laws in other common law jurisdictions and, where appropriate, other legal systems around the world.

The final chapter concludes with recommendations for statutory reform and makes some suggestions for further research into the present treatment and potential new classes of priority creditors. I hope that the book serves as a starting point for much more analysis of this crucial area of insolvency law.

Christopher F. Symes

Acknowledgements

I thank my academic colleagues who have given me their time to discuss matters of my research including Professor Andrew Keay, University of Leeds, Professor Rosalind Mason, Queensland University of Technology, Professor David Milman, University of Manchester, Associate Professor David Brown, Victoria University of Wellington (and soon to be University of Adelaide) and Emeritus Professor Suzanne Corcoran, Flinders University School of Law. I particularly thank Professor Andrew Stewart, University of Adelaide for his support, confidence, advice and outstanding scholarship.

I acknowledge the assistance of the Australian Law Reform Commission for making available to me the submissions to ALRC 45 and Justice Paul Heath (NZ) for forwarding to me the relevant International Bar Association survey results.

I thank my wife, Dr Anna Vnuk who has made this book possible.

Chapter 1
Introducing Statutory Priorities in Corporate Insolvency

In many countries there is a statutory regime of priority creditors used in corporate insolvency. In order to understand the regime, we must undertake a theoretical, historical and descriptive analysis of who enjoys a statutory preferred creditor status from a legal viewpoint. This book's analysis uses the Australian jurisdiction, although other jurisdictions, particularly those that embrace the common law, are used for comparative purposes.

Statutory priorities militate against the fundamental principle of *pari passu* (equal) distribution to the detriment of ordinary unsecured creditors. Therefore, persuasive justifications must exist for jurisdictions to maintain statutes that continue to prefer these 'priority' creditors over other creditors and contributories. These justifications are the central theme of this work.

Priority creditors are entitled to a statutory right of payment although they are not secured creditors. Traditionally, the major categories of priorities include the administrative costs of insolvency, employees' claims for wages and other entitlements of the insolvent company, and government claims for taxes and debts. This book analyses these major categories, as well as exploring potential new categories for statutory priority status, and suggests these could include environmental clean-up costs, consumer prepayments, small business and international creditors, tort claimants and other miscellaneous (and most likely) non-consensual creditors.

Insolvency research is still in its infancy even though insolvency laws have been present for centuries. Those outside the insolvency field may assume that a great deal is known about debtors and creditors, and about the reasons and justifications for the particular provisions that occur in our insolvency statutes. They may assume there would be agreed theories and principles in the common law world as to insolvency law and practice. Furthermore, they may assume that governments or practitioners, if not the wider society, would have an accurate picture of the nature and extent of corporate insolvency's impact on debtors, creditors and the community. Unfortunately, nothing could be further from the truth.

Insolvency in Australia is divided into corporate and personal legal procedures. There is a clear distinction between the two in the terminology which is in common use. Personal insolvency procedures are known as 'bankruptcy' and corporate insolvency procedures are referred to as 'corporate insolvency'. While this book is concerned only with corporate insolvency, reference is made to the law of bankruptcy at various points.

Corporate insolvency is predominantly a creature of statute and, in Australia, its legal form is mainly found in the principal corporate law statute, the *Corporations Act 2001* (Cth).[1] Clearly then, it is a branch of Australian corporate law,[2] although one commentator has now described it as 'being regarded as a separate field of law; no longer is it merely a part of company law and commercial law'.[3] Corporate insolvency law is based on concepts originally developed by the common law and so case law is important, particularly in areas with less statutory regulation such as receivership. While this book deals with liquidation and not receivership, case law is becoming an important source of law in liquidations as well.[4]

Corporate insolvency law is often influenced by other areas of law such as property law, equitable duties and the law of contract,[5] although much of this influence is not in matters pertaining to the issues considered here. Corporate insolvency law is also becoming increasingly influenced by extraterritorial and cross border aspects as business becomes more globalized.[6] Although the topic can be examined from a local Australian perspective with appropriate comparisons drawn from other jurisdictions, it has not to date been considered essential for unified cross border legislation.[7]

In keeping with the book's focus, only statutory priorities will be investigated. Those priorities established by the special treatment that exists or might exist by virtue of using retention of title or subordination claims will not be covered.[8] Many insolvency problems that are related to statutory priorities are excluded including the extent of the use of floating charges, the maintenance of the secured creditor's position and priorities created by other statutes outside corporate insolvency. The statutory priorities investigated here include claims by past, present and possible future claimants.

Chapter 3 analyses some of the major theories underlying insolvency law in the context of statutory priorities. The creditors' bargain model, drawn from the

1 The *Corporations Act 2001* (Cth) is a comprehensive statute, providing for the registration of corporations and then their governance, liability, finance, control and restructuring, as well as their insolvency.

2 Tomasic, R. and Whitford, K. *Australian Insolvency and Bankruptcy Law* (2nd ed. 1997) 1.

3 Keay, A. 'The Unity of Insolvency Legislation: Time for a Re-think?' (1998) 7 *Insolvency Law Journal* 4, 10.

4 Australian courts have had jurisdiction over insolvency matters since 1823: *Act for the Administration of Justice in New South Wales and Van Diemens Land, 1823* 4 Geo IV c 96 s 22. Chapter 2 below details the evolution of the relevant law.

5 Tomasic, R. and Whitford, K. *Australian Insolvency and Bankruptcy Law* (2nd ed. 1997) 1.

6 Ibid.

7 Cross border insolvency legislation has been promoted by UNCITRAL and Australia New Zealand and the United Kingdom have all adopted the Model Law.

8 See e.g., Australian Law Reform Commission, *General Insolvency Inquiry*, Report No 45 (1988) ('Harmer Report'), paras 752–755, 765–768.

law and economics literature and expressed by writers such as Jackson[9] in the United States, is by far the most commonly held view on insolvency legal theory. The chapter acknowledges this position, yet points to communitarianism or value based theory,[10] when appropriate, to show a broader understanding of viewpoints, essentially by discussing the 'moral, political, personal and social' elements of insolvency.[11] Recognising these broader issues shows that multiple interconnected perspectives are needed to fully justify the statutory priorities.

Little work has been done in Australia, and in many other parts, in developing a theoretical framework for corporate insolvency law and practice, especially in the area of priorities. While a chapter in a book on statutory priorities is not going to settle upon a definitive theory it will seek to advance the debate, particularly by submitting more discussion on communitarianism. Critical approaches to corporate insolvency law and practice are still developing and the chapter cursorily deliberates these.

Corporate insolvency law is truly significant. Insolvency law has been claimed to be 'the root of commercial and financial law because it obliges the law to choose' whom to pay as 'there is not enough money to go around'.[12] 'The choice cannot be avoided or compromised or fudged'.[13] It is in this context that statutory priorities sit. The law is clearly choosing, or favouring, the priority creditors.

It has been suggested corporate insolvency has a 'profound effect on normal legal relationships', as 'contracts are shattered and their terms interfered with or negated', 'people lose their jobs' and the 'economy of the state itself may be sapped'.[14] Corporate insolvency then is the 'destroyer and spoliator'.[15] Statutory priorities attempt to soften such a profound effect by giving a preference in the form of priority to payment to certain favoured groups, such as those who lose their jobs, the state and those charged with administering the insolvent estate.

The notion of equality between creditors has long been a principle of corporate insolvency law and has been described as preventing 'an undignified scramble by creditors over available assets'.[16] Furthermore, another principle of insolvency law is the orderly processing of insolvencies.[17] This, too, is important to avoid

---

9 See e.g., Jackson, T.H. *The Logic and Limits of Bankruptcy* (1986).

10 See e.g., Korobkin, D.K. 'Rehabilitating Values; A Jurisprudence of Bankruptcy' (1991) 91 *Columbia Law Review* 717.

11 See e.g., Gross, K. *Failure and Forgiveness; Rebalancing the Bankruptcy System* (1997) 24.

12 Wood, P.R. *Principles of International Insolvency* (1995) 1–1.

13 Wood, P.R. 'Principles of International Insolvency (Part 1)' (1995) 4 *International Insolvency Review* 94.

14 Wood, P.R. op.cit.

15 Ibid.

16 O'Donovan, J. 'Corporate Insolvency: Policies, Perspectives and Reform' (1990) 3 *Corporate and Business Law Journal* 11.

17 Principles of insolvency law are broadly similar in different Western legal systems and have been identified by the Australian Law Reform Commission (Harmer Report para

the 'unseemly scramble by creditors' so as to achieve a fair distribution of the available assets.[18] Such descriptions suggest that there is a race of creditors to be paid and statutory priorities are part of the race. The legislature has formalized the 'race rules' so principles can be applied and that 'scramble' can be avoided. The analogy springs to mind of a formal race conducted by strict rules and under the gaze of the public, like the Melbourne Cup or the English Derby, compared to a picnic race meeting held in rural Australia with few formalities.

In terms of their size and impact on Westerners' lives, corporate insolvencies are of much greater significance than individual bankruptcies.[19] The opposite was arguably true some decades ago and many might still argue that individual bankruptcy has more significance in the social research domain.[20] Corporate insolvency's greater economic impact provides further reason for concentrating on the corporate rather than individual side of insolvency statutory priorities, although such an inquiry should not exclude some social element.

Research into priorities should also be seen as truly significant. Wood, in 1995 when writing on the principles of international insolvency, dedicates three pages to possible research topics 'based on relative originality and usefulness'.[21] Supporting the choice of research on statutory priorities are his suggestions of 'creditor equality in insolvency law',[22] 'insolvency law and fairness to debtors and creditors'[23] and 'insolvency law and political policies',[24] all topics that extend into this book.

Flessner[25] states that the corporate insolvency procedure is a drastic remedy; at the outset the debtor will be dispossessed or be placed under supervision and the creditors will be denied their right to enforce their claims. At the end of the

---

33) as 'aims', in Roy Goode's book *Principles of Corporate Insolvency Law* (1997) as 'objectives', and criticized by Ian F. Fletcher in 'The Genesis of Modern Insolvency Law – An Odyssey of Law Reform' (1989) *Journal of Business Law* 365 in that they were 'honoured more in the breach than in observance and that the somewhat theoretical and idealized accounts of the law's working to be found in print were often a long way removed from practical reality'.

18 Tomasic, R. *Australian Corporate Insolvency Law* (1993) 5.

19 Wood, P.R. 'Principles of International Insolvency (Part 1)' (1995) 4 *International Insolvency Review* 94, 95.

20 See e.g., Sullivan, T.A., Warren, E. and Westbrook, J.L. *As We Forgive our Debtors – Bankruptcy and Consumer Credit in America* (1989) and Ryan, M. *The Last Resort: A Study of Consumer Bankrupts* (1995).

21 Wood, P.R. *Principles of International Insolvency* (1995) 355.

22 Ibid. 356.

23 Ibid.

24 Ibid.

25 Flessner, A. 'Philosophies of Business Bankruptcy Law: An International Overview' in Jacob S. Ziegel (ed.), *Current Developments in International and Comparative Corporate Insolvency Law* (1994) 19.

procedure there may be expropriation of the debtor through liquidation of his assets, and of the creditors through the extinction or reduction of their claims.

He concludes that it 'seems natural then from time to time we should explore the reasons that justify such drastic treatment of private (and very often simply unfortunate) debtors and creditors'.[26] This book explores these 'reasons that justify' such treatment.

What follows contributes to the investigation of statutory priorities in Australia and beyond, by providing evidence that is of far greater weight than previous anecdotal work and descriptive generalizations of statutory priorities. Such discussion allows for debate upon whether the present legislative provision is achieving its objectives or should be amended. This book provides, in particular, a resource to assist other 'claimants' seeking to lobby government for inclusion in the preferred treatment outlined in the statutory priority provision.

One particular concern to those involved with insolvency is the distributional problem. By its very existence, corporate insolvency means that not all debts are going to be met. Therefore, we can expect that there is a serious monetary effect on creditors. But what do we know about this particular problem? Does it affect debtors, creditors and the community? And, if so, to what extent? How are the laws that govern this occurrence justified? Are they working and for whom? Are there theories, perspectives or principles which have been or should be developed to guide lawmakers and practitioners on this particular problem? These questions are debated here.

Statutory priorities have rarely featured in corporate insolvency law scholarship to date. However, there are five important works that outline the present understanding of priority creditors. Important papers on the topic have been written by José Garrido from Spain,[27] Paul Heath from New Zealand, [28] and Jacob Ziegel from Canada.[29] With regard to books, no one's work has been dedicated solely to the topic,[30] although recent books by Vanessa Finch in the UK[31] and Karen Gross in the US[32] offer some specific coverage.

Each of these works are discussed in later relevant chapters. Nonetheless, it is useful at this point to present broad summaries of the works of Garrido, Heath and

26 Ibid.

27 Garrido, J.M. 'The Distributional Question in Insolvency: Comparative Aspects' (1995) 4 *International Insolvency Review* 25.

28 Heath, P. 'Preferential Payments on Bankruptcy and Liquidation in New Zealand: Are They Justifiable Exceptions to the Pari Passu Rule?' (1996) 4 *Waikato Law Review* 24.

29 Ziegel, J.S. 'Preferences and Priorities in Insolvency Law: Is There a Solution?' (1995) 39 *St Louis University Law Journal* 792.

30 The exception could be Hardy, A.E. *Crown Priority in Insolvency* (1986), a Canadian book dedicated to the topic of Crown priorities and including discussions on statutory liens and statutory deemed trusts.

31 Finch, V. *Corporate Insolvency Law Perspectives and Principles* (2002).

32 Gross, K. *Failure and Forgiveness: Rebalancing the Bankruptcy System* (1997).

Ziegel. The ideas of Finch and Gross are set out in some detail in later chapters, particularly the theoretical constructs of Gross in Chapter 3. Parts of Finch's scholarship have also been extremely useful in the analysis of new priorities in Chapters 7, 8 and 9.

Garrido's International Commentary

Professor José Garrido from University of Vigo in Spain has contributed to the history of statutory priorities by presenting material that transverses both the civil and common law worlds. His most relevant English publication is 'The Distributional Question in Insolvency: Comparative Aspects' in 1995.[33] A second article, 'Some Reflections on the EU Bankruptcy Convention and its Implications for Secured and Preferential Creditors',[34] also contains a small but relevant discussion on the topic of statutory priorities.

Garrido attempts to advance ideas in order to reach a better understanding of what he terms the 'distribution problem'. He argues that distributional outcomes are regarded as one of the main sources of discontent during insolvency proceedings in most industrial countries.[35] Garrido divides his 1995 article into two major sections, with the first dealing with the importance of the distributional question and its opposition to some trends in the economic analysis of law. The second section shows the evolution of distributional systems and their differences.

According to Garrido, to grasp the meaning of the close logical relationship between insolvency and distribution, it is essential to research the historical origins of the modern insolvency proceeding.[36] He outlines the different paths of general law and insolvency law which eventually were absorbed together, granting priorities to creditors deserving of protection and minimizing the impact on creditors by spreading losses through proportional distribution. Garrido notes that the protection of certain creditors can be a highly commendable function of the law, although it is performed at a serious cost.[37] The cost of credit protection is imperceptible outside insolvency and Garrido suggests that while many countries have introduced statutes with new preferential credits, they have failed to take account of the previous existence of a long list of preferential creditors in and outside the insolvency statute.[38] He argues that the more priorities are granted

33 Garrido, J.M. 'The Distributional Question in Insolvency: Comparative Aspects' (1995) 4 *International Insolvency Review* 25.

34 Garrido, J.M. 'Some Reflections on the EU Bankruptcy Convention and its Implications for Secured and Preferential Creditors' (1998) 7 *International Insolvency Review* 79.

35 Op.cit.

36 Ibid. 28.

37 Ibid. 32.

38 Ibid.

by general law, the more preferential creditors there are that will be unpaid in insolvency.[39]

In the second section to his 1995 paper, Garrido describes the evolution of credit protection. Garrido observes that the evolution saw a change from merchant law to state law and so credit protection became a political instrument in the hands of states.[40] As a result, the number of priorities increased. Supporting his argument of credit protection as a political instrument, he notes that, as priorities are granted by legislation, every pressure group tries to influence parliaments in order to achieve better treatment.[41] Garrido suggests that it is not politically marketable to destroy preferential credits and so displacement happens, rather than elimination, and the fight among preferential credits is for the top position, not for mere existence.[42]

Heath on New Zealand Priorities

Paul Heath (formerly Queens Counsel and now Judge of the New Zealand High Court) has considered, from a New Zealand perspective, whether preferential payments, presently in force for bankruptcies of individuals and company liquidations, can be justified in light of the *pari passu* rule.[43] He also considers the fundamental importance which has been attached to the *pari passu* rule both in New Zealand and overseas and the policy issues underpinning preferential payments.[44]

Supporting the principle that *pari passu* distribution is the most fundamental principle of insolvency law, Heath discusses the courts' reinforcement of the *pari passu* rule on public policy grounds.[45] In the second part of his article, he refers to other jurisdictions' treatment of the inter-relationship between preferential payments and the *pari passu* rule. Heath dedicates the third part of his paper to an exploration of issues that are present in preferential debts.[46] In the fourth part, Heath briefly identifies a number of philosophical bases upon which insolvency law reform can proceed.[47] In part five, Heath chronicles the history of preferential

39 Ibid.

40 Ibid. 34.

41 Ibid.

42 Ibid.

43 Heath, P. 'Preferential Payments on Bankruptcy and Liquidation in New Zealand: Are They Justified Exceptions to the *Pari Passu* Rule?' (1996) 4 *Waikato Law Review* 24.

44 Ibid., indicating the intent to highlight issues rather than to suggest definitive answers.

45 Heath, P. 'Preferential Payments on Bankruptcy and Liquidation in New Zealand: Are They Justified Exceptions to the *Pari Passu* Rule?' (1996) 4 *Waikato Law Review* 24, 26.

46 Ibid. 30.

47 Ibid. 32.

payments in New Zealand. Employees, Crown debts, administration costs and rent are all included in his discussion of the historical development.[48] He recalls that the first time preferential claims were set out in legislation was in the *Bankruptcy Act 1867* (NZ).[49]

In part six, Heath discusses the 1996 New Zealand position of preferential payments and divides these up into four distinct categories.[50] Firstly, administration costs, secondly, employee related claims, thirdly, Crown related claims and fourthly, miscellaneous debts which have for various reasons been afforded a priority. In each, he determines the underlying basis in principle or policy and considers whether each can be justified. In his study on the status for employees, he notes they have been in a preferred position since 1867.[51] He concludes that it is difficult to make out a case for the retention of Crown debts[52] and he calculates that the hotchpotch of items which from time to time have gathered sufficient momentum to receive priority have no future as preferential debts.[53]

Heath's work is essentially repeated in the Advisory Report on Preferential Debts for the New Zealand Ministry of Commerce by the New Zealand Law Commission.[54] Heath was indeed the Commissioner who prepared this Report. With New Zealand legislative developments closely shadowing Australia, there is much similarity with the history mapped out in Chapter 2 below.

Ziegel on Canadian Priorities

Emeritus Professor Jacob Ziegel has posed the question whether there is a 'solution' to preference and priorities in insolvency law.[55] In 1995, he reported upon a small empirical study which he conducted during 1988 in metropolitan Toronto of 95 bankruptcies. Secured creditors in his study recovered on average 43 percent of their claims, unsecured creditors recovered 5 percent and the insolvency practitioner (trustee) recovered 99 percent.[56] In his St Louis University Law Journal paper, he considered whether Canada can justify such disparate treatment of creditors.

48 Ibid. 34–38.

49 Ibid. 35.

50 Ibid.

51 Ibid. 47, see *Bankruptcy Act 1867* (NZ) s217.

52 Ibid. 52.

53 Ibid. 53.

54 New Zealand Law Commission, *Priority Debts in the Distribution of Insolvent Estates An Advisory Report to Ministry of Commerce* (1999).

55 Ziegel, J.S. 'Preferences and Priorities in Insolvency Law: Is there a Solution?' (1995) 39 *Saint Louis University Law Journal* 793.

56 Ibid. 794.

Ziegel examined the rationales for secured creditors' preferred treatment, suggesting that

> [T]here are many factors that explain [the] modern insolvency systems' departure from the basic equality of creditors and the preferred treatment accorded to a particular class or subclass of creditors: political clout, self-serving legislation (in the case of government claims), vulnerability of creditors (as in the case of the preferred status of employee claims), protection of the [*fiscus*], title concepts, and, not least, the foundational respect for freedom of contract.[57]

Ziegel has explored the justifications for the exceptions that 'frequently demote the secured party's priority in favour of other groups of creditors'.[58] These limits on freedom of contract include the subordination of security rights in favour of employees, governmental claims, other involuntary creditors and then unsecured consensual creditors. Ziegel finishes his discussion by concluding that unsecured 'trade creditors are the heavy losers'.[59] He identifies that the risk is greater for smaller trade creditors and notes how Canada has a security in place for growers and producers 'of agricultural products for money owing by a manufacturer for products delivered to the manufacturer'.[60]

Ziegel's work illustrates the type of scholarship that may be possible for further exploration of other common law countries' statutory priorities. Some of these possibilities are discussed later in Chapter 10.

Government Reports

One rich area of secondary legal sources for insolvency research is provided by law reform and parliamentary committee reports. Many jurisdictions have had major government and quasi-government law reform and parliamentary committee reports prepared on the subject of insolvency during the 1980s or 1990s and these, along with their interested party submissions, provide fertile information and are valuable research resources. The review process undertaken by agencies charged with this task usually results in an interim discussion or working paper plus a final report. The law reform and parliamentary committee reports are well suited for use in research because they usually set out the existing local (e.g., Australian or United Kingdom) and overseas law, criticize the shortcomings of this law, cover philosophical or jurisprudential aspects and recommend changes to the present law. They are also useful in their production of bibliographies of articles and books, plus tables of cases and legislation. They also draft provisions for suggested new

57 Ibid. 796–800.
58 Ibid. 799.
59 Ibid. 802.
60 Ibid. 803.

laws. In summary, they provide one means of interpreting or finding the purpose behind particular legal positions. In view of this, much use is made of these secondary sources.

In Australia, the Australian Law Reform Commission (ALRC) has produced four reports related to insolvency: Report No 6 on 'Insolvency: The Regular Payment of Debt', No 36 on 'Debt Recovery and Insolvency', No 45 on 'General Insolvency Inquiry' (The Harmer Report) and, more recently, No 80 on 'Legal Risk in International Transactions'.

In keeping with the abovementioned model, the ALRC released Issues Paper No 6 in 1985 and Discussion Paper No 32 in 1987, both preceding the Harmer Report. Earlier, in 1978, the Senate Standing Committee on Constitutional and Legal Affairs had released a paper on Priority of Crown Debts. By far the most comprehensive, however, was the Harmer Report of 1988 and it is a most detailed source for any research into statutory priorities.

The Harmer Report had its origin in 1983, when the ALRC was asked by the Federal Attorney-General to examine all aspects of the law and practice relating to insolvency. As expected with such wide terms of reference, there was a chapter in the final report dedicated to priority among creditors. Chapter 15 noted that the companies' legislation and bankruptcy legislation of the day contained provisions that had 'the effect of specifying the order of priority in which creditors are to be paid from the realized assets of an insolvent company or individual'. The legislative effect was to create three classes of unsecured creditors:

- priority or preferential creditors – those creditors given priority by section 441 of the Companies Code (now section 556 of the *Corporations Act*) and section 109 of the *Bankruptcy Act*;
- ordinary unsecured creditors; and
- deferred creditors – those creditors who may only make a claim after all other debts have been paid.[61]

The Report also noted the permanent priority in the *Income Tax Assessment Act 1936* (Cth) accorded to the Commissioner of Taxation in respect of certain taxes. The Report reviewed the fundamental principle of *pari passu* distribution and expressly supported its maintenance, subject to the qualifications that it 'should not intrude unnecessarily upon the law as it otherwise' affected 'property rights and securities and that it should encourage the effective administration of insolvent estates'.[62] The Report acknowledged that any departure from *pari passu* 'should only be countenanced by reference to clearly defined principles and policies and then only when they enjoy general community support'.

On the basis of that general approach, the ALRC recommended the repeal of some of the priorities that existed at that time and the re-ordering of others. They

61 Harmer Report, para 712.

62 Ibid. para 713.

proposed just two broad categories of claims: administrative costs and employee benefits. The Report's numerous recommendations on this and other aspects of insolvency law were slowly implemented by the Federal Government.[63] The discussion of priorities in the Harmer Report remains an important starting point for analysis of the area and its recommendations will be discussed in detail in the chapters that follow.

In terms of reports from other countries, the Cork Report (UK) in 1982,[64] the Colter Report (1986) from Canada,[65] the New Zealand report already mentioned,[66] and the Scottish Law Commission (1982)[67] all provide in-depth commentary on the state of play in statutory priorities at the time of their publishing. These reports too will feature in later chapters.

Definitions

It is important from the outset to attain clarity in the terminology used in this book. Frequently in the literature the term 'bankruptcy' is used to describe corporate insolvency, because some jurisdictions refer to corporate insolvency as corporate bankruptcy. This will not be employed throughout the book and so any mention of bankruptcy can be taken to mean personal bankruptcy, unless it is found in a reference to material from an overseas jurisdiction.

The term 'liquidation' is used interchangeably with the phrase 'winding up' in most literature and the following chapters will attempt to use the word 'liquidation' although there may be occasions where the substituted phrase 'winding up' will be employed.

Although priority creditors are not only found in insolvency statutes, in this book when priority creditors are referred to this term means priority in the insolvency context. Priority creditors are paid their debt (hopefully) and so there is the possibility of describing the priority in terms of the debt and not the person owning the debt. Hence, these creditors are preferred to others and so the term 'preferential debt' is used in some literature instead of the term 'priority creditors'. Again, the term priority creditor or preferential debt can be used interchangeably. The terms vary across jurisdictions: for example, the United Kingdom's Cork

---

63 In relation to priorities, the *Corporations Law* in 1993 made certain changes as outlined in Chapters 2 and 5 below.

64 Report of the Review Committee, *Insolvency Law and Practice* (Cmnd 8558, 1982).

65 Advisory Committee on Bankruptcy and Insolvency, Canada, *Proposed Bankruptcy Act Amendments Report of the Advisory Committee on Bankruptcy and Insolvency* (1986).

66 New Zealand Law Commission, Priority Debts in the Distribution of Insolvent Estates An Advisory Report to Ministry of Commerce (1999).

67 Scottish Law Commission, Bankruptcy and Related Aspects of Insolvency and Liquidation, Report No 68 (1982).

Committee[68] titled its chapter 'Preferential Debts', while the Australian Harmer Report used the heading 'Priority Among Creditors' to cover the same material. This book refrains from using the word 'preferential' when describing priority creditors. This is important, for in the Australian context 'preferences' are usually taken to be the antecedent transactions undertaken by the company prior to liquidation.

Specific Australian Legislation

The major Australian provision on priorities in corporate insolvencies is section 556(1) of the *Corporations Act 2001* (Cth). This provides that:

> in the winding up of a company the following debts and claims must be paid in priority to all other unsecured debts and claims:
>
> first, expenses (except deferred expenses) properly incurred by a relevant authority in preserving, realising or getting in property of the company, or in carrying on the company's business;
>
> if the Court ordered the winding up – next, the costs in respect of the application for the order (including the applicant's taxed costs payable under section 466);
>
> (ba) if:
>
> (i) during the period of 12 months ending when the winding up commenced, an application (the first application) was made under section 459P for the company to be wound up in insolvency; and
>
> (ii) when the first application was made, the company was not under administration; and
>
> (iii) the company began to be under administration at a time after the first application was made; and
>
> (iv) the first application was not withdrawn or dismissed before the administration began; and
>
> (v) the Court did not, in response to the first application, make an order under section 459A that the company be wound up in insolvency;

---

68 Review Committee, *Report of the Review Committee Insolvency Law and Practice* Cmnd 8558 (HMSO, London, June 1982) Chair Sir K. Cork, 'Cork Report'.

Next, the costs in respect of the first application;

next, the debts for which paragraph 443D(a) or (aa) entitles an administrator of the company to be indemnified (even if the administration ended before the relevant date), except expenses covered by paragraph (a) of this subsection and deferred expenses;

[repealed];

(da) if the court ordered the winding up – next, costs and expenses that are payable under

subsection 475(8) out of the company's property;

(daa) if the company resolved by special resolution that it be wound up voluntarily – next, costs and expenses that are payable under subsection 446C(8) out of the company's property;

(db) next, costs that form part of the expenses of the winding up because of subsection 539(6);

(dc) [repealed];

(dd) next, any other expenses (except deferred expenses) properly incurred by a relevant authority;

(de) next, the deferred expenses;

(df) if a committee of inspection has been appointed for the purposes of the winding up – next, expenses incurred by a person as a member of the committee;

subject to subsection (1A) – next, wages and superannuation contributions and superannuation charge payable by the company in respect of services rendered to the company by employees before the relevant date;

next, amounts due in respect of injury compensation being compensation the liability for which arose before the relevant date;

subject to subsection (1B) – next, all amounts due:

(i) on or before the relevant date; and

(ii) because of an industrial instrument; and

(iii) to, or in respect of, employees of the company; and

(iv) in respect of leave of absence;

subject to subsection (1C) – next, retrenchment payments payable to employees of the company.

Section 556(2) goes on to define the terms 'company', 'deferred expenses', 'employee', 'excluded employee', 'non-priority day', 'official manager', ' relevant authority', 'retrenchment payment', 'spouse' and 'superannuation contribution'.

Each of the various categories of priority in section 556(1) will be discussed in later chapters. Earlier Australian provisions dealing with statutory priorities will be outlined in Chapter 2. In later chapters, where it is appropriate, provisions from other jurisdictions are also replicated.

Structure of the Book

In this chapter certain introductory matters have been addressed. Some of the relevant literature has been mentioned and the argument has been made that the topic is a worthwhile one to investigate. Chapter 2 goes on to outline the fascinating history of statutory priorities. Chapter 3 relates the topic to the creditors' bargain perspective and a developing perspective in corporate insolvency law, namely, communitarianism. In doing so other theories and approaches are also described and discussed.

Chapters 4 and 5 identify and describe the present classes of priorities. Chapter 4 examines administration costs and Chapter 5 examines employee wages and entitlements. Chapter 6 describes the priority previously given to taxation and explores whether the reasons for its removal were valid. The chapter also discusses the previous priority given to crown or government debts, particularly in light of overseas experiences. Chapter 7 discusses and analyses the merits of including a new priority for environmental clean up costs. Chapters 8 and 9 open up a discussion on the possibility of other new priorities and again draw on support and analysis from other jurisdictions. Chapter 8 focuses on consumers and Chapter 9 on other possible priorities.

Chapter 10 concludes by summarizing the position of the priorities mentioned. From the research in statutory priorities comes an understanding of the current law, of who enjoys priority creditor status, and of the justification for the enjoyment of such priority. This chapter considers whether these priorities work and should continue in the statute, and whether there is a need for reform which can assist in achieving fairness and equity in corporate insolvency distributions that involve priority creditors. The chapter makes recommendations that specifically address the present legal positions suggesting some adjustment to the *Corporations Act*. It also contemplates how further research might be conducted to ascertain empirical information on statutory priorities.

Chapter 2
The Evolution of Statutory Priorities

Modern corporate insolvency law can trace its history to the Italian merchants of the Middle Ages.[1] Their merchant law included some rules on insolvency and, amongst them, a rule of proportional distribution.[2] Importantly, exceptions to that principle have also existed since these early times. Italian cities of the Middle Ages taxed their merchants and the first insolvency priority was for tax claims.[3] The earliest insolvency practises assimilated priorities invented by Roman law and French customary law and the state was able to impose their policies on the principles elaborated by the merchants. In the fifteenth century, when merchant law was incorporated into state law in Europe, the differences in priorities began to be significant because whoever held the priorities was dependent upon the political system. No longer were the priorities designed to suit the merchants' needs but, more typically, were a political instrument exercised under the influence of pressure groups.[4] In England the Crown's ancient prerogative treatment rights also imposed an exception to proportional distribution.[5]

Before the concept of insolvency became a formal part of the English legal system in the mid-sixteenth century, English creditors took whatever collection measures they could through the ordinary process of the courts. Under such a system the creditor who took the action reaped the rewards for promptly collecting his/her own debt and no provision was made by the courts for distributing the debtor's estate for the benefit of all creditors or even those who deserved special treatment.[6] This led to an undesirable situation of a 'scramble' to be paid amongst creditors. English case law dating back to 1628[7] suggests that the judiciary in some cases thought it was appropriate to treat creditors in insolvency in an

1 Garrido, J.M. 'The Distributional Question in Insolvency' (1995) 4 *International Insolvency Review* 25, 34.

2 Ibid. 33, Garrido queries whether secured credit was always given a priority arguing that secured forms of credit played a minor role in the early history of commercial practice.

3 Ibid.

4 Ibid.

5 Keay, A. and Walton, P. 'Preferential Debts: An Empirical Study' [1999] *Insolvency Lawyer* 112.

6 Markham Lester, V. *Victorian Insolvency* (1995) 13.

7 See *Audley v Halsey* (1628) Cro Car 148, 79 ER 731; *R v Pixley* (1725) Bunb 202, 145 ER 647; *R v Bewdley* (1712) 1 PWms 207, 24 ER 357; *Lechmere v Thorowgood* (1689) Comb 123, 90 ER 381; *Rorke v Dayrell* (1791) 4 TR 402, 100 ER 1087; *R v Cotton* (1751) 2 Ves 295, 28 ER 186.

unequal manner when occasionally a justification was made. While no relevant statute existed at the time to give special treatment to some creditors, it revealed a potential future pathway for legislators. Since 1825[8] the legislature, initially in Britain and shortly after in colonial Australia, has been willing to debate and then legislate to create an expectation of equal treatment amongst creditors and also dilute this principle with exceptions.

This chapter narrates the history of legislation dealing with statutory priorities and the early case law that interpreted it. The chapter traces the history in both Britain and in pre- and post-colonial Australia, as the origins of Australian law, and a number of other countries, in this area lie with British law.

The Earliest British Statutes

The British parliament in 1542 passed a law known as 'An Act Against Such Persons as Do Make Bankrupts'.[9] This was the first insolvency legislation in Britain. In s1, the Act required that assets of the estate be paid to creditors in 'portion rate and rate like, according to the quantity of their debts'. Lester observes that this Act 'marked England's acceptance of one of the substantive principles of bankruptcy law: when a debtor becomes insolvent, his (sic) remaining property rightfully belongs to all of his creditors and should be distributed rateably among them'.[10] At the time this distribution was made by the Chancellor and not by an insolvency practitioner, as occurred in later practice. This principle, developed from the Roman law of equally dividing the assets of a debtor amongst their creditors (*Vendito Bonorum*), is the precursor to any development of statutory priorities.

Bankruptcy Acts in Britain

Much of the substantive legal principles of personal insolvency were established by 1800 in Britain.[11] Certainly, the rateable distribution of the bankrupt's assets among creditors that was established in 1542 remained an integral part of all future statutes.[12] Lester opines that '[B]ankruptcy law originated from the need to solve the practical commercial problem created by failed businesses … [D]rafters

8 The first bankruptcy legislation enacted in 1542 contained no designated categories of priorities, though the Crown, not being bound by the statute, remained able to have recourse to the debtor's assets before these came into the hands of the bankruptcy authorities: Goode, R.M. 'The Death of Insolvency Law' (1980) 1 *Company Lawyer* 123, 127.

9 *An Act Against Such Persons as Do Make Bankrupts 1542* (UK) 34 and 35 Henry VIII c 4.

10 Markham Lester, V. *Victorian Insolvency* (1995) 15.

11 Ibid. 37.

12 Ibid.

of legislation hit early upon the practical solution for a trader's failure: treat all creditors equally, rateably dividing the bankrupt's estate as quickly and as inexpensively as possible'.[13] While this may be true, treating all creditors equally did not remain law for long because, by 1825,[14] special mention was made in the legislation of some creditors, although no priority as such was accorded.[15]

In the *Bankruptcy Act 1842* (UK), a priority was given to any 'Servant or Clerk' who was owed wages or salary. A maximum limit was placed upon the priority of three months' wages or salary and the amount was not to exceed £30.[16] Labourers and workmen were included, but their wages were limited to forty shillings. In 1869, the *Bankruptcy Act 1869* (UK) changed the limits for clerks or servants to four months' wages or salary and the amount was not to exceed £50, and for labourers or workmen, the limit was not to exceed two months' wages.[17] Such treatment, as outlined in more detail later in the chapter, provides a fine example of a statutory exception to the principle of treating all creditors equally.

British Company Law[18]

The modern company dates from the British *Companies Act* of 1844[19] and so the law and practice of winding up would be expected to occur for the first time shortly afterwards. Prior to 1844, incorporation as a company was permitted by Royal Charter or through a specific Act of Parliament. The *Companies Act* provided that upon registration of the deed of settlement with the Register of Companies the

---

13 Ibid.

14 *An Act to Amend the Laws Relating to Bankrupts 1825* (UK) s48.

15 *An Act to Amend the Laws Relating to Bankrupts 1825* (UK) s48. The Act did not state that the creditors should be paid in priority, merely that any servant or clerk could be paid six months wages or salary by the Commissioners and the servant or clerk was at liberty to claim any amount incurred outside this time frame. Armour, J. 'The Chequered History of the Floating Charge' (2004) 13 *Griffith Law Review* 25, 33 fn 36 wrongly interprets this as the first statutory priority. Keay, A. and Walton, P. 'The Preferential Debts Regime in Liquidation Law: In the Public Interest?' [1999] *Company Financial and Insolvency Law Review* 84, 86 describe it as a 'preference in bankruptcy for certain employees', which is more accurate.

16 *Bankruptcy Act 1842* (UK) ss28, 29. The *Commentaries on the Laws of Scotland* in 1826 did though give hints to an insolvency priority when it suggested that wages of domestic servants should be given a priority to be paid out of the deceased estate just as funeral expenses were, and the quote cursorily concluded that 'bankruptcy is sure to be in the same footing', Bell, *Commentaries on the Laws of Scotland* (1826) Vol. II 159.

17 *Bankruptcy Act 1869* (UK) s32.

18 A fuller treatment of the history of company law is contained in Gower, *Modern Company Law* (2nd ed. 1957) chapters 2 and 3.

19 *Joint Stock Company Registration and Regulation Act 1844 (Companies Act)* (UK).

entity became a body corporate, although there was still unlimited liability for shareholders. This Act has been described as 'the legislative ancestor of modern company law'.[20] Limited liability was introduced in Britain by the *Limited Liability Act* of 1855 and the modern form of Memorandum and Articles of Association was adopted to replace the deed of settlement in 1856 in the *Joint Stock Companies Act* of that year.

The first statute dedicated to winding up was also introduced in 1844.[21] Known as the *Winding up Act 1844* (UK), it was silent on matters of priority. However, it did state that the law and practice of bankruptcy 'then in force shall extend so far as the same may be applicable'[22] to the Act. Under s20 it was the court that could settle distributions and in these provisions were express consideration for the costs of the winding up, an item that also features as a statutory priority in later legislation.

The *Joint Stock Companies Act 1856* provided in Part III for winding up and, in s87, allowed the court to make an order 'as to the Priority and Payment out of the Estate of the Company of the Costs, Charges, and Expenses incurred in winding up any company as it thinks just'.

Companies Act 1862 (UK)

The various statutes dealing with companies were consolidated in the *Companies Act 1862* (UK). This piece of legislation still forms the basis of many common law countries' Companies Acts.[23] In Australia, most of the colonies passed legislation modeled on this British statute and one commentator has observed, in a critical tone, that there was a large measure of uniformity because colonial legislators simply adopted what had been passed in Britain.[24]

Part IV of the Act contained 100 sections that were dedicated to the winding up of companies. Just four are relevant to priorities and these were ss 110, 133, 144 and 168. In light of their later influence and importance to Australian statutory priority law each of the sections will be considered below.

Section 110 provided that the court, in the event of insufficient assets to satisfy all liabilities, could order payment of the 'Costs, Charges, and Expenses incurred in the winding up … in such Order of Priority as the Court thinks just'. This provision is a little peculiar, as most of the winding up provisions in the Act appear to have been framed in the expectation that the company would be solvent

20 Austin, R.P. and Ramsay, I.M. *Ford's Principles of Corporations Law* (12th ed. 2005) 40.

21 *An Act for Facilitating the Winding up the Affairs of Joint Stock Companies Unable to Meet their Pecuniary Engagements 1844 (Winding up Act)* (UK).

22 *Winding Up Act 1844* (UK) s11.

23 See e.g., in New Zealand, Wishart, D. *Company Law in Context* (1994) 54.

24 McQueen, R. 'Limited Liability Company Legislation – The Australian Experience' (1991) 1 *Australian Journal of Corporate Law* 22, 24.

when wound up or at least be that way once contributors had honoured their calls. However, this section allowed for the court to determine priorities based on its sense of what is 'just' in circumstances where the company that was being wound up was insolvent.

The remaining three sections with some component of priority (ss133, 144 and 168) did not expressly contemplate insolvency in the winding up. In s133, a list of ten consequences of a voluntary winding up was provided. The first stated that the property of the company should be applied in satisfaction of its liabilities *pari passu*. Such a statement still remains in modern insolvency and company legislation.[25] The section assumed that the voluntary winding up would be solvent and that assumption is less likely in many modern day closures.

Section 144 provided for a priority, that of '[A]ll Costs, Charges, and Expenses properly incurred in the Voluntary Winding-up of a Company, including the Remuneration of the Liquidators'. These amounts were to be paid out of the assets of the company 'in priority to all other Claims'. Thus the equal sharing amongst creditors would occur only after administration expenses had been given a priority by the statute. It is to be noticed that this provision did not expressly contemplate insolvency, as compared to s110, and so there was no judicial discretion granted for these priorities.

The final provision in the *Companies Act 1862* that addressed a priority in this highly influential legislation was s168. Here, the provision permitted liquidators to prosecute directors and officers and to collect 'all Expenses properly incurred ... in such Prosecution' as a priority. Again it was an administration expense that gained a statutory priority and the provision seemed to assume a solvent winding up.

The detailed winding up provisions first expounded in the *Companies Act 1862* were replicated in all successive British Companies Acts until 1986. From 1986, and up until the present, a separate *Insolvency Act 1986* (UK) has contained statutory priorities for both corporate and personal insolvency.[26]

The Absorption of Priorities in Company Legislation

As described above there were some priorities that were expressed specifically in companies legislation, while others were expressed in bankruptcy legislation and by extension applied to corporate insolvency. During the nineteenth century the Companies Acts, both in England and Australia, incorporated by express reference

25 See e.g., *Corporations Act 2001* (Cth) s555.

26 See Review Committee, *Report of the Review Committee Insolvency Law and Practice* Cmnd 8558 (1982). This Report (the Cork Report) led to a major overhaul that resulted in inter alia, statutory provisions being taken from the companies legislation and placed in the new insolvency legislation.

certain provisions of the Bankruptcy Acts or bankruptcy rules, including those dealing with provable debts, fraudulent dealings and some statutory priorities.

A further complication in the late nineteenth century was the British move in 1875 to introduce a second *Judicature Act*,[27] which extended and simplified practice rules and provided a uniform system of law in all courts. Despite a provision to apply the rules under the *Bankruptcy Act* to companies,[28] this legislation had limited operation on corporate statutory priorities.[29]

A number of colonies followed the British move.[30] For example, Victoria after a decade of debate adopted the British changes in 1883.[31] Section 9 of the *Judicature Act 1883* (Vic) provided for the administration by the court of the assets in the winding up of any company with the same rules to prevail as were 'in force for the time being under the law of insolvency'.

Preferential Payments Legislation

In Britain in the early 1880s, the *Judicature Act* had left uncertainty surrounding the issue of statutory priorities. This was due to the fact that some debts were given priority by companies' legislation and some still only found mention in the bankruptcy statute, although the priority applied also to corporate insolvency. Three further aspects contributed to the disquiet: there were collusive agreements occurring that disadvantaged some creditors, the legal developments were in contradiction to other European countries and there was concern regarding the generous treatment for landlords. Rigorous parliamentary debate occurred, as detailed below, and in 1888 the *Preferential Payments in Bankruptcy Act* was passed in Britain. Its long title was 'An Act to Amend the law with respect to Preferential Payments in Bankruptcy, and in the Winding up of Companies'. This gave certainty to its application to both forms of insolvency. It received Royal Assent on Christmas Eve 1888 and became effective on 1 January 1889.

---

27 The first *Judicature Act* (UK) was enacted in 1873.

28 Section 10 of the *Judicature Act 1875* (UK) applied rules under the *Bankruptcy Act* to companies in liquidation, so that, for example, local rates which were due from a bankrupt's property were given priority over other debts.

29 A number of decisions provide support: see for example *Crumlin Viaduct* (1879) 11 Ch D 755, where the court held the bankruptcy order of payment was not to apply; and *Re Albion Steel and Wire Company* (1877–1878) 7 Ch D 547, where the court held the partial priority to rates and taxes found in the Bankruptcy legislation was not applicable. Moreover, the provisions of the *Bankruptcy Act 1883* (UK) which took away the priority of the Crown over other creditors in the distribution of assets in bankruptcy were held not to have been incorporated into the *Companies Act 1862* (UK) by virtue of the *Judicature Act 1875* (UK) s10: see *Re Oriental Bank Corporation; Ex parte R* (1884) 28 Ch D 643.

30 See Bennett, J.M. 'Historical Trends in Australian Law Reform' (1969–1970) 9 *University of Western Australia Law Review* 211, 227–232.

31 Ibid. 229.

The Act was just seven sections long. However, the first section was the only one of major importance. Section 1 provides:

> (1) In the distribution of the property of a bankrupt, and in the distribution of the assets of any company being wound up under the *Companies Act,* 1862, and the Acts amending the same, there shall be paid in priority to all other debts –
>
> (a) All parochial or other local rates due from the bankrupt or the company at the date of the receiving order or, as the case may be, the commencement of the winding up, and having become due and payable within twelve months next before that time, and all assessed taxes, land tax, property or income tax assessed on the bankrupt or the company up to the fifth day of April next before the date of the receiving order, or, as the case may be, the commencement of the winding up, and not exceeding in the whole one year's assessment;
>
> (b) All wages or salary of any clerk or servant in respect of services rendered to the bankrupt or the company during four months before the date of the receiving order, or, as the case may be, the commencement of the winding up, not exceeding fifty pounds; and
>
> (c) All wages of any labourer or workman not exceeding twenty five pounds, whether payable for time or for piece work, in respect of services rendered to the bankrupt or the company during two months before the date of the receiving order or, as the case may be, the commencement of the winding up:
>
> Provided that where any labourer in husbandry has entered into a contract for the payment of a portion of his wages in a lump sum at the end of the year of hiring, he shall have priority in respect of the whole such sum, or a part thereof, as the court may decide to be due under the contract, proportionate to the time of service up to the date of the receiving order, or, as the case may be, the commencement of the winding-up.

All three instances resembled closely the provisions of the *Bankruptcy Act 1869*. Section 1(2) then expressed the principle *pari passu* by providing that the debts from s1 ranked equally between themselves and were to be paid in full, unless the property of the bankrupt or the assets of the company were insufficient to meet them and then they abated in equal proportions between themselves.

Section 1(3) directed that, subject to keeping some amount to satisfy later costs of administration or otherwise, the debts in subsection (1) were to be paid 'so far as the property of the debtor, or the assets of the company, as the case may be, is or are sufficient to meet them'.

Section 1(4) provided that:

> In the event of a landlord or other person distraining or having distrained on any goods or effects of an bankrupt or a company being wound up within three months next before the date of the receiving order or the winding up order respectively, the debts to which priority is given by this section shall be a first charge or the goods or effects so distrained on, or the proceeds of the sale thereof:
>
> Provided, that in respect of any money paid under any such charge the landlord or other person shall have the same rights of priority as the person to whom such payment is made.

The final two subsections (5) and (6) of s1 made subsection (1) applicable to property of bankrupts and deceased estates.[32]

The Early Common Law

As bankruptcy predated corporate insolvency, the courts in England have dealt with cases relating to insolvency payment priorities over the last five centuries. The English common law contains judgments on priorities from seventeenth century England where the Crown would pursue its debts and, because of the Crown's prerogative, it was able to claim priority over creditors including those who had initiated the bankruptcy action.[33] As the Crown was not expressly stated to be bound by any bankruptcy statute until 1883, it enjoyed 'a kind of super priority', [34] which was a subject for disputation. If the bankrupt's property could pass from bankrupt to trustee upon his or her appointment then it was no longer subject to the Crown's process. However if this was yet to be achieved then there was a Crown's writ of extent. In addition, the Crown also had specific rights under legislation like the Excise Acts in the eighteenth century that imposed duties and occasionally liens over the subject matter of the duty.[35] The early jurisprudence period ended

32 Section 2 precluded the Act from applying to the *Friendly Societies Act 1875* (UK), the priority given to the payment of funeral and testamentary expenses or the *Stanaries Act 1887* (UK). Section 3 gave the Act effect only to new bankruptcies and winding ups after the commencement of the Act. Section 4 prevented any application in Ireland and s5 provided the commencement date as 'immediately after the last day of December one thousand eight hundred and eighty eight'. Section 6 repealed sections of earlier Acts mentioned in a schedule to the Act and s7 gave the Short Title.

33 See *Audley v Halsey* (1628) Cro Car 148, 79 ER 731; *R v Pixley* (1725) Bunb 202, 145 ER 647; *R v Bewdley* (1712) 1 PWms 207, 24 ER 357; *Lechmere v Thorowgood* (1689) Comb 123, 90 ER 381; *Rorke v Dayrell* (1791) 4 TR 402, 100 ER 1087; *R v Cotton* (1751) 2 Ves 295, 28 ER 186.

34 Keay, A. and Walton, P. 'The Preferential Debts Regime in Liquidation Law: In the Public Interest?' [1999] *Company Financial and Insolvency Law Review* 84, 86.

35 See *Stacey v Hulse* (1780) 2 Doug 411, 99 ER 264; *Attorney-General v Senior* (1739) 2 Doug 416, 99 ER 267; *Re Day* (1824) 1 M'Cle 384, 148 ER 160.

with the *Bankruptcy Act 1849* (UK) providing a Crown priority over unsecured creditors for 'assessed duties' limited to 12 months unpaid assessed taxes.

The Supreme Courts of the Australian colonies were established from 1823[36] and they were granted jurisdiction in relation to bankruptcy and insolvency, with the prevailing English legislation[37] generally being adopted.[38] There are few reported Australian cases on insolvency priorities from the nineteenth century.[39]

In England, the growth of a specialized corpus of law and procedures dealing with corporate insolvency was manifest in dedicated statutes and was also encouraged when issues relating to such matters became the exclusive jurisdiction of the Chancery Court from 1862.[40] This court was suited to hearing corporate insolvency, given its experience in trust estates, deceased estates and individual bankruptcy estates. From this time, cases were decided which facilitated certain priorities in insolvency. The reasoning in these judgments reflected the contemporary importance placed upon property and those creditors of substance who could petition for the winding up. Also, the central role of the Crown was illustrated. In particular, it was the Master of the Rolls, Lord Romilly, who shaped the early jurisprudence and gave many of the earliest and richest directions on the matter of insolvency priorities.

In 1868, Lord Romilly held that the creditor (who was the petitioner) was entitled to a priority for the petitioning costs and the costs of the liquidator should also be paid before the ordinary creditors. He referred to the petitioner's costs as enjoying a 'first charge on the estate'.[41] There was no consideration of any statutory provisions. Then, in 1870, Lord Romilly blazoned the issue of priorities when petitioned on a matter of whether the costs of the winding up or the remuneration of liquidator should be paid when there were insufficient funds for both. He held that:

---

36 *Act for the Administration of Justice in New South Wales and Van Diemens Land, 1823* 4 Geo IV c 96, s22. The other colonies followed later. See An Act for the better Administration of Justice in the District of Moreton Bay 1857 s20; noting that Victoria became a colony in 1850 and before that the people in south eastern Australia were subject to the *Administration of Justice Act 1840* (NSW) which had established a Resident Judge for Port Phillip with powers over matters of insolvency. In the Western Australian colony, the *Act for the Administration of Justice 1842* 6 Vic 11, s1 applied the British insolvency laws from the commencement of white settlement.

37 Most likely the *Bankruptcy Act 1732* (UK) 5 Geo II c 30.

38 Rose, D. Lewis' *Australian Bankruptcy Law* (11th ed. 1999) 19.

39 Some cases are discussed in later chapters. Examples include *Re International Smelting and Reducing Co Ltd* (1887) 13 VLR 896; *Re Bower* (1887) 8 ALT 159; *Re Green* (1890) 4 QLJ 23.

40 *Companies Act 1862* (UK) s81.

41 *Re Audrey Hall Cotton Spinning Company* (1868) LR 6 Eq 245. Lord Romilly said that he had 'always held that the Petitioner is entitled to have his costs paid first; he is the person who has brought the matter before the court, and obtained the order to wind up, and his costs are the first charge on the estate': Ibid. 247.

> In the absence of any special agreement I consider that these costs are to be paid according to law; and the rule of the Court is this, that in the first place the costs of the petition for winding-up are to be paid out of the assets, next the costs of the winding-up, and then the remuneration of the official liquidator; but no remuneration can be given until all the costs of the winding up are paid, including the costs of any provisional liquidator who may have been appointed.[42]

Another judgment, demonstrating Lord Romilly's clear acceptance that there will be cases that justify a priority in the distribution of assets, occurred in 1869. Counsel, in dealing with other matters in *Madrid Bank v Pelly*,[43] broached the topic of whether costs against a company in liquidation are to be paid by the liquidator out of the assets or are 'merely the subject of proof, as in the case of an ordinary creditor'.[44] Lord Romilly curtly replied: 'He must pay the costs out of the assets. You have not to prove for the costs'.[45]

What is interesting to note is the lack of acceptance of employees' wages and salaries as a priority under corporate insolvency law. The *Companies Act 1862* (UK) was completely silent as to this priority. In 1866 Lord Romilly was asked to grant a clerk a priority for approximately £12 that was owed to him for work undertaken within three months of the winding up order and any payment in lieu of notice.[46] Lord Romilly had been prepared to interpret existing priorities statutory provisions widely but, here, there was no base provision to expand. He stated he could not put the clerk 'on a different footing from other creditors',[47] explaining that the court had no power to order payment because there was no express priority provision in the *Companies Act*. The express provision in the *Bankruptcy Act* that gave employees a priority worked against the clerk, as the Master of the Rolls interpreted parliament's omission to include a similar priority in the companies legislation as deliberate. Provisions to allow a cross vesting of provisions from the bankruptcy legislation to the companies legislation only appeared in later statutes.

The importance of real property is demonstrated in an example from Canada in 1869,[48] where a railway company which became insolvent was subject to legislation which allowed for a priority treatment for creditors who had sold land to the company but remained unpaid. When the allowed amount proved to be more than sufficient to meet these special creditors, the court ordered the balance be distributed amongst other creditors.

---

42 *Re Massey; Re Freehold Land and Brickmaking Company* (1870) LR 9 Eq 367, 369.

43 *Madrid Bank v Pelly* (1869) LR 7 Eq 442.

44 Ibid. 449.

45 Ibid.

46 *Re General Rolling Stock Company (Chapmans Case)* (1866) LR 1 Eq 346, 347.

47 Ibid.

48 *Re Coburg and Peterborough Railway Company* (1869) 16 Gr 571.

Another English case highlighting the importance of real property to priority law was decided in 1878, where landlords were given a right to distrain for rent accrued after the appointment of a liquidator.[49] While the *Companies Act 1862* specifically provided that a landlord could not distrain for rent and he or she should stand as an ordinary creditor,[50] this changed in situations where the company had retained actual possession of the property for the purpose of carrying on the business of the liquidation. Under the exception granted by the courts landlords enjoyed a priority, but only for the post-appointment rent.

Re Henley and Co[51] in 1878 provides the first authority that the Crown is entitled to be paid out of assets in priority to all other creditors.[52] James LJ stated the principle that 'whenever the right of the Crown and the right of a subject with respect to the payment of a debt of equal degree come into competition, the Crown's right prevails'.[53] On the facts of this case the Crown was owed taxes upon the liquidation but had not taken any steps to recover the debt. This case decided that the right of the Crown was not taken away by the 1862 *Companies Act*, even though there was no express statutory provision binding the Crown. Later legislation addressed this omission.

British Parliamentary Debates of the 1880s and 1890s

It is appropriate to detail the British parliamentary debates of this period as they were the first to provide substantial commentary and discussion on the topic. The Australian colonies gladly accepted developments from the mother country without debate and so local colonial Hansards reveal little.

The first of these debates concerned the Preferential Payments in Bankruptcy Bill 1888. According to the Attorney-General, Sir Richard Webster, the object of the Bill was to enable the wages of a servant to be paid.[54] The Attorney-General pointed to many cases where this was not possible because of collusive arrangements made 'behind the back' of the servant between the debtor and other creditors. The new Act provided a means of getting the employees paid by direct action of the creditor.

In the course of the debate in the House of Commons, the member for Stockport, Sydney George, objected to an amendment provision to the Bill that would see a creditor presenting a bankruptcy petition even if the debt did not exceed £50. The

49 *Re North Yorkshire Iron Company* (1878) 7 Ch D 661.

50 *Companies Act 1862* (UK) s163.

51 (1878) 9 Ch D 469.

52 For later cases, see e.g., *Re Bonham Ex parte Postmaster General* (1879) 10 Ch D 595; *Re Oriental Bank Corporation* (1884) 28 Ch D 643; *West London Commercial Bank* (1888) 38 Ch D 364; *Exchange Bank of Canada v R* (1886) 11 App Cas 157.

53 (1878) 9 Ch D 469, 481.

54 England, House of Commons, *Debates*, 6 December 1888, 1381.

Attorney General's retort was that if a man could not pay wages of £50, he ought to be made bankrupt.[55]

In the House of Lords, the Bill was read a second time on 18 December 1888. The Earl of Dunraven introduced it on behalf of the government. In his opinion 'the government believed the Bill would give workers the same conditions of justice that they would receive in other [unnamed] countries in respect to their wages priority in cases of bankruptcy and liquidation'.[56] The Bill also proposed that in cases where the landlord distressed for recovery of rent, it would give priority to local authorities and wages up to a certain limit. In the event of distress not being sufficient to meet all the requirements of the case, the landlord should have the right of priority over the general assets and total estate of the bankrupt or company in liquidation. According to the Earl, the Bill did not take away any practical rights from the landlord, but would do away with much hardship to the wage earning classes of Britain.[57] The Bill was ultimately passed by Parliament.

The subject again returned to the Commons in 1897 when the legislature considered whether workers' wages should enjoy a better statutory priority and greater fairness upon their employer's insolvency. A new Bill, The Preferential Payments in Bankruptcy Amendment Bill, was presented to the House in early 1897. The House debated five significant issues; the impact on workers, the undesirable practices of debenture-holders, the provision of information to persons outside the company, the nature of the priority and the contribution of workers toward the value of the assets available for distribution. At that time, workers were missing out on wages in insolvencies because there was a higher priority given to debenture-holders through private agreements, mainly as a result of floating charges. Support for the workers' plight in the Commons was widespread.

In moving the second reading of the Bill, the Hon George Kemp[58] outlined to members that provision had not been made in the *Preferential Payments in Bankruptcy Act 1888* for wages claims when a company was being wound up and the assets were not sufficient to cover both them and the claims of the debenture-holder. The new legislation proposed to give priority to the existing priority debts, but also over 'the claims of debenture-holders under a floating charge on the assets, effects or uncalled capital of the company'. Kemp noted that the number of cases in which workers suffered loss from wages through the winding up of companies was small, because wages were as a rule paid weekly, but payments for 'piecework' were different.[59] Kemp gave instances to the Commons where a weaver might work for two or three weeks to complete a task and then be deprived of his wages priority by the floating charge.[60] He claimed clerks who were paid

55 England, House of Commons, *Debates*, 6 December 1888, 1381.

56 England, House of Lords, *Debates*, 18 December 1888, 621.

57 Ibid.

58 England, House of Commons, *Debates*, 10 February 1897, 71.

59 Ibid.

60 Ibid.

quarterly also ran high risks of being left unpaid.[61] He drew the Commons' attention to the fact that debenture-holders missed out on some of their money and it was a small matter, but for workers to forego their wages was more crucial.[62] He told the House that 'to them the loss of one or two weeks wages was a very considerable thing. It was, in fact, a matter of bread and cheese to them'.[63]

In a debate that could have happened today and not 1897,[64] the Hon Robert Ashcroft spoke in support of the amendment to the legislation venting his disappointment in the practice of the day by debenture holders who would take a floating charge which covered 'every stick and stone possessed by the company'.[65] The result, as it would be today without statutory intervention, was to deprive workers and other priority creditors of a distribution. He drew the House's attention to examples where companies had been wound up and the workers had missed out on the payment of wages.[66] He cited an example of 24 women reelers whose average wage did not reach 16 shillings a week and whose employer was wound up without them receiving 'a single penny'.[67]

The *Preferential Payments in Bankruptcy Act 1888* had been passed with no discussion on the principle of payment of priorities before chargeholders and, in 1897, Sir Albert Rollit told the House that the real remedy was in securing information for employees and others dealing with the company. He argued for a registration system for debentures and floating charges.[68] The Hon J.A. Mundella supported the Bill and possibly also gave support to Rollit's principle of access to information. He said that a 'workman ought to have prior claim over all others on the ground first, that workmen had not the means, and it was not their business, to inquire into the solvency of the parties for whom they worked'.[69] He noted that the position of the worker differed from that of the ordinary creditor, who inquired into the solvency of the people they were dealing with and took risk with the rest of the creditors.[70] In a justification that could have been submitted in more recent litigation, Mundella argued for wages' priority 'because every stroke of work the

61 Ibid. 72.

62 Ibid. 74.

63 Ibid.

64 Compare the 2005 debate in the Canadian Parliament on the Bill C-55 for a *Wage Earner Protection Program Act*: Canada, *Debates*, House of Commons, 5 May 2005, 1815–1835.

65 England, *Debates*, House of Commons, 10 February 1897, 76.

66 Ibid.

67 Ibid.

68 Ibid. 80.

69 Ibid. 84.

70 There was further support from the Hon Herbert Whitely who suggested a worker was unable to gauge the credit of his employer and so the priority before chargeholders was appropriate: Ibid.

workman did to the last moment of his employment contributed to increase the value of assets for all the creditors'.[71]

One member supporting the Bill likened the workman to the seaman.[72] A seaman was entitled to what was known as a maritime lien upon the vessel on board which he served, and a maritime lien took precedence over the claims of a mortgagee of the vessel, so the member questioned why a worker should not have a similar priority against debenture-holders. This would have had a significant impact in the House at such a time, remembering the importance of British maritime history and law.

One lone voice in the Commons spoke with reservation about the proposed preferential payments. The Hon W.E.M. Tomlinson expressed his concern that the debate had been unjust to the commercial community who had a desire, wherever it was possible, to find some means to pay wages and he did not think that many occurrences of workers' injustice had happened.[73]

In summing up the debate, the Solicitor General observed that 'in every part of the House [there was] a general agreement as to the fairness of the principle on which the Bill was founded'.[74]

As enacted, the *Preferential Payments in Bankruptcy Amendment Act 1897* contained just five sections. Sections 2 and 3 were crucial.[75] Section 2 provided:

> In the winding up of any company under the Companies Act, 1862, and the Acts amending the same, the debts mentioned in section one of the Preferential Payments in Bankruptcy Act, 1888, shall, so far as the assets of the company available for payment of general creditors may be insufficient to meet them, have priority over the claims of holders of debentures or debenture stock under any floating charge created by such company, and shall be paid accordingly out of any property comprised in or subject to such charge.

Section 3 then required a receiver to pay the priority debts as mentioned in the *Preferential Payments in Bankruptcy Act 1888* before the payment of any principal or interest in respect of any debenture.

These debates were not the source of any express judicial comment, although the two pieces of legislation, the *Preferential Payments in Bankruptcy Act 1888* and the *Preferential Payments in Bankruptcy Act 1897* were accepted as significant and 'resolute'.[76]

---

71 England, House of Commons, *Debates*, 10 February 1897, 84.

72 England, House of Commons, *Debates*, 10 February 1897, 84 (Hon M. Warr).

73 England, House of Commons, *Debates*, 10 February 1897, 86.

74 Ibid.

75 Section 1 gave the short title, s4 made the Act applicable in Ireland and s5 excluded Scotland from its operation.

76 See e.g., Denning LJ in *Re Barleycorn Enterprises Ltd* [1970] 1 Ch 465, 473.

Other British Legislation

In 1883, the *Companies Act* was passed in Britain and it enabled 'workpeople and clerks' to have a preference where a company went into liquidation. Also, in 1883, the *Bankruptcy Act* was passed and this Act extended preferential payments to rates as well as wages.

After the *Preferential Payments in Bankruptcy Act 1888* and the *Preferential Payments in Bankruptcy Amendment Act 1897*, subsequent companies' legislation incorporated priorities. In 1890, Britain made substantial changes to its insolvency law in the *Companies (Winding up) Act* and then consolidated many of the changes in the *Companies (Consolidation) Act 1908*. Section 207 of the 1908 Act dealing with preferential payments[77] was, in turn replicated by s319 of the *Companies Act 1948*.[78] The *Insolvency Act 1986* later provided for statutory priorities as part of a separate insolvency statute, while the recent *Enterprise Act 2002* made some impact with the removal of the tax priority, as discussed later in Chapter 6.

Australian Legislative History[79]

As mentioned above, all the Australian jurisdictions used the British insolvency law for their base and there is some conformity of priorities exhibited throughout the colonies and, later, the States of the Commonwealth. In fact, the major text on company liquidations in Australia states that '[O]f the history of winding up in Australia there is not a great deal to be said!'[80] In disputing this, it can be argued that a detailed study of corporate insolvency law in Australia is yet to be undertaken. The story, similar to Britain, is essentially one of wages and salaries being given priority first by personal insolvency legislation and later in companies' legislation. Administration expenses also find their priority too in the companies' legislation.

---

77 *Companies (Consolidation) Act* 1908 (UK) s209.

78 *Companies Act* 1948 (UK) s319.

79 Australian corporate law history has been researched and recorded by Prof Rob McQueen in particular. See e.g., McQueen, R. 'Company Law as Imperialism' (1995) 5 *Australian Journal of Corporate Law* 1; McQueen, R. 'Limited Liability Company Legislation – The Australian Experience' (1991) 1 *Australian Journal of Corporate Law* 1; McQueen, R. 'Why High Court Judges Make Poor Historians: The Corporations Act Case and Early Attempts to Establish a National System of Company Regulation in Australia' (1990) 19 *Federal Law Review* 245; McQueen, R. 'An Examination of Australian Corporate Law and Regulation 1901–1961' (1992) 15 *University of New South Wales Law Journal* 1.

80 Keay, A.R. *McPherson The Law of Company Liquidation* (4th ed. 1999) 20.

Colonial Australia

Statutory priorities appeared in only the second Act dealing with insolvent debtors in the colonies.[81] In 1841, s42 of 'An Act for giving Relief of Insolvent Debtors' in the NSW colony[82] stated

> And be it enacted that it shall be lawful for the trustee or trustees to provide payment to any clerk or servant of six months salary or wages in full out of the insolvent estate provided so much shall be actually and bona fide due at the time of the order for sequestration made.

This section was to be satisfied before ordinary creditors and it was unlimited as to the amount paid, provided it did not exceed six months.

Then in 1847 the *Winding up Act 1847* in New South Wales[83] (and applying also in Queensland) mirrored the 1844 British company winding up legislation. As noted above, the British Act was silent on priorities and this was reflected in the colonial Act. Section 10 of the NSW Act also included a direction that bankruptcy law and practice was to be followed in winding ups. Following this, South Australia enacted legislation in 1854[84] that emulated the British predecessors of 1844 and 1848.

No other colony adopted the British Winding up Acts and after Britain had enacted the *Joint Stock Companies Act* in 1856, Western Australia and Tasmania chose to follow suit in 1858[85] and 1859[86] respectively. Both these Acts remained silent on priorities.

In South Australia, the *Insolvent Act 1860* (SA) became the second piece of legislation to treat servants and clerks to a priority by providing that 'it shall be lawful for the Court, upon proof thereof, to order so much as shall be due, not exceeding three months' wages or salary, and not exceeding Thirty Pounds, ... and such servant or clerk shall be at liberty to prove any sum exceeding such amount'. '[L]abourers or workmen' could also be ordered payment of claims, upon proof, that were not exceeding four pounds. This 1860 legislation mirrored the British

---

81 The first was the *Absent Debtors Act 1840* (NSW), where no issue of priorities was included.

82 *An Act for Giving Relief to Insolvent Persons and Providing for the Due Collection Administration and Distribution of Insolvent Estates within the Colony of New South Wales and for the Prevention of Frauds affecting same 1841* (NSW) 5 Vict No 17.

83 *An Act for facilitating the Winding-up of Joint Stock Companies unable to meet their Pecuniary Engagements 1847* (NSW) 11 Vict No 10, s10.

84 *An Act to facilitate the dissolution and provide for the winding up the affairs of Joint Stock Companies 1854* (SA).

85 *Joint Stock Companies Ordinance 1858* (WA).

86 *Joint Stock Companies Act 1859* (Tas).

Bankruptcy Act 1842 both in its provisions for the amounts of wages and time limits for servants and clerks and its inclusion of 'labourers or workmen'.[87]

The new consolidated *Companies Act 1862* in Britain was enacted first by Queensland in 1863,[88] and then by Victoria[89] and South Australia[90] in 1864. These were the first examples of Australian company legislation that contained insolvency provisions. Like the related English Act, there were provisions for priorities, albeit limited to administration costs, charges and expenses incurred in the winding up.[91] In Queensland, the *Insolvency Act 1864* also provided a wages priority for clerks, servants, labourers and workmen without distinction. In comparison to other jurisdictions this Act provided for higher amounts to be claimed, for example a maximum of £50.

As mentioned above, the British legislation of 1869 saw further development, in which the time frame increased by 1 month to 4 months. In another development the express mention of a maximum amount for labourers and workman was eliminated. New legislation in Tasmania in 1870 reflected the new British position.[92] While Western Australia introduced a similar priority in 1871,[93] using the same treatment for clerks and servants, it remained completely silent on the fate of labourers and workman.

In 1874, the Queensland parliament enacted an *Insolvency Act*,[94] which replicated its earlier 1864 treatment of a priority for wages or salary of a clerk, servant, labourer or workman that amounted to not more than £50 over 3 months. So it can be seen the treatment of clerks and servants in Queensland was a little harsher, in the sense that they could claim priority for only 3 months' wages, while Britain had changed its legislation 5 years before to grant a period of 4 months. On the other hand, the Queensland provision gave one more month's entitlement to a priority for labourers' wages than in Britain, where the limit for such workers was two months.

Tasmania and New South Wales also enacted companies' legislation based on the British *Companies Act 1862*. Tasmania passed its *Companies Act* in 1869 and New South Wales in 1874. As observed above, these Acts gave priority only to administration expenses. Western Australia took until 1893[95] to enact legislation based on the British *Companies Act*.

87 Harmer, R. 'Employee Creditors and Corporations' in McCallum, R., McCarry, G. and Ronfeldt, P. (eds) *Employment Security* (1994) 232.

88 *Companies Act 1863* (Qld).

89 *Companies (Trading) Act 1864* (Vic).

90 *Companies Act 1864* (SA).

91 See e.g., *Companies (Trading) Act 1864* (Vic) ss101, 127.

92 *Bankruptcy Act 1870* (Tas) s31.

93 *Administration of Justice (Bankruptcy) 1871* (WA) s34.

94 *Insolvency Act 1874* (Qld) s143.

95 *Companies Act 1893* (WA) s154.

Under the *Insolvency Act 1880* (SA), the priority period for unpaid wages of clerks and servants was extended to 'four months and not exceeding Fifty Pounds', while priority was given to the wages of any labourer or workman for two months.[96] This brought South Australia into line with the British *Bankruptcy Act* of 1869. In 1886, however, the *Insolvent Act 1886* (SA) provided for a priority for servants' or clerks' wages or salary that did not exceed three months or £30.[97] Hence, this legislation provided a worse outcome for workers than the previous Act of 6 years earlier and reflected the 1860 legislation! The reason for this appears to be that new insolvency legislation in Britain in 1883 was followed without dissent by the colonial legislature and the deterioration of the worker's position upon his or her employer's insolvency was simply not realized. For labourers and workmen the 1880 Act[98] provided a priority for 2 months wages without specifying an amount. By the 1886 Act[99] they were limited to £6 but had no expressed time limitation.

The *Bankruptcy Act* of 1887 in New South Wales[100] granted a priority to clerks or servants, labourers or workmen for wages of up to £50, though limited to the previous 6 months. This was the most generous treatment to date.

A Convergence of Priorities

As we have seen, the *Judicature Act* in 1875 in Britain provided that the rules relevant to the rights of creditors in bankruptcy also applied to the winding up of companies.[101] Then in 1888, the *Preferential Payments in Bankruptcy Act 1888* extended priorities to the winding up of companies. In 1890, Britain made substantial changes to its insolvency law in the *Companies (Winding up) Act 1890*. The main purpose of this Act was to assimilate procedures in winding up and bankruptcy.

Following these developments, the colonial legislatures drafted *Companies Acts* that included provisions dedicated to insolvency. As described above, the colonies had earlier developed laws dealing with the winding up of companies but had left out express mention of priorities.[102] Now these were included. However, by the late 1880s the adoption of the Judicature Act in the colonies, while assisting in other areas, had also created uncertainty in the approach that was to be taken for

96 *Insolvency Act 1880* (SA) s63.
97 *Insolvent Act 1886* (SA) s201.
98 *Insolvency Act 1880* (SA) s63.
99 *Insolvent Act 1886* (SA) s202.
100 *Bankruptcy Act 1887* (NSW).
101 *Judicature Act 1875* (UK) s10.
102 See e.g., *An Act to facilitate the dissolution and provide for winding up the affairs of Joint Stock Companies 1854* (SA).

priorities. As seen above this was a factor that led the British parliament to enact the *Preferential Payments in Bankruptcy Act 1888.*

In 1885, Victoria enacted the *Companies' Wages Act 1885*, which remains the only piece of legislation in Australia's history dedicated entirely to a statutory priority in insolvency. The Act referred to the distribution of assets on the winding up of a company using the companies' legislation of 1864[103] and the *Mining Companies Act 1871.* Section 3 of the Act stated that the wages of clerks and servants 'shall be paid in priority to all other debts of whatsoever kind secured or unsecured'. The priority was limited to one month's service and for an amount of no more than £25.[104] Such a priority, indeed such an Act, was surprising, particularly placing employees before the secured creditors in the distribution. In Chapter 5, there is discussion of the idea of a 'superpriority' for employee entitlements over secured creditors. This was floated by the Federal Government in 2001 and finally rejected in 2005. Had it been accepted it would have achieved exactly the outcome that the Victorian Act did, albeit more than a century later!

The first colony to pass a Companies Act that made express mention of employee priority was South Australia in 1892. Section 151 of the *Companies Act 1892* (SA) provided for employees' wages of up to £25 to have priority upon insolvency. The Crown was not bound by this Act.[105] Despite this, it was held that 'the prerogative of the Crown to require payment of debts owing to it in priority to the claims of creditors in equal degree is not taken away.'[106]

In Western Australia, the *Companies Act 1893*[107] provided for priority of wages and administration expenses. The treatment for unpaid wages was similar to previous bankruptcy legislation,[108] granting a £50 maximum for clerks and servants within 4 months. For labourers and workmen, the limit was £25 within 2 months. Previous West Australian insolvency legislation had not expressly provided a limit for labourers or workmen.

In 1895, Tasmania enacted a *Companies Act* and statutory priorities in this new legislation included both wages priority and administrative expenses. [109] The wages priorities were identical to the earlier *Bankruptcy Act* provisions in 1870. This is somewhat surprising given the 25 year time lapse, as one would expect that average weekly wages would have risen during this time. Clerks and servants still received only £50 within 4 months while labourers and workmen enjoyed a priority without specific mention of a maximum amount and limited to claims within 2 months.

103 *Companies Act* (aka '*The Companies Statute*') *1864* (Vic).

104 *Companies' Wages Act* 1885 (Vic) s3.

105 *Re Commonwealth Agricultural Service Engineers Ltd* [1928] SASR 342.

106 *Re Millingen's Ltd* [1934] SASR 72, 82 (Murray CJ).

107 *Companies Act 1893* (WA) s154.

108 *Bankruptcy Act 1871* (WA) s34.

109 *Companies Act 1895* (Tas) s29.

Australia in the 20th Century – The First 30 years of Federation

The establishment of the Australian Constitution in 1901 saw the Commonwealth being given power over bankruptcy and insolvency,[110] and trading, financial and foreign corporations, [111] although there was little legislative activity in these areas for the first 15 years. The High Court was established with jurisdiction over Commonwealth powers and decided in *Huddart, Parker and Co Pty Ltd v Moorehead*[112] that the Federal Parliament's legislative power over corporations was somewhat restricted.

The *Companies Act 1862* (UK) continued to be the major influence on corporate law and so all States had Companies Acts that included detailed insolvency provisions.[113] During this period in Britain the provisions of the *Preferential Payments in Bankruptcy Act 1888* were incorporated into the *Companies (Consolidation) Act 1908*. No changes to existing Companies Acts in Australia followed and it was only when new legislation was enacted that priorities more akin to the British developments were reflected in Australia.

During World War 1, Victoria enacted a *Companies Act 1915*. It followed the now traditional line of granting a priority for clerks and servants of the maximum amount of £50 within four months. The Act also permitted claims by workmen and labourers although it limited these claims to four months without specifying a limit on the amount of money claimed.[114] This was an increase of two months over most of the existing legislative treatment. Administration costs were also given a priority.[115]

Tasmania passed new companies legislation in 1920 and the Act increased the priority for wages or salary of a clerk or servant to a maximum of £100.[116] Workmen and labourers were also given four months (an increase of two months over the 1895 Act[117]) without an express mention of amounts.[118] As could be expected from earlier legislative examples, administration costs, including remuneration of the liquidator, were given a priority.[119]

The Commonwealth eventually used the power in s51(xvii) of the *Australian Constitution* 'to make laws for the peace, order, and good government of the Commonwealth with respect to … bankruptcy and insolvency'. It first exercised

110 *Australian Constitution* s51(xvii).

111 *Australian Constitution* s51(xx).

112 (1909) 8 CLR 330.

113 *Companies Act 1899* (NSW); *Companies (Trading) Act 1864* (Vic); *Companies Act 1863* (Qld); *Companies Act 1892* (SA); *Companies Act 1893* (WA); *Companies Act 1895* (Tas).

114 *Companies Act 1915* (Vic) s208.

115 *Companies Act 1915* (Vic) s197.

116 *Companies Act 1920* (Tas).

117 *Companies Act 1895* (Tas) s29.

118 *Companies Act 1920* (Tas) s209.

119 *Companies Act 1920* (Tas) s198.

this power when Parliament enacted the *Bankruptcy Act 1924* (Cth), which was based on the *Bankruptcy Act 1914* (UK). The *Bankruptcy Act 1924* is the first example of the Commonwealth parliament legislating for statutory priorities. However, it was an Act that applied to personal insolvency. Despite this, the authors of *The Australian Companies Acts Reconciled and Annotated* in 1937 discussed a difficulty in application of statutory priorities. They noted that by 1937 all the States in their companies' legislation had adopted the Bankruptcy Rules as to the priority of debts in winding up, but had also 'enacted certain definite rules as to priorities that differ materially in scope and principle from the Bankruptcy scheme'.[120] The authors did not give a conclusive answer to the question of whether the 'adoption' should permit the Bankruptcy Rules as to priorities to have precedence. They suggested the companies' legislation was 'not exhaustive' in regard to priorities.[121] In the 1920s the position was even more uncertain as a number of States had companies legislation dating back 25 years.[122]

The *Bankruptcy Act 1924* (Cth), in s84, provided a detailed list of 'priority of debts' which trustees had to apply in the distribution of the estate. These included: expenses and remuneration of the administration; the taxed costs of the petitioning creditor; wages or salary of any clerk, servant, labourer or workman not exceeding £50 and incurred within four months of the administration commencing; workers' compensation of up to £200; apprentice payments; municipal and other local rates, and land tax and income tax of up to one year's assessment; and, finally, rent for a period not exceeding three months. The comprehensive nature of this statutory provision followed the lead provided by s33 of the British *Bankruptcy Act 1914*.[123]

In the late 1920s, State based Companies' Acts compared less favourably in some matters of priority debt treatment due to their lack of comprehensive cover. For example there was no express priority for workers compensation in the *Companies Act 1915* (Vic), the Act that applied to company employers during the 1920s. As already indicated, in Tasmania from 1920 the worker's maximum wages priority was £100 if their employer was a company, yet under the *Bankruptcy Act* (which applied if the worker's employer was an individual and now bankrupt) it was £50. Even during the 1930s, workers enjoyed different treatment for wages depending on whether their employer was subject to the *Bankruptcy Act 1924* or the State based companies' legislation. An example of this was the treatment of labourers, who had a limit on the wages priority of £25 under the South Australian *Companies Act 1934* compared to £50 under the *Bankruptcy Act 1924* (Cth); or

120 Pilcher, N.G., Uther, A.H. and Baldock, W.J. *The Australian Companies Acts Reconciled and Annotated* (1937) 800.

121 Ibid. 801.

122 See e.g., *Companies Act 1893* (WA); *Companies Act 1892* (SA).

123 *Bankruptcy Act 1914* (UK).

the workers' compensation debt that was limited to a maximum of £100 under the State Act[124] and was twice as much under the *Bankruptcy Act*.

Australian Legislation 1930–1959

The *Companies Act* of 1929 in Britain served as a model for Australian States passing their own Companies Acts during the thirty year period of 1930–1959.

Queensland passed the first Act to reflect the British *Companies Act 1929* in 1931.[125] Section 273 provided for the right of the Crown to be paid debts of the Crown in priority and s274 provided 'preferential payments' to clerks, servants, workmen and labourers. The administration costs also had a priority under s259. In s272, the legislation incorporated the bankruptcy rules to apply to priorities. This legislation replaced the *Companies Act 1863* (Qld) after many complaints of antiquity and obsolescence concerning that law.[126]

South Australia passed a *Companies Act* in 1934.[127] A Parliamentary Joint Committee on the Companies Bill 1933 reported that 'in recent years a definite move has been made throughout Australia and New Zealand to revise the company legislation along the lines of the British acts of 1929–1930, adapting such measures to local conditions'.[128] This piece of legislation is fairly representative of the Acts of this era and is therefore explained more fully in the paragraphs that follow.

Section 234 of the *Companies Act 1934* (SA) reads:

> The Court may, in the event of the assets being insufficient to satisfy the liabilities, make an order as to the payment out of the assets of the costs, charges, and expenses incurred in the winding up in such order of priority as the Court thinks just.

This provision is representative of the administration costs provisions of this era. The *Companies Act 1929* (UK) also provided a priority for administration costs but without the need for a court order.[129]

Then, in Part IV of the Act, proof and ranking of claims were specified. Section 279 provided that:

> Subject to subsections 7 and 8 of this section, in a winding up there shall be paid in priority to all other debts after all costs, liquidator's remuneration, and expenses of or incurred in the winding-up as provided by this Act –

124 *Companies Act 1934* (SA) s279.

125 *Companies Act 1931* (Qld).

126 Editorial, *Law Institute Journal*, 1 April 1931, 81.

127 *Companies Act 1934* (SA).

128 South Australia, House of Assembly, Debates, Report No 70 (1934) 1.

129 *Companies Act 1929* (UK) s254.

> All wages or salary (whether or not earned wholly or in part by way of commission not being an overriding commission) of any clerk, servant, or commercial traveller in respect of services rendered to the company during four months next before the relevant date not exceeding Fifty Pounds;
>
> All wages of any workman or laborer not exceeding Twenty-five Pounds, whether payable for time or for piecework, in respect of service rendered to the company during four months next before the relevant date;

These two subsections dealt with the employee priority for wages and it can be seen that the priority was ranked behind the administrative expenses. The *Companies Act 1929* (UK) expressed these provisions in a similar manner, limiting the workman and labourer priority to just two months.[130] The reference to a 'commercial traveller' seems to have been the result of local conditions and had not appeared in the British statute.[131]

Section 279(1)(c) provided for workers compensation payments and taxes to be specified as priority payments:

> Unless the company is being wound up voluntarily merely for the purposes of reconstruction or of amalgamation with another company or unless the company has at the commencement of the winding-up under such a contract with insurers as is mentioned in section 13 of the Workmen's Compensation Act, 1932, rights capable of being transferred to and vested in the workman, all amounts (not exceeding in any individual case One Hundred Pounds) due in respect of compensation, or liability for compensation, under the said Act accrued before the relevant date;

Finally, s279(1)(d) provided priority for:

> All assessed land tax and income tax assessed prior to the relevant date and having become due and payable within the preceding twelve months, but not exceeding in the whole one year's assessment.[132]

---

130 *Companies Act 1929* (UK) s264.

131 There was substantial case law as to who was a clerk or servant within the meaning of the statutory priority. See *Re Klien* (1906) 22 TLR 664, [1906] WN 78 (where a commercial traveller was paid partly by periodical payments and partly by commission, the commission was salary and received the priority); *Ex parte Homburg* (1842) 2 MD & D 642 (a person engaged as a traveller at an annual salary was a clerk or servant); *Re Ashley and Smith Ltd* [1918] 2 Ch 378 (outside paid contributors to newspaper were held not to be entitled to claim priority); *Re Hartwick Fur Co* (1914) 17 DLR 853 (person engaged for selling furs on commission held to be entitled to claim priority).

132 *Companies Act 1934* (SA) s279(1)(d).

Section 279(1)(c) used the exact wording that appeared in the *Companies Act 1929* (UK), with only the section number and name of the local Act inserted to replace the British equivalent.[133] Section 279(1)(d) reflected part of the British statute[134] with the priority for land and income tax, but did not go as far as the earlier Act in including a preference to 'parochial or local rates'. None of the State Acts during this period included these rates.

The framers of s273 of the South Australian Act foresaw the possibility of a need for subrogation, particularly for payments made to employees. Subsection (3) provided that where any payment had been made on account of wages or salary to any of the employees mentioned in s279(1)(a) and (b), then the person advancing the money would have a 'right of priority in respect of the money so advanced'. They were to be paid up to the amount by which that employee 'would have been entitled to priority in the winding up'.

In s273(1) debts, that is for wages, workers compensation and taxes, were all ranked equally among themselves and were to be paid in full unless the assets were insufficient to meet them in which case subsection (4) provided that 'they shall abate in equal proportions'.

The section also gave some additional treatment to taxes. Where the assets were not able to stretch so far as the 'general creditors', then the priority debts of subsection (1) had priority over the claims of debenture-holders under any floating charge created by the company and were to be paid out of any property that comprised or was subject to the floating charges. This was not the case for s273(1)(d) debts, namely, the taxes. The tax debts did not need to be paid prior to the floating charge holder.

Landlords were also considered in the priority provisions of the 1934 Act. Section 273(6) provided that in the event of a landlord or other person distraining or having distrained on any goods or effects of the company within three months before the relevant date, then the priority debts shall be a first charge on the goods or effects so distrained or on the proceeds of their sale.

Finally, s273(8) of the South Australian Act provided for the court to make orders that it deemed 'just' where there were assets redeemed after an indemnity for the costs of litigation had been given by certain creditors. The court could make an order giving the indemnifying creditors an advantage in consideration of the risk that they had run by giving the indemnity.

The other subsection mentioned in the proviso at the very beginning of the s273 is subsection (7), which provided for insurance moneys to be passed on to third parties to whom such liability was incurred.

New South Wales passed a *Companies Act* in 1936 and Victoria in 1938. Western Australia followed in 1943. All these Acts reflected the *Companies Act 1929* (UK). Tasmania was the only State not to follow the British statute. From the

133 *Companies Act 1929* (UK) s264(d) which mentions s7 of the *Workmen's Compensation Act* 1925 (UK).

134 *Companies Act 1929* (UK).

point of view of priorities in the Tasmanian *Companies Act*, the limits on wages and salary were much lower. For example, in Queensland workers qualified for a priority in respect of services rendered during the six months before the winding up of an unlimited amount,[135] whereas workers in Tasmania from 1920 until 1959 had limits as low as four months and £100 for unpaid work.[136]

The New South Wales *Companies Act* differed from its South Australian counterpart in the area of priorities. The following paragraphs highlight the specific differences between these two States and serve as an illustration of the difficulties created in one country with many different pieces of priorities legislation and many States.[137] Workers compensation had a cap of £200 in respect of any individual case, whereas the South Australian *Companies Act* provided for amounts up to just £100. The rent priority required a calculation so that no more than three months rent was given a priority, when in South Australia there was no such restraint and unlimited amounts of rent could gain priority. Section 297(1)(b) of the *Companies Act* (NSW) provided identical treatment to the South Australian Act for clerks, servants and commercial travelers to enjoy a wages priority, but also generously included labourers and workmen in the one subsection. This meant the cap found in the South Australian legislation for labourers and workmen was much smaller than that which applied in New South Wales.

In referring to administrative expenses, the New South Wales Act included specific mention of 'the costs of the audit pursuant to section three hundred and sixteen of this Act'.[138] The South Australian *Companies Act 1934* (SA) was silent on a priority for audit costs, although there was a general reference in s279(1) to 'expenses ... incurred in winding-up as provided by this Act'.[139] Hence, an audit undertaken for the liquidator could still have been expected to fall under the priority for liquidation expenses.

The New South Wales Act provided for a tax priority and was a little more comprehensive than the South Australian Act as it referred to 'all land tax and income tax assessed or to be assessed under any Act or Commonwealth Act'.[140] The South Australian Act did not refer to the Commonwealth and its taxes, even though the taxation power constitutionally is a concurrent power.[141] The Commonwealth started using the power for income tax in during World War 1 and there was a two-tiered system of paying income tax between 1915 and 1942. Both New South Wales and South Australia kept the same time limits and prohibition on a priority of no more than one year's assessment.[142]

135 *Companies Act 1931* (Qld) s274.
136 *Companies Act 1920* (Tas) s209.
137 *Companies Act 1936* (NSW) s297(1)(c).
138 *Companies Act 1936* (NSW) s297(1)(a).
139 *Companies Act 1934* (SA) s279(1).
140 *Companies Act 1936* (NSW) s297(1).
141 *Australian Constitution* s51(ii).
142 *Companies Act 1936* (NSW) s297(1)(d); *Companies Act 1934* (SA) s279(1)(d).

The rent priority in the New South Wales *Companies Act 1936* was worded in somewhat more plain English terms than the South Australian subsection. Section 297(1)(e) read:

> So much rent reckoned from day to day, for a period not exceeding three months, as was due and payable to the landlord of the company at the relevant date.
>
> Provided that no payment shall be made under this paragraph in excess of the value of the goods on the premises, such value to be fixed by the court in a summary manner in the event of the liquidator and landlord not agreeing as to the amount.

There is no use of words like 'distrain' or mention of 'goods' or a 'first charge', yet the effect is similar. The time period is kept consistent with the earlier South Australian statute.

Finally, in the New South Wales Act the right to subrogation and use of the phrase 'right of priority' is maintained to provide a person who makes payment on account of wages or salary to 'stand in the shoes' of the employee for priority purposes. The Act describes the position of such a person as 'equal to that of' the employees.[143]

Western Australia did not grant as extensive a list of priorities as the other States, with no mention of rent or workers' compensation in the provision dealing with priorities.[144] However, these may have been granted priority by application of the 'cross-vesting section'. During this period, all States had a provision that applied bankruptcy rules to winding up. This included priorities, as illustrated by the Western Australian provision:

> [E]xcept so far as is otherwise enacted in the winding-up of an insolvent company the same rules shall prevail and be observed with regard to the respective rights of secured and unsecured creditors, ... and as to the priorities of debts and liabilities, as are in force for the time being under the law of bankruptcy.[145]

A fine example of the problems created by priorities and separate corporate insolvency provisions in the Australian States is the annotated 'The Australian Companies Act' publication,[146] which had to provide a 'reconciliation' to its practitioner readership for each section of the differing Acts during this period.

143 *Companies Act 1936* (NSW) s297(3).

144 *Companies Act 1943* (WA) s271.

145 *Companies Act 1943* (WA) s269; see also *Companies Act 1936* (NSW) s296; *Companies Act 1938* (Vic) s262; *Companies Act 1934* (SA) s278; *Companies Act 1931* (Qld) s272; *Companies Act 1920* (Tas) s208; *Companies Act 1929* (UK) s262.

146 Pilcher, N.G., Uther, A.H. and Baldock, W.J. *The Australian Companies Acts Reconciled and Annotated* (1937) 801.

When dealing with the main priorities section and the words 'in priority to all other debts,' it quotes:

> These words would appear to give preferential claims mentioned in this section an absolute priority over the other preferential claims brought into play by s296 (*that is the bankruptcy rules*) and the other relevant statutes which came into force prior to this Act, that is if the present section is to be taken as non-exhaustive as suggested above. All the State Acts give the preferential debts mentioned respectively therein priority over the claims of holders of debenture under any floating charge where the assets of the company available for the payment of general creditors are insufficient to meet them, excepting that (a) Victoria in subsec. (2) extends the priority in respect of claims for salary and wages to make it effective as against all mortgages, charges and liens created by the company; (b) New South Wales in subsec. (4) restricts the priority against the said debenture holders to wages and salary only; and (c) South Australia excludes land and income taxes from any priority against such debenture holders.

For many in business, not the least debenture-holders, such a circumstance must have led to much confusion when commerce was being transacted across State borders. It is likely that expert advice was regularly sought.

An Attempt to Add a New Priority

The proceedings of the South Australian Parliament reveal that there was an attempt in 1933 to add to the list of priority debts. During debate[147] on the Companies Bill, there was an amendment moved to include the following:

> Where the company carried on the business of a grain merchant, all amounts due or accruing due to any person in respect of grain delivered by him to the company under any contract for the sale or storage of such grain or under any other contract of the like nature relating to such grain.

A vote was taken and the motion was lost 19 votes to 16. This would really have been 'adapting' to local conditions as South Australia at the time was a large producer of wheat and other grain and wheat farmers were a powerful lobby group.[148] It was also at the time following the Great Depression and drought when

147 South Australia, *Parliamentary Debates*, House of Assembly, 31 October 1934, 168 (the House of Assembly having resolved itself into a Committee).

148 See e.g., Dean Jaensch, *The Flinders History of South Australia Political History* (1986) 235. There is some similarity with United States and Canadian priorities law, where specific local nuances see people like fishermen and foresters having special treatment. Some of these are discussed in Chapter 9 below.

feelings were still strong about the hardships suffered.[149] The debate also followed a case heard by the South Australian Supreme Court, *Verco Bros and Co Ltd*,[150] where the court was asked to provide a Crown priority in a corporate insolvency for wheat held on trust by a Board of Management set up to administer the *Farmer's Relief Act 1931* (SA). Nonetheless, to allow a new priority would have added to a lack of uniformity with the other States, a matter that had already been expressed by commentators of the day to be an important motivation to reform companies' legislation.[151]

The Uniform Companies Acts in the Period 1960–1981

The *Uniform Companies Acts* were the first attempt by the States to standardize their companies legislation and, in many respects, the Acts followed the *Companies Act 1948* (UK). For statutory priorities, it was the first time in Australia's history that all parts of the country had exactly the same provisions. Two States, Victoria and Tasmania, had legislated in 1958[152] and 1959[153] respectively to accept this British Act 'in toto'.

During 1961, all States enacted essentially identical legislation and so it was possible to speak of the statutory priorities section which was identical in the *Companies Act* of each State.[154]

In s292 of the *Companies Act 1962* (SA), the statutory priorities were expressed as follows:

> (1) Subject to the provisions of this Act, in a winding up there shall be paid in priority to all other unsecured debts –
>
> firstly, the costs and expenses of the winding up including the taxed costs of a petitioner payable under section 224, the remuneration of the liquidator and the costs of any audit carried out pursuant to section 281;

149 Ibid. 240–241.

150 [1933] SASR 264.

151 Editorial, *Law Institute Journal* 1 April 1931, 81; 'South Australian Company Legislation' (1927) 1 *Australian Law Journal* 89 (5 July 1927), Holmes, J.D. 'A Commonwealth Companies Act' (1934) 7 *Australian Law Journal* 37 (15 February 1934). See McQueen, R. 'An Examination of Australian Corporate Law and Regulation 1901–1961' (1992) 15 *University of New South Wales Law Journal* 1, 17, where the author claims the 'matter was hotly debated amongst a variety of interest groups throughout the 1920s and 1930s'.

152 *Companies Act 1958* (Vic).

153 *Companies Act 1959* (Tas).

154 *Companies Act 1961* (NSW); *Companies Act 1961* (Vic); *Companies Act 1961* (Qld); *Companies Act 1961* (WA); *Companies Act 1961* (Qld); *Companies Act 1962* (SA); *Companies Act 1962* (Tas); *Companies Act 1962* (ACT); *Companies Act 1962* (NT).

> secondly, all wages or salary (whether or not earned wholly or in part by way of commission not being an overriding commission) including any amount payable by way of allowance or reimbursement under any contract of employment or award or agreement regulating conditions of employment, of any employee not exceeding Five hundred dollars whether for time or piecework in respect of services rendered by him to the company within a period of six months before the commencement of the winding up;
>
> thirdly, all amounts due in respect of workmen's compensation under the Workmen's Compensation Act, 1932, as amended, and accrued before the commencement of the winding up;
>
> fourthly, all remuneration payable to any employee in respect of annual leave or long service leave or sick leave or all three, or in the case of his death to any other person in his right, accrued in respect of any period before the commencement of the winding up; and
>
> fifthly, the amount of all municipal or other local rates due from the company at the date of the commencement of the winding up and having become due and payable within the twelve months next preceding that date, the amount of all land tax and income tax assessed under any Act or Act of the Commonwealth before the date of the commencement of the winding up and not exceeding in the whole one year's assessment; and any amount due and payable by way of repayment of any advance made to the company, or in payment of any amount owing by the company for goods supplied or services rendered to it under any Act or Act of the Commonwealth or law of a Territory of the Commonwealth relating to or providing for the improvement, development or settlement of land or the aid, development or encouragement of mining.

In comparing this Act to earlier legislation, there was not a great deal of reform across the statute and the priorities section is similarly not much different. The New South Wales *Companies Act 1961* had an identical five subsections covering the subject matter aligned to what is mapped out above for South Australia.[155] However, in an example that nicely demonstrates problems with 'uniform' legislation that is not national, the limited amounts for the wages' priority were £300 and 4 months in New South Wales,[156] Queensland[157] and Western Australia,[158] compared to the limits of £500 and 6 months in South Australia.[159] For the workers' compensation priority, South Australia had no limit, while in the

155 *Companies Act 1961* (NSW) s292(1).
156 *Companies Act 1961* (NSW) s292(1)(b).
157 *Companies Act 1961* (Qld) s292(1)(b).
158 *Companies Act 1961* (WA) s292(1)(b).
159 *Companies Act 1962* (SA) s292.

Companies Act 1961 (NSW) (and the other states in the uniform scheme!) it was limited to just £1,000.[160]

The other section that concerned priorities in this uniform companies' legislation was s217, which in substance stated that the provisions of the Companies Act relating to the remedies against property, priorities of debts and the effect of arrangements with creditors were binding on the Crown.[161] As these were State Acts, the constitutional concept of inconsistency by virtue of s109 of the Australian Constitution applied. Therefore, if a State Act provided an order of priorities for the payment of debts in a winding up and a Commonwealth Act made a different order of priorities, the State Act would be invalid to the extent of the inconsistency. The State Act in such a situation was not repealed, as only the State concerned could repeal it, but the provision was ineffective. In a State Companies Act, the effect of binding the Crown in the right of a State was to waive its normal right to first priority in payment of debts. Further, while there was a subsection that recognized that income tax would be paid, but after other priorities, the law of a State could not take from the Commonwealth its right to first priority for payment; only a Commonwealth Act or an agreement by the Commonwealth could have effectively changed the Commonwealth's order of priority.[162]

Section 221 of the Commonwealth *Income Tax Assessment Act 1936* provided an order of priority for tax due in the winding up of a company, yet referred only to the order of priority in the *Bankruptcy Act 1924.* There was no mention of the Companies Acts as they were State Acts under the uniform companies' legislation.

The Commonwealth enacted a new *Bankruptcy Act* in 1966. It did not represent a radical departure from the general pattern of bankruptcy law as reflected in the earlier Act of 1924. It is still in operation. Section 109 of this Act is the provision directing priority payments. It maintains priorities for administration costs, funeral and testamentary expenses, salary wages and commissions up to a maximum (currently $1500), workers' compensation and other entitlements, and child support payments. It also recognizes some sections of the *Income Tax Assessment Act 1936* (Cth). However, since its enactment the role of the *Bankruptcy Act 1966* (Cth) has had a diminished impact upon corporate insolvency priority law.[163] This is dissimilar to the role described earlier of the *Bankruptcy Act 1924* (Cth) in the

160 *Companies Act 1961* (NSW) s292(1)(c).The same provision also appeared in the Queensland and Western Australian Acts.

161 *Companies Act 1961* (NSW) s217 and all other States' Companies Act at the same section number.

162 Mason, H.H. and O'Hair, J.S. *Australian Company Law* (2nd ed. 1973) 350.

163 There was still some impact of the *Bankruptcy Act 1966* (Cth) on corporate insolvency priorities in the 1960s. The Commonwealth's *Income Tax Assessment Act 1936* in s221 provided an order of priority for tax due in the winding up of a company and referred to the order of priority in the *Bankruptcy Act*.

1920s and through the years until the extended treatment of priorities reflected in the companies legislation in the 1960s.

A National Cooperative Scheme for Company Law

A cooperative scheme was developed in the 1980s to further establish a national regulatory approach for companies and, by association, the winding up provisions. Again, the reform was an attempt at uniformity as some States had moved away from this ideal by making legislative changes in their own Companies Acts.

The Commonwealth passed legislation that applied only in the Australian Capital Territory and each State passed legislation applying the Commonwealth legislation as its own law. This legislative package of the Commonwealth Acts and State Application Acts was referred to as a Code.[164] Hence in South Australia, for example, the companies' legislation was referred to as the *Companies (South Australia) Code*. The uniform legislation came into force on 1 July 1981 for all six States and the ACT.

Section 441 of the Companies Code, which operated throughout all of Australia between 1981 and 1990, provided for statutory priority payments. As originally enacted, the section read …

> Section 441 Priority Payments
>
> Subject to the following provisions of this Subdivision, in the winding up of a company the following debts shall be paid in priority to all other unsecured debts;
>
> first, the costs, charges and expenses of the winding up, including the taxed costs of an applicant payable under section 366, the remuneration of the liquidator and the costs of any audit carried out under section 422;
>
> if the winding up was preceded by the appointment of a provisional liquidator – second, the costs, charges and expenses properly and reasonably incurred by the provisional liquidator during the period of his appointment and the remuneration of the provisional liquidator;
>
> where the winding up commences within 2 months after the end of a period of official management of the company – third, the costs, charges and expenses of and incidental to the official management properly and reasonably incurred by the official manager during the period of official management, including the remuneration of the official manager, of any deputy official manager and of any auditor appointed in accordance with Division 3 of Part VI;

164 Lipton, P. and Herzberg, A. *Understanding Company Law* (12th ed. 2004) 6.

where the winding up commences within 2 months after the end of a period of official management of the company – fourth, debts of the company properly and reasonably incurred by the official manager in the conduct by him of the business of the company during the period of official management;

fifth, wages in respect of services rendered to the company by employees before the relevant date, but not exceeding $2000 in respect of an excluded employee of the company;

sixth, all amounts due in respect of injury compensation, being compensation the liability for which arose before the relevant date;

(g) seventh, all amounts due –

(i) on or before the relevant date;

(ii) by virtue of an industrial instrument;

(iii) to, or in respect of, employees of the company; and

(iv) in respect of leave of absence,

but not exceeding $1,500 in respect of an excluded employee of the company;

(ga) eighth, retrenchment payments payable to employees of the company (other than excluded employees of the company);

(h) ninth –

(i) all amounts of rates, being rate that are, or are in the nature of, municipal or other local rates (other than rates imposed by an Act or law of the Territory) that were due and payable at the relevant date and the liability for which accrued within the 12 months that next preceded that date;

(ii) all amounts of income tax that were assessed under any State Act or law of another Territory before the relevant date, not exceeding in the whole one year's assessment;

(iii) all amounts of land tax that were assessed under any State Act or law of another Territory before the relevant date, not exceeding in the whole one year's assessment;

(iv) all amounts of pay-roll tax (other than pay-roll tax imposed by an Act) that were due and payable at the relevant date; or

(v) all amounts that were due and payable, at the relevant date –

by way of repayment of any advance made to the company; or

in respect of goods supplied or services rendered to the company, under any State Act or law of another Territory relating to or providing for the improvement, development or settlement of land or the aid, development or encouragement of mining; and

(j) tenth, any amount that, pursuant to an order under section 309 of this Act or under section 33 of the *Securities Industry Act* 1980, the company was at the relevant date under an obligation to pay.

In comparison to earlier Acts already discussed in this chapter, there was a lot more specific detail for administration expenses, particularly incorporating the phrase 'official management' and not just limiting the priority to liquidation expenses. The employee priorities remained, although they were again given more detail and the Code specified the broad types of employment that were covered. Introduced by this legislation was the limitation placed upon excluded employees, which is discussed in Chapter 5. Tax priorities continued in some form and in 1985 s441(1)(j) was included to introduce a Crown priority for the costs of a statutory investigation. Such investigation costs were denied under earlier case law.[165]

The effect of the *Bankruptcy Act 1966* (Cth) upon statutory priorities in corporate insolvency was finally resolved by s438(2) of the Code. This subsection provided that the rules of bankruptcy were made subject to s441 of the Code, so that s441 represented the principal source of statutory priorities in winding up.

The Corporations Act (or Law) 1990 – Present

The Commonwealth took an expansive view of constitutional power in the late 1980s and passed a *Corporations Act 1989* that largely replicated the Companies Code. After a successful constitutional challenge by the States,[166] and then agreement between the Commonwealth and the States, the States each passed an

165 *Re Denton Sub-Divisions Pty Ltd* (1968) 89 WN NSW 231.

166 *New South Wales v Commonwealth* (1990) 169 CLR 482, 8 ACLC 120. The legislative package passed by the Commonwealth in September 1989 was challenged by several States in the High Court alleging that it was unconstitutional, particularly the provisions concerning the incorporation of companies. The Court held that the Commonwealth did not have power to pass laws with respect to the incorporation of trading

Act applying to companies using the *Corporations Act* of 1989 as a basis. The State legislation was entitled *Corporations* (*name of State*) *Act 1990* and was in force from 1 January 1991. The legislation was referred to as the 'Corporations Law'. In August 2000, after more constitutional and cross-vesting challenges,[167] all the States and the Northern Territory referred their legislative powers with respect to corporations to the Commonwealth Parliament. This meant that a comprehensive Commonwealth statute on corporate law could then be enacted under s51(xxxvii) of the Constitution and apply nationally in the same way as any other Commonwealth statute.[168] This statute is known as the *Corporations Act 2001* (Cth) and is currently in operation.

Throughout this period the statutory priority provision in s556, reproduced in Chapter 1, remained relatively unchanged. Section 556 varied from its predecessor s441 in a number of matters, albeit mostly superficial. Chapters 4 and 5 below will discuss the changes to administration expenses and employee entitlements respectively. With administration expenses, the addition of a voluntary administration regime required additional priority considerations since 1993. With the employee entitlements, the major variation between s441 and the present s556 is the removal of monetary limits for most employees. The most recognizable change from s441 to the present provisions is the complete removal of rates and taxes and this is discussed in Chapter 6 below.

Conclusion

This chapter has reviewed the relevant history of statutory priorities. The review suggests that the Australian legal position with respect to priorities at the present time, as outlined in Chapter 1, is not so radically different from previous versions from the Australian colonies and later States. Comparisons with Britain and other common law countries are appropriate given the closeness of the mother country and her colonies particularly in the nineteenth century. Perhaps there is a conservatism demonstrated by the history that suggests a need to constantly justify the position of priority creditors and not depart from the status quo. However, there is evidence presented in this chapter that there has been a gradual amassment of priorities' law to deal with a reasonably settled list of creditors. Later chapters will explore potential new priorities keeping in mind the history as outlined here.

---

and financial corporations and therefore did not have the power to completely take over corporate regulation.

167 See *R v Wakim* (1999) 198 CLR 511, 17 ACLC 1055; *Bond v R* (2000) 201 CLR 213, 169 ALR 607; *R v Hughes* (2000) 202 CLR 535, 171 ALR 155.

168 Austin, R.P. and Ramsay, I.M. *Ford's Principles of Corporations Law* (12th ed. 2005) 42–45.

Chapter 3

Theoretical Perspectives and Visions for Statutory Priorities

Many countries including Australia do not have a developed theoretical perspective on statutory priorities in corporate insolvency. Indeed an advanced common law country like Australia cannot claim to have developed theoretical perspectives on any aspect of corporate insolvency. At best there is some agreement that certain principles influence good local insolvency law-making.[1] Given this absence it is apposite to explore statutory priorities perspectives by commencing with some thoughts on corporate law in general.

Australian and British corporate law has developed in a pragmatic and piecemeal way, with different perspectives exerting varying degrees of influence over the present law.[2] It is rare to find these perspectives expressly stated, as such conceptual frameworks tend to remain 'beneath the text of the statute or judicial decision'.[3]

The corporation is most commonly regarded as being capable of reduction to a series of contracts, albeit a large number, and this is referred to as a 'nexus of contracts' perspective. Such a perspective is given statutory support in the Australian *Corporations Act 2001* (Cth) as there is an express provision[4] recognizing a statutory contract between the company and its directors, the company and its members and the members with each other.[5]

Internationally it has been argued that corporate insolvency law also operates through a contractual perspective, as its features are conveniently viewed as being

1 See, the principles of insolvency first listed as 'aims' in Australian Law Reform Commission, *General Insolvency Inquiry*, Report No 45 (1988) 'Harmer Report', para 33.

2 Tomasic, R., Bottomley, S. and McQueen, R. *Corporations Law in Australia* (2nd ed. 2002) 52.

3 Ibid. The authors mention concession theory, aggregate theory, economic theories, natural entity theory, communitarian theory, feminist theories, corporate social responsibility, and an organizational perspective.

4 *Corporations Act 2001* (Cth) s140(1) reads 'A company's constitution (if any) and any replaceable rules that apply to the company have effect as a contract: (a) between the company and each member; and (b) between the company and each director and company secretary; and (c) between a member and each other member'.

5 See e.g., Lipton, P. and Herzberg, A. *Understanding Corporate Law* (12th ed. 2004) 91–96.

grounded in contract.[6] This is understandable as the law of corporate insolvency focuses on the rights of creditors and their corporate debtor, and such rights tend to arise from a contractual relationship.

In quite recent times, this dominant perspective of the contract in corporate law and its influence on corporate insolvency law has been challenged by a few scholars, whose vision for these areas of law suggests the application of broader considerations. Such challengers have developed perspectives that go beyond contractual analysis to incorporate other factors such as a range of community interests, recognition of ethical issues and accepting that multiple values can apply.

This chapter begins by acknowledging and explaining the dominant perspective in corporate law and its tendency to be the most widely accepted perspective in corporate insolvency law as well. Next, the challenges to these dominant perspectives are considered. Following this, the chapter introduces other less traditional perspectives such as the inclusion of the community and broader notions of influence on corporate insolvency law. The topic of statutory priorities in corporate insolvency lends itself to such broader notions and so the chapter concludes by supporting the broader view.

The Nexus of Contracts Perspective

Recently the nexus of contracts perspective as it applies to corporate law was explained in this fashion:

> each corporation consists of multiple bilateral contracts between equity and debt investors, corporate managers and directors, and others; the corporation represents a mere series of contracts joining inputs to produce outputs.[7]

Such an explanation suggests corporate law can be interpreted as part of the wider understanding of contract law and policy, sometimes called contractarianism and linked to a law and economics analysis.[8]

---

6 See e.g., Baird, D.A. and Jackson, T.H. 'Corporate Reorganization and the Treatment of Diverse Ownership Interests: A Comment on Adequate Protection of Secured Creditors in Bankruptcy' (1984) 51 *University of Chicago Law Review* 97; Jackson, T.H. *The Logic and Limits of Bankruptcy Law* (1986).

7 Spender, P. and Bottomley, S. 'How to do things with Contractarianism' (2004) 13 *Griffith Law Review* 9, 11 using work by Bratton, W. 'The Nexus of Contracts' Corporation: A Critical Appraisal' (1989) 74 *Cornell Law Review* 407, 420.

8 See e.g., Easterbrook, F.H. and Fischel, D.R. *The Economic Structure of Corporate Law* (1991) 35–39; Bottomley, S. and Parker, S. *Law in Context* (2nd ed. 1997) 280; Spender, P. and Bottomley, S. 'How to do things with Contractarianism' (2004) 13 *Griffith Law Review* 9, 11.

The modern nexus of contract perspective was originated in 1937 by Coase,[9] with his theory of 'the firm'. He is accredited with first identifying the similarities between corporations and markets.[10] In 1972, Jensen and Meckling summarized the perspective by viewing the corporation as simply 'one form of legal fiction which serves as a nexus of contracting relationships'.[11] More recently, this has been expressed by defining the corporation 'as a specialist contracting intermediary, delineated by the several contracts entered into by persons interested in the output and cash flows produced'.[12]

From such descriptions, it is obvious that the perspective is consistent with an economic analysis.[13] 'Law and economics' encompasses an enormous amount of scholarship, directed towards 'gaining a better understanding of the economic nature and consequences of law'.[14]

Corporate law is an obvious area where the law is explicitly engaged in regulating economic activity.[15] Frequently therefore corporate law scholarship couches both normative and descriptive explanations of the corporation in terms of a nexus of contracts.[16]

---

9 Coase, R. 'The Nature of the Firm' (1936) 4 *Economica* 386. Coase explored the existence of a firm (corporation) and how it could be reconciled with resource allocation. He analysed the decentralised process of the market, which achieves an orderly movement of goods and services according to the price mechanism.

10 An earlier work had contemplated some of these visions: see Berle, A. and Means, G. *The Modern Corporation and Private Property* (1932).

11 Jensen, M.C. and Meckling, W.H. 'Theory of the Firm: Managerial Behaviour, Agency Costs, and Ownership Structures' (1976) 3 *Journal of Financial Economics* 305, 311.

12 Whincop, M. '*Gambotto v WCP Ltd*: Economic Analysis of Alterations to Articles and Expropriation Articles' (1995) 23 *Australian Business Law Review* 276, 277.

13 See Bainbridge, S.M. 'The Board of Directors as Nexus of Contracts: A Critique of Gulati, Klien & Zolt's "Connected Contracts" Model' (2002) 88 *Iowa Law Review* 1, 4 where he states 'most corporate law scholars today embrace some variant of shareholder primacy … A more recent variation, which arguably is the dominant model in today's scholarship, blends two economic theories – the nexus of contracts theory of the firm and agency cost economics'.

14 Posner, R.A. 'Foreword', *Encyclopaedia of Law and Economics* at <http://encyclo.findlaw.com/foreword.html> accessed on 12/08/05.

15 Law and economics is subject to many internal variations and these are well recognized, but it is beyond the scope of this work to explore them. See e.g., *Encyclopaedia of Law and Economics* <http://encyclo.findlaw.com>.

16 See e.g., Eisenberg, M. 'The Conception that the Corporation is a Nexus of Contracts, and the Dual Nature of the Firm' (1999) 24 *Journal of Corporations Law* 819; Blair, M. and Stout, L. 'A Team Production Theory of Corporate Law' (1999) 85 *Virginia Law Review* 247; Bratton, W. 'The 'Nexus of Contracts' Corporation: A Critical Appraisal' (1989) 74 *Cornell Law Review* 407.

Contractarianism in the corporate law context 'emphasises the importance of market forces in aligning the interests of corporate managers and shareholders … rather than legal rules'.[17] As Austin and Ramsay suggest

> [A]ccording to the contractual theory, competitive markets are more important than mandatory legal rules in providing managers with appropriate incentives to maximise shareholder wealth. These markets include the product market, the market for corporate control and the managerial labour market.[18]

Here, contractarianism suggests less need to have government-imposed regulation to require managers to act in the interests of shareholders, as this is achieved through the market forces.[19]

The contractualists assert that 'mandatory legal rules imposed by governments will rarely be preferable to individual contracting'.[20] Thus the 'role of government-imposed corporate law, under [contractarianism], is limited' to legal rules that 'deter one-off instances of management self-dealing that cannot be prevented by market forces' and to imposing 'standard form contracts which reduce the transaction costs [associated with] negotiating new contracts'.[21] Austin and Ramsay suggest that some aspects of the *Corporations Act* duties on directors are an example of government-imposed corporate law which relieves the companies from using standard form contracts with their directors for these duties.[22] It also alleviates 'the expense of incorporating the duties into individual contracts with directors'.[23]

Challenges to the Nexus of Contracts Theory in Corporate Law

Various challenges have been made to the contractarian approach to corporate law. Some commentators suggest that according to the nexus of contracts perspective, the only relevant function of a company is to maximize returns to individual investors.[24] This maximization of shareholder wealth is certainly an assumption of contractarianism in corporate law. Such an analysis treats the corporation as 'nothing more than a shorthand expression for a multiplicity of private, consensual, contract-based relations between economic actors, each seeking to

---

17 Austin, R.P. and Ramsay, I.M. *Ford's Principles of Corporations Law* (12th ed. 2005) 25.

18 Ibid. 26.

19 Ibid.

20 Ibid.

21 Ibid.

22 Ibid.

23 Ibid.

24 Tomasic, R., Bottomley, S. and McQueen, R. *Corporations Law in Australia* (2nd ed. 2002) 57.

maximise his or her own benefits'.[25] If this is the case then there appears to be little room for other considerations beyond these private relations. It is in these other considerations where government-imposed corporate law has a role. One response to this challenge has been the growth in calls for social responsibility for corporations.[26]

The nexus of contracts approach has also been criticized as insufficiently 'contractual' and lacking a 'nexus'.[27] Yet those critics continue to support contractarianism by offering a replacement perspective that still maintains a 'web of interlocking connected contracts'.[28] Bainbridge has recently argued that 'the' nexus remains in the contractarian perspective of the corporation and is found with the board of directors.[29] However, as described above, Austin and Ramsay suggest even the regulation of the board's relationship with the company requires a government-imposed corporate law and not just the nexus achieved through market forces and voluntary contracting.[30]

Australian Literature

Beginning in the 1980s, there has been a limited amount of Australian corporate law scholarship that explores broader perspectives to supplement the doctrinal discussion on legal rules.[31] Most of this scholarship draws heavily on law and economics analysis and its contractarian connection, with little modification for Australian conditions.[32]

Whincop, who has been regarded as pre-eminent in the Australian scholarship on corporate law perspectives, was one writer who strongly supported a contractarian

25 Ibid. 58.

26 See e.g., Lansdown, R. and Segal, J. 'The Social Responsibility of Modern Corporations' (1978) 2 *University of New South Wales Law Journal* 336; Sarre, R., Doig, M. and Fiedler, B. 'Reducing the Risk of Corporate Irresponsibility: The Trend to Corporate Social Responsibility' (2001) 25(3) *Accounting Forum* 300.

27 Gulati, G.M., Klien, W.A. and Zolt, E.M. 'Connected Contracts' (2000) 47 *University of California Los Angeles Law Review* 887.

28 Oman, N. 'Corporations and Autonomy Theories of Contract: A Critique of the New *Lex Mercatoria*' (2005) <http://papers.ssrn.com/sol3/papers.cfm?abstract_id=681728> 31.

29 Bainbridge, S.M. 'The Board of Directors as Nexus of Contracts: A Critique of Gulati, Klein & Zolt's "Connected Contracts" Model' (2002) 88 *Iowa Law Review* 1, 7.

30 Austin, R.P. and Ramsay, I.M. *Ford's Principles of Corporations Law* (12th ed. 2005) 26.

31 Spender, P. and Bottomley, S. 'How to Do Things with Contractarianism' (2004) 13 *Griffith Law Review* 9, 10 and 13.

32 See e.g., Tomasic, R., Bottomley, S. and McQueen, R. *Corporations Law in Australia* (2nd ed. 2002) 58.

vision.[33] Whincop attempted to develop a more sophisticated perspective to take into account the context of Australian corporate law.[34] Part of this development involved using a relational contract perspective,[35] with a recognition that contracts often involve complex and long-term relations between parties, rather than discrete transactions and so also involve significant elements of non-economic personal satisfaction.[36] This perspective emphasizes the importance of flexible and generalized obligations in contracts and the existence of multiparty contracts. Furthermore, from a corporate law perspective it focuses on the relationship between the corporate parties rather than the intended product of that relationship.[37] Additionally, it treats the parties as private, autonomous and rational decision-makers.

Creditors' Bargain – Insolvency's Nexus of Contracts Perspective

Turning now to the specific context of insolvency, the nexus of contracts perspective is difficult to apply to the insolvent corporation. Many of the contractual relationships will have terminated when the corporation is in insolvency and consequently the board of management will no longer provide the key 'nexus'. However, the notion of shareholder primacy that underpins the contractarian perspective can be substituted in an insolvent corporation by the concept of creditor primacy – a requirement to act in the interests of creditors and to maximize their distribution from the estate. Indeed, over the last two decades the dominant model of insolvency law has taken this as a starting point. The so-called 'creditors' bargain' model asserts that the most prominent features of insolvency law are best seen as reflecting the notional agreement the creditors of the corporation themselves would have struck if given the chance to bargain with each other before anyone had extended credit. It is a perspective of an *ex*

---

33 Whincop's scholarship is celebrated in volume 13 of the *Griffith Law Review* (2004) following his tragic death in 2003. His most substantial output included a book, *An Economic and Jurisprudential Geneaology of Corporate Law* (2001) and numerous articles including 'Nexuses of Contracts, Corporate Authority Doctrine and Doctrinal Indeterminacy: From Formalism to Law and Economics' (1997) 20 *University of New South Wales Law Journal* 274.

34 Whincop, M. 'A Relational and Doctrinal Critique of Shareholders' Special Contracts' (1997) 19 *Sydney Law Review* 314.

35 For an overview on relational contract analysis, see e.g., McNeil, I.R. *The New Social Contract* (1980); Paterson, J., Robertson, A. and Heffey, P. *Principles of Contract Law* (2nd ed. 2005); Campbell, D., Collins, H. and Wightman, J. *Implicit Dimensions of Contract; Discrete, Relational and Network Contracts* (2003).

36 Spender, P. and Bottomley, S. 'How to do things with Contractarianism' (2004) 13 *Griffith Law Review* 9, 13.

37 Whincop, M. 'A Relational and Doctrinal Critique of Shareholders' Special Contracts' (1997) 19 *Sydney Law Review* 314, 328.

ante bargain for a collective regime.[38] As such the model has obvious links to the contractarian perspective as it applies to corporate law.

The creditors' bargain model developed in the United States as a result of discussion regarding the aims of insolvency law. It is by far the most developed of insolvency perspectives and while 'currently rather unfashionable'[39] is the model that constitutes the 'only sustained attempt at a principled analysis of the law governing bankrupt companies'.[40] Its major advocate, Jackson,[41] proposes a restrictive view that insolvency law is to be analysed as collectivized debt collection law, whose purpose is the efficient coordination of the claims of creditors in order to enhance the value of the debtors' assets for all claimants.[42] When diverse co-owners (creditors) assert rights against a common pool and achieve the same return as if the individual creditors had enforced their own claims,[43] this is known as the 'creditors' bargain'.

The creditors' bargain perspective 'is argued to justify the compulsory, collectivist regime of insolvency law on the grounds that', if 'company creditors' were 'free to agree' to 'forms of enforcement of their claims on insolvency, they would agree to collectivist arrangements rather than procedures of individual action or partial collectivism'.[44] Jackson recognizes that this system is 'attractive to creditors' as it reduces 'strategic costs' and is 'administratively efficient'.[45] The result is then a greater pool of assets. Finch concludes (and, in a way, Jackson admits[46]) that it follows from this position that 'the protection of non-creditor interests of other victims of corporate decline, such as employees, managers and members of the community, is not the role of insolvency law'.[47]

---

38 Jackson, T.H. *The Logic and Limits of Bankruptcy Law* (1986) 17 where he suggests 'a system designed to mirror the agreements one would expect creditors to arrive at were they able to negotiate such agreements *ex ante*'.

39 Mokal, R.J. *Corporate Insolvency Law Theory and Application* (2005) 34.

40 Ibid.

41 Jackson, T.H. *The Logic and Limits of Bankruptcy Law* (1986) 3 and 39; Baird, D.G. 'The Uneasy Case for Corporate Reorganisations' (1986) 15 *Journal of Legal Studies* 127; Baird, D.G. and Jackson, T.H. 'Corporate Reorganisations and the Treatment of Diverse Ownership Interests: A Comment on Adequate Protection of Secured Creditors in Bankruptcy' (1984) 51 *University of Chicago Law Review* 97.

42 Ibid.

43 Jackson, T.H. 'Bankruptcy, Non-Bankruptcy Entitlements, and the Creditors' Bargain' (1982) 91 *Yale Law Journal* 857, 864.

44 Finch, V. *Corporate Insolvency Law Perspectives and Principle* (2002) 28.

45 Jackson, T.H. *The Logic and Limits of Bankruptcy Law* (1986) 25.

46 Ibid.

47 Finch, V. *Corporate Insolvency Law Perspectives and Principle* (2002) 28.

Critiques of the Creditors' Bargain Perspective

Recently Cole wrote

> When Thomas Jackson published *The Logic and Limits of Bankruptcy Law* in 1986 he framed virtually all bankruptcy scholarship that would follow for the next fifteen years ... This 'creditors' bargain' approach has divided the world of bankruptcy academics into two camps: the 'Law and Economics' scholars who appear to adopt the creditors' bargain as the essential purpose of bankruptcy, and the 'Progressives' who contend that the purpose of bankruptcy is to promote social welfare, ordering and redistribution that is not politically feasible through other means. The common pool, according to the Progressives, should be shared by more claimants than the Law and Economics scholars are willing to acknowledge.[48]

Critiques of the creditors' bargain model, and of the law and economics scholarship that underlies it, have been made by 'progressive' voices in the United States and the United Kingdom. The main United States critiques are presented by Warren[49] and Korobkin,[50] while in the United Kingdom the most substantial work is presented by Finch,[51] and more recently Mokal.[52]

Warren advances a case for consideration of a wider set of interests that includes those of employees and suppliers.[53] She suggests that insolvency law is 'more

48 Cole, G.M. 'Limiting Liability Through Bankruptcy' (2001–2002) 70 *University of Cincinnati Law Review* 1245, 1251.

49 Warren, E. 'Bankruptcy Policy' (1987) 54 *University of Chicago Law Review* 775.

50 Korobkin, D.R. 'Rehabilitating Values: A Jurisprudence of Bankruptcy' (1991) 91 *Columbia Law Review* 717.

51 Finch, V. *Corporate Insolvency Law Perspectives and Principles* (2002).

52 Mokal, R.J. *Corporate Insolvency Law: Theory and Application* (2005) 34.

53 There has been a longstanding debate in corporate law concerning the question of to whom a corporation owes a duty. Most commentators would agree that the officers and directors owe a duty to shareholders as they invested in the company and so are exposed to some risk. Some commentators have also suggested that solvent companies owe a duty to act as socially responsible citizens and there is evidence of a slight trend in corporate legislation toward this. For example the *Corporations Act 2001* (Cth) s299 (1) (f) requires certain disclosure of environmental issues. See generally, Lansdown, R. and Segal, J. 'The Social Responsibility of Modern Corporations' (1978) 2 *University of New South Wales Law Journal* 336; Sarre, R., Doig, M. and Fiedler, B. 'Reducing the Risk of Corporate Irresponsibility: The Trend to Corporate Social Responsibility' (2001) 25(3) *Accounting Forum* 300; Sarre, R. 'Responding to Corporate Collapses: Is There a Role for Corporate Social Responsibility?' (2002) 7 *Deakin Law Review* 1.

complex and ultimately less confined'[54] than proponents of the creditors' bargain model such as Baird and Jackson might suggest. Warren uses Congressional comments on the United States *Bankruptcy Code* to support 'concerns broader than the immediate problem of debtors and their identified creditors'.[55] Congress has stated that insolvency policies should reflect a public interest that goes beyond the debtor and creditor.[56] Although there is ready acknowledgment that the creditors' bargain perspective is attractive because it is straightforward and central, Warren observes that it can close off further inquiry into insolvency analysis.[57]

Korobkin[58] suggests that the economic approach is incapable of recognizing non-economic values such as moral, political, social and personal considerations following corporate failure. He suggests that the creditors' bargain perspective has 'misidentified the distinct function of [corporate insolvency] law' because it views the law as a response to the economic problem of collecting debt. He contends that insolvency policy should not be 'closed', as the proponents of the creditors' bargain perspective suggest.[59] He concludes that corporate insolvency law must be explained 'not as a maximizer of economic outcomes but as a system for rendering richer, more informed decisions in response to financial distress'.[60]

Finch[61] is strident in her criticism of the creditors' bargain model. She posits that '[I]n real life ... creditors differ in their knowledge, skill, leverage and [ability to bear the] costs of litigating', so that such a perspective is wrong in the way it assumes creditors 'to be de-historicised and equal'.[62] This argument challenges whether statutory priorities can ever suit a creditors' bargain perspective. The beneficiaries of these priorities clearly differ in their degree of bargaining power. For example, employees are unlikely to have the 'knowledge' to bargain and achieve an advantageous position upon the insolvency of their corporate employer. Moreover, the skill and position of a liquidator to arrange the payment of their own fees and reimbursements is clearly superior to other priority creditors. A deserving creditor like a consumer who makes a prepayment to a corporation is clearly in a poor position to leverage a special bargain should insolvency occur to their supplier. Also, the costs of litigating to improve a position against other creditors again suggests some priority creditors would not benefit from an insolvency law based upon a creditors' bargain model. Parties may also differ in their ability to

54 Warren, E. 'Bankruptcy Policy' (1987) 54 *University of Chicago Law Review* 775, 778.

55 Ibid. 788.

56 Ibid. 788 and detailed in fn 25 thereof.

57 Ibid. 812–813.

58 Korobkin, D.R. 'Rehabilitating Values: A Jurisprudence of Bankruptcy' (1991) 91 *Columbia Law Review* 717, 762.

59 Ibid.787–789.

60 Ibid. 789.

61 Finch, V. *Corporate Insolvency Law Perspectives and Principles* (2002) 28–33.

62 Ibid. 31.

keep litigation costs down, as happens with governments employing their own legal staff as opposed to very small business creditors who need to fund the litigation personally. This suggests that the function of insolvency law should be somewhat broader than merely maximizing the collective returns of creditors as the creditors' bargain model decrees.

Finch continues her rebuttal of the creditors' bargain perspective by questioning the assumption that all creditors have purely economic interests.[63] She cites the 'employee creditors who face displacement costs' and may consider that they have claims on the corporation's assets that are morally superior to those of secured creditors.[64]

The creditors' bargain model provides for pre-insolvency rights being enforced post-insolvency. However, the insolvency of a company brings into play new factors, for example, the importance of creditors and the making of new decisions about where losses will fall. The insolvency regime that will apply in a particular corporation generally depends upon the course of action taken by the creditors. For a receivership it will be the secured creditor that chooses the insolvent corporation's future, but for a corporate rescue under Australia's voluntary administration laws or the compulsory winding up of the insolvent corporation, all of the creditors are invited to participate. A similar role is granted to creditors in the United Kingdom. Insolvency law looks beyond the pre-insolvency rights and recognizes formal rights which were not in place before insolvency. Finch goes even further to suggest that while some creditors who suffer in an insolvency have formal rights, 'others without formal rights may also be prejudiced'.[65] She nominates employees who lose their jobs and also cites 'suppliers who will lose customers', or 'tax authorities whose prospective entitlements [might] be diminished', as those without formal rights who suffer prejudice.[66]

Finch argues that the creditor wealth maximization 'vision' underlying the creditors' bargain model fails to consider 'those who suffer the greatest hardships in the context of financial distress'.[67] She criticizes the narrow construct of insolvency law as, 'in essence, [merely] a sale of assets for [the benefit] of creditors, [in] what might be termed a "car-boot sale" image'.[68] Such criticism is justified if we broaden the notion of a 'creditor' beyond those identified pre-insolvency and contemplate the wider effects of insolvency. The creditors' bargain model cannot therefore support even the current degree of legislative intervention that addresses the financial needs of priority creditors. Insolvency legislation that

63 Ibid.

64 Ibid.

65 Ibid. 32.

66 Ibid.

67 Ibid. 32. This is a point made by Korobkin, D.R. 'Contractarianism and the Normative Foundations' (1993) 71 *Texas Law Review* 541, 581.

68 Finch, V. *Corporate Insolvency Law Perspectives and Principle* (2002) 29.

provides a statutory priority for employees' wages, for example, is clearly not grounded in a creditors' bargain perspective.

In a final blow to the creditors' bargain model, Finch attacks the Jackson idea of pre-insolvency legal rights being carried through to insolvent companies. She states that the argument that insolvency law should only give effect to these pre-insolvency rights can be countered by asserting that a core and proper function of insolvency law is to pursue different distributional objectives than are implied in the body of pre-insolvency rights.[69] This is what eventuates when we have statutory priorities. 'Different', because some creditors are identified for special treatment that they did not receive pre-insolvency. Finch elegantly describes this as 'insolvency law's application to the turbulence of financial crisis, as distinct from the calm waters that mark pre-insolvency contracts'.[70] The statutory priority treatment represents 'an intrusion of a number of value judgements concerning relative priorities of various liabilities and the order in which groups of liabilities should be discharged'.[71] These value judgements are not needed before the company's insolvency, nor in some cases could they have been made earlier. For example, the financial decision by a company on whether to expend money on environmental cleanup or to pay employee redundancies is unlikely to be troublesome and value laden for a solvent company, but it can be quite the opposite for an insolvent company.

The creditors' bargain model effectively means that post-insolvency distributions can only be measured in monetary amounts and seen through the eyes of each creditor.[72] Recently, Mokal, a supporter of the creditors' bargain model in the past,[73] has attempted to apply it to a feature of insolvency law, the automatic stay where the debtor is given protection from their creditors by the statute triggering an injunction against the continuance of any creditor's action.[74] He argues that the model fails as it has neither descriptive nor moral force.[75] He concludes that the model relies on nothing but creditors' preferences and it suggests no reason why those preferences ought to be considered binding.[76] The creditors, if actually asked *ex ante* to choose an insolvency regime, would in Mokal's opinion be unable to reach agreement or would pick a system designed to reflect their pre-insolvency advantages.[77] Any agreement made under the circumstances of the creditors' bargain model would likely be exploitative and oppressive of weaker

69 Ibid. 32.
70 Ibid. 32.
71 Ibid. 33.
72 Gross, K. *Failure and Forgiveness* (1997) 138.
73 Mokal, R.J. *Corporate Insolvency Law: Theory and Application* (2005) 34.
74 Ibid. 32–59.
75 Ibid. 59.
76 Ibid.
77 Ibid.

parties and would have no justificatory force.[78] This 'experiment' of Mokal's using the automatic stay, a statutory insolvency feature, gives support to this chapter's premise that the creditors' bargain is not suitable to explain statutory priorities.

The above mentioned critiques of the creditors' bargain model suggest that it fails to recognize the significant differences among creditors and this is augmented when considering priority creditors.[79]

The Australian Position on the Creditors' Bargain Model

While Australian literature discusses the aims and objects of corporate insolvency law (and these are considered to be broadly similar in all Western legal systems),[80] it remains thin on persuasive support for a creditors' bargain model or indeed any other vision. Routedge[81] in 1998 tested Australia's voluntary administration law and found it complied both in construction and judicial interpretation with the creditors' bargain model. Anderson[82] in 2001 also considered the creditors' bargain model when discussing the same voluntary administration law. These two papers remain isolated exceptions.

Observers of Australian theoretical perspectives on corporate law have been advised to be 'wary of pigeon-holing' ideas[83] under any of the perspectives, as none can claim to supply an overarching explanation of the solvent or insolvent corporation. Theoretical imprecision still exists in Australia and elsewhere and much of this area of law operates according to simple pragmatic influences.[84] Therefore it cannot be assumed the creditors' bargain model is the theoretical perspective in use in Australian corporate insolvency regulation.

---

78 Ibid.

79 Ibid. Later, in Chapters 7, 8 and 9 below, the 'inability to pay' difference is treated as a relevant factor in the criteria applied to test new priorities.

80 Tomasic, R. *Australian Corporate Insolvency Law* (1993) chapter 1 discusses 10 objectives identified by the Harmer Report, para 33; and see also Goode, R.M. *Principles of Corporate Insolvency Law* (1990) 5–9. Many other writers call upon these objectives to introduce their insolvency discussions.

81 Routedge, J. 'Part 5.3A of the Corporations Law (Voluntary Administration): Creditors' Bargain or Creditors' Dilemma' (1998) 6 *Insolvency Law Journal* 127.

82 Anderson, C. 'Commencement of the Part 5.3A Procedure: Some Considerations from an Economic and Law Perspective' (2001) 9 *Insolvency Law Journal* 4. This author also notes a 'substantial attempt to look at some of the economic issues surrounding the insolvency legislation in Australia', citing a Staff Research paper issued through the Productivity Commission: see Bickerdyke, I., Lattimore, R. and Madge, A. *Business Failure and Change: An Australian Perspective*, Productivity Commission Staff Research Paper.

83 Tomasic, R., Bottomley, S. and McQueen, R. *Corporations Law in Australia* (2nd ed. 2002) 66.

84 Ibid.

Historically, there is evidence to suggest that insolvency law developed without much thought for theories or visions. Markham Lester, writing about the Victorian era, suggests that this area of law

> originated from the need to solve the practical commercial problem created by failed businesses. Its roots were not in political philosophy or a particular theory of government, and there appears to be no evidence that it ever became a partisan political issue.[85]

Australian history does not offer any evidence to suggest any difference locally.

The Communitarian Perspective

In response to the criticism of the nexus of contract perspective in corporate law other perspectives have been presented. One of these is communitarianism.[86] This perspective regards corporations as being comprised of important constituencies in addition to shareholders. The list of constituencies is long and includes employees, secured and unsecured creditors, customers or clients, and the local communities in which a corporation operates.[87] There is no complete list and communitarians disagree about which non-shareholder constituencies should be included.[88] The communitarian vision is for the corporation to be responsive to all its constituencies.[89]

Communitarians view individuals as being connected to each other and as being 'obliged' to act in the interests of the good of the community, even if that curtails some individual freedom.[90] The communitarian perspective recognizes that legal persons 'are not all separate individuals, but part of an interconnected

85 Markham Lester, V. *Victorian Insolvency* (1995) 37.

86 See e.g., Millon, D. 'New Directions in Corporate Law: Communitarians, Contractarians, and the Crisis in Corporate Law' (1993) 50 *Washington & Lee Law Review* 1373, 1379; Morrissey, D.J. 'Toward a New/Old Theory of Corporate Social Responsibility' (1989) 40 *Syracuse Law Review* 1005; Mitchell, L.E. *Progressive Corporate Law* (1995).

87 Tomasic, R., Bottomley, S. and McQueen, R. *Corporations Law in Australia* (2nd ed. 2002) 60.

88 Mitchell, L. 'The Fairness Rights of Corporate Bondholders' (1990) 65 *New York University Law Review* 1165.

89 Bradley, M., Schipani, C.A., Sundaram, A.K. and Walsh, J.P. 'The Purposes and Accountability of the Corporation in Contemporary Society: Corporate Governance at a Crossroads' (1999) 62 *Law & Contemporary Problems* 9, 45.

90 The definitive works on communitarianism generally (ie not in the corporate or insolvency law sense) are Etzioni, A. *The Spirit of Community; Rights, Responsibilities and the Communitarian Agenda* (1993) and Etzioni, A. *The Moral Dimension: Toward a New Economics* (1988).

world'.[91] When considering to whom the company owes a duty, no distinction is to be made between the interests of the shareholders, seen as private, with the interests of the community, that is, the public.[92]

Where contractarians view law as a means of ensuring *ex ante* freedom and efficiency of contracting, communitarians see law as a vehicle to ensure distributive justice and equity from the payoffs to contracts.[93] As Bradley et al recognize, the communitarian view argues for various types of corporate constituency statutes providing an ability to choose different rules for different situations.[94] Bradley et al conclude that the conceptual battle lines between contractarianism and communitarianism are 'stark', because the contractarian finds legitimacy in the values of liberty and competition whereas the communitarian emphasizes justice and cooperation.[95]

A Communitarian Perspective of Insolvency

In the mid 1990s a radical view was outlined that both the corporate and personal insolvency systems should take into account the interests of the community, basically that insolvency law be interpreted from a communitarian perspective.[96] This alternative view was not so unusual given an environment of a dominant creditors' bargain model that provided a view of insolvency law as a narrow restricted law that merely applied to contractual creditors and the insolvent debtor. In a growing environment of scholarly debate on insolvency, North American (and to a lesser extent, British) discussions on alternative and, arguably, more appropriate visions of corporate insolvency have flourished. Some of these visions are described below.

According to Gross, 'a Communitarian perspective mandates attention to what is often ignored in contemporary policy debates: the social side of human nature; the ripple effects and long-term consequences of present decisions'.[97] 'The application of communitarian concepts to the world of [insolvency] suggests

---

91 Gross, K. 'Taking Community Interests into Account in Bankruptcy: An Essay' (1994) 72 *Washington University Law Quarterly* 1031, 1040.

92 Gross, K. *Failure and Forgiveness* (1997) 205.

93 Bradley, M., Schipani, C.A., Sundaram, A.K. and Walsh, J.P. 'The Purposes and Accountability of the Corporation in Contemporary Society: Corporate Governance at a Crossroads' (1999) 62 *Law & Contemporary Problems* 9, 45.

94 Ibid.

95 Ibid. 42.

96 Gross, K. 'Taking Community Interests into Account in Bankruptcy: An Essay' (1994) 72 *Washington University Law Quarterly* 1031.

97 Ibid. 1042, citing Etzioni, A. *The Spirit of Community; Rights, Responsibilities and the Communitarian Agenda* (1993) 253–254.

that the welfare of the community should be very much a part of corporate [insolvency]',[98] particularly given the increase of global companies.

Communitarianism in insolvency defines 'the scope of corporate and personal bankruptcy' as legal regulation 'beyond the debtor and its immediate creditors'.[99] It follows, therefore, that at the heart of the debate about insolvency policy is a 'determination of who and what the system is designed to protect'.[100]

Defining what is meant by 'community' is obviously important in this context.[101] Placing communitarianism into the insolvency context requires some thought about the identifiable players in the system, followed by looking beyond these players to identify, if possible, others affected by insolvency, whose interests should be considered. So who are these other affected players? The community in insolvency must, by its definition, involve the debtor and creditor.[102] Traditionally, insolvency has also involved a third party assigned to wind up the estate. This liquidator or trustee has had an independent role to administer and therefore assist in the efficient management of the insolvent estate. The courts have had a long involvement in insolvency, including the appointment of liquidators and the source of support and judicial direction for all parties including liquidators. The government has been a long-term member of the insolvency community. Governments have been involved not just in making laws, but also in areas such as the licensing of liquidators, and qualifying as an involuntary creditor for taxes and other government debts. The government is also a source of administrative assistance in areas such as the present Australian employees' entitlement support scheme (General Employee Entitlements and Redundancy Scheme),[103] which is designed to protect employees' wages. Statutory subrogation makes the government a creditor for the amount of their financial support to employees. Others that will make up the community in insolvency are less identifiable and include involuntary 'players' such as tort victims.[104]

---

98 Op.cit, Gross, 1043.

99 Ibid.

100 Ibid. 1046.

101 Schermer, B.S. 'Response to Professor Gross: Taking Community Interests into Account in Bankruptcy: An Essay' (1994) 72 *Washington University Law Quarterly* 1049, 1051.

102 The statutory definition of solvency is an ability to pay debts as and when they are due and payable: *Corporations Act 2001* (Cth) s95A.

103 This Scheme is outlined in detail in Chapter 5 below.

104 One recent Australian example, involving the James Hardie companies, has been the potential victims of asbestosis and their future payouts should the company not be present to pay when these claims materialize, a so called 'long tail liability'.

Support for a Communitarian Perspective from the Law Reform Commissions

In 1982 the influential Cork Report[105] in the United Kingdom referred to the law of insolvency as embodying a 'compact to which there are three parties: the debtor, his creditor and society'.[106] Any system which is to cope with the consequences of an insolvency has to bear in mind the interests of these three parties.[107] Each of the principles (or aims) of insolvency, as outlined by the Cork Report,[108] could fit into this perspective. In what could be taken as support for the communitarian perspective, the Cork Report stated:

> We believe that a concern for the livelihood and well-being of those dependent upon an enterprise which may well be the lifeblood of a whole town or even a region, is a legitimate factor to which a modern law of insolvency must have regard. The chain reaction consequent upon any given failure can potentially be so disastrous to creditors, employees and the community that it must not be overlooked.[109]

In Australia, the Harmer Report in 1988 stated, in its opening paragraph, that insolvency 'law concerns not only the principal participants' of debtor and their creditors but it has 'a direct impact on many others'.[110] The Harmer Report expressly mentions employees, family, customers and agencies of government, such as those concerned with the revenue and administration of the law,[111] as the 'others' upon whom insolvency law has a direct impact.[112]

In summary, both the United Kingdom and Australian Law Reform Commissions have made ready acknowledgement that insolvency law is made up of more that just debtors and creditors and their relationship. Such support for a broader view accords with communitarianism and implicitly refutes the creditors' bargain model.

---

105 Review Committee, *Insolvency Law and Practice* Cmnd 8558 (1982) 'Cork Report'.

106 Cork Report, para 192.

107 Tolmie, F. *Introduction to Corporate and Personal Insolvency Law* (1998) 3.

108 Cork Report, para 198.

109 Ibid. para 204.

110 Harmer Report, para 1.

111 Ibid.

112 Ibid. para 33, where nine principles are discussed under the heading of *Aims of insolvency law*. None of the principles address perspectives or the community other than in a general way, although the Harmer Report notes that 'on a more abstract level insolvency law is viewed by some as the guardian of values that seem appropriate in the conduct of the credit economy', ibid.

Present Support for a Broad Perspective

Recent discussions on perspectives in corporate insolvency have supported broadening the focus even beyond the creditors' bargain model and the concept of communitarianism. Keay[113] has for instance discussed the importance of the public interest in insolvency; while Finch[114] has described her 'visions' which include creditors' bargain and communitarianism, but also three other 'benchmarks'– forum vision, ethical vision and a multiple values/eclectic approach.

The concept of the public interest, when considered in the corporate insolvency context, has an admirable width. Scholars have defined 'public interest' by default as the interest of those other than the debtor. Keay suggests it is the interests of anyone who has a stake, financial or otherwise, in the business of the insolvent company.[115] This is supported by Gross' community approach where she includes many as having a community interest, a term that Keay suggests can equate to public interest.[116] Keay concludes that, rather than formulating a conclusive definition, the legal system should interpret the public interest as 'taking into account interests of those parties directly involved in any given insolvency situation'.[117] Certainly insolvency law as part of a legal system appears to take into account the interests of some parties that consider they deserve statutory priorities, and to that extent meets their needs. Other parties that do not enjoy a statutory priority can argue that it is in the 'public interest' that insolvency law extends further to embrace their position.

Insolvency is traditionally categorized as a matter of private law because of the private nature of the rights of creditors against particular debtors and the amounts those creditors will receive by way of payment.[118] Keay argues that 'insolvency law is wider than that'.[119] No 'legal issue can be seen as off limits to a consideration of the public interest',[120] and insolvency law has the potential to involve substantial numbers of the public. A concept such as the public interest is certainly a consideration for the formulation of statutory priorities. The legislators have had to consider whether various modifications to the principle of *pari passu* are appropriate. In doing this, serious social issues, such as employees going

113 Keay, A. 'Insolvency Law: A Matter of Public Interest?' (2002) 51 *Northern Ireland Legal Quarterly* 509.

114 Finch, V. *Corporate Insolvency Law Perspectives and Principle* (2002) Chapter 2.

115 Keay, A. 'Insolvency Law: A Matter of Public Interest?' (2002) 51 *Northern Ireland Legal Quarterly* 509.

116 Ibid. 524.

117 Ibid. 525. However Keay then appears to limit his interpretation of the insolvency system to the debtor and the creditors: ibid. 525.

118 Ibid. 509.

119 Ibid. 509.

120 Ibid. 510.

without their wages due to the insolvency of their corporate employer, must be considered as matters of public interest.

Keay asserts that parliaments, law reform commissions and the courts do take the public interest into account when considering significant insolvency law issues.[121] As outlined in Chapter 2, there has been a steadily expanding range of interests considered in the history of statutory priorities. Keay concludes that '[U]nless the public interest is considered it is likely that rudimentary elements of our society will be damaged and the law will be regarded with contempt and as something which is aloof from everyday life'.[122] This factor influences the later chapters of this book that contemplate new priorities to be considered by the legislators.[123]

Finch[124] acknowledges that '[A]n important aspect of communitarianism is the centrality that is given to distributional concerns' that include statutory priorities.[125] For her, the 'problem is not … that community interests cannot be identified, but that there are so many potential interests in every insolvency' and, so, the 'selection of interests worthy of legal protection' or special treatment like a statutory priority 'is liable to give rise to considerable contention'.[126]

In an attempt at pushing the contemplation of perspectives beyond the creditors' bargain model, Finch presents a vision of the insolvency process establishing a 'forum' in which all interests, not just monetary, that are affected by business failure would be recognized.[127] This would shift the focus beyond creditors to all participants in the company's financial distress. While underdeveloped at this point in time, it has been described as requiring the law to establish a 'space' that would provide 'not just interested parties' with a 'medium of … discourse'.[128] Another 'vision' recognized (and questioned) by Finch is the 'ethical' one[129] which is promoted by Shuchman.[130] This perspective does not broaden the number of 'players', but proposes that the foundations of insolvency law take into account the 'situation of the debtor, the moral worthiness of the debt, and the size, situation and intent of the creditor'.[131] Finally, Finch recognizes a 'notion that insolvency

121 Ibid.

122 Ibid. 534.

123 See below Chapters 7, 8 and 9.

124 Finch, V. *Corporate Insolvency Law Perspectives and Principle* (2002) 25–56.

125 Ibid. 36.

126 Ibid. 37.

127 Ibid. 38.

128 See e.g., Flessner, A. 'Philosophies of Business Bankruptcy Law: An International Overview' in Ziegel, J.S. (ed.), *Current Developments in International and Comparative Corporate Insolvency Law* (1994); Korobkin, D.R. 'Rehabilitating Values: A Jurisprudence of Bankruptcy' (1991) 91 *Columbia Law Review* 717.

129 Finch, V. *Corporate Insolvency Law Perspectives and Principle* (2002) 39.

130 Shuchman, P. 'An Attempt at a Philosophy of Bankruptcy' (1973) 21 *University of California Los Angeles Law Review* 403.

131 Op.cit.

law serves a series of values'.[132] This 'vision' encapsulates 'economic and non-economic dimensions and the principle of fairness as a moral, political, personal and social value'.[133] Found predominantly in the work of Warren[134] and Korobkin,[135] the multiple value/eclectic approach attempts 'to achieve such ends as distributing the consequences of financial failure amongst a wide range of' players' and 'protecting the investing public, jobs, the public and community interests'.[136] This approach is recognized by Finch as broad enough to incorporate communitarian philosophies and the 'forum' vision.[137]

As this discussion shows, both Keay and Finch are endeavouring to move the theoretical perspective of insolvency law beyond the creditors' bargain model. As for statutory priorities, there has been no detailed consideration of any particular perspective. Finch has suggested that while there is silence on which perspective should be used for distributional matters in insolvency, such matters are 'too serious to be overlooked by those concerned with fairness and justice'.[138] She concludes that valuing factors other than economic efficiency, as the creditors' bargain model does, is an important step towards analysing and justifying distributional fairness.[139]

The Future for the Broader Perspective of the Progressives

The theoretical perspective that could emerge as the vision to be applied to statutory priorities may well come to embrace a communitarian's concept of distributional fairness and justice. Meanwhile one can expect the law of statutory priority to continue to support established insolvency principles such as those articulated in the Cork Report.[140] These include the aim to 'realise the assets of the insolvent which should be properly be taken to satisfy debts with the minimum of delay and expense', and the aim to 'distribute the proceeds of realisations amongst creditors fairly and equitably'.[141] Another aim expressed by the Cork Report and relevant to statutory priorities is

132 Ibid. 40.

133 Warren, E. 'Bankruptcy Policy' (1987) 54 *University of Chicago Law Review* 775.

134 Ibid.

135 Korobkin, D.R. 'Rehabilitating Values: A Jurisprudence of Bankruptcy' (1991) 91 *Columbia Law Review* 717.

136 Finch, V. *Corporate Insolvency Law Perspectives and Principle* (2002) 40–41.

137 Ibid. 41.

138 Ibid. 53.

139 Ibid. 55.

140 Cork Report, para 198; and see also Roy M. Goode, *Principles of Corporate Insolvency Law* (1990) 5–9; Roman Tomasic, *Australian Corporate Insolvency Law* (1993) 4–12.

141 Cork Report, para 198.

> to recognise and safeguard the interests not merely of insolvents and their creditors but those of society and other groups in society who are affected by the insolvency, for instance not only the interests of directors, shareholders and employees but also those of suppliers whose livelihoods depend on the enterprise and the community.[142]

To the extent that such an aim already exists, it may serve to provide the base from which wider theoretical perspectives will develop.

Conclusion

The literature on Australian corporate insolvency law is in its infancy when discussing theoretical perspectives. It is impossible to describe an insolvency theory or theoretical framework that completely or convincingly explains the existing regime. The closest attempts can be found in the 'aims' paragraph of the Harmer Report,[143] and in the text by Tomasic[144] where the author uses objectives earlier identified by Goode[145] in the United Kingdom. Corporate insolvency principles are usually considered to include fairness, expedition, efficiency and impartiality. Such principles are often incorporated into these expressed aims or objectives and as such will be discussed in the following chapters.

International perspectives on insolvency, especially those from the United States, position the proper function of insolvency law as one that maximizes the collective return to the creditors and provides a compulsory, economically efficient, collective system for dealing with the debts. This 'proper function' connects the local and international perspectives on corporate law where the nexus of contracts theory and its related creditors' bargain visions are dominant, although regularly criticized. This chapter has expressed the need for a broader approach and invited further development of perspectives that incorporate the community. Under this view the proper function of insolvency law recognizes and protects the rights and interests of others as well as the private rights of creditors. The rights of the community at large can be encompassed into statutory priorities and the redistribution of assets. While at present the conceptual frameworks for statutory priorities in corporate insolvency tend to remain beneath the text of the statute or judicial decision in the same way as they do in corporate law, future scholarship will no doubt expand the current understanding.[146]

---

142 Cork Report, para 198(i).

143 Harmer Report, para 33.

144 Roman Tomasic, *Australian Corporate Insolvency Law* (1993) 4–12.

145 Goode, R.M. *Principles of Corporate Insolvency Law* (1990) 5–9, 54–63.

146 As described in the introduction to this chapter above: see e.g., Tomasic, R., Bottomley, S. and McQueen, R. *Corporations Law in Australia* (2nd ed. 2002) 52.

Chapter 4

The Statutory Priority of Administrative Expenses: A Matter of Rent, Requisite Expenses and Administrator Remuneration

As described in Chapter 1, s556 of the *Corporations Act 2001* (Cth) prescribes the statutory order of priorities that must be followed by a liquidator. This chapter discusses the expenses of the winding up and associated administration costs,[1] including the liquidator's remuneration priority. These administrative expenses are going to be part of every winding up and include the rent and other miscellaneous expenses usually expended in a liquidation or in the company's prior insolvency administrations. These miscellaneous expenses will be referred to in this chapter as requisite expenses. This chapter then is divided into discussions on three major expenses: *rent; requisite expenses,* covering the many expenses incurred during the liquidation such as litigation costs, special expenses, rates and miscellany; and finally the liquidator's *remuneration*. This is the order in which these items appear in the *Corporations Act 2001* (Cth).

Section 556(1)(a) through to (1)(df) of the Act can be grouped together and referred to as the administrative costs or administrative expenses priorities. The legislation provides for a priority to be given to:

> (a) first, expenses (except deferred expenses) properly incurred by a relevant authority in preserving, realising or getting in property of the company, or in carrying on the company's business;
>
> (b) if the Court ordered the winding up – next, the costs in respect of the application for the order (including the applicant's taxed costs payable under section 466);
>
> (ba) if (i) during the period of 12 months ending when the winding up commenced, an application (the first application) was made under section 459P for the

1 Both 'costs' and 'expenses' are used interchangeably in describing outgoings made by the liquidator in the administration of the estate. Perhaps 'costs' in a legal context is more correctly used to describe 'sums payable for legal services', although even when describing 'solicitors costs' this is interpreted as the *profit costs* representing profit and overheads and *disbursements* representing out-of-pocket expenses. See e.g., *Oxford Dictionary of Law* (3rd ed. 1994) 99.

> company to be wound up in insolvency; and (ii) when the first application was made, the company was not under administration; and (iii) the company began to be under administration at a time after the first application was made; and (iv) the first application was not withdrawn or dismissed before the administration began; and (v) the Court did not, in response to the first application, make an order under section 459A that the company be wound up in insolvency; next, the costs in respect of the first application;
>
> (c) next, the debts for which paragraph 443D (a) entitles an administrator of the company to be indemnified (even if the administration ended before the relevant date), except expenses covered by paragraph (a) of this subsection and deferred expenses;
>
> (d) [repealed];
>
> (da) if the Court ordered the winding up – next, costs and expenses that are payable under section 475(8) out of the company's property;
>
> (db) next, costs that form part of the expenses of the winding up because of subsection 539(6);
>
> (dc) [repealed];
>
> (dd) next, any other expenses (except deferred expenses) properly incurred by a relevant authority;
>
> (de) next, the deferred expenses;
>
> (df) if a committee of inspection has been appointed for the purposes of the winding up – next, the expenses incurred by a person as a member of the committee;

The justification of the administration expenses priority can be expressed using the High Court of Australia's reasoning in *Re Universal Distributing Co Ltd (in liq)*.[2] The court held that 'where persons are entitled to share in the distribution of a fund', then 'the costs and expenses of recovering, caring for, preserving and realising assets to create the fund are a fair charge on the fund'.[3] The House of Lords in 1995 supported this reasoning in commenting upon the adoption of contracts by a liquidator.[4] They acknowledged a *salvage principle* in liquidation

---

2 (1933) 48 CLR 171.

3 See discussion and interpretation by Australian Law Reform Commission, *General Insolvency Inquiry*, Report No 45 (1988). 'Harmer Report', para 717.

4 *Powdrill v Watson* [1995] 2 All ER 65, 84.

such that 'if a liquidator adopts a contract for the purpose of the more beneficial conduct of a liquidation all such liabilities under such contract after the date of adoption are entitled to priority'.[5]

The costs and expenses of recovering, preserving and realizing the property of the company or carrying on its business enjoy the first ranking, because it is said all creditors have a 'community of interest'[6] in maximizing the amount available for distribution. These expenses must be properly incurred, and by a relevant authority. This includes insolvency practitioners who have acted as external administrators such as liquidators, provisional liquidators and Part 5.3A (corporate rescue) administrators.

These statutory administrative expense priorities occur so high up in the order of payments that unsecured creditors and even other priority creditors like employees can blame such favourable treatment as the cause of small or no dividends for themselves. An example, admittedly an extraordinary one, is provided by *Re Peregrine Investments Holdings Ltd and Ors*,[7] where Le Pichon J heard that the amount of fees and disbursements for a provisional liquidator were revised down to $76 million for the period of 63 days! Clearly the law cannot permit liquidators to develop an attitude that they may incur certain expenses or run up their fees, with little scrutiny, simply because they have great confidence they will be paid, due to their priority position in the statute.[8]

The legislation provides some requirements for scrutiny of administration expenses but adds little explanation to what expenses are covered and there is little discussion of such priorities in secondary sources. The case law, with precedents dating back to the 1880s, appears at times to be underdeveloped and under-reported in detail.[9]

Expenses are not prescribed by the legislation and Street J has suggested that:

> [T]here is no purpose in attempting to enumerate exhaustively the heads of expenses that will fall within this [priority]. They must, however, be capable of

---

5 Ibid.

6 A phrase used in the Harmer Report, para 717.

7 [1998] 3 HKC 1.

8 The other major case that shed light on large insolvency fees occurred in the United Kingdom. In *Mirror Group Newspapers v Maxwell* [1998] 1 BCLC 638 a receiver collected £1.67m from asset realizations and then left £40,000 for other creditors. This led to the Ferris Report and recommendations for remuneration scales, reasonableness, disclosure and proportionality. See Shandro, S. and Osborne, L. 'Insolvency Practitioner fees in the UK' (2004) Fourth Quarter *INSOL World* 6. Australia is yet to have a major case, although *Korda, in the matter of Stockford Ltd (subject to Deed of Company Arrangement)* [2004] FCA 1682 (21 December 2004) created much discussion on external administrators' fees.

9 A number of cases that follow in this chapter suggest litigation activity on these matters during the late 1800s when many of the reported judgements were very brief, some taking no more than a page of the published reports.

> being seen to relate to the winding up in the sense of being costs or expenses accruing in the course of the winding up. Rent is a classic instance.[10]

This chapter seeks to provide a more detailed understanding of the priority by discussing some of the cases, both recent and historical, that have formed the law in this area. It also discusses the expressed justifications for inclusion of certain expenses that have become deemed to fall within the statutory priority.

As seen in Chapter 2, the use of a priority for administration costs was embedded in the winding up statutes both in colonial Australia and England.[11] It is one of the oldest statutory priorities in corporate insolvency.

Prior to the introduction of the *Corporate Law Reform Act 1992* (Cth), s556(1)(a) included the various types of costs and expenses associated with winding up that now appear in s556(1)(a), (1)(b), (1)(da), (1)(dd) and (1)(de). Section 556(1)(a), before 1993, used to accord a first priority for payment of the costs, charges and expenses of the winding up (which included the taxed costs of the applicant payable under s466), the liquidator's remuneration and the costs of any audit carried out under s539. The cases that refer to s556(1)(a) in its prior form are still relevant to the new subsections as they now appear in s556(1).

Corporations Act 2001 (Cth) Section 556(1)(a) – Rent

Under s477(1)(a) of the *Corporations Act 2001* (Cth), a liquidator has the power 'to carry on the business of the company so far as is necessary for the beneficial disposal or winding up of that business'. Carrying on the business will usually involve operating or using some premises that the company has been using prior to the commencement date of the appointment of the liquidator and, if these are rented, then the liquidator is going to incur rental expenses. These expenses will be incurred during the time of 'preserving, realising or getting in property of the company, or in carrying on the company's business', as s556(1)(a) provides, and, therefore the liquidator receives a priority over unsecured creditors.

The English Position on Rent Priorities

Section 10 of the *Judicature Act 1875* (UK), that introduced the bankruptcy rules to corporate insolvency into Britain, did not expressly give a priority to a landlord for rent.[12] Interestingly, in Scotland in the late 1800s the landlord was considered a secured creditor and so had the best priority of all![13] In any event, the English

10 *Re Denton Sub-divisions Pty Ltd (in liq)* and the *Companies Act* (1968) 89 W.N. (Pt. 1) (NSW) 231, 234.

11 See e.g., *Joint Stock Companies Act 1856* (UK) s87.

12 See e.g., *Thomas v Lionitev Co* (1881) 17 Ch D 250.

13 See e.g., *Wanzer Ltd* (1891) 1 Ch 305.

position tended to oscillate from granting all outstanding rent a priority, to limiting the priority to only rent incurred post-appointment and then only if there was an intention to use the premises for carrying on the business.

In 1871, Chancery first decided the implications of a rent priority by ignoring the concept. In *Re Lundy Granite Co ex parte Heavan*,[14] Lord Justice Sir W M James commented that '[A]s a general rule, I shall have no hesitation in granting leave to a landlord to pursue his rights by distress for rent accrued during the time when the official liquidator chooses to leave the goods on the land'.[15] He was supported by Lord Justice Sir G. Mellish, who expressed the view that if the official liquidator, for the convenience of winding up, did not surrender the lease but continued to keep possession for the purpose of obtaining a better price for the goods, the landlord should not be deprived of the right to recover rent. This merely reinforced the established property law and overruled an attempt by Lord Romilly MR, at first instance to interpret the *Companies Act 1862* (UK) as having the objective 'to put everybody who had claims upon the company upon an equal footing',[16] including landlords.

Ten years later, *Re South Kensington Co-operative Stores*,[17] sought to clarify the position as to when it was that the rent provable in the winding up ceased to be an expense and when the rent incurred by the liquidator commenced. At that time it appears that rent was considered acceptable as an expense of the winding up, although there were no relevant authorities cited in the reported case. Fry J decided to draw the line[18] and conceded that it was 'hardly in controversy ... that rent which accrued before the liquidation should be a matter of proof and the subsequent rent a matter of full payment'.[19] This was presumably on the basis that the later rent was incurred as a liquidation expense and hence, was acceptable at law.

In *Re Oak Pits Colliery Co Ltd*,[20] a year later, the mere abstention on the part of the liquidator to disclaim was held not to mean that the property had been retained for the benefit of the liquidation. The liquidator in this case was unable to use the land that the company had leased due to the coal pits located on the land being full of water. Hence the liquidator did not take possession of the colliery (there were mortgagees) or the land where the coal pits were located. Plant and machinery had been brought onto the site of colliery and so the landlord sought leave to distrain on the plant and machinery and/or have the proceeds paid to him. Justice Kay decided that the landlord must have his full rent, and this meant the rent accrued since the commencement of the winding up. The liquidator appealed against this decision.

---

14 *Re Lundy Granite Co ex parte Heavan* (1871) 6 Ch App 462.
15 Ibid. 467.
16 Ibid. 464.
17 (1881) 17 Ch D 161.
18 Ibid. 165.
19 Ibid. 164.
20 (1882) 21 Ch D 322.

On appeal, the Court of Appeal brought to the fore some fine distinctions on the facts. The colliery was in the possession of separate mortgagees and the land at the surface was still in possession of the landlord and never leased to the company.[21] However, the court did go on to discuss the aspects of rent in liquidations. A joint judgment delivered by Lindley LJ set up a requirement that:

> [I]n all cases in which a landlord seeks to distrain after a winding up or seeks to be paid his rent in priority to other creditors he must shew why he should have such an advantage over the other creditors.[22]

The Court of Appeal accepted that if a liquidator retains the property for the purpose of advantageously disposing of it, or continues to use it, then the rent ought to be regarded as a debt contracted for the purpose of winding up and ought to be paid in full, like any other debt or expense properly incurred by the liquidator for the same purpose.[23]

Jumping forward to 1970, in *Re ABC Coupler and Engineering Co Ltd (No 3)*,[24] a landlord argued that rent and other liabilities were liquidation expenses and therefore payable in full and in priority to other debts. Justice Plowman held that rent accrued before the commencement of the winding up could not be a liquidation expense, but that rent accruing after the commencement could be.[25] This appears to be a straightforward and sensible resolution to the issue of rent. However, if the liquidator merely took formal possession of the company's rented premises, in order to protect the goods and equipment of the company stored there, then the court would not direct the liquidator to pay rent accruing as an expense of the liquidation.[26] This rejection of rent expenses as an administration expense is applicable only if there is no intention to use the premises for the carrying on of trade. So the true test is whether the liquidator maintained the premises for the convenience of winding up or whether he/she retained it for the purpose of trade. The motivation of the liquidator thus becomes critical.[27]

The Australian Position on Rent Priority during Liquidation

The position in the United Kingdom does not seem to be consistent with a South Australian case, decided in 1934. The case describes the priority of rent very clearly and how it arises. In *Re Flour and Grain Exchange Ltd, ex parte Rix*[28]

21 Ibid. 328.
22 Ibid. 329.
23 Ibid. 330–331.
24 [1970] 1 All ER 650.
25 Ibid. 668.
26 Ibid. 657.
27 Milman, D. 'The Liquidation Expense Principle' [2000] *Insolvency Lawyer* 126.
28 [1934] SASR 386.

the company rented premises to carry on its business as flour millers and grain merchants. They installed plant, machinery, elevators and other trade fixtures. In September 1933 they went into voluntary liquidation and the liquidator carried on the company's business, continuing to use the rented premises in the ordinary course of the business. In November the liquidator ceased to carry on the business in the rented premises and removed the company's goods, but not their fixtures. The liquidator held onto the keys of the premises and advertised the lease for sale. In April 1934 the liquidator sold the company's assets within the premises and, in May, delivered the keys to the owner. The liquidator argued that the rent accruing, between his appointment in September 1933 and when he handed back the keys in May 1934, did not attract a priority because he did not use the premises for beneficial occupation. Justice Piper ordered that the landlord was entitled to be paid rent up until May 1934 as a priority. His Honour stated that the liability for rent out of a company's assets by a liquidator is 'not dependent on or to be measured by the degree to which the use of the premises has been profitable to him or the company'.[29] He relied on authority from earlier English rates cases, specifically *Re National Arms and Ammunition Co*,[30] and not on authority from the earlier rent cases decided throughout the common law world.

Justice Piper focused on the question of 'use', as distinct from 'profitable use'. The liquidator had kept the premises to store the assets until they were sold. His Honour stated:

> [N]o doubt a lessor cannot recover rent as a liquidation expense unless the liquidator does something in the way of enjoying the property, but once the liquidator has, so to speak, taken the leased premises into use, the lessor's right to rent as a liquidation expenses arises (sic), and, in my opinion, it continues until the liquidator unambiguously determines the use.[31]

His Honour concluded that the continuance of use depends on the will of the liquidator.[32] In this case, if the liquidator wanted to, he could have moved all assets out when he stopped operation some six months before he determined the lease. Had this case been followed, the rent priority would have developed subject to an 'intention' test that would have contributed to more litigation and to the detriment of the relative simplicity that presently exists.

29 Ibid. 388.

30 *Re National Arms and Ammunition Company* (1885) 28 Ch D 474.

31 [1934] SASR 386, 388.

32 Ibid. 388.

The Modern Approach to Rent Priority

By 1974, the United Kingdom position was very clear. In *Re Downer Enterprises Ltd*[33] the court supported the 'well established principles' with respect to rent.[34] In this case, there was a 'chain of assignments'[35] to the lease and the company, Downer Enterprises, was under a creditor's voluntary winding up. The applicant, an assignor to the company and an earlier assignee of the premises, was seeking an entitlement to be paid in full (out of the assets of the company) a sum representing rent accrued after the commencement of the winding up. The applicant had paid this sum to the landlord. During the liquidation of the company the premises had subsequently been leased to yet another party. The applicant was trying to recover the amount they had paid 'under pressure of proceedings'.[36] Evidence was given that the liquidator had not used the leased premises during the relevant time of his liquidation.[37] Pennycuick VC observed '[T]he law on this point has been the subject of a number of judicial decisions, most of the leading cases having been decided just about a century ago; that is, in the 1870s.'[38] He went on to refer to *ABC Coupler* and the earlier cases of *Re Lundy Granite* and *Re Oak Pits Colliery* to show these 'well established principles'. In obiter dicta he stated: '[T]here is no relevant distinction between a landlord's right to distrain and a landlord's right to receive payment of the rent in full.'[39] This statement brought together some of the earlier cases dealing only with distress and those dealing only with rights to be paid.

Pennycuick VC decided a date from when the rent acquired its priority, that being the date when the liquidator had instructed a firm to find a purchaser of the lease.[40] He then decided that it was necessary for the liquidator to have remained in possession from this time and to have done so with a view to the realization of the property in the lease to the best available advantage.[41] Such a finding meant that the applicant could receive a priority and that this rent formed part of the administration expenses. This outcome differed substantially from that of the earlier cases because there was no question of use, despite a clear intention to dispose.

In *Re Linda Marie Ltd*[42] rent was owed for premises where the company's business had been carried on for a short period of time by the liquidator, but then

33 *Re Downer Enterprises Ltd* [1974] 1WLR 1460.
34 Ibid. 1467.
35 Ibid. 1464.
36 Ibid. 1463.
37 Ibid. 1462.
38 Ibid. 1465.
39 Ibid. 1466.
40 Ibid. 1467.
41 Ibid. 1467.
42 [1989] BCLC 46.

the premises were closed. The liquidator eventually surrendered the lease upon the payment of an agreed sum. The argument was whether the agreed sum was an expense arising out of the preservation of property or a 'necessary disbursement'. The latter enjoyed only a fifth position among the ranking of priority creditors, whereas the former enjoyed first position. Justice Warner suggested that there is a distinction between the preservation of property which connotes some positive action taken in relation to it and the mere retention of property which may be the result of inaction.[43] His Honour contemplated a situation where a payment like this one could be made by a liquidator in order to avoid the forfeiture of a lease so as to enable her to realize the lease advantageously.[44] No similar argument on the distinction between preservation expense[45] and necessary disbursements[46] has arisen in Australia.

Justification for a Rent Priority

As Sullivan, Warren and Westbrook describe it: 'some landlords qualify as reluctant creditors ... [as the insolvency] will force them to extend credit they prefer to avoid'.[47] To ease the burden of being a reluctant creditor, the response from parliament has been to grant a priority for at least the rent incurred during the insolvency administration.

Another way of explaining the priority is that the landlord is the owner of immovable property, which is deemed to be an important cog in the economic world and so deserves better treatment than the suppliers of goods and services and other creditors.[48] This reasoning supported an early separate priority (non-administrative expense) for rent in Canadian law which was subsequently rejected by the 1985 Colter Report.[49] The Colter Report did though support the continuation of what was termed 'occupation rent' as an administrative expense and thus a beneficiary of a continued priority.

In seeking other ways to justify the rent priority, consideration can be given to a justification identified in a recent New Zealand Law Commission Report.[50] The

43 Ibid. 52.

44 Ibid.

45 See e.g., *Corporations Act 2001* (Cth) s556(1)(a).

46 See e.g., *Corporations Act 2001* (Cth) s556(1)(dd) and referred to as 'other expenses incurred by the relevant authority'.

47 Sullivan, T.A., Warren, E. and Westbrook, J.L. *As We Forgive Our Debtors* (1989) 297.

48 Advisory Committee on Bankruptcy and Insolvency, Proposed Bankruptcy Act Amendments Report of the Advisory Committee on Bankruptcy and Insolvency (1986), 'Colter Report', 80.

49 Ibid.

50 New Zealand Law Commission, Priority Debts in the Distribution of Insolvent Estates, An Advisory Report to Ministry of Commerce (1999).

Report did not specifically address rent, but dealt with general administration costs as part of the overall subject matter of priority debts. The Report argued that the priority was 'an appropriate price to pay for proper co-ordination and management of the bankruptcy or liquidation process'.[51] In other words, the reason for rent being an administrative expense priority is simply that, to efficiently manage the process, the law needs to support the insolvency practitioner paying the rent. A more complicated reason is not required.

It is more difficult to find a justification specifically for rent as expressed in Australian literature. Leaving aside case law, the Harmer Report is the most obvious source. Yet the Harmer Report expresses only a general rationale to cover all administration costs and charges. The rationale is expressed as giving a priority to administration costs because all 'creditors have a community of interest in having a common agent to maximise a fund for distribution among them'.[52] When specifically considering rent, this rationale is insufficient, as creditors only receive an indirect benefit when 'occupation rent' is given a priority. It is an indirect benefit because paying the rent will enable the premises to be used to generate profit that can subsequently be distributed among creditors. In this way there is some community benefit. Additionally, the expense of rent is an indirect benefit for all creditors who may receive a distribution after the company's assets have been realized, as these may have been housed safely in the rental premises until their sale. At best the rationale can be said to offer only vague support for the rent priority.

Corporations Act 2001 (Cth) Section 556(1)(a) – Requisite Expenses

The phrase 'requisite expenses' has been coined in order to facilitate a convenient discussion of other miscellaneous costs and expenses that enjoy a priority.[53] It appears an apt description. The dictionary defines 'requisite' as 'required by the nature of things or by circumstances'.[54] In the insolvency context, this describes how these costs and expenses will arise once the insolvency practitioner is in place. For instance, the liquidator may have to incur litigation costs by bringing proceedings or defending them. These, then, are requisite costs. Similarly the

---

51 Ibid. 18.

52 Harmer Report, para 717.

53 The writer first used this phrase in a paper presented at the 2000 Australian Corporate Law Teachers' Association National Conference at the University of Wollongong and participants generally accepted that it was an accurate reference to the manner in which these types of expenses were considered. The paper was subsequently published as Symes, C.F. 'Remuneration, Rent and "Requisite" Costs: The 3 R's of Insolvency's Administrative Expense Priority' (2000) 11 *Australian Journal of Corporate Law* 149.

54 Funk and Wagnall's *Standard Desk Dictionary* (1977).

liquidator may have to engage an auctioneer to sell the company's property and the fees of the auctioneer can be categorized as requisite expenses.

If 'expenses' is not a term of art,[55] but is to have a wide meaning,[56] then what is it to include? The following discussion illustrates the diversity of reported cases, which are not recent nor numerous, and it appears that liquidators do not have a problem classifying what constitutes an expense that will enjoy the priority. Perhaps there is no confusion what an expense is because it is the unsecured creditors who are affected and out of pocket if an expense is wrongly classified. Such unsecured creditors are not in a good position to challenge the requisite cost that has gained the priority. The cause of this may be a failure to discover details that could be disputed. Even if the unsecured creditor did know such details they would probably not want to spend more money on litigation.[57]

In determining whether a particular post-liquidation dealing is an expense of the winding up and worthy of a priority, the court has to consider whether it is a distinct transaction or if it can be characterized by reference to one entire transaction having its origin before the commencement of the winding up.[58] If it is the latter then the priority status is not granted.

The following discussion deals with requisite administrative expenses including litigation costs, other special expenses and rates.

Litigation Costs Owed by Liquidator as Requisite Costs

Early cases from the 1800s established the trend to pay for litigation costs as part of the administrative expense priority. For example, in *Re Trent and Humber Ship-Building Company, Bailey and Leetham's Case*[59] the Equity Court was willing to include both the costs of a contractual damages action and the costs of the application for leave to bring the action, given that the company was in liquidation. The original action was commenced by a plaintiff who had suffered damages from a breach of contract for late delivery of a ship. The contract was to be paid by four instalments – when the vessel was 'in frame', 'plated', 'launched' and, finally, when 'delivered'. The judgment damages were £6,083 and the taxed costs of the action were £516. The successful litigants asked for this amount to be paid in full while the liquidator wanted to pay a proportional dividend. Counsel for the liquidator noted that an early text[60] recorded that both a verdict and judgement,

---

55 *Re Beni-Felkai Mining Co* [1974] 1 Ch 406, 410.

56 Commonwealth, *Explanatory Memorandum, Corporate Law Reform Act 1992* (1992), para 909.

57 Colloquially this is known as not wanting to 'throw good money after bad!'

58 CCH, *Australian Corporations & Securities Law Reporter*, Vol. 3, 162–720.

59 (1869) LR 8 Eq 94.

60 The text referred to was Griffith and Holmes, *Bankruptcy*, however the writer could not locate the year of publication (which is presumably before 1869).

if subsequent to a bankruptcy, would not be accepted into proof by a liquidator unless there was a special contract.

However, Sir W.M. James VC found against the liquidator and with some force. He stated that '[T]he result of the action in this case shews that it was improperly resisted, and if it was improperly resisted on behalf of the assets, then I think the assets ought to pay the costs of that improper resistance'.[61] This is a somewhat tough-minded approach given that, on the facts, the liquidator after appointment had sought the court's approval to perform the contract to complete building and deliver the ship, and he had done so. Yet he still had to contend with the action because of the non-delivery within the contract timeframe. The liquidator also had the court's leave to defend such an action.

The liquidated company was ordered to pay the plaintiff's costs of the action, the costs of the application for leave to bring the action, and his costs of the application to the Court for an order establishing his right to such payment.[62] All these amounts were to be paid in full out of the assets of the company.

In *Re Silver Valley Mines*,[63] a lower court refused two liquidators' actions and the resultant litigation costs, concluding that the application was 'improper and wrong.'[64] The court wanted it known that official liquidators must conduct litigation entirely at their own risk as to costs in the event of failure.[65] On appeal Jessel MR was slightly more sympathetic to the liquidator's cause. He stated that the official liquidator must be treated as a person who, as a general rule, is entitled to his costs of the liquidation properly incurred.[66] He also recognized the discretion of a judge to refuse costs, for instance, if the matter that was appealed was frivolous.[67]

Chancery in 1913 gave an expansive interpretation to a litigation costs priority. In *Re Pacific Coast Syndicate Ltd*[68] the court held that the litigation costs are to be paid as a priority regardless of whether the order simply directed payment of costs, or directed that the costs be paid out of the assets of the company, or directed that the liquidator pay the costs with liberty to recoup them out of the assets.[69]

---

61 (1869) LR 8 Eq 94.

62 *Re Trent and Humber Ship Building Company Bailey and Leetham's Case* (1869) LR 8 Eq 94, 98.

63 (1882) 21 Ch D 381.

64 Ibid. 385.

65 Ibid. 388.

66 Ibid. 385.

67 Ibid. 390.

68 [1913] 2 Ch 26.

69 Ibid. 28.

An Illustrative Case Example of Requisite Costs

In 1884, the principal case in the area of requisite costs was decided. In *Re Dominion of Canada Plumbago Company*[70] the company being wound up changed solicitors and the first solicitor claimed his costs as a priority. Unfortunately, there were insufficient assets to pay the costs incurred in winding up the company. After the sale of assets and the payment of necessary other expenses there was approximately £35 left in the estate.[71] After the change of solicitors, the liquidator was unsuccessful in an action against a contributory (shareholder), Kirby. As a result of this litigation the liquidator was ordered to pay Kirby the taxed costs of the application amounting to almost £23. At the same time the liquidator was at liberty to retain the amount of the liquidator's costs in the action out of the assets of the company. This left approximately £12 in the estate.[72] This amount was quite insufficient to pay the first solicitor's costs and was needed by the liquidator to pay his out of pocket expenses.

The first solicitor argued that the liquidator should not have satisfied the contributory.

Justice Pearson decided that the question to answer was whether, in the administration of the assets, the liquidator is bound to pay a litigant his costs in priority to the general costs of the liquidation.[73] If that was the case, then the payment to the contributory was correct and the £12 was all that was left to pay the first solicitor. He examined the principle and concluded that the costs of a party who has succeeded at law could not become costs in *pari passu* with the general costs of the liquidation.[74] Justice Pearson went on to decide to apportion the £12 by £5 to the first solicitor and the balance to the liquidator.[75] The first solicitor appealed this decision. The Court of Appeal supported Pearson J. There is little by way of principle or reasoning expressly provided in the report.

On appeal, Baggallay LJ decided that the payment of the litigation costs by the liquidator to the contributory, in accordance with the court order, was correct and the liquidator had the ability to recoup this amount out of the assets of the company. This amount was a priority over all other creditors in the liquidation.[76] Lord Justice Baggallay held that there was a statutory discretion in the *Companies Act 1862* (Eng) to apportion.[77] Lord Justice Cotton supported Pearson J's priorities' decision, stating that 'it would have been wrong for a judge … to give the solicitor

70 (1884) 27 Ch D 33.
71 Ibid. 34.
72 Ibid. 34.
73 Ibid. 36.
74 Ibid. 37.
75 Ibid. 40.
76 Ibid. 42.
77 Ibid. 42.

a priority for his costs over the official liquidator in respect of expenses properly incurred'.[78]

Other Support for Requisite Costs

In the late 1890s, the decision in *Re Dominion of Canada Plumbago Company* was followed in *Re London Metallurgical Co.*[79] Here, the liquidator of the company placed a name of a person on a list of contributories. As this person did not want to be in the position of having to contribute toward meeting a shortfall, they took out a summons to have their name removed from the list and were successful in the order they sought. They had incurred costs in taking out the application and the court ordered the liquidator should pay. The order directed the liquidator to pay out of the assets of the company, and that these costs should form part of the costs in the winding up.

The liquidator drew attention to the fact that an immediate demand for the costs would go unsatisfied as he already had large costs of realization not yet paid, another order of the court for costs in a separate application and three more actions in the courts where he was to pay amounts as securities for costs.

Justice Vaughan Williams started with the proposition that 'successful litigants and other persons who become creditors of the company after the winding up order, are prima facie entitled to be paid in full'.[80] He directed that successful litigants are not to be placed in competition with unsecured creditors.[81]

His Honour conceded that 'until insolvency is shewn the right of the successful litigant is to be paid in full'[82] and then there is an onus on the liquidator to show that the condition of the assets is such that the successful litigant is not entitled to what is prima facie their right. Justice Vaughan Williams rebutted any suggestion that there was a priority of these court orders dependent upon the date on which each is made.[83] His Honour did acknowledge that a liquidator may show that there are persons who have prior rights to the successful litigant and then the court will not make any order without making provision for these claims.[84]

Justice Vaughan Williams observed that the successful litigant's payment is not to be postponed until 'all possible claims, contingent or otherwise, have come in'[85] and that the order gives the successful litigant the prima facie right to immediate payment in full. This is subject to existing claims that are prior in right or equal to

78 Ibid. 43.
79 (1895) 1 Ch 758.
80 Ibid. 763.
81 Ibid. 766.
82 Ibid. 764.
83 Ibid. 765.
84 Ibid.
85 Ibid. 766.

those of the litigants. Essentially, the successful litigant does not have to wait until the whole of the assets are recovered.[86]

Justice Vaughan Williams rebuffs the proposition that to pay at once the costs of successful litigants might have policy implications. He argues that where there is doubt as to the sufficiency of the assets, liquidators will be deterred from commencing proceedings because those who have present claims may swallow up the assets. He reasons that, if necessary, creditors in liquidations must provide an indemnity fund for liquidators to litigate.

Requisite Costs When Liquidators are being Sued

There are a series of cases where the liquidator has been sued and this has resulted in a priority. On one occasion the court expressed some sympathy toward the liquidator while in other cases, the liquidator was made to pay when they were the unsuccessful litigant. However, the area lacks discussion, good argument and judicial direction.

In *Re S Davis and Co Ltd*,[87] a company went into liquidation and they were the bailees of some furniture at the time. Three years later, the bailor received back his furniture but some of it was missing and some damaged. There was a suggestion that this may have been caused by the war during those years. The bailor received judgment for £601 and he issued a summons for this amount to be taxed and paid in priority to the unsecured creditors.

Justice Cohen held that the liquidator carried on the business, including the business of holding the applicant's goods, in bailment for reward. The judge reiterated the legal position that all debts and liabilities incurred in the course of carrying on the business by the liquidator, being in the nature of salvage, rank for payment in priority to the general debts and liabilities of the company. Among such liabilities was the obligation to deliver up the goods to the applicant in proper condition at the termination of the bailment upon commencement of the liquidation.[88] Hence the liquidator had adopted the contract and breached the obligation, and the bailor was entitled to payment of damages. Justice Cohen did concede that the liquidator would not be liable if 'the loss or damage was not due to negligence – e.g. that it was due solely to war damage – or that it was due to an event occurring before the commencement of the liquidation'.[89] However the liquidator had not discharged the onus of proof in such matters. The liquidator was ordered to pay the damages and the taxed costs as costs of the winding up.[90] The judgment reinforced the principle that the liquidator, as unsuccessful litigant, must be prepared to pay these costs as priority expenses.

86 Ibid. 770.
87 [1945] 1 Ch 402.
88 Ibid. 407.
89 Ibid.
90 Ibid. 408.

In a rare Australian judgment on the subject no direction was forthcoming on the treatment of litigation costs as requisite priority costs. In *Re Kratzmann Holdings Pty Ltd (in liq)*,[91] prior to entering liquidation the company had used subcontractors. Money had been paid into court pursuant to legislation in Queensland known as the *Subcontractors Charges Act 1974–76* (Qld). The liquidator had admitted the charges of various subcontractors and was seeking an order from the court to pay these charges. The liquidator was also asking the court to extinguish some other contractors' claims to charges. This would result in a balance of the money held in court going back to the liquidators for use in paying a dividend to creditors. In addition, there was an issue as to the court's judgment on costs of these proceedings. A solicitor for one of the subcontractors argued for an order of costs in favour of his client, following on from receiving the court's judgment in favour of his client's charge being met. The liquidator agreed to their costs being met as an ordinary debt but not as a priority over other creditors.

Master Lee followed Dunn J in *Ex parte Pavex Constructions and others*[92] where there was a fund in court which exceeded the amount of several charges. Counsel for the liquidator referred the Master to the order made by Dunn J in *Kratzmann* and suggested an order in the similar terms was appropriate. Master Lee decided that he should make the order for costs in favour of the subcontractors, but avoided the priority issue by stating: 'if the order for costs ... must result in priority, then no special order is required from me'.[93] Such a statement did little to assist in the interpretation of litigation costs as entitlement for priority.

Special Expenses as 'Requisite' Costs

In *Corporations Act 2001* (Cth) s556(1)(a), the general subparagraph dedicated to costs and expenses, it is implied and expected that there will be unusual or special expenses incurred during the external administration that will attract the priority.

In *Crest Insurance Co of Australia Ltd v Rosser*,[94] a provisional liquidator appointed to the insurance company had the power to carry on the business. However, he merely succeeded in terminating all of the contracts upon which the business was based. One former client summoned the liquidator for the return of their premium arising out of the cancellation of their policy and for liability to pay an accident claim. The plaintiff claimed both of these were a 'cost, charge or expense of the provisional liquidator'.[95] Justice Cohen did not see the action of cancelling the contracts as a 'positive step in carrying on the business'.[96] Furthermore, he did not regard the right to the return of the premium as being an

91 *Re Kratzmann Holdings Pty Ltd (in liq)* (1982) 1 ACLC 320.
92 [1979] Qd R 318.
93 *Re Kratzmann Holdings Pty Ltd (in liq)* (1982) 1 ACLC 320, 322.
94 (1985) 10 ACLR 109, 112.
95 Ibid. 110.
96 Ibid. 111.

expense incurred in the carrying on of business, rather it was something that the client could prove for in the liquidation.[97] Justice Cohen, in commenting as to what expenses a voluntary liquidator might incur, suggested that they are entitled to pay the day to day costs and expenses involved. These would include rent, insurance and the current accounts of suppliers, as no business can be conducted for any length of time without the payment of ongoing expenses.[98]

The Expenses Paid on Finance Bills can be Requisite Expenses

In *K D Morris and Sons Pty Ltd v Bank of Queensland Ltd*,[99] the members of the High Court of Australia were equally divided as to the effect of certain financial transactions. It was held that the amount paid by the company's bank when rolling over commercial bills drawn by the company after the commencement of the liquidation did not form part of the costs and expenses of the winding up. While some texts use this case as an authority on priorities,[100] it must be said it is a dubious one despite its significance in other legal areas. The headnote suggests a 3:2 decision upholding the appeal from the Queensland Supreme Court. Such a result would mean that there is no priority for expenses that are ultimately paid by the acceptor of accommodation bills, when drawn by the company and rolled over by its liquidator under the terms of a commercial bill acceptance facility. These terms are established before the liquidation.

However, Murphy J, whilst in the majority, gave no consideration to the administrative expense priority (certainly in no express terms). He chose to uphold the appeal because he did not like the liquidator entering into transactions that, upon his interpretation of the companies' legislation of the day, did not grant such powers.

Taking Murphy J's neutrality on the priority into account, that leaves the priority point evenly decided 2:2. Justices Mason and Aickin, said to be in the minority, held that the acceptance of the last of the series of bills gave rise to a liability that fell within the description 'the costs and expenses of the winding up'. Such a finding would have meant a priority.[101] Their Honours supported the Bank's contention that the relevant transactions took place after the commencement of the winding up and were entered into by the liquidators in the course of, and for the purposes, of the winding up.[102] This happened because the original agreements were seen to have come to an end and were superseded by substituted agreements

97 Ibid. 112.

98 Ibid. 113.

99 (1980) 54 AJLR 424; ACLC 34,292.

100 See e.g., Andrew Keay, *McPherson The Law of Company Liquidation* (4th ed. 1999) 588–589.

101 *K D Morris and Sons Pty Ltd v Bank of Queensland Ltd* (1980) 54 AJLR 424, 436.

102 Ibid. 438.

entered into by the liquidators (and earlier by the provisional liquidators) and all after the date of the commencement of the liquidation.[103]

This reasoning was rejected by Stephen and Williams JJ, who held that the agreements between the liquidators and the Bank did no more than provide a means of prolonging the already established cyclical character of the liability.[104] They were seen as merely rollover operations that did not justify being interpreted as a cost or expense of winding up. Since then their Honours' judgment has been interpreted as the majority view, due to Murphy J finding against the priority on other grounds. It has not been subjected to much criticism on the administrative expense point. It stands as a source of disappointment that the High Court of Australia did not embrace this rare opportunity to really explore the cost and expenses priority, nor have they since. The case, while questionable as a specific guide to what constitutes a special requisite expense for the purposes of the administrative expense priority, has gained acceptability as an authority for other principles applied in finance law.

Requisite Expenses in the Form of Payments for Professional Help

In *Re Barleycorn Enterprises Ltd*[105] a firm of chartered accountants had prepared a statement of affairs after the winding up order had been made and the Official Receiver had sanctioned their fees. When an administrative receiver was appointed, the assets were insufficient to pay the preferential claims and the debenture holder. The Court of Appeal decided that the accountants should be paid in priority to both.

Other cases have discussed priority payments to directors, accountants and liquidators engaged in preliminary liquidation matters where the work qualified as administration expenses. In *Re Mawcon Ltd*,[106] expenses incurred by directors, as special managers, in carrying on the company's business for the benefit of the winding up, were held to be liquidation expenses. In *Re Introductions Ltd (No 2)*,[107] the company accumulated funds from ultra vires trading. As there were no other available assets, Stamp J allowed the liquidator to meet his own costs and charges and the accountant's charge for the preparation of the statement of affairs. These costs outranked other creditors.

A liquidator may also be able to recover payment for preliminary work before the decision is taken to wind up the company. In *Re Berkley Applegate (Investment Consultants) Ltd*[108] the cost of preliminary work, completed when the company

103 Ibid.

104 Ibid. 427.

105 *Re Barleycorn Enterprises Ltd Mathias and Davies (A Firm) v Dunn* [1970] 1 Ch 465.

106 [1969] 1 WLR 78.

107 [1969] 1WLR 1359.

108 [1989] 1 Ch 32.

was not in a formal liquidation, was still held to be an expense of the winding up. However, there were exceptional circumstances in this case and a liquidator performed preliminary work that would usually have been undertaken by a trustee with an indemnity. Yet, as a note of caution a situation should not be allowed to develop where liquidators ensure they are paid, as a priority creditor, for work done when the company is still under the control of its directors. In such a circumstance they must be treated in the same way as any other professionals; that is as unsecured creditors if the company subsequently appoints a liquidator.

Rates as Requisite Expenses in a Winding Up

Rates, such as land taxes and local government rates, could be considered as a component within requisite expenses. Rates due at the time of commencement of the winding up have no priority,[109] and certainly no special statutory priority in the *Corporations Act 2001* (Cth).[110] Where a liquidator keeps the rateable property with a view to selling, he or she may be ordered to pay rates and taxes falling due subsequently as part of the expenses of winding up.[111]

In *Re National Arms and Ammunition Company*[112] Fry LJ commenced his judgment with the principle of equal sharing, commenting that:

> when a company is wound up, the creditors who are such at the commencement of the winding up stand on an equal footing as between themselves. But if after that period the company or the liquidator on its behalf … enter into contracts or occupy land … neither the persons with whom the contracts are entered into, nor the persons to whom sums in respect of the land are payable … are bound to accept a dividend on their claims.[113]

He decided, therefore, that rates owed to a local government for street improvement and borough improvement 'must be paid in full'.[114]

Lord Justice Bowen, in the same case, stated that the true test was whether there had been a beneficial occupation within the ordinary meaning of those words and, if so, then the rates enjoyed the priority of an administration expense.[115] He had earlier stated the principle to be applied to administrative expenses in its clearest terms;

---

109 See e.g., *Dry Docks Corporation* (1888) 39 Ch D 306.

110 As outlined in Chapter 2, the early companies' legislation provided for a priority attaching to a year's arrears of rates.

111 *Re National Arms and Ammunition Co* (1885) 28 Ch D 447.

112 (1885) 28 Ch D 447.

113 Ibid. 481.

114 Ibid.

115 Ibid. 482.

> A broad line is to be drawn between obligations which have occurred before the commencement of the winding up and those which accrue after the commencement of the winding up. Persons having claims which have accrued due before the winding up must come in as creditors *pari passu*, and on principle there is no reason why a debt properly incurred by the liquidator after the commencement of the winding up should not be paid in full, nor can I see why sums becoming due after the commencement of the winding up, in respect of property of which the liquidator retains possession for the purposes of the company, should not be paid.[116]

Lord Justice Baggallay provided the major judgment, relying on precedent[117] to develop the requirement of beneficial occupation before the cost could fall within the administrative expense priority. The liquidator had been appointed over a company that manufactured rifles. The company had a stock of unfinished rifles when the liquidator was appointed. These were finished and sold at a profit by the liquidator. Lord Justice Baggallay, therefore, was convinced that there had been a beneficial enjoyment of the premises and so the rates were deemed to be part of the administration expenses.

In more recent times the mandatory expenditure incurred in connection with land, such as rates, has been confirmed as part of the requisite costs that enjoy the administrative expenses priority. In *Re Nolton Business Centres Ltd*[118] council rates, which were raised in instalments and so fell due for payment after the date of appointment of a liquidator, were held by the Chancery Division to be liquidation expenses. Judge Weeks affirmed *Re National Arms and Ammunition Company*,[119] particularly Bowen LJ's clear interpretation of the priority.

Justification of Requisite Expenses

The Harmer Report[120] in Australia suggested that administrative expenses, represented by the sorts of cases mentioned above, should rank highly. The Harmer Report's rationale for the administration priority provides that 'creditors have a community of interest in having a common agent to maximise a fund for distribution' among them.[121] Therefore, this 'common agent' should enjoy their

116 Ibid. 479.

117 Those cases mentioned by Baggally LJ are *In re West Hartlepool Iron Company* (1875) 34 LT (NS) 568; *In re Watson, Kipling and Co* (1883) 23 Ch D 500; *In re International Marine Hydropathic Company* (1885) 28 Ch D 470.

118 [1996] BCC 500.

119 28 Ch D 447.

120 Australian Law Reform Commission, *General Insolvency Inquiry*, Report No 45 (1988), 'Harmer Report', para 720.

121 Ibid. para 717.

right to remuneration and an indemnity for expenses. However, this rationale can only be indirectly applied to indemnity expenses such as litigation costs, special expenses and rates.

It has been observed that administration costs are not, strictly speaking, preferential debts because they are not debts which would otherwise have been payable by the insolvent company.[122] The reasoning runs that the company would not have incurred these costs had it been continuing as a solvent company. The Harmer Report concluded that administration costs are not to be treated as a pre-existing debt of the insolvent entity but are costs incurred on behalf of the general body of creditors, which should be borne by those creditors.[123] While this is indirectly true of rent, however, it is not the case with administrative expenses like rates. It seems superficial to suggest that rent benefits all creditors but it is much less convincing to argue rates benefit them!

In summary, no obvious justification has been developed by the courts for the priority of requisite costs. However, one of the aims of insolvency is to provide an equal, fair and orderly procedure[124] and the priority for requisite costs certainly adds to making an orderly insolvency process. Again this is a superficial justification.

Corporations Act 2001 (Cth) Section 556(1)(b) – Applicant's Costs

In the case of a court-ordered (compulsory) winding up, the costs of the application to the court are given a priority. This priority includes the taxed costs of the applicant payable under s466 of the *Corporations Act 2001* (Cth).

In earlier legislation such as the *Companies Code*, s441(1)(a) provided for all administration expenses in the one subparagraph. It read 'first, the costs, charge and expense of the winding up, including taxed costs of an applicant payable under section 366, the remuneration of the liquidator and the costs of any audit carried out under section 422'. This caused the applicant's costs to be in competition with other administrative expenses. If there were insufficient funds to satisfy all of these expenses, the rule was that the applicant's costs were to be paid first.[125] This was rationalized on the basis that these costs were incurred for the benefit of all creditors and without them there would be no winding up.[126]

One Australian text suggests that 'the fact that the [applicant's] costs are now in second position [indicates that] the legislature has … decided not to accept' the

122 New Zealand Law Commission, *Priority Debts in the Distribution of Insolvent Estates,* An Advisory Report to Ministry of Commerce (1999) 40.

123 Harmer Report, para 719.

124 See e.g., Tomasic, R. and Whitford, K. *Australian Insolvency and Bankruptcy Law* (2nd ed. 1997) 5.

125 *Re Audrey Hall Cotton Spinning Co* (1868) LR 6 Eq 245; *Re Massey* (1870) LR 9 Eq 367.

126 *Re New York Exchange Co* [1893] 1 Ch 371.

earlier rationale.[127] However, parliamentary papers do not indicate the legislature even considering the downgrade in priority ranking when adopting the current provisions. Nevertheless, they are clearly ranked behind administrative expenses discussed above in s556(1)(a).

Endangering the Applicant's Costs Priority

The relatively recent case of *Morepine Pty Ltd v Crush Pacific Industries Pty Ltd*[128] concerns a priority for applicant's costs. Morepine successfully applied to the court for a winding up of Crush Pacific Industries Pty Ltd based on the insolvency of the company. Prior to this, Morepine had been trying to wind up upon other grounds, including that it would be just and equitable to liquidate. This had taken a substantial amount of time and effort. Morepine's solicitors had submitted a bill of costs of $28,562.97 and disbursements of $30,029.85.[129] The applicant's taxed costs therefore amounted to over $58,000.

This court was asked to determine if these amounts were given priority under s556(1)(b). If so then there were no funds left for unsecured creditors. This is not such an uncommon situation but what made the situation unique were the high costs of over $58,000. The usual cost of obtaining an order for winding up is between $3,000–$5,000.

Section 466(2) of the *Corporations Act 2001* (Cth) provides that the liquidator will reimburse the taxed costs incurred by the applicant for a winding up out of the property of the company. Justice Young held that the court has a discretion as to what order it will make as to costs.[130]

Justice Young stated: 'there is no power in the *Corporations Act* for a court to do what it feels is just in its own eyes with respect to the priorities set out in s556'.[131] He observed that the Act took the form of requiring *pari passu* of creditors[132] subject to the priorities in s556.[133] Section 556(1) used the mandatory word 'must', requiring the claims mentioned in the section to be paid in priority to all other unsecured debts. His Honour held that if the claim by Morepine was 'for "costs in respect of the application for the order" then it wholly ranks'[134] in s556(1)(b). He felt a wide interpretation could be given to the words 'in respect of' even though they were, in his opinion, 'difficult of definition'.[135]

---

127 Keay, A. *McPherson The Law of Company Liquidation* (4th ed. 1999) 592.

128 (1996) 14 ACLC 898.

129 Ibid. 899.

130 Ibid. 901. Here the court cites with approval *Re Mailrite Pty Ltd* (1985) 3 ACLC 528.

131 *Morepine Pty Ltd v Crush Pacific Industries Pty Ltd* (1996) 14 ACLC 898, 900.

132 *Corporations Act 2001* (Cth) s555.

133 *Morepine Pty Ltd v Crush Pacific Industries Pty Ltd* (1996) 14 ACLC 898, 900.

134 Ibid.

135 Ibid. 901.

Justice Young sympathized with the situation which the parties faced in Morepine. He said '[W]hen one looks at the bill ... one can see considerable problems with it if one is looking at it in terms of fairness between the plaintiff (Morepine), the liquidator and the unsecured creditors'.[136] On one hand it was a bill that would be allowed by a costs assessor as it conformed to the costs agreement, but on the other hand, it was based on a costs agreement which should not be taken into account by a cost assessor if he or she is considering what costs are to be paid pursuant to an order of the court. Although the bill may be a proper one because of the costs agreement it was to be paid for by a third party and in such circumstances it would be discounted. Justice Young knew that the work had been done for an abandoned purpose: that of trying to establish a cause for winding up along just and equitable grounds. Giving a priority seemed to be unfairly prejudicial on the unsecured creditors. Furthermore, the legal work undertaken for Morepine seemed slow to Young J. Noting that Morepine's lawyers took 6 hours 45 minutes to peruse 830 pages and charged $1,552.50, he commented in disbelief that judges 'are usually allowed about an hour to do so!'[137] Justice Young went on to say that it

> makes one wonder whether solicitors should be paid for spending an extremely long period of time just looking at documents when the result will be that they will be rewarded for sitting and reading, whilst the unsecured creditors and the liquidator will be left without a cent.[138]

Despite obvious concerns as to the fairness of the claims for the applicant's costs in this case, Young J could find little authority to assist in a determination of what is normally included in the costs allowed by the subparagraph.[139] Plaintiffs do not have open slather to incur applicant's costs although the courts do take a fairly benign view of what is normally included in the costs allowed.[140]

The case is a fine example of the impact and importance of statutory priority provisions. Throughout the judgment, one of Australia's senior judges, Young J, struggled with the lack of fairness that the statutory priority provided. Yet in the end he was merely able to suggest that the parties attempt to arrive at a settlement.[141]

The Miscellany of Specific Administration Expenses Granted a Statutory Priority

Section 556(1) provides specific priorities for the following: s556(1)(c) indemnified debts of an administrator of the company; s556(1)(da) if the Court

136 Ibid.
137 Ibid. 901–902.
138 Ibid. 902.
139 Ibid.
140 See e.g., *Re A&N Thermo Products Ltd* [1963] 1 WLR 1341.
141 *Morepine Pty Ltd v Crush Pacific Industries Pty Ltd* (1996) 14 ACLC 898, 902.

ordered the winding up – next, costs and expenses that are payable under s475(8) out of company's property; s556(1)(db) costs that form part of the expenses of the winding up because of ss539(6); s556(1)(dd) any other expenses properly incurred by a relevant authority.

All of the above have had administrative expense priority in a less specific way in the past and have now been included in the legislation to rank from third through to eighth priority. There are no significant cases decided on these subparagraphs, despite them being specifically included in the *Corporations Act 2001* (Cth) and its predecessor since 1993.

Section 556(1)(c) gives a priority order of payment to the debts incurred by an administrator during the course of the administration of a company in accordance with Part 5.3A. Under s443D(a) the administrator is entitled to an indemnity for debts incurred in the exercise or performance of the administrator's functions or powers. These relate to services rendered, goods bought, and property hired or leased, used or occupied as described by ss443A, 443B and 443BA. It would include rent during the administration and amounts payable to the Commissioner of Taxation. The administrator's remuneration is a deferred expense and is not included in s556(1)(c) but found in s556(1)(de), as discussed below.

In 2007 the former priority found in s556(1)(d) was repealed. It dealt with official management and had little interest or relevance as the concept of official management was repealed in 1993. The auditor's remuneration for a company in official management also enjoyed a priority under s556(1)(dc), until it too was repealed in 2007.

In the case of a compulsory, court-ordered winding up there is a priority under s556(1)(da) for the costs and expenses of making a report as to the affairs of the company. Section 475 of the *Corporations Act 2001* (Cth) requires the directors and secretary of the company, being forced into winding up, to prepare a report. Subsection 8 allows for the liquidator to pay the directors and secretary reasonable costs and expenses in this connection.

The liquidator must lodge half-yearly accounts and ASIC may choose to arrange an audit of these accounts. ASIC will fix the costs of the audit. These form part of the expenses of winding up with a priority in s556(1)(db). Often there will be a close connection between auditors and insolvency practitioners and the opportunity exists for collusion amongst the accounting professionals. This collusion regarding audit costs can prejudice other creditors given the benefit received through this priority and so independence and careful scrutiny are required.[142]

Section 556(1)(dd) allows for other expenses that do not qualify under s556(1)(a).[143] It has been suggested that this might include costs awarded against

142 The recent changes to the *Corporations Act 2001* (Cth) in Part 2M.4 on auditor independence and appointment did not address the insolvent company.

143 Keay, A. *McPherson The Law of Company Liquidation* (4th ed. 1999) 593.

a liquidator in relation to an unsuccessful action. Such a suggestion is doubtful given the established position of litigation costs in s556(1)(a) as discussed above.

Corporations Act 2001 (Cth) Section 556(1)(de) – Remuneration – 'The Deferred Expenses'

The *Corporations Act 2001* (Cth) in s556(1) assumes that all of the costs and expenses of the winding up are to be paid before the remuneration of the relevant authority.[144] A 'relevant authority' is defined in s556(2) to include a liquidator, a provisional liquidator and an administrator of a company or of a deed of arrangement. The remuneration of a liquidator or other relevant authority comes within the concept of 'deferred expenses', which is defined in s556(2) to include any 'remuneration, or fee for services, payable to the relevant authority'. Where the liquidator is improperly appointed, however, they are not entitled to remuneration.[145]

The liquidator, out of the assets of the company, pays expenses that he or she has incurred as far as he or she is able to recover them. If the liquidator's position is that, having provided for such costs, there is no remuneration available, the practise is to ask the creditors or shareholders to put up a fund for his or her benefit.[146]

Creating a high priority requires caution as it may encourage a corresponding 'devil may care' approach. Liquidators should adopt the perspective that they should expend money and incur fees only if that represents 'value for money'. Otherwise money that could have been used for other priority creditors' payments and dividends to creditors is taken to meet the remuneration expenses of the liquidator. Liquidators are favoured by the legislation and so should spend company funds or incur debts as if they were using their own money.[147]

The Early Criterion for a Liquidator's Remuneration Priority

Case law on the remuneration priority established very early on in insolvency law history that the liquidator would be paid only after other important expenses.

144 CCH, *Australian Corporations & Securities Law Reporter*, Vol. 3 para 162–810, 244,094. All expenses except expenses of members of committee of inspection under s556(1)(df).

145 See e.g., *Re John Plunkett Consolidated Pty Ltd (in liq) (No 3)* (1979) CLC 40–545 for proper appointments and *Re Kyra Nominees Pty Ltd* (1980) CLC 40–659 for improper appointments.

146 There is no legislative requirement in this regard.

147 It is acknowledged that a lien is present for external administrators. See e.g., *Re Biposo Pty Ltd (No 4)* (Unreported, Supreme Court of NSW, 12 December 1995). However, as referred to in Chapter 1, in an attempt to contain the work to a manageable size, the treatment of liens must be considered beyond the parameters of this work.

Cases from as early as 1868[148] determined that liquidators should wait for their fees until other expenses have been paid. Case have established the need to distinguish expenses and fees to recover secured assets from other expenses and fees incurred in the orderly close down of a company.

The earliest case, *Re Audley Hall Cotton Spinning Company*,[149] is not really about liquidators' remuneration although it is used by some texts as a suggested authority.[150] It involved a liquidator, once appointed, changing solicitor's firms, although the reason for the change is not reported. The first solicitor had been solicitor for the petitioner as well! The liquidator paid a dividend to creditors and held some money back. However, this remaining balance was insufficient to pay the whole of his costs. He then took out a summons for the delivery of the file and other documents from the first solicitor, who received an undertaking to be paid in full out of the estate. An order directed that the petitioner's costs would be paid as the highest priority, followed by the liquidator's costs as incurred before the change of solicitor and then his costs after the change. On two occasions the liquidator had received £100 for expenses and remuneration. The liquidator sought permission of the court to apply the balance by paying, as the order had said, all that was owed to the first solicitor and to apply rateably the balance between the first solicitor and second solicitor. Obviously, the case is not really about liquidators' remuneration. It does though give an insight that in the early days of corporate insolvency law, liquidators did not wait for all expenses to be paid before satisfying their fees in priority.

Lord Romilly MR granted the permission.[151] He observed that it was unfortunate that the liquidator had paid out a larger dividend to creditors than was warranted and looked after himself by paying out a sum for his services, but conceded that neither factor affected the question about the payments to the solicitors.[152] It is hard to think that such an action would be forgiven today.

Further Clarity from Lord Romilly[153] – That the Liquidator Must Wait for their Remuneration

In another early case, *Re Massey re Freehold Land and Brickmaking Company*,[154] there were again insufficient funds to pay both the solicitor and the liquidator. The liquidator argued that his costs should be met and the balance applied rateably

148 *Re Audley Hall Cotton Spinning Company* (1868) LR 6 Eq 245.

149 (1868) LR 6 Eq 245.

150 Keay, A. *McPherson The Law of Company Liquidation* (4th ed. 1999) 592. Keay is describing the former legal position for this priority.

151 *Re Audley Hall Cotton Spinning Company* (1868) LR 6 Eq 245, 247.

152 Ibid. 247 and 248.

153 Lord Romilly's judgements were featured in the history of statutory priorities in Chapter 2.

154 (1870) LR 9 Eq 367.

between himself and the solicitor. Lord Romilly MR decided that the 'liquidator cannot get any remuneration until all the costs of the winding up are paid'.[155] The present position in s556 of the *Corporations Act 2001* (Cth) approximately 140 years later expresses this, despite the fact that in practice interim payments are expected and approved by creditors.

Australian Criterion for Liquidator's Remuneration Priority Over Secured Assets

The first Australian reported case on the issue of priority for the liquidator's remuneration is *Re Universal Distributing Co Ltd (in liq)*.[156] It stands as authority for the proposition that 'a liquidator who is involved in realizing an asset that is subject to security is entitled to deduct from the proceeds to be delivered to the secured creditor that portion of the liquidator's remuneration that [is] related to the realization of the security'.[157]

The liquidated assets of Universal Distributing Co Ltd were insufficient to satisfy the liability secured by its debentures, as there was a charge over the whole company's undertaking and its uncalled capital. Not surprisingly, the High Court of Australia held that the debenture debt took priority over the general costs, charges and expenses of the liquidation. This was subject to the expenses incurred by the liquidator in the actual realization of the assets subject to the security. Part of the official liquidator's time had been expended in recovering the uncalled capital and other moneys from which the debenture holder was entitled to a priority of payment. Therefore the expenses and so much of the liquidator's remuneration as represented these services were directed to be paid out of the assets in priority to the debenture debt.[158] The court decided that only after payment of these expenses, and then the debenture debt, would the rest of the expenses and the rest of the remuneration be paid.

Justice Dixon held that:

> [T]he court cannot overreach or postpone a security in exercising its statutory power 'in the event of the assets being insufficient to satisfy the liabilities' to make an order as to the payment out of the estate of the company being wound up of the costs, charges and expenses incurred in winding up in such order or priority as the Court thinks just. A security even over uncalled capital has prevailed over the claim of a petitioning creditor under an order for his costs. (*Re Anglo-Austrian Printing and Publishing Union*; *Brabourne v Same* (1895) 2 Ch 891).[159]

155 Ibid. 368.

156 (1933) 48 CLR 171.

157 Keay, A. *McPherson The Law of Company Liquidation* (4th ed. 1999) 594.

158 *Re Universal Distributing Company Ltd (in liquidation)* (1933) 48 CLR 171, 174–175.

159 Ibid. 173–174.

Justice Dixon also commented: '[T]he security is paramount to the general costs and expenses of the liquidation but the expenses attendant upon the realisation of the fund affected by the security must be borne by it' (*Re Oriental Hotels Co*; *Perry v Oriental Hotels Co* (1871) LR 12 Eq 126).[160] He expressed the priority in this way: 'I see no reason why remuneration for work done for the exclusive purpose of raising the fund should not be charged upon it'.[161]

A Liquidator's Remuneration Priority versus the Crown

A year later in England, in *Re Beni-Felkai Mining Co Ltd*[162] a liquidator claimed that his remuneration should have priority before an income tax debt. The liquidator swore an affidavit stating that he had used his personal assets in an effort to maintain himself when things went wrong in the company he was liquidating. He was 'practically destitute'[163] and desired to resign but had been unable to induce anyone to relieve him.[164] The Court recognized that, as a liquidator, 'he is the person who can see what the position is'[165] and is entitled to seek a fund for his benefit from creditors or shareholders or others if he decides he cannot go on unless there is funding.[166] Counsel for the Attorney General put it bluntly: 'The liquidator is his own master ... [T]he real question here is whether the Crown should risk losing income tax or the liquidator should risk losing his remuneration'.[167]

Justice Maugham held that, when the assets of a company in voluntary liquidation are insufficient to discharge its liabilities, the court had the power to make an order in the exercise of its discretion as to the payment out of the costs, charges and expenses (including the liquidator's remuneration).[168] The court could direct such order of priority as it thinks just,[169] and that prima facie all the expenses ought to be paid before the liquidator's remuneration.[170] In an appropriate equitable way, Maugham J allowed the 'destitute' liquidator to keep the amounts of remuneration he had taken by consent, before he knew there were insufficient assets to meet all the priority expenses of the liquidation.[171]

160 Ibid. 174.
161 Ibid. 175.
162 *Re Beni-Felkai Mining Co* [1934] Ch 406.
163 Ibid. 410.
164 Ibid.
165 Ibid. 422.
166 Ibid.
167 Ibid. 415.
168 Ibid. 419.
169 Ibid.
170 Ibid. 422.
171 Ibid. 423.

The Modern Australian Statement on Liquidator's Remuneration Priority

In 1971 the New South Wales Supreme Court gave the clearest statement yet on the liquidator's remuneration priority. In *Re Buena Vista Motors Pty Ltd*,[172] the liquidator had been in place for five years. This helpfully added to a judicial examination of administration expense priorities. This case demonstrated that the purpose that there be equal treatment of priority creditors was 'unworkable'.[173] Justice Street noted that this was so because there had already been a great many disbursements by way of costs and expenses during the 5 year period that the company's business was being carried on after the winding up order.[174] Equal treatment of priority creditors was not possible despite what the legislation might prescribe.

Justice Street decided the liquidator had acted with *bona fides* and would suffer a shortfall in remuneration. However, claims for rent, long service leave and holiday pay of employees employed by the company's business and operated by the liquidator should be paid in priority to the remuneration. He was guided by the Companies Rules of the day,[175] and conferred the expense priority behind the other expenses mentioned. It is still true that, if there are insufficient funds to satisfy all the creditors, then the liquidator's remuneration is normally the last to be paid. The common law is likely to look to other administration claims to be satisfied earlier in the order.

In *Buena Vista*,[176] Street J described the circumstances of a liquidator's remuneration expenses aptly. He said:

> [O]ne may concede the bona fides of the liquidator during the course of his having carried on the business, and one may recognise the substantial shortfall which he may suffer in the remuneration which would otherwise be due to him if the assets were sufficient to pay his remuneration in full. On the other hand, however, the other claimants within the winding up whose claims fall for consideration have equally strong justification for expecting to have their claims paid in full.[177]

The Present Situation

Australian courts have the power under s485(3) of the *Corporations Act 2001* (Cth) to 'make an order as to the payment out of the property of the costs, charges

172 (1971) ACLC 40–019, 27,213.
173 Ibid. 27,214.
174 Ibid.
175 Now *Corporations Act 2001* (Cth) s556(1)(de).
176 *Re Buena Vista Motors Pty Ltd* (1971) ACLC 40–019.
177 Ibid. 27,215.

and expenses incurred in the winding up in such order of priority as the court thinks just' in the event that the property of the insolvent company is insufficient to satisfy the liabilities.

By 1989, in the United Kingdom, Warren J had commented in *Re Linda Marie Ltd (in liq)*[178] that only in exceptional circumstances will the court exercise discretion to change the order so as to improve the ranking of the liquidator's remuneration.[179]

It would now be most unlikely for an Australian court to exercise a discretion in favour of a more sympathetic stance and provide a higher ranking for the liquidator's remuneration. This is due to the debate about the high fees of liquidators,[180] that was illuminated by Ferris J in *Mirror Group Newspapers plc v Maxwell*,[181] the subsequent Ferris Report,[182] and some condemnation by some members of the insolvency profession towards the end of the 1990s.[183] A recent voluntary administration case has contributed to the debate after the Federal Court considered the need to clarify the basis on which creditors should 'fix' the remuneration of administrators.[184] Justice Finkelstein in *Korda, in the matter of Stockford Ltd* (subject to Deed of Company Arrangement)[185] outlined guidelines for insolvency practitioners in relation to disbursements and to provide sufficient information so fees can be properly assessed. His Honour felt that following such guidelines, practitioners would restore public confidence in this area of commercial life.[186] He provided factors that a court should consider when any claim for fees

178 [1989] BCLC 46.

179 Ibid. 54.

180 See e.g., in the USA, Eisenberg, T. 'Differing Perceptions of Attorney Fees in Bankruptcy Cases' (1994) 72 *Washington University Law Quarterly* 979; Palans, L.A. 'Comments on Eisenberg, Differing Perceptions of Attorney Fees in Bankruptcy Cases' (1994) 72 *Washington University Law Quarterly* 997; Symposium, 'Paying the Piper: Rethinking Professional Compensation in Bankruptcy' (1993) 1 *American Bankruptcy Institute Law Review* 231.

181 *Mirror Group Newspapers plc v Kevin Maxwell and Ian Maxwell and the personal representatives of Robert Maxwell (deceased)* [1998] BCC 324.

182 Justice Ferris' Working Party on the Remuneration of Office Holders <http://www.dca.gov.uk/civil/ferrisfr.htm>.

183 See e.g., Wallace, P. 'Ferris revisited – SIP9 updated' (1998) 10 (4) *Australian Insolvency Journal* 36; Justice Lightman, 'Officeholders' Charges: Cost Control and Transparency' (1998) 19 *Company Lawyer* 72, 76. Judicially see Ferris J in *Mirror Group Newspapers plc v Kevin Maxwell and Ian Maxwell and the Personal Representatives of Robert Maxwell (deceased)* [1998] BCC 324. Approved by *Korda, in the matter of Stockford Ltd (subject to Deed of Company Arrangement)* [2004] FCA 1682 (21 December 2004) (2005) 23 ACLC 150.

184 *Korda, in the matter of Stockford Ltd (subject to Deed of Company Arrangement)* [2004] FCA 1682 (21 December 2004) (2005) 23 ACLC 150.

185 Ibid.

186 Ibid. para [51].

is assessed, suggesting the use of a 'lodestar' amount[187] to be the fairest and most reasonable for all parties in light of the absence of legislation.

Section 473 of the *Corporations Act 2001* (Cth) has been extended to require greater reporting before the remuneration is determined and some sections direct the court as to matters to which it must have regard.[188]

Certainly now in the *Corporations Act 2001* (Cth) the positioning of the remuneration priority does not suggest it has parliament's support for more favourable treatment.

Justification for a Liquidators' Remuneration Priority

A liquidator is entitled to reasonable remuneration for work done. The problem is that the liquidator's remuneration comes in priority to, and at the expense of, deserving priority creditors and unsecured creditors who are entitled to the net assets of the company. It is interesting to recall that during the nineteenth century liquidators were remunerated by reference to results. They received a percentage of recoveries. This approach led to unacceptably high remuneration. Later their remuneration was calculated using a rate per hour basis.[189] In the United Kingdom, in response to the Ferris Report, it has been debated that a form of success or contingency fee could be (re) introduced.[190] It is the opinion of one academic that the costs of liquidation often eat up the whole estate.[191] It will alarm the supervising court and others, including unsecured creditors, if the liquidator is to receive, by way of remuneration, a large part of the company's assets. This was the case in *Re Peregrine Investments Holdings Ltd and Ors*.[192] Here, Le Pichon J discovered fees of $27 million for 34 days work![193]

---

187 Ibid. para [47] describing the United States approach to fixing the fees of trustees and attorneys under the Bankruptcy Code. A 'lodestar' amount should be understood simply to mean an amount by way of guidance for insolvency practitioners.

188 *Corporations Act 2001* (Cth) s473(10) (11) and (12) and s495(5)which were inserted in 2007.

189 Justice Lightman, 'Office holder' Charges: Cost Control and Transparency' (1998) 19 *Company Lawyer* 72, 76.

190 Wallace, P. 'Ferris revisited – SIP9 updated' (1998) 10 (4) *Australian Insolvency Journal* 36, 38.

191 Tyler, E.L.G. 'Has the Judge Gone Too Far? Le Pichon J and Office-holders' Remuneration' (Paper presented at the INSOL Pacific 1999 Conference Academics Forum, Auckland, New Zealand, 21 February 1999). Oddly the author claims that the liquidators are not in competition with creditors.

192 *Re Peregrine Investments Holdings Ltd and Ors* [1998] 3 HKC 1.

193 Ibid.

The Debate on Appropriate Liquidators' Remuneration

Liquidators' and other external administrators' remuneration has been under close scrutiny in recent times. In part this must be due to their statutory priority. In the United Kingdom, Ferris J chaired a working party investigating the topic during 1998. This response stemmed from *Mirror Group Newspapers plc v Maxwell*,[194] in which Ferris J was particularly critical of liquidators simply taking fees by reference to hours spent at hourly rates. He said the practitioner must explain the nature of each main task undertaken and the considerations that led him/her to embark upon that task or to persevere with it. The time spent must be linked to this explanation so that the amount of time devoted to each task can be seen. In 1999, Margaret Quinn, a Registrar in the Federal Court of Australia, wrote a series of Discussion Forum articles on the topic of remuneration for New Directions in Bankruptcy.[195] She discussed recent cases and concluded sufficient information must be provided to satisfy a court of the remuneration calculated. Much of the discussion is silent on the priority aspect of the remuneration, although it is clear that any priority over creditors should be justified.

There is no fixed scale of remuneration and yet the consumer-conscious public and unsecured creditors are requiring more detail. They demand reasons for time spent and evidence of value for money. Remuneration in insolvency matters was for many years assisted by the printed IPAA (Insolvency Practitioners Association of Australia) Guide to Hourly Rates. Recently, the Guide has been removed and new arrangements are in place. The IPAA released a Statement of Best Practice – Remuneration in July 2000.[196] The Statement directs liquidators to claim fees based on their own internal structures having regard to the complexity of demands in each liquidation. There is now statutory intervention from 2007 in the form of changes to the *Corporations Act 2001* (Cth) providing for fixing and reporting on 'reasonable remuneration' before being supported by members or creditors.[197]

The climate has clearly changed, in part, because of the observations in the judgments of Ferris J in *Maxwell's* case[198] and Le Pichon J in *Re Peregrine*[199] that have exposed abuses in liquidators' remuneration payments. Not to expose such abuses would have been to the financial detriment of lower priority and unsecured creditors in both cases.

194 *Mirror Group Newspapers plc v Kevin Maxwell and Ian Maxwell and the personal representatives of Robert Maxwell (deceased)* [1998] BCC 324.

195 Quinn, M. 'Remuneration' (1999) 9 (1) *New Directions in Bankruptcy* 14; (1999) 9 (3) *New Directions in Bankruptcy* 14.

196 The Statement is available at <http://www.ipaa.com.au/default.asp?menuid=242 &artid=512>, now superseeded.

197 *Corporations Act 2001* (Cth) s473(10), (11) and (12), s495(5).

198 *Mirror Group Newspapers plc v Kevin Maxwell and Ian Maxwell and the personal representatives of Robert Maxwell (deceased)* [1998] BCC 324.

199 *Re Peregrine Investments Holdings Ltd and Ors* [1998] 3 HKC 1.

Justice Ferris in the *Maxwell* case said that fees paid to liquidators should reward value and not simply indemnify against cost.[200] It is interesting to contemplate what the priority treatment does to this line of thinking. The priority treatment certainly achieves a possible indemnification against costs and ease of recovery yet the granting of a priority says little regarding the quality of the work performed.

The Harmer Report on the Topic of Liquidators' Remuneration

It is interesting to recall that in the submissions to the Harmer Report[201] in 1988, there 'was general acceptance that the fees and expenses of the liquidator, in protecting or realizing assets or running the business, should rank first in the administration costs'. A joint submission of the Insolvency Practitioner's Association of Australia (IPAA), the Institute of Chartered Accountants in Australia and the Australian Society of Accountants (now Australian Society of Certified Practising Accountants)[202] argued that the remuneration of the insolvency practitioner should rank higher than fifth. They suggested second or third. All these professional bodies have members who are insolvency practitioners. It was not surprising to have them lobby for a higher position for their constituents. The professional bodies argued in favour of this particular ordering on the basis that the liquidator consents to perform the liquidation with no indemnity other than from the assets and therefore should be rewarded with a high priority.

The Australian Law Reform Commission (ALRC), in preparing the Harmer Report, also heard oral presentations and recorded them as transcripts. An oral submission was made by Russell Heywood-Smith as part of the joint ICA/ IPAA (SA divisions) formal response to the earlier ALRC Discussion Paper No 32. Heywood-Smith referred to the existing ranking of the remuneration and called upon the ALRC to recommend an order that saw 'the current number 5 priority ... rank number 3'. Heywood-Smith commented that:

> [T]here appears no justification for a director or officer of an insolvent company being paid his costs for providing a liquidator with information from the company in the form of a report as to the companies [sic] affairs and (in) priority to the liquidator's remuneration. [203]

---

200 *Mirror Group Newspapers plc v Kevin Maxwell and Ian Maxwell and the personal representatives of Robert Maxwell (deceased)* [1998] BCC 324.

201 Australian Law Reform Commission, *General Insolvency Inquiry*, Report No 45 (1988), 'Harmer Report', para 719.

202 Harmer Report, Submission No 38, 17-18. Copy of this submission is on file with candidate.

203 Australian Law Reform Commission, *General Insolvency Inquiry*, Report No 45 (1988) Transcript 210, 215.

As a liquidator and a representative of insolvency practitioners, Heywood-Smith found it hard to accept such a low ranking for liquidator's remuneration. His views are likely to reflect those of other insolvency practitioners. The *Corporations Act 2001* (Cth) has not, however, evolved to reflect their viewpoint.

In complete contrast to the submissions received by the Harmer Inquiry, it has been suggested by a current loose-leaf service that the liquidator's remuneration should be low on the list of priorities.[204] The rationale for such a suggestion is that the liquidator is in a position to know whether the assets will be sufficient and, if not, they may refuse to continue the winding up process unless the creditors and contributories give security for their fees.[205] This assumes the maintenance of the priority while suggesting a different position in the statute.

Further debate is required on both the method for charging and the position of the priority for remuneration. Remuneration should be measured on a performance basis and the priority could be amended to specify a fixed fee or percentage with the balance being subject to an incentive scheme.

Corporations Act 2001 (Cth) Section 556(1)(df) – Priority for Committee of Inspection Expenses

A committee of inspection can be appointed to a company being wound up after meetings of creditors and contributories.[206] Such a committee is usually made up of creditors or contributories. While there is no statutory provision for remuneration of members of this committee, they may incur expenses in the course of their duties and these may be reimbursed. Such reimbursement is given priority in s556(1)(df).

Conclusion

This chapter has illustrated the major administrative expenses that are granted a statutory priority during insolvency. There is no question that these administrative expenses will continue to enjoy a statutory priority in corporate insolvency.

The *Corporations Act 2001* (Cth) in Australia fragments administrative expenses to a much greater degree than ever before. Some of this fragmentation is particularly appropriate, such as keeping liquidators' remuneration apart from the other costs and charges incurred when the insolvency practitioner preserves, realizes and collects the property of the company or carries on the company's business. The fragmentation provides more ranking than past legislation and gives parliament's

204 Butterworths, *Australian Corporations Law*, 5.6.0275.

205 *Corporations Act 2001* (Cth) s556(1)(de).

206 *Corporations Act 2001* (Cth) s548. In the United Kingdom these committees are known as liquidation committees: *Insolvency Act 1986* (UK) ss101, 141.

intention as to what expenses are most important. The *Corporations Act 2001* (Cth) is silent however, on what constitutes much of the 'administrative expenses'. The common law, happily supporting such vague descriptions, is often contained in brief judgments that involve little discussion of other judgments in the same or related areas. Very little cross-referencing of cases is apparent.

This chapter has offered an exhaustive description of the administrative expenses priority as it appears in the Australian *Corporations Act 2001* (Cth). Other jurisdictions will have similar administrative expense priorities given their origin in the British statutes of the nineteenth century. The justification for each administrative expense is the 'community of interest' that serves to maximize the fund for distribution. Rent is justified to achieve the orderly process of winding up, liquidator's remuneration is justified to enable the very process to occur and the requisite costs and the miscellany that are listed in the *Corporations Act 2001* (Cth) complete the legislative picture but are incongruous to justify. However exorbitant liquidator's remuneration or specific expenses like audit costs clearly serve no 'community of interest'. It is these areas that require further scrutiny.

Chapter 5

Employees as Priority Creditors: Still the Focus of Attention after 180 Years of Statutory Protection

This chapter discusses the most common and largest group of statutory priority creditors, the employees. The treatment of employees as priority creditors has been longstanding. In this chapter the relevant early statutory history is depicted to complement what has already been said in Chapter 2.[1] After a brief discussion on some judicial comment as to the employee priority, the relevant subsections of s556 of the present Australian *Corporations Act 2001* (Cth) are analysed. Today there is considerable debate with respect to the employees' position in an insolvent company. The Australian Federal Government has played a major role in this debate. There has been a dramatic shift in the role that employees play in corporate insolvency. This has been grounded, in part, in the long-term statutory priority.

Australian and British employees have had a priority in the distribution of an insolvent estate since 1825.[2] This treatment originally covered wages. Over time it was extended to accrued entitlements, which include severance pay and annual and long service leave.

There has been debate over the removal of other priorities that were afforded similar status to employees throughout the last 180 years.[3] However, employee priorities given to wages and entitlements claims have not been subject to extensive scrutiny. Far from any pressure to remove employee entitlements as a priority, there have been major developments in the form of an entitlements scheme to assist employees to fare better upon employer insolvency. It would be expected that the employee priority would be the last to be considered as a target for removal.[4]

---

1 Chapter 2 has extensively described all priority history, including that of the employee priority.

2 The Supreme Court of New South Wales was set up in 1825 and used British legislation that included Acts dedicated to insolvent persons. See e.g. *An Act to Amend the Laws Relating to Bankrupts 1825* (UK) 6 Geo 4 c 16.

3 The debate on the removal of the tax priority is discussed in Chapter 6.

4 Although as mentioned later in the chapter there is some English comment to this effect.

Back in 1994, Australia ratified and accepted Part 2 of the Protection of Workers' Claims (Employer's Insolvency) Convention 1992 (C173) Article 3 of the International Labour Organization (ILO). This document gives a privilege in the ranking of claims in insolvency to employees. The Australian Federal Government did not review in detail the statutory treatment of employees in insolvent companies at that time. The ILO had considered the issue of employee priority in insolvency much earlier, in Article 11 of the ILO's Convention No 95 on Protection of Wages (1949).

The employee priority presently recognized under the Australian *Corporations Act* provides the employee with a likelihood of payment, which is even greater than that enjoyed by unsecured creditors and the government for any of their debts. The priority is an extensive one. The legislature has supported an inclusive approach that presents no ceilings on wages, superannuation contributions, retrenchment pay and leave entitlements. Even excluded employees like directors are not forgotten. They may receive payments to a prescribed maximum amount. There is no discrimination across industry or hierarchy of employment. Equal treatment is given to all employees regardless of their jobs.

The distributional outcome of the insolvent company's assets among its creditors is regarded as one of the main sources of discontent with insolvency proceedings in most industrialized countries.[5] Despite this, the treatment of giving an employee wage priority has had continued support and appears sacrosanct. Malins V-C in *Re Association of Land Financiers*[6] summed it up in this way, as early as 1881: 'it seems absurd that a poor man whose week's wages are unpaid should have to wait and come in with the general body of creditors'.[7] He went on: 'it is monstrous to suppose that the Legislature could have intended the servants of a company to be left utterly destitute'.[8] Such feelings as to the justice of paying wages upon insolvency continue today.[9]

---

5 Garrido, J.M. 'The Distributional Question In Insolvency' (1995) 4 *International Insolvency Review* 25.

6 (1881)16 Ch D 373.

7 Ibid. 374.

8 Ibid. 375.

9 See e.g., *In the matter of Ansett Australia Ltd and Mentha* [2001] FCA 1806 (14 December 2001) Goldberg J para 62; Priest, M. 'More companies face payouts', *The Australian Financial Review* (Sydney), 24 September 2003 quoted the NSW IR Commission's Marks J who suggested it was a 'contemporary community value in NSW that employees were fundamentally entitled to receive outstanding entitlements'.

The Past Treatment of Employees

It is uncertain when employees were first given a priority in insolvency administrations.[10] As outlined in Chapter 2, Civil law countries recognized a preferential protection of workers' claims even before labour laws were established. Once merchant law was incorporated into state law in all European countries, differences in priorities arose and the law no longer reflected merchant needs but became a political instrument.[11] The system progressively recognized the demands of various pressure groups. Priorities, including employee priorities, were the result of political lobbying.[12]

The French Civil Code (Napoleonic Code) provided for protection in the early nineteenth century.[13] Legislation in 1830 extended the treatment from domestic servants to cover workers and employees, commercial travellers, theatrical performers and other categories of wage earners.[14] The *Laws of Scotland* in 1826 described Britain's first foray into giving the wages of domestic servants a priority to be paid out of the bankrupt or deceased estate, just like funeral expenses.[15] The Cork Report[16] in Britain suggested the priority was first introduced into insolvency legislation for social welfare reasons. The priority would ease the financial hardship caused to a relatively poor and defenceless section of the community.[17] The reasons for the introduction of this policy approach were the: 'emphasis on encouraging work and industriousness'[18] and the need for protection of wages in the absence of social welfare.[19] Without protection, it was feared, 'employees may decide not to work for a struggling or new employer', or, if times got tough, would be tempted to leave rather than risk non-payment of wages.[20]

---

10 Bronstein, A.S. 'The Protection of Workers' Claims in the Event of the Insolvency of their Employer. From Civil Law to Social Security' (1987) 126 *International Labour Review* 715, 718.

11 Garrido, J.M. 'The Distributional Question In Insolvency' (1995) 4 *International Insolvency Review* 25.

12 Baird, D. 'Loss Distribution, Forum Shopping, and Bankruptcy: A Reply to Warren' (1987) 54 *University of Chicago Law Review* 815, 824.

13 Bronstein, A.S. 'The Protection of Workers' Claims in the Event of the Insolvency of their Employer. From Civil Law to Social Security' (1987) 126 *International Labour Review* 715, 718.

14 Ibid.

15 Bell, *Commentaries on the Laws of Scotland* (1826) Vol. II, 159.

16 Review Committee, *Insolvency Law and Practice* Cmnd 8558 (1982), 'Cork Report' para 1428.

17 Ibid.

18 Harmer, R.W. 'Employee Creditors and Corporations' in McCallum, R., McCarry, G. and Ronfeldt, R. (eds), *Employment Security* (1994) 227, 229.

19 Ibid.

20 Ibid.

In the *Bankruptcy Act 1842* (UK)[21] a priority was expressly mentioned for servants or clerks who were owed wages or salary. A maximum limit[22] was placed on the priority and this was the way the legislature in Britain and Australia chose to deal with it until the 1980s. The distinction between 'clerks or servants' and 'labourers or workmen' was also reflected in Australian colonial legislation[23] and the *Bankruptcy Act 1914* (UK).[24] The statutes maintained the distinction and broadened the ambit to include piecework.[25]

Unfortunately, the use of such phrases invited litigation to determine which employees were to benefit from the priority. For example the Victorian Supreme Court in 1887[26] decided that a manager was neither a clerk nor a servant and, in 1929,[27] it decided that a director, company secretary, floor manager and musicians were not 'clerks or servants'.

It has been recognized that throughout the nineteenth century the courts appeared to facilitate the existence of at least three distinct classes of work relationship: the master/servant relationship, the principal/contractor relationship and an emerging employer/employee relationship.[28] The principal division in the law of employment at the time was different groups of wage and salary earners according to their social rank and status.[29] Therefore, the insolvency treatment merely reflected the laws that regulated employment.

All colonies in Australia were responsible for their own insolvency legislation. A priority section appeared in the earliest of insolvency statutes. Differences, as outlined in Chapter 2, were sometimes significant in terms of what limits were

---

21 *Bankruptcy Act 1842* (UK) 5 and 6 Vict c 122.

22 Originally three months' wages or salary and the amount was not to exceed £30. Labourers and workmen were included, but their wages were limited to forty shillings. In 1869, a further amendment changed the limits for clerks or servants to four months' wages or salary and the amount was not to exceed £50, and for labourers or workmen, the limit was not to exceed two months' wages. *Bankruptcy Act 1869* (UK) s32 (2).

23 For example, *Insolvency Act 1880* (SA) s63. See Chapter 2 for details of all the relevant colonial Acts.

24 *Bankruptcy Act 1914* (Cth) 4–5 Geo V c 59.

25 Kloss, D.M. and Milman, D. 'The Rights of Employees on Corporate Insolvency' (1982) 46 *Conveyancer* 99.

26 *Re Intercolonial Smelting Company Ltd* (1887) 13 VLR 896.

27 *Re Esplanade Theatre Ltd* [1929] VLR 236.

28 Howe, J. and Mitchell, R. 'The Evolution of the Contract of Employment in Australia: A Discussion' (1999) 12 *Australian Journal of Labour Law* 113, 115.

29 Ibid. 117.

placed upon the amounts to be claimed and how far back into the life of the company a claim could extend.[30] In 1841, s42 of the relevant NSW Act[31]stated:

> And be it enacted that it shall be lawful for the trustee or trustees to provide payment to any clerk or servant of six months salary or wages in full out of the insolvent estate provided so much shall be actually and bona fide due at the time of the order for sequestration made.

This section was to be satisfied before ordinary creditors. Much of the colonial legislation mirrored the *Bankruptcy Act 1842* (UK).[32] Each contained provisions for the amounts of wages and time limits for servants and clerks and included labourers or workmen.[33]

As highlighted in Chapter 2 there were early changes and differences made by colonial parliaments. For example, in 1880, in South Australia, the period was extended to 'four months and not exceeding Fifty Pounds' and wages of any labourer or workman for two months.[34] In 1886, the *Insolvent Act 1886* (SA)[35] provided a priority for servants or clerk's wages or salaries, not exceeding three months or £30. This is in comparison to the colonial legislation of New South Wales, enacted a year later in 1887[36] that used six months and £50 for these occupations. There was also a lack of consistency across the colonies. For example, where South Australia limited its priority for labourers or workmen to £6, at the same time the New South Wales statute allowed £50![37]

As mentioned in Chapter 2, there was no insolvency priority for wages in the earliest company legislation in Britain or Australia, although the *Judicature Act 1875* (UK)[38] provided that the rules applied to bankruptcy would also apply to corporate insolvency.

Many of the States in the 1930s passed new *Companies Acts* and gave employees' wages a priority.[39] The differing descriptions of occupations were carried forward

---

30 For a New Zealand history see Heath, P. 'Preferential Payments on Bankruptcy and Liquidations in New Zealand: Are they Justifiable Exceptions to the Pari Passu Rule?' (1996) 4 *Waikato Law Review* 24.

31 *An Act for giving relief to Insolvent Persons and providing for the due Collection Administration and Distribution of Insolvent Estates within the colony of New South Wales and for the prevention of Frauds affecting same 1841*(NSW) 5 Vict No 17 s42.

32 *Bankruptcy Act 1842* (UK).

33 See Chapter 2. See also Harmer, R. 'Employee Creditors and Corporations' in McCallum, R., McCarry, G. and Ronfeldt, P. (eds), *Employment Security* (1994) 227, 232.

34 *Insolvency Act 1880* (SA) s63.

35 *Insolvent Act 1886* (SA).

36 *Bankruptcy Act 1887* (NSW).

37 *Insolvent Act 1886* (SA) s202.

38 *Judicature Act 1875* (UK) s10.

39 See e.g., *Companies Act 1934* (SA).

from the previous century.[40] In South Australia the legislation added 'commercial traveller' to the group of occupations that previously mentioned 'clerks, servants, labourers and workmen'. The 'blue collars' of workman and labourers were given a priority with a cap of £25[41] for calculations based on piecework or time. Section 279(1)(b) carried a proviso:

> where any labourer in husbandry has entered into a contract for the payment of a portion of his wages in a lump sum at the end of the year of hiring, he shall have priority in respect of the whole of such sum, or a part thereof, as the court may decide to be due under the contract proportionate to the time or amount of service up to the relevant date.

This reflects the special nature of the employment and lifestyle of employees engaged in rural industries, and the commitment of the legislators to stay closely to the principle of *pari passu.*

To round off, the employees' special treatment[42] provided a priority for workers' compensation amounts in respect of compensation or liability for compensation arising under, what was then, very recent legislation[43] in that area. Here again there was a capping of £100 per individual case.

The *Uniform Companies Acts* of the 1960s dedicated a particular section to employees.[44] The legislation stopped referring to clerks, servants, et cetera and used 'employee'. For example, the *Companies Act 1962* (SA) in s292 (1) put the employees' priority immediately after the administration costs priority. Subsection (b) states:

> secondly, all wages and salary (whether or not earned wholly or in part by way of commission) including any amount payable by way of allowance or reimbursement under any contract of employment or award or agreement regulating conditions of employment, of any employee not exceeding one thousand five hundred dollars whether for time or piecework in respect of services rendered by him to the company before the relevant date.[45]

---

40 For example, *Companies Act 1934* (SA) s279 provided '(a) all wages or salary (whether or not earned wholly or in part by way of commission not being an overriding commission) of any clerk, servant, or commercial traveller in respect of services rendered to the company during four months next before the relevant date not exceeding fifty pounds'.

41 *Companies Act 1934* (SA) s279(1)(b).

42 *Companies Act 1934* (SA) s279 (1)(c).

43 *Workmen's Compensation Act 1932* (SA) s13.

44 See e.g., *Companies Act 1962* (SA) s292. As it was 'uniform' all States had the same section number.

45 *Companies Act 1962* (SA) s292(1)(b).

While there were still limits being placed on the amounts allowed as a priority the use of the term 'contract of employment' put an end to litigation to determine which employees would be covered.[46]

In the *Companies Code* that applied during the 1980s s441 provided a similar treatment. The Code separated wages, injury compensation, leave and retrenchment payments. It introduced the term 'excluded employee' and put monetary limits on the wages and other entitlements claims of this group of employees. Furthermore, it removed the former monetary limit of $1500 for all other employees.

By virtue of the States' referral of their powers, company law is now covered by Federal legislation. Section 556 of the *Corporations Act 2001* (Cth) continues to address priorities for employees of corporations. It uses the all-embracing term 'employees' and places no limits on what can be claimed by most employees. The section is addressed more comprehensively later in the chapter.

Judicial Comments on the Employee Priority

The employees' position as a priority creditor has not created much in the way of judicial commentary despite, or perhaps due to, statutory regulation. Indeed, it is rare for a judge to comment on the principle of the employee's priority position. The cases that are reported are commonly concerned with matters of statutory interpretation. Perhaps the small number of reported cases is due to the inability of employees to fund litigation once they have lost their job. In 1866, Lord Romilly commented that he was not prepared to put the employee 'on a different footing from other creditors of the company'.[47] As noted in Chapter 1 this position seems to have changed by 1881, when Malins V-C, as quoted earlier, plainly took a different view.[48]

The most significant judicial comment on insolvency and employees in recent years in Britain occurred in a series of cases involving Powdrill, Leyland DAF and Ferranti.[49] In 1994, Lightman J in the Chancery Division was called upon to interpret the *Insolvency Act 1986* (UK) provisions as they dealt with employees. He noted that employees, with respect to their labour, should not to be treated in the same way as other creditors supplying goods and services under continuing contracts. He stated:

> They merit special protection. They are specially vulnerable and unlikely to have the muscle to insist (as may some other suppliers under continuing contracts) on

---

46 As observed above. See e.g., cases like *Standard Rubber and Leatherboard Company Pty Ltd* [1912] VLR 236 and *Esplanade Theatres Ltd* [1929] VLR 237.

47 *Re General Rolling Stock Company Chapmans Case* (1866) LR 1 Eq 346, 347.

48 *Re Association of Land Financiers* (1881)16 Ch D 373, 374–375.

49 *Powdrill v Watson, Re Leyland DAF Ltd Re Farranti International plc* [1995] 2 All ER 65.

> payment or special treatment in respect of sums already accrued due or to accrue in the future.[50]

This attitude was not supported on appeal. Lord Browne-Wilkinson said that:

> even if it would be right to attribute to parliament a special tenderness towards employees, it is most improbable that parliament intended to produce such an unfair disparity between some employees and others.[51]

This appeal considered whether the receiver of a company had 'adopted' employees' contracts of employment and if so whether the sums claimed under the adopted contracts were sums payable as administration expenses for the time when the employees had worked for the receiver as well as having the effect of liability to the receiver for all past employee entitlements. The court held that the consequence of the adoption of contracts of employment was to give priority only to the administration expenses portion of the employment during the tenure of the receivership.

In 1916 in Canada[52] Meredith CJ observed that:

> salaries and wages are generally needed for, and generally expended in, the support and maintenance of the persons earning them, their wives and families and others dependent upon them, and so may well be given priority, for a short period, over other debts due to other creditors ... (which are) generally more nearly related to the profit and loss account of the creditor than his sustenance or that of those dependent upon him.[53]

He went on to suggest that a liberal construction should be given to statutes conferring preferences on employees of insolvent companies. This was unlike the United States of America, where there was some suggestion that the employee preference was a derogation of the common law and so statutes conferring it must be strictly construed.[54]

In Australia, courts have addressed employees and insolvency in a matter-of-fact manner. They have not dwelt in detail upon the special position. In a recent example, Goldberg J in the *Ansett* case[55] expressed concern for the unsecured creditors on more than one occasion in his judgment before expressing that 'it is appropriate, in order to mitigate the hardship being suffered by the employees of

---

50 *Re Leyland DAF Ltd, Re Ferranti International plc* [1994] 4 All ER 300 at 318.

51 *Powdrill v Watson, Re Leyland DAF Ltd, Re Farranti International plc* [1995] 2 All ER 65, 80.

52 *Re Parkin Elevators* (1916) 31 DLR 123, 125.

53 Ibid.

54 Ibid.

55 *In the matter of Ansett Australia Ltd and Mentha* [2001] FCA 1806.

the Ansett group ... to put them in a position of being able to receive the employee entitlements'.[56] Finkelstein J in *Incat*[57] noted that the court was in no position to vary the statutory priorities and that the history of the employee priority was 'initially a social measure' but commented no more.

The Present Position of Employee Priorities – The Australian Corporations Act

Four classes of debts given priority in s556 are related to employees and their various rights. This gives statutory recognition to employees as a preferred class of unsecured creditors who ought to receive special protection. Each of the employees' priorities for wages, injury compensation, leave and retrenchment are addressed below.

Definitions – Section 556(2)

Section 556(2) contains a limited definition of 'employee' which is: 'a person who has been or is an employee of the company whether remunerated by wages, salary, commission or otherwise'. Since the term 'employee' is not itself defined, it would be given its ordinary common law meaning.[58] And hence, for instance, independent contractors would be excluded. The employee's employment must have started before the 'relevant date'. The relevant date is defined in s9 of the *Corporations Act 2001* (Cth) as the day on which the winding up is taken, because of Division 1A of Part 5.6, to have begun. This division contains four sections and contemplates different starting dates depending on whether the liquidation is compulsory or voluntary or if the company has had an earlier voluntary administration.

Also provided in s556(2) is a definition of 'excluded employee':

> an employee of the company who has been: (i) at any time during the period of 12 months ending on the relevant date; or (ii) at any time since the relevant date; or who is, a director of the company;
>
> an employee of the company who has been: (i) at any time during the period of 12 months ending on the relevant date; or (ii) at any time since the relevant date; or who is, the spouse of an employee of the kind referred to in paragraph (a); or

56 *In the matter of Ansett Australia Ltd and Mentha* [2001] FCA 1806 para 62.

57 *McEvoy v Incat Tasmania* [2003] FCA 810.

58 See for a fuller discussion on the common law, Creighton, B. and Stewart, A. Labour Law (4th ed. 2005) Chapter 11 'The Creation and Categorisation of Employment Relationships'.

an employee of the company who is a relative (other than spouse) of an employee of the kind referred to in paragraph (a).

The legislation places various limits in respect of excluded employees' claims to a priority during non-priority days. [59] The concept of non-priority days was introduced so that any person becoming a director just before the relevant day would not suffer any injustice for benefits accrued to the time before they became a director. Some of these definitions are considered again later in the chapter.

Corporations Act 2001 (Cth) Section 556(1)(e) – Wages

Section 556(1)(e) gives a priority to wages, superannuation contributions and superannuation guarantee charges payable by the company in respect of services rendered to the company by employees before the date of the winding up order or before the date of the commencement of the winding up order, whichever is appropriate.

'Wages' are defined by s9 of the *Corporations Act 2001* (Cth) to mean: 'amounts payable to or in respect of an employee of the company (whether the employee is remunerated by salary, wages, commission[60] or otherwise) under an industrial instrument'. 'Wages' can include amounts payable by way of allowance or reimbursement but excludes amounts payable in respect of leave of absence. An industrial instrument is defined in s9 of the *Corporations Act 2001* (Cth) to mean: 'a contract of employment or a law, award, determination or agreement relating to terms or conditions of employment'. A letter given to an employee setting out such terms has been held to be an industrial instrument.[61] There is no limit to the amounts that can be claimed as wages under s556(1)(e) for employees other than 'excluded employees'. That said, 'unpaid wages are usually an insignificant item in an insolvency'. [62] Excluded employees are limited to $2,000 by s556(1A).

A liquidator must deduct tax payable to the Australian Tax Office pursuant to Pay As You Go (PAYG) obligations. Section 12–35 of Schedule 1 of the *Taxation Administration Act 1953* (Cth) provides that an entity must withhold an amount from salary, wages, commission, bonuses or allowances it pays to an individual as an employee (whether of that or another entity). In a recent case, *Deputy Commissioner of Taxation v Applied Design Development Pty Ltd (in liq)*,[63] heard

59 *Corporation Act 2001* (Cth) s556(1A) for wages, s556(1B) for leave and s556(1C) for redundancy payments.

60 'Commission' was required to be expressed in the statute because there had been doubt raised in Britain upon whether employees on commission enjoyed an insolvency priority: see *Bankruptcy (Amendment) Act* 1926 (UK) s2.

61 *Re Farmer Furniture Pty Ltd* (1998) 16 ACLC 1,110.

62 Holding, P. 'Who Bears the Risk? Protecting Employee Entitlements Upon Insolvency' (1995) 69 *Law Institute Journal* 789, 790.

63 [2002] FCA 205.

in the Federal Court, Mansfield J found that the employees' 'right to wages earned before liquidation arose as a matter of law from an employee/employer relationship and so s12–35 does not require that there exist an employer/employee relationship at the time of payment by the liquidator'.[64]

Bonuses are included in this wages priority, provided that the employment contract imposed an obligation on the employer company to pay the bonus and did not merely give it a discretion to make such payments.[65]

Corporations Act 2001 (Cth) Section 556(1)(e)– Superannuation

Superannuation contributions are defined by s556(2) to mean: 'a contribution by the company to a fund for the purposes of making provision for obtaining superannuation benefits for an employee of the company or for dependants of such an employee'. The *Corporate Law Reform Act 1992* (Cth) amended the previous wages priority provisions to make it clear for the first time that superannuation contributions are given the same priority as wages and hence appear in s556(1)(e). This means that where an employee has forgone wage increases in exchange for enhanced superannuation contributions by their employer, the employee will not be disadvantaged in a winding up.[66]

In the event that property of the company is insufficient to meet the claims under s556(1)(e) then the claims must be paid proportionately.[67] The claims under s556(1)(e) are payable in priority to claims of a chargee in relation to a floating charge created by the company and thus payments may be made from property comprised in or subject to the charge.[68]

From 2007 the Superannuation Guarantee Charge has been included in this subsection and then subsections (1AB), (1AC), (1AD), (1AE) and (1AF) have helped define and determine how much is to be treated as a priority. This followed a Federal Government announcement in October 2005 that it was proposing amendments to clarify the status and priority of the Superannuation Guarantee Charge by aligning it with the treatment of superannuation as outlined immediately above.[69] In the announcement it was stated that the initiative would 'improve the prospect of recovery of outstanding superannuation obligations'.

---

64 See e.g., Symes, C. 'The $44 Question – To Make Tax Instalment Deductions or Not?' (2002) 2 (9) *Insolvency Law Bulletin* 156.

65 See e.g., *Walker and Sherman v Andrew* (2002) 20 ACLC 1476; *Re Galaxy Media Pty Ltd (in liq)* (2002) 20 ACLC 73.

66 Commonwealth, *Corporate Law Reform Bill 1992* (Cth) *Public Exposure Draft,* para 1081.

67 *Corporations Act 2001* (Cth) s559.

68 *Corporations Act 2001* (Cth) s561.

69 See <www.treasury.gov.au/contentitem.asp3pageId=&contentID=1022> *Corporate Insolvency Reform*, 2.

Injury Compensation - Section 556(1)(f)

Section 556(1)(f) provides for a priority to be given to amounts due in respect of injury compensation in liquidations where the liability to pay arose before the relevant date.[70] Again, s9 provides a definition of 'injury compensation' to mean: 'compensation payable under any law relating to workers compensation'. There is no limit to the amount that may be claimed under s556(1)(f) although it is not a priority over the claims of a holder of a floating charge.

Section 556(1)(f) will not apply in respect of a winding up of a company, undertaken merely for the purposes of a reconstruction or amalgamation, in which the right to injury compensation has been preserved.[71] The section also has no effect upon statutory workers compensation schemes as the amounts under such schemes are payable on contracts of insurance engaged in between the company and the insurers.[72] Section 563 also provides that s556(1)(h) does not apply where a company has entered into a contract with an insurer in respect of any liability for injury compensation. The impact of s563 is to override the priority and maintain one of the basic principles of insolvency, fairness, as it would be unfair to give a priority to employees for amounts already protected from the employers' insolvency.

Injury compensation as a priority has become a feature of the insolvency legislation since the enactment of legislation on workers compensation. The *Bankruptcy Act 1914* (UK)[73] first mentioned a priority not exceeding in any individual case £100, due in respect of the *Workmen's Compensation Act 1906* (UK). The British *Companies Act 1929* referred to a priority for amounts under the *Workmen's Compensation Act 1925* (UK) and provides for a priority for all amounts due 'in respect of any compensation or liability for compensation under the said Act'.[74] Australian insolvency legislation enacted after the mid 1920s included this priority and referred to State legislation on workers compensation.[75]

Leave Entitlements – Section 556(1)(g)

Under s556(1)(g) employees are given a priority to receive all amounts due in respect of leave of absence up to the 'relevant date'. These amounts will arise under an 'industrial instrument', defined in s9 to mean: 'a contract of employment

70 'Relevant date' is explained above.

71 *Corporations Act 2001* (Cth) s563.

72 See e.g., *SGIO (Queensland) v Rees (Liquidator of KD Morris and Sons Pty Ltd)* 1979 CLC 40-586.

73 *Bankruptcy Act 1914* (UK) s33(1)(d).

74 *Companies Act 1929* (UK) s264(1)(d).

75 See Chapter 2 above. For example, the New South Wales *Workers' Compensation Act 1926* is mentioned in the *Companies Act 1936* (NSW) and in South Australia, the *Workmen's Compensation Act 1932* is mentioned in the *Companies Act 1934* (SA).

or a law, award, determination or agreement relating to terms or conditions of employment'. Section 9 also defines 'leave of absence' to include: 'long service leave, extended leave, recreation leave, annual leave,[76] sick leave or any other form of leave of absence from employment'. It is here that the largest debts owed to employees are usually found.[77] No limit is imposed upon the amount of such leave of absence claims made by an employee. Whether or not the employee fails to receive wage entitlements in insolvency, this is the most likely debt to be left unpaid.[78] Outstanding leave entitlements, when unfulfilled in insolvency, lend evidentiary support to the International Labour Organisation's view that priority rights are inadequate protection for employees.[79] There is, however, potential for abuse, if the employee was able to bargain for an extraordinarily generous leave of absence with their employer during the renewal of employment contracts. This may happen with some inside knowledge that the employer is well along the path to liquidation. What could result is a higher entitlement than would have occurred without the inside knowledge of pending closure.

Section 556(1B) does limit the amount of leave of absence claims for an 'excluded employee' to $1,500 for non-priority days. This has the effect of allowing these 'excluded employees' normal statutory priority in respect of entitlements gained from service as an ordinary employee.[80]

The wording of s556(1)(g) places the payment in context. It must arise due 'to, or in respect of, employees of the company'. Similar wording was the subject of interpretation by the South Australian Supreme Court in *Re E&L Constructions Pty. Ltd. (in liq)*[81] under previous legislation. The wording was interpreted narrowly. It used 'employee' not 'employees', and so the priority did not extend to the employer's contribution to build up a statutory fund for long service leave in the building industry. O'Donovan argues that the present subsection might extend to include such contributions because of the phrase 'to, or in respect of, employees of the company'.[82]

76 'Annual leave', referred to earlier as 'holiday pay', had been interpreted as 'wages' under s84(1)(e) of the *Bankruptcy Act 1924* (Cth) and was capped as to that amount that had accrued within 4 months immediately preceding the date of the sequestration order. See e.g., *Re W J Taylor and Sons* (1934–1936) 8 ABC 88.

77 Holding, P. 'Who Bears the Risk? Protecting Employee Entitlement Upon Insolvency' (1995) 69 *Law Institute Journal* 789, 790.

78 See e.g., *Re Falcolm Sportswear Pty Ltd, Hart v Barnes* (1983) 1 ACLC 690.

79 Bronstein, A.T. 'The Protection of Workers' Claims in the Event of the Insolvency of their Employer. From Civil Law to Social Security' (1987) 126 *International Labour Review* 715, 719.

80 O'Donovan, J. *McPherson The Law of Company Liquidation* (Student Edition) (1994) 212.

81 (1981) 28 SASR 154.

82 O'Donovan, J. *McPherson The Law of Company Liquidation* (Student Edition) (1994) 212.

Duthie, in his arguments on retrenchment priorities,[83] also suggests that the phrase 'in respect of' is very wide and there is no reason to read it down.[84]

Despite these opinions, in *Irving v Construction Industry Long Service Leave Board*,[85] Justice O'Loughlin followed *Re E&L Constructions Pty Ltd*. The outcome was the rejection of a priority under s556(1)(g) for funds[86] set up to collect levies for employees from employers in particular industries; because of their itinerant nature. These funds pay out to employees when they have reached their long service leave entitlement. The narrow construction was supported on appeal to the full Federal Court.[87]

The history of the leave entitlements priority in Australia reflects the changing industrial laws of the 1950s and British precedents. In 1958 the *Companies Act 1958* (Vic) was extensively redrafted and the priority for wages and salary was extended to debts due in respect of annual leave and long service leave. Section 216 deemed any amount due for annual leave and long service leave as salary and wages. There was a cap of £250. Tasmania copied this legislative move a year later.[88] The *Uniform Companies Acts* from 1961 incorporated the Victorian developments for leave entitlements and they gave an unlimited priority for amounts of annual leave and long service leave in all states.

In Britain the *Companies Act 1948* (UK) provided for an annual leave priority.[89] It read: 'all accrued holiday remuneration becoming payable to any clerk, servant, workman or labourer (or in the case of his death to any other person in his right) on the termination of his employment before, or by the effect of the winding up order or resolution'.[90] Subsection (8) then explained the expression 'accrued holiday remuneration' as including:

> in relation to any person, all sums which, by virtue either of his contract of employment or of any enactment (including any order made or direction given under any Act), are payable to him in respect of a period of holiday had his employment with the company continued until he became entitled to be allowed the holiday.[91]

---

83 Duthie, L. 'The Priority of Retrenchment Payments in a Liquidation or Receivership' (1992) 20 *Australian Business Law Review* 378, 384.

84 Ibid.

85 (1997) 15 ACLC 95.

86 Funds like the Victorian Contract Cleaning Industry Portable Long Service Leave Fund and the Building Industry Long Service Leave Fund in Victoria and a similar fund in South Australia known as Construction Industry Long Service Leave Fund.

87 (1997) 145 ALR 158.

88 *Companies Act 1959* (Tas) s 227(2).

89 *Companies Act 1948* (UK) s 319(1)(d).

90 *Companies Act 1948* (UK) s 319(1)(d).

91 *Companies Act 1948* (UK) s319(8)(b).

Australian law, by contrast, did not provide any explanation of what constituted annual leave.

New Zealand had also provided a priority for leave before Australia. The *Companies Act 1955* (NZ) provided for a similar treatment to that found in Britain. The New Zealand Act expressed the priority as 'all holiday pay becoming payable to any servant or worker' and then went further to limit the total wages and leave priority to £200.[92]

The reasons for Australia trailing Britain and New Zealand in implementing the leave priority were primarily due to the difficulty of getting the States to have uniformity in corporate law during the 1940s and 1950s. Furthermore, the States were in the post war period and new corporate legislation was scarce. For example, during the 1940s only one State passed a Companies Act; Western Australia. That Act was really catching up to the other States' companies' legislation of the 1930s. Even in the 1950s only two States passed legislation (Victoria and Tasmania) and this was late in the decade and closely followed the *Companies Act 1948* (UK).

Retrenchment Payments – Section 556(1)(h)

An area which particularly affects employees after the appointment of a liquidator is the priority obtained by them for retrenchment payments. Section 556(1)(h) of the *Corporations Act* provides that these payments will rank ahead of the claims of a chargee in relation to a floating charge.[93] There is surprisingly little authority concerning this priority. As a result, liquidators have little to guide them in their deliberations upon distribution.[94] Retrenchment payments include severance pay and payments in lieu of notice. For an employee to obtain the benefit of s556(1)(h), they must satisfy three criteria. First that an amount is payable by the company to the employee;[95] second, that such an amount has arisen by virtue of an industrial instrument[96] that is, a contract of employment or a law, award, determination or agreement relating to terms or conditions of employment;[97] and third, that this amount is payable in respect of the termination of employment by the company.[98] It does not matter whether the amount become payable before or after the relevant date, that is in general terms, before or after the liquidation.[99] An employee cannot however, claim the priority if they are an excluded employee, such as an employee director of the company, or a spouse or relative of such an employee director.

92 *Companies Act 1955* (NZ) ss308 (1)(b), 308(2).

93 *Corporations Act 2001* (Cth) s561(a).

94 Duthie, L. 'The Priority of Retrenchment Payments in a Liquidation or Receivership' (1992) 20 Australian Business Law Review 378.

95 *Corporations Act 2001* (Cth) s556(2).

96 *Corporations Act 2001* (Cth) s556(2).

97 *Corporations Act 2001* (Cth) s9.

98 *Corporations Act 2001* (Cth) s556(2).

99 *Corporations Act 2001* (Cth) s556(2).

Duthie[100] submits that s556(1)(h) should be interpreted so as to protect the interests of employees of the company ahead of creditors. He cites 'legislative and judicial history and the construction of Section 556 itself'[101] as evidence that the interests of the employee should be pre-eminent. Any interpretation should appreciate that the amount is payable in respect of a termination.

Where a notice of termination period is stipulated by contract or by an award or registered agreement it is common practice for an employer to be able to make a payment of wages for the period in lieu of requiring the employee to serve out the notice. Therefore, a liquidator may make such a payment.[102] Section 170CM of the *Workplace Relations Act 1996* (Cth) expressly gives the employer, hence the liquidator, this option. Where s170CM is inapplicable and a contract allows for termination by notice but does not expressly mention the payment of wages in lieu then there is a question of whether the employer is legally entitled to do so.[103] In the past it was said that where there is no express provision to pay an amount in lieu of notice, such a term could be implied into the contract and then result in a priority in a liquidation. Duthie argued that if a Court were to imply such a term 'allowing the giving of notice by a payment in lieu',[104] then it became part of the contract and should be treated similarly to any express provisions in a contract. However, the High Court in *Sanders v Snell*[105] held that no term could be implied to permit payment in lieu of notice if this was inconsistent with other express terms in the contract. In the case there was a contract with two separate provisions allowing termination on notice although only one provision contemplated payment in lieu of notice and the other provision was silent. While the case can be confined to its particular facts some uncertainty remains in employment law.[106]

It appears that payments made in lieu of notice could be interpreted as amounts payable 'by virtue of a contract of employment'.[107] While there is no case law directly on point, such an interpretation could result in these payments forming part of the priority debt provided by s556(1)(h).

Where an employee brings an action against their employer for wrongful dismissal, an award of damages can result. These damages can be considered to be entitled to a priority under s556(1)(h). For s556(1)(h) to apply, however, it is important to determine whether or not these damages are amounts payable 'by

100 Duthie, L. 'The Priority of Retrenchment Payments in a Liquidation or Receivership' (1992) 20 *Australian Business Law Review* 378.

101 Duthie, L. 'The Priority of Retrenchment Payments in a Liquidation or Receivership' (1992) 20 *Australian Business Law Review* 378, 384.

102 Creighton, B. and Stewart, A. *Labour Law* (4th ed. 2005) 420.

103 Ibid.

104 Duthie, L. 'The Priority of Retrenchment Payments in a Liquidation or Receivership' (1992) 20 *Australian Business Law Review* 378, 384.

105 (1998) 196 CLR 329.

106 See e.g., Creighton, B. and Stewart, A. *Labour Law* (4th ed. 2005) 420.

107 *Corporations Act 2001* (Cth) s556(2) definition of 'retrenchment payment'.

virtue of an industrial instrument' – that is, by virtue of a contract of employment'. Duthie argues that the wide construction of the phrase 'by virtue of' would reach awards of damages as such a payment is 'in consequence of, or because of, the contract of employment'.[108] Areas outside of insolvency law have provided authority for the proposition that damages may be included, as there is no case law directly on point in the area.

Firstly, in *Wheeler v Philip Morris Ltd*[109] the Federal Court held that damages awarded for breach of the employment contract were paid in consequence of the termination of the person's employment and hence fall within the definition of an eligible termination payment under the *Income Tax Assessment Act 1936* (Cth).[110] The damages were seen to be a payment made because of the contract of employment.

Secondly, in the English case *Delaney v Staples*,[111] a payment was made by an employer to an employee in lieu of proper notice on account of damages for breach of contract. The payment was a payment relating to the termination of employment and not a payment of wages since the employee/employer relationship had ended by the summary dismissal and the employee was under no obligation to render further services under the contract.[112] This again suggests that damages may be included, provided there is sufficient nexus to a priority by virtue of the contract of employment.[113]

Two recent English cases show the difficulty presented by this priority. In *Allders Department Stores Ltd (In Administration)*[114] Collins J held that redundancy payments in an administration were not "wages or salary" and so had no priority under paragraph 99 (schedule B1) nor could they be payments under Rule 2.67(1) of the Insolvency Rules. Then *in the matter of Huddersfield Fine Worsteds Ltd (known as Ferrotech)*[115] the Court of Appeal also supported the position that payments in lieu of notice in respect of employees of a company in administration did not have a priority.

108 Duthie, L. 'The Priority of Retrenchment Payments in a Liquidation or Receivership' (1992) 20 *Australian Business Law Review* 378, 390.

109 (1988) 32 IR 323; (1988) 97 ALR 282.

110 (1988) 97 ALR 282, 313; See also, *Grout v Gunnedah Shire Council (No 3)* (1995) 59 IR 248.

111 [1992] 1 All ER 944.

112 [1992] 1 All ER 944, 949.

113 The contention that the *Delaney v Staples* decision on payments in lieu of notice equates to payments relating to the termination of employment was made in the writer's LLM dissertation, Symes, C.F. *Deserving the Law's Sympathy* (LLM thesis, University of Adelaide, 1996) and then cited in Keay, A. *McPherson The Law of Company Liquidation* (4th ed. 1999) 601.

114 *Allders Department Stores Ltd (in administration)* and *in the matter of the Insolvency Act 1986* [2005] EWHC 172 (Ch), BCC 289.

115 *Huddersfield Fine Worsteds Ltd, Ferrotech Ltd, Granville Technology Group Ltd* and *in the matter of the Insolvency Act 1986* [2005] EWCA Civ 1072.

In *Perry v Aboriginal Legal Service Ltd*,[116] Santow J resorted to the doctrine of equitable estoppel to award an employee the priority he deserved for the award of an unfair dismissal and retrenchment payment. This was because the retrenchment payment did not fit into the s556(1)(h) specifications. The employee's duties were not considered to place him in a position to be covered by the appropriate award because of his managerial position and so the retrenchment payment was voluntary. The decision could suggest a lacuna in s556(1)(h) and lead to more litigation if insolvency practitioners refuse the priority to obvious employee claimants.

The history of the retrenchment payment priority is brief.[117] The first Companies Code in 1981 did not contain an express priority. In *Re VIP Insurances Ltd (in liq)*[118] it was held that such payments did not fall within the predecessor of s556(1)(e), the wages priority. From 31 March 1986 the Companies Code was amended to contain s441(1)(ga).This gave a priority for retrenchment payments for the first time. Section 556(1)(h) now uses the same wording as its predecessor.

Payments of Employee Priorities Before Floating Chargeholders – Section 433

The *Corporations Act 2001* (Cth) in s433 obliges the receiver or other person taking possession or assuming control of property to pay certain preferential debts out of the assets subject to the floating charge, before accounting to the chargeholders for their principal and interest.[119] Fixed charges are not affected by the section and generally, the property law protects their priority.

Section 433 applies to receivers and managers, and other controllers. It applies whether the receiver was appointed by the court or privately. The obligation to pay preferential debts under s433 crystallizes at the date of the receiver and manager's appointment.[120]

If the receiver is appointed under a charge, it is usual that the charge is composed of separate parts, fixed and floating. In ss433(5) and (3)(c) there are provisions for certain unsecured debts to be paid in priority to debts that are secured by a floating charge. Section 433 provides that, where a receiver is appointed on behalf of the holder of any debenture of a company, secured by a floating charge, or where possession is taken by or on behalf of debenture holders of any property comprised in or subject to a floating charge, then certain debts are paid in priority to any debenture-holders' claims for principal or interest. These debts can include wages,

116 *Perry v Aboriginal Legal Service Ltd* [1997] Equity Division Supreme Court of NSW Number BC 90007618 (unreported, Santow J, 9 December 1997).

117 Duthie, L. 'The Priority of Retrenchment Payments in a Liquidation or Receivership' (1992) 20 *Australian Business Law Review* 378, 380–381.

118 *Re VIP Insurances Ltd (in liq)* [1978] 2 NSWLR 297.

119 The history of s433 and its predecessor, s196 of the *Uniform Companies Act 1961*, are detailed in *McEvoy v Incat Tasmania Pty Ltd* [2003] FCA 810, 8–16.

120 See e.g., *Russell v AGC (Advances) Ltd* (1987) 12 ACLR 79.

and other entitlements, pursuant to s556(1)(e), (g) and (h). Section 433 does not include claims for injury compensation.[121]

Section 433 draws a distinction between property which is subject to a fixed charge and property which is subject to a floating charge,[122] and only protects employee priorities against the floating charge. This may be justified by the fact that the debt secured by a floating charge is similar in kind to unsecured debts. Neither would hinder the company in pursuit of its business.[123] Another rationale for the distinction, in light of employee priorities, may be a determination that employees' efforts have increased the value of assets subject to a floating charge, and should therefore deserve the law's sympathy.[124]

Where the charge does include both fixed and floating parts, the order for payment would be as follows: first, the value of the fixed charge to the charge holder; second, preferential claims, for example, employees' wages; and third, the charge-holder's claim as covered by the floating charge.

Section 433(3)(c) gives a preference to any debts or amounts which in a winding up are payable in priority to other unsecured debts. It applies where an advance is made by a person, such as a lender to the company, for the purpose of paying amounts in respect of wages, superannuation contributions, leave entitlements or retrenchments payments,[125] to the employees.[126] This subsection is another demonstration of the legislature's desire to assist employees in insolvency.

Recently Finkelstein J in *McEvoy v Incat Tasmania Pty Ltd*[127] decided that s433 did not oblige the receiver to pay annual leave, long service leave and retrenchment entitlements to employees who were accruing these entitlements when the entitlements were not due and payable. He suggested that the three previous cases on this section, *Love v Image Centre Pty Ltd*,[128] *Whitton v ACN003266886 Pty Ltd*[129] and *Re Office-Co Furniture Pty Ltd*[130] were 'not altogether helpful'.[131]

In summary, s433 creates a positive obligation upon the receiver or other controller to pay the employees' priorities out of any assets coming into their hands. This is crucially important, as the employees' priorities would be ineffective if they were required to await a distribution until after the chargeholder had been paid from the company's property. A chargeholder will frequently take a floating

121 *Corporations Act 2001* (Cth) s433(3)(c).

122 O'Donovan, J. *Company Receivers and Managers* (2nd ed. 1992) 4087.

123 Ibid.

124 See e.g., *Stein v Saywell* (1969) 121 CLR 529.

125 See e.g., *Fisher v Maddern* [2002] NSWCA 40521/01.

126 O'Donovan, J. *Company Receivers and Managers* (2nd ed. 1992) 4092.

127 *McEvoy v Incat Tasmania Pty Ltd* [2003] FCA 810.

128 *Love v Image Centre Pty Ltd* (unreported, NSW Supreme Court, Young J, 13 February 1991)

129 (1996) 42 NSWLR 123.

130 [2000] 2 Qd R 49.

131 *McEvoy v Incat Tasmania Pty Ltd* [2003] FCA 810, 17.

charge over all of the company's assets. Without s433 taking into account these priorities, employees could expect to receive very little.

The Concept of Employee Entitlements Priorities – Justifications

The employee priority presently provides the employee with a likelihood of payment that is even greater than that enjoyed by unsecured creditors and the government. However the priority does not impact on the secured credit market because of its inferior position. The priority is an extensive one in Australia where the legislature has supported an inclusive approach that presents no ceilings on wages, superannuation contributions, retrenchment pay and leave entitlements. Even excluded employees, such as directors, are not forgotten. They may receive payments to a maximum amount. Equal treatment is given to all employees, regardless of the industry they are employed in or their level of employment.

Employees have a substantial stake in their company. This stake will be represented by such intangibles as the security of employment linked to a standard of living. More concretely, it may also be represented by the right to receive wages, leave entitlements, superannuation, retrenchment payments and other tangibles found in the employment contract or in awards and industrial agreements. Therefore, when the employer can no longer meet its financial obligations, the employee may be exposed to the risk of unpaid wages and unprotected entitlements.

Traditionally, the free-market economy has treated the employee 'in the same manner as it treats other unsecured creditors'.[132] It is assumed that the employee is giving an 'unsecured and interest-free loan to the [corporate] employer' and has therefore 'anticipated the possibility of [insolvency]'.[133] However, unlike a financial institution, the employee usually will not have looked at the financial health of the corporate employer to determine the risk involved, or sought to minimize their exposure by taking a security, often in the form of a mortgage, over corporate assets.

Additionally, it is unlikely that the employee would have negotiated into the price of their labour amounts to compensate for the risk of non-payment.[134] The topic of insolvency would almost never arise during an employment interview or negotiation of an employment contract between an employer and a prospective employee. Even at ongoing performance reviews and negotiations for workplace agreements, the topic of the employer's insolvency is unlikely to be discussed, except perhaps where unions (or at least certain unions) are involved. This issue is in fact now commonly dealt with in collective agreements in some large manufacturing workplaces – for example, the 'Manusafe' arrangements (now called

132 Gleig, D.B. 'Unpaid Wages in Bankruptcy' (1987) 21 *University of British Columbia Law Review* 61.

133 Ibid.

134 Ibid.

NEST – National Entitlement Security Trust), other 'bond' or 'trust' arrangements et cetera.[135] Thus many employees are commonly placed in a position of self-insurance without adequate power or compensation to absorb the loss of unpaid entitlements.

Employees tend to have imperfect information about the financial state of the employer and have no access to security devices to 'sure up the debt'. Even if it were mandatory that all employees receive financial information, the benefits would be questionable.[136] A financial report to employees tends to appear as a 'unique document, distinct from the annual report'.[137] In instances where reports are prepared by companies for their employees, the information presented has been analysed and the conclusion reached that these reports are pitched at an unduly high level of difficulty relative to the abilities of their intended audience. However, studies examining the identified benefits to employees of having reports prepared for them do not refer to any aspects of insolvency being mentioned in the reports. Employees simply do not have access to the information to achieve greater positioning in the case of employer insolvency. Even if an employee had access to the financial information, it is unlikely that the employee would be able to gain a strong bargaining position to cover the risk of corporate insolvency – at least when acting alone. Currently unions, acting in the interests of their members, are much more likely to raise this issue as part of their negotiations with management than at any time in the past. This is due mainly to a greater understanding by union officials of the legal consequences of insolvency law and practice brought about by some high profile corporate collapses over the last ten years.

Employees' priorities can be justified for other reasons too. For other unsecured creditors, their debt most likely represents a minor source of income, whereas to the employee, their wages and entitlements are often the main or only source of income.[138] If the receiver or administrator chooses not to keep the employee in employment or there is automatic termination because of a compulsory liquidation, the employee is faced with the loss of future employment as well as possible lost wages and entitlements. Of course, the ripple effect of a failure to pay employees' wages will mean that employees may be placed in a position where they are unable to pay their own creditors.

Another difference between employees and unsecured creditors involves knowledge and access to legal rights. As a group, and again in the absence of

135 Creighton, B. and Stewart, A. *Labour Law* (4th ed. 2005) 375.

136 Forsyth, A. 'Corporate Collapses and Employees' Right to Know: An Issue for Corporate Law or Labour Law?' (2003) 31 *Australian Business Law Review* 81.

137 Parker, L.D. *The Reporting of Company Financial Results to Employees*, Research Committee Occasional Paper No 12, London, Institute of Chartered Accountants for England and Wales (1977).

138 Ibid. 62.

support from a union, employees are less likely to enforce their rights.[139] The cost of legal assistance may well outweigh any amount of unpaid wages and entitlements and make legal action to recover these payments unviable.

It is been argued that 'it is common place for employees of insolvent companies to walk away with absolutely nothing or with paltry amounts like 25 cents in the dollar'.[140] While this may be the best that can be done for unsecured creditors, it is unjust treatment of employees for all the reasons mentioned above. Therefore, in Australia, the employee has been given special status with the statutory priority. It is well justified.

Australian Perspective

The Harmer Report accepted 'that there is strong support for the retention of the existing priority accorded to employees', despite leaning towards a wage earner protection fund.[141] The Harmer Report made no recommendations 'as to the range of benefits that should be available for priority (such as leave, retrenchment payments [and] superannuation)', nor on benefit ceilings. The reasons given for this omission were that these were policy matters to be determined by Government 'as part of' its 'social welfare and income support policies'.[142] Interestingly, there was no positive recommendation to keep the employee priorities, unlike the priorities for costs, charges and expenses of administration.

Other Australian literature nevertheless supports the treatment of employee priorities. O'Donovan has acknowledged that employees deserve the law's sympathy.[143] However, he remarks that giving preferential status to substantial retrenchment payments is a contentious issue, given the eroding of floating securities.[144] Arujan considers employees as 'innocent victims of a corporate collapse'.[145] He observes that there is 'precious little' in the *Corporations Act 2001* (Cth) touching on the 'rights, if any, of employees who stand to lose their entire means of livelihood'.[146]

---

139 Zatzman, Z. 'The Unpaid Employee as Creditor: Case Comment on Homeplan Realty' (1980) 6 *Dalhousie Law Journal* 148, 150.

140 Holding, P. 'Who Bears the Risk? Protecting Employee Entitlement upon Insolvency' (1995) 69 *Law Institute Journal* 789.

141 Australian Law Reform Commission, *General Insolvency Inquiry* Report No 45 (1988) para 727.

142 Ibid.

143 O'Donovan, J. 'Corporate Redundancy' (1976) 4 *Australian Business Law Review* 257.

144 Ibid.

145 Arjunan, K. 'Locus Standi of Employees in Companies Winding Up' (1993) 11 *Company and Securities Law Journal* 141, 142.

146 Ibid.

With the financial collapse of some high profile companies in Australia between 1999 and 2002,[147] the topic of employee entitlements became a popular subject for academics and social commentators.[148] Riley has argued that worker representatives should use the legal tools that are already available in the commercial world.[149] She advocates no radical revolution and her use of legal tools in employer insolvency is premised on retaining the existing employee priorities.[150] Noakes has done substantial work concentrating on corporate groups, employee entitlements and the impact of strategic insolvency.[151] Again, he premises his scholarship on the position that the employee priorities should remain in the *Corporations Act 2001* (Cth). Darvas has contemplated a number of proposed solutions and cautiously hinted at removing the statutory priority, but only if the accrued rights and entitlements of employees were secured.[152]Others have also joined the debate and without exception have premised their discussions on maintaining the priority.[153]

Overseas Comments

Overseas literature also supports the favourable treatment of employees. Shanker sees employees as involuntary creditors 'who deserve priority status'.[154] For him, they do not, in any realistic sense, intend to extend credit to their employers.

---

147 Examples are National Textiles (2000), Ansett (2001), One-Tel (2001), Cobar Mines (1999).

148 See e.g., Clarke, A. 'The Relative Position of Employees in the Corporate Governance Context: An International Comparison' (2004) 32 *Australian Business Law Review* 111; Forsyth, A. 'Corporate Collapses and Employees' Right to Know: An Issue for Corporate Law or Labour Law?' (2003) 31 *Australian Business Law Review* 81.

149 Riley, J. 'Protection of Employee Entitlements: A Legal Perspective' (2003) 29 *Australian Bulletin of Labour* 44. See also Riley, J. 'Bargaining for Security: Lessons for Employees from the World of Corporate Finance' (2002) 44 *Journal of Industrial Relations* 491.

150 Ibid.

151 Noakes, D. 'Corporate Groups and the Duties of Directors: Protecting the Employee or the Insolvent Employer?' (2001) 29 *ABLR* 124; Noakes, D. 'Reform to the Law of Corporate Groups in Australia to Protect Employees' (2000) 34 *University of British Columbia Law Review* 239, Noakes, D. 'Measuring the Impact of Strategic Insolvency on Employees' (2003) 11 *Insolvency Law Journal* 9.

152 Darvas, P. 'Employees' Rights and Entitlements and Insolvency: Regulatory Rationale, Legal Issues and Proposed Solutions' (1999) 17 *Company and Securities Law Journal* 103, 122.

153 See e.g., Kinsey, S. 'A Triumph for Labour over Capital: Employee Entitlements in Insolvency in the Wake of the Ansett Collapse' (2002) 10 *Insolvency Law Journal* 132; Campo, R. 'The Protection of Employee Entitlements in the Event of Employer Insolvency: Australian Initiatives in Light of International Models' (2000) 13 *Australian Journal Labour Law* 236.

154 Shanker, M.G. 'The Worthier Creditor (and a Cheer for the King)' (1976) 1 *Canadian Business Law Journal* 340, 350.

He concludes that 'where one extends credit voluntarily expecting a profit or advantage and voluntarily assuming the risk of the insolvency, then his claim to the bankrupt's assets ought to be junior to those who did not so act'.[155] He places employees, therefore, in the senior position of creditors and categorizes employees as involuntary creditors.

Garrido notes that 'all legal systems in the western world protect the worker's wages and related credits (in insolvency)'.[156] The employees' credit is given a very high priority status and is seen as the 'most protected' in virtually all legal systems. In his argument for an insolvency system to be 'much lighter and more agile'[157] to assist international considerations, he would restrict priorities to those creditors who 'really need protection'.[158] He concludes that employees are the only creditors whose protection is most unlikely to be challenged.[159]

Paul Heath,[160] writing about the cautious approach in New Zealand to statutory priorities, suggests that it is clear that tension exists between the need to protect employees while not causing undue detriment to other creditors or harm to the overall economy. This tension was addressed by the Joint Insolvency Committee of the New Zealand Society of Accountants and the New Zealand Law Society when it advised against redundancy claims being included in the employee priority in New Zealand.[161] The reasons cited by the Committee included difficulty in identifying any policy grounds, social or economic, to prefer employees over unsecured creditors on this issue.[162] Such a conclusion would be unlikely in Australia, given its inclusive provisions grounded in part on social perspective of protecting both wages and entitlements of employees.

It is possible to extrapolate from Shanker's three ways of justifying a government debt's priority to justify employee statutory priorities.[163] Shanker's first way is to look at the ability to distribute loss.[164] Employees typically have no

155 Ibid.

156 Garrido, J.M. 'The Distributional Question in Insolvency: Comparative Aspects' (1995) 4 *International Insolvency Review* 25, 44.

157 Ibid. 52.

158 Ibid. Citing Schumann, P.A. 'An Attempt at a "Philosophy of Bankruptcy"' (1973) 21 *University California Los Angeles Law Review* 403, 446.

159 Ibid. 52.

160 Heath, P. 'Preferential Payments on Bankruptcy and Liquidation in New Zealand: Are they Justifiable Exceptions to the *Pari Passu* Rule?' (1996) 4(2) *Waikato Law Review* 24, 42.

161 Submission of Joint Insolvency Committee to Labour Select Committee on the Status of Redundancy Payments Bill 1996 as detailed in Heath, P. 'Preferential Payments on Bankruptcy and Liquidation in New Zealand: Are They Justifiable Exceptions to the *Pari Passu* Rule?' (1996) 4(2) *Waikato Law Review* 24, 44–46.

162 Ibid.

163 Shanker, M.G. 'The Worthier Creditors (and a Cheer for the King)' (1975–1976) 1 *Canadian Business Law Journal* 341.

164 Ibid. 343.

ability to distribute loss of wages and other entitlements, which surely puts them in need of a priority. Of course, to use the ability to bear a loss or distribute it based on the depth of a creditor's pocket is unfair as a justification for any priority. Creditors such as governments may be able to absorb revenue loss better than employees can absorb unpaid wages, as governments have deeper pockets. Nevertheless, it seems that it would be an unsatisfactory insolvency system which would determine the worthiness of creditors' claims by the depth of the pocket.

Shanker's second way to justify a priority is to explore the dynamics that give rise to the creditors' claim.[165] The dynamics that give rise to employees' claims for unpaid wages and entitlements involve the employment interview, the acceptance of the job on certain conditions and then the ongoing performance of that contract of employment.

Unlike secured and unsecured creditors, employees do not usually have a choice (after they have accepted the job) as to whether to do business or not with the debtor company. The employee could always terminate their contract, but it is unlikely they have other ready sources of income, unlike a trade creditor.

Shanker's third way to justify a priority is to accept that there is creditor apathy in liquidations.[166] Employees as creditors in liquidations are generally apathetic about their claim. Shanker points out that 'one seriously doubts that creditors will find it profitable to expend their time and energy dealing with the affairs of their now insolvent debtor'.[167] This must generally be true for employees and their representatives. Former employees will be much more likely to be devoting their energies to searching for new work than involving themselves in the pursuit of unpaid wages and entitlements.

Shuchman[168] suggests that justification is made by examining the need and deserts of the creditors and moral worthiness, to determine who should get greater rights to payments. Using such a test, there is a clear need on the part of employees to be paid (as has been argued above). The employee's moral worthiness has indeed been recognized by the legislature and the judiciary since the 1820s.[169]

What Position Should the Employee's Priority Hold?

If it can be accepted that the employee priorities should be retained in the *Corporations Act 2001* (Cth), then it is apposite to consider whether the present

---

165 Ibid. 344.

166 Ibid. 346.

167 Ibid. 347.

168 Shuchman, P. 'An Attempt at a "Philosophy of Bankruptcy"'(1973) 21 *University of California Los Angeles Law Review* 403, 444.

169 *An Act to Amend the Laws Relating to Bankruptcy 1825* (UK) 6 Geo 4 c 16, s48.

positioning amongst the field of creditors should be maintained. Here there are three alternatives.

Maintaining the Status Quo – Keeping s556(1)(e) – (g)

Firstly, ss556(1)(e), (f)and (g) could be kept intact and the status quo maintained. This is likely to be the most palatable option with governments, secured creditors and employers.

Unsecured creditors are resigned to accepting a lower ranking on the justification that employees do deserve special protection and administration expenses assist all creditors. Financiers are able to take floating charges and with the operation of s433 the position of employee priorities is of some concern. From the point of view of employees and unions, concerns over low distributions from the assets of employers drive their pleas for better treatment. Inevitably, the pleas are for a higher positioning in the ranking of claims; although in recent years with the development of the GEERS entitlement scheme (detailed later in this chapter), the call is not so loud.

Employees and Secured Creditors with Equal Billing

Secondly, employees could be positioned alongside secured creditors. It is a common device used in Canadian provinces to legislate security for unpaid wages through statutory liens or statutory trusts.[170] The statutory lien has the effect of turning the wages claim into secured debt. Then it is common to appoint someone to represent the debt. The debt would then be payable and enforceable in priority over all other claims, except a previously registered charge (for example, a registered mortgage over the employer's land). By contrast, the statutory trust has the effect of turning the wages claim into a trust fund to be handled by a trustee – for example, the employer – for the benefit of the employees. It stands apart from the asset pool of the company.

Clarification for this statutory security approach would be needed in some areas before Australian drafters could contemplate change. First, the extent to which the lien extends over the employer's assets must be clarified. If the lien is deemed to cover only unencumbered assets then the employee may not see much improvement to their existing position. Second, at what time will the interest arise under such a lien? The interest could arise when the wages or entitlements are earned, or it could arise when the insolvency process is commenced. This factor would be crucial to the outcome. Moreover, other creditors will want to know before extending credit, so as not to be prejudiced later if the employees' interest commenced at the time wages were earned. Employees would want the interest

170 See e.g., Gleig, D.G. 'Unpaid Wages in Bankruptcy' (1987) 21 *University of British Columbia Law Review* 61.

to begin as soon as possible: for example, at the time wages were earned, to give them the best chance of attaching a security to their employer's assets.

For a statutory trust to work, decisions must be made as to whether the normal requirements of a trust will be kept. Requirements such as the tracing of funds would need a deeming provision in the legislation. To do so would then cause difficulties for other creditors, who would want to know their position with regard to the parallel security, but which may be clouded by a deeming of some assets to the trust. Australian law with respect to liens – for example, accountant's lien – has been plagued with uncertainty.[171] In light of this, any suggestion for a lien here would require caution.

Gleig[172] observes that in Canada the statutory security for employees has not proven to be the ideal solution. Canadian courts are very reluctant to read any statute liberally which purports to grant a security ahead of the vested property interests of an earlier secured creditor. The Canadian experience has revealed that statutory liens are ineffective.[173] Even with careful drafting, the impact on the credit market and the need to incorporate a registration procedure suggest the legislature should not follow this path.

Employees Before Secured Creditors

The third alternative is to amend the *Corporations Act 2001* (Cth) such that employees come before secured creditors in all insolvency administrations. To do so would greatly enhance the chances of the employees being paid. They would obtain first call over the employer's assets. The outcome would be a great deal of certainty for employees. However, even such a 'super priority' is not an absolute answer. Those companies with few assets and high labour components will still provide little distribution for employees in a wind up situation. The super priority would also have an extreme impact on the credit market. Secured creditors who granted credit at a price commensurate with the known risk would have their expectations frustrated when the risk changed, significantly and unexpectedly, by the introduction of a statutory imposition of a superior call on the company's assets. Perhaps the super priority could be established in respect of securities created only after the introduction of the new provision. Initially the credit market would have difficulty evaluating the employees' interest in a security, although over time the problem could be expected to diminish. Another problem for the creditors of a super priority would result from any change of circumstances in a business. If an employer were to change their operations to a more labour intensive one, the risk for the creditor would be greater than previously determined, due to the employee

171 See e.g., Kale, L. 'Can I Hold the Books if my Client Doesn't Pay?' (1988) 58 (1) *Australian Accountant* 59.

172 Gleig, D.B, 'Unpaid Wages in Bankruptcy' (1987) 21 *University of British Columbia Law Review* 61, 75.

173 Ibid.

super priority. It would perhaps be unusual for a company to move in the direction of greater labour intensity. In any event, it is likely creditor documentation would alter to require such information as a condition subsequent to the extension of credit.

If employees were to receive a super priority some of the risk of insolvency would be shifted to secured creditors. A super priority would diminish the incentive of employees to monitor debt.[174] The task of monitoring the risk would be transferred from the inefficient employee to the efficient secured creditor.[175] The result might be a more timely intervention by an outsider into the affairs of the company that may be approaching insolvency. The secured creditor would have an incentive to correct bad management at an earlier stage. There would be a significant expansion in the scope of risk monitoring undertaken by secured creditors. The cost of secured debt would rise because of this intensity. In a super priority situation, the employees piggyback the secured creditors yet still arrive first. With no super priority, the secured creditors' concerns diminish as they stand first in line to recover their money.

The Australian Federal Government has recently contemplated the creation of an employee super priority. Yet in the four years after the Federal Government originally revealed its plans, no draft legislation was made available for comment and in October 2005 they announced they were not proceeding with the proposal.[176] By comparison, the Canadian parliament in mid 2005 debated draft legislation, *Bill C-55*, on this matter and they first considered it in 1972![177]

The original (and at the time, astonishing) announcement was made in September 2001 by the Prime Minister, John Howard. He declared that the Federal Government was considering amending corporate laws to rank statutory employee entitlements ahead of all secured creditors, including financial institutions.[178] Clearly it was the *Corporations Act 2001* (Cth), as administered by the Federal Government, which was the likely statute into which any new provision to facilitate the change to a maximum priority for employee entitlements would be inserted. The Treasurer, Peter Costello, was to introduce this legislation after consultation with the finance industry and small businesses. The Prime Minister's announcement received immediate condemnation and rejection by the finance

174 Cantlie, S.J. 'Preferred Priority in Bankruptcy' in Jacob D. Ziegel (ed.), *Current Developments in International and Comparative Corporate Insolvency Law* (1994) 443–444.

175 Ibid.

176 <http://www.treasury.gov.au/contentitem.asp?NavId=037&ContentID=1303> provides a paper *Corporate Insolvency Reform* and on page 3 the Government's decision not to proceed is noted. (para 21).

177 Industry Canada outlines the history of this issue: see <www.strategis.ic.gc.ca>.

178 Hon J Howard, Transcript of the Prime Minister's Joint Press Conference with Deputy Prime Minister and the Minister for Foreign Affairs, Parliament House, Canberra, 14 September 2001.

sector.[179] Over the next four years the idea was mooted from time to time without much substance or vigour.

On 30 July 2002, the Treasury released a Departmental Discussion Paper on this very topic.[180] Then in April 2003 the Parliamentary Secretary to the Treasurer, Ian Campbell, reported that the government was considering the outcomes of stakeholder consultation. In May 2003, the Parliamentary Joint Committee on Corporations and Financial Services released an Issues Paper on 'Improving Australia's Corporate Insolvency Laws'.[181] This committee had earlier, in November 2002, agreed to consider and report on the operation of Australia's insolvency and voluntary administration laws. It invited interested persons and organizations to make submissions. Amongst other issues it raised the maximum priority for employee entitlements.

The Government received very few submissions supporting the proposal, with the support being limited to trade unions and the Federal Labor Opposition.[182] Most submissions were concerned about the impact of the proposal on the availability of credit; commenting that it would lead to a contraction of credit.

The view of the Australian Chamber of Commerce and Industry was that only the Government stood to benefit from the adoption of a super priority for employees.[183] Such a priority would serve to defray the government's exposure under the General Employee Entitlements and Redundancy Scheme.[184] The Chamber believed that the proposal would have a widespread economic and social impact and the costs of the proposal would be passed on to business. It supported the maintenance of the existing order of priorities under the *Corporations Act 2001* (Cth).[185]

Problems cited with changing the employee priorities include fears that a maximum priority rule would lead to artificial commercial arrangements designed

---

179 Buffini, F. and Fenton-Jones, M. 'New laws change lending outlook' *The Australian Financial Review* (Sydney) 18 September 2001, 12; 'Banks fight worker priority payouts' *The Australian Financial Review* (Sydney) 23 April 2003 that suggested: 'the attack is being led by the Australian Bankers Association but is supported by the legal profession, company directors and accountants'.

180 Letter from MJ Kooymans (A/g General Manager, Corporate Governance Division, The Treasury, to Tony Abbott, President Law Council of Australia, 30 July 2002. The letter includes a 4 page Departmental Discussion Paper entitled *Maximum Priority for Employee Entitlements*.

181 Parliamentary Joint Committee on Corporations and Financial Services, Commonwealth Parliament, *Issues Paper on Improving Australia's Corporate Insolvency Laws* (2002).

182 Submissions are available at <www.aph.gov.au/senate/committee/corporations_ctte/completed_inquiries/2002-04/ail/submissions/sublist.htm>.

183 ACCI submission is available at <www.acci.asn.au>.

184 This Scheme known as GEERS is explained in detail below.

185 Oldfield, S. 'Banks fight workers priority payment' *The Australian Financial Review* (Sydney) 23 April 2003, 3.

to avoid the operation of the rule, create a proliferation of companies employing no staff and holding no assets other than receivables from a related operating or trading company and impact severely on companies with long serving work forces.

The Australian Bankers Association indicated that a maximum priority would have a significant impact on the lending and loan security arrangements of many businesses, and would not benefit employees.[186] It claimed that the direct impact of the proposal would be higher lending rates, reduced availability of credit to many businesses and the withdrawal of credit in some cases. If a secured creditor found themselves in this position, they would have to base lending decisions to extend credit on the knowledge that recovery would be subject to payment of employee entitlements. That would mean that when approaching a lender some estimation of the amounts owed in employee entitlements would have to be furnished. Follow up figures on this very same issue would be needed. During the term of the loan, further updates as to the amounts of outstanding employee entitlements would need to calculated and furnished to the lender. Secured creditors would also want to draft a set of clauses in loan documentation allowing them to exit the loan contract. If an unfavourable report as to the amount of employee entitlements owed by the debtor company was received during the term of the loan, then the secured creditor could terminate.

The Australian Bankers Association was clearly opposed to such a move because it 'would undercut the whole basis of much of business lending, raise bank costs and perhaps cut the credit worthiness of their loan books'.[187] Employer companies could expect demands for more security, higher loan repayments and higher interest charges.

In summary then, three outcomes can be predicted from the creation of a super priority. In the first place, the cost of finance would rise if financial institutions were forced into high risk lending. That would apply to new and renegotiated borrowing, as such a legislative change could never have retrospective force. Second, the financial institutions would look to avoid lending to many risky companies and look to increase security taken from directors, or issue finance by retaining title in assets, exercising a hire-purchase type control. Thirdly, financial institutions would be forced into a monitoring role, the cost of which would be passed on and certain industries would require greater scrutiny. Financial institutions might choose not to lend to certain industries or certain employer companies, particularly those with more generous redundancy obligations.

186 Ibid.

187 Ibid.

Public Debate and the Role of the Media

The media, particularly television, have become a major participant and have set some of the agenda in the debate that has occurred in Australia since 1998 over employee entitlements on insolvency. One of the features of the debate has been the discussion of the position of employees who are paid only after a financial institution holding a security over company property. Television coverage of miners leaving their mine and being told their employee entitlements are lost has had a huge impact on sympathetic public feeling and Government policy. Such coverage certainly pressured the Federal Government to consider changes to legislation and to undertake other ad hoc measures to protect employees.[188] The television coverage then generated talkback radio and social comment programmes. Many of these programmes also gave airtime to the possibility of changing the order of payment so as to favour the employees of insolvent companies.

Despite this the Federal Government showed a lack of interest in the proposal and following the Parliamentary Joint Committee of Corporations and Financial Services' recommendation against the proposal announced their decision not to proceed.[189]

Statutory Subrogation

Subrogation involves substituting one party's rights for the rights of another. The statutory priority rights of employees' wages and entitlements can be 'subrogated' if those entitlements are paid by another party such as a financier or the government. Statutory subrogation in insolvency is permitted by s560 of the *Corporations Act 2001* (Cth).[190]

The section provides a statutory right of subrogation to employee priorities in favour of a person who, prior to the winding up, advances money to the company for the purpose of paying debts of this description. If the money is applied by way of payments to an employee, on account of such debts, then the person who made the advances is entitled to claim to be a priority creditor. The person receives the employee's right of priority to the extent that the sum in respect of which the employee was entitled to priority.[191] If the person advancing the money pays wages and income tax is deducted, it is still the gross amount that attracts the subrogation treatment.

188 Riley, J. 'Lessons from Ansett: Locating the Employees Voice in Corporate Enterprise' (2002) 27 *Alternative Law Journal* 112.

189 <http://www.treasury.gov.au/contentitem.asp?NavId=037&ContentID=1303> *Corporate Insolvency Reform*, 3.

190 For the same treatment in the United Kingdom see s386 and Schedule 6 of the *Insolvency Act 1986* (UK).

191 Keay, A. *McPherson The Law of Company Liquidation* (UK version) (2001) 178.

One justification for allowing a claim for money lent to be substituted for employee claims is that 'it alleviates the hardship which might otherwise result from employees having to wait until those claims were satisfied by the liquidator in winding up'.[192] A concomitant disadvantage of statutory subrogation, for insolvent employers, is that it enables the trading life of a company with no prospect of success to be protracted by one creditor or group of creditors to the prejudice of others.[193]

Section 560 of the *Corporations Act 2001* (Cth) requires that the person making the advance establish that money was both advanced and actually used for the purpose of paying a debt that would have enjoyed a priority in winding up.[194] It is not 'fatal' if the money advanced was not advanced exclusively for the payment of employees, provided the employee payments were one of the purposes.[195] However, only the portion used for paying employees will enjoy the subrogated status.

Until recently banking institutions would have been the principal beneficiaries of statutory subrogation in insolvency. Keay observes that '[F]ew problems arise where the bank adopts the straightforward approach of refusing to honour cheques drawn on a company's overdrawn account except for the purpose of paying wages'.[196] When a bank makes such payments they become 'entitled to priority in place of the employee who has essentially been paid' by them.[197] Of course, there are difficulties when banks insist that 'every withdrawal for wages should be followed immediately by the crediting of a similar amount to the overdrawn account to ensure that the overdraft is not increased by payment of the wages cheque'.[198] This and other variations expose the bank to breaches of the antecedent transactions and unfair preferences regimes in the *Corporations Act 2001* (Cth).[199]

Since the introduction of the GEERS scheme (discussed below) that provides employees with most of their entitlements,[200] there has been a new focus on statutory subrogation. In the United Kingdom legislation known as the *Employment Rights Act 1996* (UK) provides for payments to be made under a scheme known as the National Insurance Fund. The Secretary of State pays employees and is then subrogated to the employees' preferential rights. The subrogation is to the extent

192 Ibid.

193 Brooker (1962) 26 *Conveyancer (NS)* 294.

194 Also found in the United Kingdom. See *Insolvency Act 1986* (UK) Schedule 6 para 11 (cf paras 9 and 10).

195 Keay, A. *McPherson The Law of Company Liquidation* (UK version) (2001) 178.

196 Keay, A. *McPherson The Law of Company Liquidation* (4th ed. 1999) 602–603.

197 Ibid.

198 Ibid. 603.

199 *Corporations Act 2001* (Cth) ss588FA and 588FE.

200 The schemes are Employee Entitlement Support Scheme (EESS) from January 2000 and General Employee Entitlements and Redundancy Scheme (GEERS) from 12 September 2001.

that the payments made are in respect of liabilities that have preferred status under the *Insolvency Act 1986* (UK). The *Employment Rights Act 1996* provides for up to eight weeks arrears of pay, payment in lieu of notice, holiday pay for up to six weeks and an award for unfair dismissal.

In Australia, as described later in this chapter, the GEERS scheme has no statutory implementation, and is administratively introduced and driven. In contrast, the United Kingdom has a clear reference between the two Acts. Similar to the Australian scheme, payments are calculated by reference to weekly pay and there is a maximum amount that can be used in calculations. What presents as a problem and impacts upon the subrogation issue in Britain is the difference in maximum amounts between the two Acts.[201] Also, unfair dismissal awards do not have express priority under the *Insolvency Act 1986* (UK) yet can be paid by the Secretary of State out of the National Insurance Fund. In Australia, as described below, there is a cap in the scheme and there has not been a maximum limitation for ordinary employees under the statutory priority section of the companies' legislation since 1985.[202] Therefore, there is a difference in the amounts between the administrative scheme and the statutory priority in Australia.

Statutory subrogation is very important for governments who are supporting employee entitlements upon insolvency. Keay and Walton use British data from 1995–6 to show that out of £762 million owed by insolvent employers to employees, £177 million ranked as preferred and the remaining £585 million was unsecured debt.[203] The National Insurance Fund was an unsecured creditor for that huge sum. Australia is following a similar path now that the GEERS scheme is in place. A report by the Australian National Audit Office[204] shows that $62 million had been paid out to 30 June 2002 and all of this would be a priority debt under ss556(1)(e), (g) and (h). The government had to date recovered only $2 million of that debt. In October 2005 the government announced it had paid out in excess of $661 million since January 2000 but no mention was made of the amounts recovered.[205]

Keay and Walton observe that the United Kingdom's preferred debt regime appears to benefit the Crown and employees, but really it is the Crown through

201 *Insolvency Act 1986* (UK) s386 and Schedule 6 c8, *Employment Security Act 1996* (UK) s31.

202 *Companies Code* s441(1)(e) from 1985 provides the cap only for 'excluded employees'.

203 Keay, A. and Walton, P. 'Preferential Debts: An Empirical Study' (1999) 3 *Insolvency Lawyer* 112, 113.

204 Australian National Audit Office *Audit Report Employee Entitlement Support Schemes 2002* at <www.dewr.gov.au> accessed 17/2/03 pages 19–20.

205 <http://www.treasury.gov.au/contentitem.asp?NavId=037&ContentID=1303> *Corporate Insolvency Reform*, 2.

the National Insurance Fund that takes over the claims of the employees in a very large proportion of the cases.[206]

It is likely that statutory subrogation will continue as an important facet of protecting employee wages and entitlements. Such arrangements are justified by governments because they have an escalating outstanding debt from schemes such as GEERS payments yet they stand to recover little.

Some Issues to be Debated for Change while Maintaining the Employees' Priorities

Australia is fortunate to have a comprehensive employee priority. As industrial rights have emerged, they have been addressed as part of the employee priorities. Areas such as workers compensation, superannuation, leave and retrenchment have all been added, as is evident from the discussion above. The categories of eligible employees have also been broadened from the very limited initial coverage. Hence, it seems that existing industrial entitlements have been identified and are covered. However, there are still some issues which should be debated. These include excluded employees, employee-like persons, definitional problems concerning 'spouses', discrimination, and statutory funds for long service leave.

Excluded Employees

The current legislation defines 'excluded employees' and prevents such persons from having priority for certain wages and entitlements.[207] This exception is unfair and should be revised. Since the Companies Code in 1981 there has been a ceiling on the amounts owed to excluded employees that receive priority. Presently the maximum priority benefit is set at $1500 for leave payments and $2000 for wages. Beyond this, amounts owed to excluded employees are treated as unsecured debts. Excluded employees include directors, spouses and relatives. The Harmer Report[208] observed that the definition did not extend to a de facto spouse and recommended that it should. The present legislation has now made this change.[209]

The current ceilings for excluded employees are, of course, inexact. As average weekly earnings rise there is pressure to change the ceilings upwards. The present ceilings have been the only one featured in the legislation since the concept of an excluded employee was introduced in 1985. Average male weekly

---

206 Keay, A. and Walton, P. 'Preferential Debts: An Empirical Study' (1999) 3 *Insolvency Lawyer* 112, 113.

207 See the discussion earlier in this chapter on *Corporations Act 2001* (Cth) ss556(1)(e) and (1)(g).

208 Australian Law Reform Commission, *General Insolvency Inquiry*, Report No 45 (1988) para 728.

209 *Corporations Act 2001* (Cth) s556(2).

earnings have gone from $281.40[210] to $954.10[211] since 1985. In 1982 there was a ceiling of $2000 placed on all employees receiving a priority in insolvency.[212] In 1985, amendments to s441 of the *Companies Code* removed the maximum limit in respect of all employees and left the limit to apply only to excluded employees' wages. This was the first time there was discrimination between employees and excluded employees. It was then that the $1500 limit was placed on leave payments. Furthermore, in those amendments there was no priority for excluded employees' retrenchment entitlements.

Directors and related parties are targeted for special treatment in the distribution of assets of a company. This is despite the fact that directors and their families may well have been employed in work-type situations with the insolvent company.

The justification for delaying a portion of excluded employees' wages and entitlements claims suggests that unscrupulous directors could manufacture large claims of remuneration. The unscrupulous director would presumably have been in a position to know about the likely future insolvency and so keep their wages paid and their entitlements up to date. After all, there are no unfair preference provisions relating to employees' wages and entitlement payments before insolvency.

When considering arguments for retaining the exemption, one is readily confronted with thoughts of the directors as being responsible[213] for the demise of the company, so why then should not they suffer by missing out in part with their entitlements? This argument, however, is harsh. Corporate insolvency, perhaps even more than personal insolvency, is often unpredictable and can have a multitude of causes.

Another argument for retaining the directors' excluded employee status is that directors would miss out in only a very small number of cases. This is based on reasoning that suggests that because directors are in a superior position with regard to information on the financial situation of the company,[214] they would always ensure that they were paid their wages and other entitlements during the company's lifetime of solvency. When things start to go bad, as the reasoning would have it, directors would address any outstanding entitlements of their own. Again, this argument fails to consider the likely pandemonium, particularly in small companies, just before insolvency. It is just such a chaotic scenario that

210 Taken from *1981 Year Book Australia No 62* (1982) R J Cameron Australian Statistician, 153. This would have been the amount available to the legislators in 1982 when the $2,000 ceiling was introduced.

211 Taken from *2004 Year Book Australia No 86* (2004) D Trewin Australian Statistician, 159.

212 *Companies Code* s441.

213 Responsibility is one of the arguments put forward by Van Wezel Stone, K. 'Policing Employment Contracts within the Nexus of Contract Firm' (1993) 43 *University of Toronto Law Journal* 353.

214 One that is required by the *Corporations Act 2001* (Cth) in the directors' duties ss180–183 and in the common law on directors' duties.

might contribute to directors overlooking the ability to set themselves right as far as wages and other entitlements are concerned.

It has indeed been suggested that it is unfair to treat directors performing 'employee-like' functions in a different manner to all other employees.[215] These directors might be putting in long hours in an eleventh-hour bid to save the company from insolvency. They may not have taken holidays in recent times due to the extra work created by the financially unstable company. Such behavior, and the fact that the company's reasons for failure maybe beyond the directors' control, does point to unfair treatment. For example, in the United Kingdom directors who are owed wages and entitlements are treated just as any other employee.

Finch considers the introduction of some form of discriminatory treatment for the United Kingdom and counters that it 'might be considered to be too draconian'.[216] She suggests that to discriminate might 'exaggerate the extent to which company directors are able to self-inform concerning their company's insolvency risks, to influence financial risk-taking or to exit from excessively risky situations'.[217]

Perhaps there is a middle road in the debate. Directors could enjoy like treatment to all other employees for their first (and possibly their second) corporate insolvency in which they have been directors. That is a type of 'three strikes and you miss out' treatment.[218] This would safeguard against treatment that is too favourable toward those intent in engaging in 'phoenix' type corporate management,[219] while still showing fairness to directors who are unfortunate enough to find themselves directing a failed company.

Such a change would be simple to introduce, as the wording of 'excluded employee' could change akin to the disqualification section. The caps that appear now could be maintained (or slightly increased) for the director on their third insolvency.

---

215 The writer has put this position in Symes, C.F. 'Are Directors (and Their Families) Treated Too Harshly under Insolvency Entitlements Law?' (2003) 3 (8) *Insolvency Law Bulletin* 137. The article draws upon a suggestion by Vanessa Finch in her book *Corporate Insolvency Law Perspectives and Principles* (2002).

216 Finch, V. *Corporate Insolvency Law Perspectives and Principles* (2002) 437.

217 Ibid.

218 In the UK the Federation of Small Business have argued for a designation of 'provisional director' where a director has been at the helm of several failed companies. They would then have to disclose this to trade creditors.

219 See e.g., Guest Committee, 'Curbing the Phoenix Company', First Report, Law Reform Committee, Parliament of Victoria (Melbourne, 1994), Second Report (May 1995) and Third Report (November 1995); Tomasic, R. 'Commercial Morality and Public Policy as "Principles" of Corporate Insolvency Law' in Cranston, R. (ed.), *Essays in Honour of Roy Goode* (1997) 461.

Aside from their exclusion under s556 of the *Corporations Act 2001* (Cth), Australia deals directors a further blow by making them ineligible to make claims under the GEERS scheme.[220]

It is time to abolish this discriminatory treatment. Now that the GEERS scheme is in place, directors and other excluded employees could be treated like fellow employees. If this is not yet palatable, then Australia should place a higher ceiling on claims of directors, spouses and relatives so that they can receive the equivalent to, say, four weeks' average weekly earnings for both wages and leave entitlements. The lack of any change in the amount of the ceiling screams out for a change to drafting techniques. For example, the present technique employed for statutory offences (such as the use of 'penalty units' and not dollar amounts) could be usefully adopted, whereby the amounts are not included in the legislation but in an appropriate schedule which is then adjusted by regulation. The ceiling could perhaps be defined with reference to average weekly earnings in the same way as the *Income Tax Assessment Act 1936* (Cth) uses the Consumer Price Index in its calculations of an indexed cost base for capital gains tax assessments.

Relative and Spouse Definitions for 'Excluded Employee'

A claim by a wife, husband, child, parent, brother or sister of a bankrupt in respect of unpaid salary or wages has been ineligible for priority payment under the *Bankruptcy Act* in Australia for many years. A similar treatment is given in the *Corporations Act 2001* (Cth). Section 556(2) of the *Corporations Act 2001* (Cth) mentions 'relative' in its definition of 'excluded employees' but does not define the term. Section 9 of the *Corporations Act 2001* (Cth) defines 'relative' as '... the spouse, parent or remoter lineal ancestor, son, daughter or remoter issue, or brother or sister'. This means that grandchildren and grandparents are potential 'excluded employees'. 'Spouse' is not defined in the *Corporations Act 2001* (Cth), other than to make it clear that a 'de facto spouse' is included.[221] Perhaps it would be helpful to have a brief description included in s9, so as to give certainty to the application of the s556(2) definition of 'excluded employees'. For example, the *Income Tax Assessment Act 1936* (Cth) defines 'spouse' in the following way: 'In relation to a person includes another who although not legally married to the person, lives with the person on a bona fide domestic basis as the husband or wife of the person'.[222] Given the similar commercial nature of these Acts, this definition would suit the *Corporations Act*.

220 Discussed later in the chapter.

221 *Corporations Act 2001* (Cth) s556(2).

222 *Income Tax Assessment Act 1936* (Cth) s6.

Employee-like Persons

During the preparation of the Harmer Report, the Australian Law Reform Commission (ALRC) received submissions that the 'employee' definition for the priority should be extended to include persons who work in an employee-like capacity.[223] The Harmer Report recommended that the definition should not be changed.[224] Its reasons for such a recommendation were that persons who work as independent contractors should not have their status categorized artificially when the company to which they contracted their services goes into liquidation.[225] To allow this would give the contractor an advantage from the present position of being an unsecured creditor and make them a priority creditor.

The Harmer Report acknowledged that in 1988 the industrial law in at least one State provided the power to declare void or amend contracts which classify persons as contractors when they might appear to be employees.[226] Even more law has been generated since then on the distinction between the categories of independent contractor and employee[227] and so there are many commentators calling for reform of this aspect of industrial law.[228]

When legislation referring to clerks, servants, workers and labourers (amongst others), was changed to use the word 'employee' to describe the priority from 1961 in the *Uniform Companies Acts*, difficulties were likely to be encountered in distinguishing employees from independent contractors.[229] This distinction was not a concern for the Harmer Report in 1988 and has not been the subject of any reported case law on s556. The expertise of accountants and others in the tax

223 Australian Law Reform Commission, General Insolvency Inquiry Report No 45 (1988) para 731. These included submissions from Hon R Willis Submission 192 (on file with candidate) and W B Creighton Sydney Transcript 579, 80.

224 Ibid.

225 Ibid.

226 Ibid.

227 See e.g., *Hollis v Vabu Pty Ltd* [2001] HCA 44 (2001) Aust Torts Reports 81615 (2001) 207 CLR 21.

228 See e.g., Stewart, A. 'Redefining Employment? Meeting the Challenge of Contract and Agency Labour' (2002) 15 *Australian Journal of Labour Law* 235; Davies, P. and Freedland, M. 'Employed or Self-Employed? The Role and Content of the Legal Distinction: Labor Markets, Welfare and the Personal Scope of Employment Law' (1999) 21 *Comparative Labor Law and Policy* 231; Linder, M. 'Employed or Self-Employed? The Role and Content of the Legal Distinction: Dependent and Independent Contractors in Recent US Labor Law: An Ambiguous Dichotomy Rooted in Simulated Statutory Purposelessness' (1999) 21 *Comparative Labor Law and Policy Journal* 187; Langille, B.A. and Davidov, G. 'Employed or Self-Employed? The Role and Content of the Legal Distinction – Beyond Employees and Independent Contractors: A View from Canada' (1999) 21 *Comparative Labor Law and Policy Journal* 7.

229 O'Donovan, J. *McPherson The Law of Company Liquidation* (3rd ed. 1987) 402.

and industrial areas should make the decision of determining whether a person is an employee or independent contractor relatively straightforward. Definitions in tax related legislation regularly provide that an employee in general terms is a person who receives payment in the form of salary or wages in return for work or services or payment for work under a contract that is wholly or principally for the person's labour, and the person liable to make the payment is the employer.[230] It seems hard to see much confusion with this extensive definition of 'wages' in s9. It is harder still to argue that there is any injustice in the priority not extending to all appropriate persons. Independent contractors should have priced into their contract the risk of the insolvency of the contracting company and they do not need the special protection afforded by a statutory priority. The difficulty with this stance is the blurred nature of 'contractor'. Many contractors are not running a business and have no control over the price of this labour as they have been coerced into arranging their employment to appear as a contractor.

Discrimination Between Employees

In its early history the employee priority provision was clearly directed to lower ranking employees. As we have seen, the early Acts used terms such as 'clerk', 'servant', 'labourer' and 'workman'.[231] Later, the adoption of a simple test of employment as the principal criterion in the *Companies Code* meant that there was no reason to continue any case by case constructions. The current statute, in referring to employees, is therefore unaffected by previous decisions[232] that prejudiced some employees such as company secretaries.[233] In 1912, Cussen J in the Victorian Supreme Court held that a company secretary was a 'clerk or servant'.[234] Then in 1929 the same court held a director, company secretary, floor manager and a band of musicians of a theatre were not 'clerks or servants'.[235] Of course, the present lack of discrimination amongst different ranks of employees is entirely appropriate. The importance of regular pay and entitlements is probably equal across the different ranks. Perhaps the culpability of the corporate failure could rest more on middle or senior management, but that seems little reason to remove their priority.

230 Various definitions are given in tax-related legislation. For example, *Superannuation Guarantee (Administration) Act 1992* (Cth) s12(1); *Fringe Benefits Assessment Act 1986* (Cth) s136(1); *Taxation Administration Act 1953* (Cth) subdivn 12B Sch 1 and in Payroll Tax legislation see for example, *Payroll Tax Act 1971* (NSW) 3AA (1).

231 For example, *Companies Act 1936* (NSW) s297(1)(b).

232 O'Donovan, J. *McPherson The Law of Company Liquidation* (3rd ed. 1987) 402.

233 See e.g., *Re R W Lees Ltd; Ex parte Pender* [1938] St R Qld 220.

234 *Re Standard Rubber and Leatherboard Co Pty Ltd* [1913] VLR 236.

235 *Re Esplanade Theatre Ltd* [1929] VLR 237.

Long Service Leave Statutory Funds

Funds have been set up to ensure that employees in certain itinerant occupations receive long service leave accumulated from service with a series of firms.[236] Where a company becomes insolvent and the Fund is owed a contribution then this money should be paid into the Fund. Hence the Fund should be treated in a similar fashion to employees outside these industry funds who have their amounts paid to them in priority by virtue of s556(1)(g).

The justification for treating long service leave funds in the same way as employees who are entitled to long service leave is clear cut. When an itinerant worker goes to claim their entitlement they must go to the Fund and it may not be in the position to pay if it has not received contributions from numerous failed insolvent company employers. This would leave these itinerant workers in a less favourable position simply because of the nature of their particular industry.

Unfortunately, the decision in *Irving v Construction Industry Long Service Leave Board*[237] ignored such policy considerations and held that the statutory fund was not entitled to be treated as a priority creditor. Reform could be achieved by a minute expansion of s556(1)(g)(iii) to read: 'to, or in respect of, employees of the company or a statutory fund set up on their behalf'. Such a change would assist the financial viability of the Funds by providing them with an opportunity to receive the levies out of the assets of all companies solvent and insolvent.[238]

The GEERS Scheme and its Priority

Now that Australia has a scheme to pay employees' wages and entitlements upon insolvency it is appropriate to consider the effect upon the existing statutory priority.

The History of the Scheme

In the late 1990s, the employee priority became the focus of much attention and the Federal Government was moved to contemplate its function. The Government was unsure how effective the priority was and lacked any empirical evidence. The problem appeared to be that even though employee statutory priorities existed, they did not mean employees were paid what they were owed in wages and other entitlements. In 1988 the Harmer Report recommended that a wage earner

236 See e.g., Building Industry Long Service Leave Fund in Victoria.

237 (1997) 15 ACLC 95.

238 Symes, C.F. 'It Would be "Bettaform" to Give a Priority: Irving v Construction Industry Long Service Leave Board' (1997) 10 *Corporate and Business Law Journal* 101.

protection fund be established[239] and in 1997 this recommendation received a renewed public airing.[240]

In August 1999, the then Minister for Employment, Workplace Relations and Small Business (the Hon Peter Reith) released a Ministerial Discussion Paper entitled 'The Protection of Employee Entitlements in the Event of Employer Insolvency'.[241] The paper welcomed comments about the protection of employee entitlements in the event of employer insolvency. The paper proposed two options: a scheme for basic payments of employee entitlements funded by government, known as a 'basic payments scheme'; or a 'compulsory insurance scheme' which would cover employee entitlements and be paid for by all employers with the exception of small businesses, whose employees would be paid their entitlements by the government.

Both options aimed for a 'fair and reasonable level of protection' without guaranteeing full payment of all entitlements. Both options envisaged 'capped payments' that would guarantee employees up to 29 weeks of pay (at ordinary time rates). This framework would consist of a guarantee to pay up to 4 weeks unpaid wages, 4 weeks annual leave (accrued in the last year), 5 weeks pay in lieu of notice, 4 weeks redundancy payment, and 12 weeks long service leave, assuming any of these were outstanding to eligible employees.

The 1999 Discussion Paper also floated the idea of setting maximum rates of payment for each week of entitlements and suggested the maximum correspond to an annual salary at ordinary time earnings, then around $40,000.

The Paper suggested that a basic payments system would share the burden across all Australians through the taxation systems of all State and federal governments. One advantage of the basic payment system option was that there would be no incentive to engage in a tactic of shifting assets into other companies within the same group of companies and, therefore, legally avoiding the existing entitlements to a workforce left behind in a mere shell of a company.

The Federal Government chose the option of a basic payments scheme and established the Employee Entitlement Support Scheme (EESS) for employees who were terminated on or after 1 January 2000 as a result of their employer's insolvency. This scheme was set up using the framework outlined above including a payment of four weeks unpaid wages and four weeks annual leave. However, EESS was set up with the expectation that the States would contribute half of the

---

239 Australian Law Reform Commission, *General Insolvency Inquiry*, Report No 45 para 723-725.

240 Symes, C.F. 'The Protection of Wages When Insolvency Strikes' (1997) 5 *Insolvency Law Journal* 196, 203 where the writer made a suggestion of a statutory employees' protection fund based upon a surcharge of $10 collected by the government when companies lodged their annual returns.

241 The Hon Peter Reith, MP, Minister for Employment, Workplace Relations and Small Business, Ministerial Discussion Paper 'The Protection of Employee Entitlements in the Event of Employer Insolvency', August 1999.

amount payable to employees and when they refused to join in employees received only half the amount promised by the scheme. Where a claim was made against EESS the Federal Government took over that employee's priority in relation to any assets of the employer that might eventually become available for distribution, thus allowing the government to recoup a proportion of the expenditure required to establish the scheme and be subrogated for the part of the priority it had paid.

In early 2001, the Federal Government released a first report into the Scheme.[242] The Report indicated that the first payment was made in March 2000 and by 30 June 2000 there were 134 employers across Australia whose former employees had made claims. The number of employees making claims by 30 June 2000 was 892. In the period from July to December 2000, there were 308 employers whose insolvency caused a claim to be made upon the Scheme and this saw payments made to 2,499 employees. The average payment per eligible employee under the Scheme was $2,177. The Report said this represented 'a significant proportion of their [employees'] outstanding entitlements'.[243]

A new scheme known as the General Employee Entitlements and Redundancy Scheme (GEERS) has applied since 12 September 2001. It replaced EESS and it pays all unpaid wages, all accrued annual leave, all accrued long service leave, all accrued pay in lieu of notice, and up to sixteen (previously eight) weeks' redundancy entitlements. It too was based on the basic payments scheme option. In GEERS the State Governments are not expected to fund the scheme. Two caps or upper limits exist in GEERS: a wages and salary upper limit of $101,300 (2007/8) per annum, and a sixteen week limit on redundancy payments regardless of the employee's entitlement. The wages and salary limit is increased yearly.

In a press release on 20 September 2001 the then Minister (Hon Tony Abbott) stated that over 90 percent of workers who lost their entitlements would receive 100 percent of their entitlements under the more generous GEERS. The Government claimed this Scheme met the statutory and community standard entitlements. *The Australian* newspaper reported that it was 92 percent of workers who would be covered and that only one in 12 workers would be left short.[244]

Insolvency practitioners administer the scheme and so employees may approach the liquidator of their employer (or obtain a form through the GEERS Hotline, the Australian Workplace website or other government agencies such as Centrelink) within 12 months of the liquidation. The completed form can then be processed through the liquidator and the government's Employee Entitlements Branch within the Department of Employment and Workplace Relations. The employee will be paid promptly by the liquidator.

---

242 *Employee Entitlement Support Scheme – Year One Activity Report*, Department of Employment, Workplace Relations and Small Business, January 2001.

243 Ibid.

244 Henderson, I. 'Workers Left in the Lurch to get Entitlements', *The Australian* 20 September 2001, 8.

Where a claim is made against GEERS the Federal Government takes over that employees' priority in relation to any assets of the employer that might eventually become available for distribution, thus allowing the government to recoup a proportion of the expenditure required to establish the scheme and be subrogated for the part of the priority it had paid. The Commonwealth gets this priority by stepping into the employees' priority position using s560 of the *Corporations Act 2001* (Cth) which allows advances to be paid before other debts in winding up.[245] After the liquidator has sold some assets or gains access to company funds by some other means then they are in a position to pay back the government for its payment to the employees though of course these advances can remain unpaid for a number of years. The Commonwealth considers its payment as a loan, which the insolvency practitioner agrees to use only for paying employees owed the legal entitlements.

Since 1 November 2005 the exclusions from GEERS have included 'excluded employees' that are eligible for entitlements beyond $3,500 and employees of companies where the liquidator has funds and expects to be able to pay entitlements within 16 weeks of the Department of Employment and Workplace Relations receiving their claim form.[246] Contractors, subcontractors or agents are also excluded from GEERS.

ANOA Report into GEERS

In December 2002 the Commonwealth Parliament received the Australian National Audit Office's report (ANOA report) on the administration of EESS and GEERS.[247] The operation of the two schemes is noted in the ANOA Report as having been characterized by rapid change and development since their inception with a further administrative challenge being the inherently unpredictable workload.[248]

---

245 The subrogation of the employee for the Commonwealth has been the subject of recent judicial comment suggesting that the Commonwealth did not obtain enforcement rights based upon GEERS payments to employees of a company that had receivers and administrators appointed. See Finkelstein J *Commonwealth of Australia v Rocklea Spinning Mills Pty Ltd (Rec and Mgr Apptd)* [2005] FCA 902, 5. Changes from 1 November 2005 diminished the impact of this decision, handed down in July 2005, as GEERS no longer applies to receiverships or administrations and the changes prevent a Deeds of Company Arrangement from lowering the priority of payment to employees without their permission. See <http://www.treasury.gov.au/contentitem.asp?NavId=037&ContentID=1303> *Corporate Insolvency Reform*, 2. and <www.workplaceexpress.com.au>. 'GEERS Extended to Cover More Lost Wages and Ineligible Employees' 12 October 2005.

246 <www.workplace.gov.au/NR/rdonlyres> accessed 1/12/05.

247 Australian National Audit Office, *Audit of Employee Entitlement Support Schemes* January 2003. The 'ANOA Report' is available at <www.anao.gov.au>.

248 ANOA Report, 3.

Timeliness The Scheme's auditors identified a range of opportunities for improvement in the administration of the schemes. The main area in which the performance of the schemes' administrators, the Department of Employment and Workplace Relations, was said not to be meeting expectations was in the timeliness of making payments.[249] The Department was assessed as taking 26 weeks to clear 80 percent of claims and this was 'well short' of the Department's original published standard of 80 percent in 12 weeks and compared poorly with their revised standard of 80 percent in 16 weeks. [250] Nevertheless, the Minister claimed that the time taken to pay claims was 'within five weeks'. This is comparable to other countries that operate similar schemes.[251]

Statistics According to the ANOA Report, an estimated 7.5 per cent of Australian businesses cease operating each year and one in every fifteen of these closures is a business insolvency. Of this category, some will fail to pay employees their entitlements.[252]

From the beginning of EESS (2000) and including the first nine months of GEERS (September 2001- June 2002), almost 17,500 employees received a total of $87.5 million in assistance. To 30 June 2002 there had been 2172 cases comprising 1508 under EESS and 664 under GEERS. More recently, in October 2005 the government reported that over 54,000 employees had received in excess of $661 million in assistance.[253]

In 2002, the number of claims was around 90 new cases per month and the median number of employees per insolvent business was three. Some 80 percent of cases involved 10 employees or less. The mean number of claimants per insolvent business to 30 June 2002 was 9.7 employees. However, the mean was skewed by a small number of large cases. Fifteen cases involved more than 100 claims and three exceeded 500 claims. Such figures demonstrate strongly that the main problem of unpaid employee entitlements upon insolvency is in the small business sector. These figures seem to confirm suggestions that it is not the employees of large businesses

---

249 ANOA Report, 3.

250 In commenting on the ANOA Report the *Workplace Express* highlighted ANOA's discovery that DEWR is only processing six out of 10 claims within its 16 week target. See <www.workplaceexpress.com.au>. 'DEWR Failing to Meet Entitlement Payouts Timeline' 11 December 2002.

251 Bronstein, A.T. 'The Protection of Workers' Claims in the Event of the Insolvency of Their Employer: From Civil Law to Social Security' (1987) 126 *International Labour Review* 715.

252 ANOA Report, 9.

253 <http://www.treasury.gov.au/contentitem.asp?NavId=037&ContentID=1303> *Corporate Insolvency Reform*, 2.

in the regulated and unionized industries that are at great risk, but those working for employers with few staff and, in some cases, less knowledge of their obligations.

While the entitlements from GEERS can include wages, it was always suggested that it was other entitlements that were the substance of most claims. This is borne out by the figures that show that around 10 percent of money paid out by the schemes up to June 2002 went to pay wages. About 25 percent were claims for payments in lieu of notice and another 25 percent in respect of annual leave. Approximately 20 percent were for claims for redundancy pay and 20 percent were for long service leave payments.[254]

Recovery of funds The ANOA Report concludes that Department of Employment and Workplace Relations could improve the management and operation of the schemes by taking a more active role in pursuing recovery of funds from the assets of the insolvent.[255] Although it was acknowledged that recovery took time, the average recovery time was around two years. The ANOA Report also noted that by August 2002 the Department had recovered only $2 million. That said, the records showed that the Commonwealth had begun to receive significant amounts of recovered funds in 2002. More substantial amounts should have begun to flow in from then on.

The Disadvantages of GEERS

GEERS is a taxpayer funded scheme and so suffers from some criticism.[256] Criticism of GEERS can be leveled because, in the first place, it is not a complete protection of all entitlements. The scheme uses a maximum income threshold that is used to calculate payments and there is the limit of redundancy payments to sixteen weeks. Many workers at middle or senior levels in companies may well suffer from the first limitation. However it is the capping of redundancy payments that 'hits particularly hard at the many long-serving workers whose severance pay entitlements well and truly exceed' the eight week limit as it was until 2006.[257] Eight weeks was formerly the standard cap for redundancy pay under federal awards but this figure has since been raised.[258] Furthermore many employees that were covered by workplace agreements or employment contracts had an entitlement of

---

254 ANOA Report, 19.

255 ANOA Report, 4.

256 Campo, R. 'The Protection of Employee Entitlements in the Event of Employer Insolvency: Australian Initiatives in the Light of International Models' (2000) 13 *Australian Journal of Labour Law* 236; Hughes, C.M. 'Towards Pinstriped Unionism: Protecting Employee Entitlements Through Securitisation' (2000) 12 *Bond Law Review* 7; Riley, J. 'Protection of Employment Entitlements: A Legal Perspective (2003) 29 *Australian Bulletin of Labour* 31.

257 Creighton, B. and Stewart, A. *Labour Law* (4th ed. 2005) 375.

258 Ibid. 433.

more than eight weeks redundancy pay.[259] The number disadvantaged is lessened now that the cap has risen to sixteen weeks.

Secondly, it may be questioned how long the Federal Government will stay with funding a scheme if it starts to hurt financially. The recoveries from the subrogation could be so low that there will be a larger than expected cost to Treasury. One measure available to the government is the ability to use the provisions in Part 5.8A of the *Corporations Act 2001* (Cth)[260] to take action against directors who intentionally try to prevent recovery of employee entitlements. Successful actions against directors would see the directors compensating the company for the employee entitlements and if the employees had already been paid by GEERS then the compensation could be paid to the government.

Thirdly, GEERS was introduced administratively so that it is easy to adjust. This works both ways and so it remains at the government's discretion to reduce the percentage of the coverage (that is, back from covering all long service leave, for example) or the maximum wage cap. A recent example of this was the government's move to restrict GEERS to liquidations. The scheme had previously been used in receiverships and voluntary administrations but from 1 November 2005 the government narrowed its application. As GEERS has no legislative foundation then moves such as the recent restriction is not debated on the floor of parliament and the variations can happen 'at the stroke of an executive pen'.[261]

Fourthly, it continues the debate on whether the taxpayer should fund what is a corporate debt. Companies could have had these amounts as contingent liabilities, paid profits in lieu of setting aside amounts to cover the entitlements and later find that tough times see profits stop and when the employees' liability cannot be met then the GEERS is there. The scheme, being publicly funded, 'does nothing to encourage businesses to avoid the problem in the first place by making proper provision for the payment of employee entitlements: that is, by setting aside necessary funds, as opposed to treating monies owed or potentially owed to employees as part of the firm's working capital'.[262] This use of employee entitlements as working capital is the same behaviour that occurs when a business fails to pay the entitlements because they believe the statutory priority will fix the problem after liquidation.

259 Ibid. 375.

260 *Corporations Act 2001* (Cth) Part 5.8A introduced liability for directors who purposely steer the company into agreements or transactions that avoid employee entitlements. For commentary see Noakes, D. 'Measuring the Impact of Strategic Insolvency on Employees' (2003) 11 *Insolvency Law Journal* 91; Symes, C.F. 'A New Statutory Directors' Duty for Australia – A "Duty" to be Concerned about Employee Entitlements in the Insolvent Corporation' (2003) 12 *International Insolvency Review* 133; Reynolds, M. 'The Corporations Law Amendment (Employee Entitlements) Act 2000: To What Extent Will It Save Employee Entitlements?' (2001) *Queensland University of Technology Law Journal* 134.

261 Creighton, B. and Stewart, A. *Labour Law* (4th ed. 2005) 375.

262 Ibid.

Fifthly, it could push the government (through the Australian Securities and Investments Commission) into funding litigation into 'trading whilst insolvent' actions against directors (although directors are not the cash cow or repository for huge assets that some people think).[263] Successful litigation in this area would provide additional funds for distribution and the government may receive greater GEERS reimbursement.

Comparison of Australia's Administrative Scheme with the United Kingdom

Consideration of funds such as GEERS is important not just because they can provide an alternative to a statutory priority, but because they also enjoy the same priority by subrogation. But should the fund enjoy the priority? It is possible that the fund could be treated as an unsecured creditor. In response to such questions it is helpful to compare GEERS with the National Insurance Fund ('NIF') of the United Kingdom.

Employees of a company that has entered insolvency proceedings are entitled to claim against the NIF on terms set out in ss166–70 and 182–190 of the *Employment Rights Act 1996* (UK). These provisions enable employees to claim in respect of unpaid wages, but limited to eight weeks and to a weekly wage of £240. This amount has risen twice since the introduction of the Act. Employees can also claim for notice pay, holiday pay, the basic award for unfair dismissal compensation, statutory redundancy pay and any award made by an industrial tribunal for failure to consult with representatives of the workforce. Where the Secretary of State pays out in respect of the claim of the employee, the Secretary of State enjoys the position of being subrogated to the claim of the employee against the insolvent company.[264]

In the United Kingdom, the Cork Report[265] accepted that employees should continue to receive special treatment and through the medium of claims on the Redundancy Fund (later the NIF). The Cork Report was keen to remove the preferential claims system[266] and there was narrow support for maintaining rights of subrogation for those who had lent money to pay preferential arrears of wages.[267]

263 See e.g., Noakes, D. 'Corporate Groups and the Duties of Directors: Protecting the Employee or the Insolvent Employer?' (2001) 29 *Australian Business Law Review* 124; Burgess, J., Dark, J., Lewer, J. and Waring, P. 'Employee Entitlements in Australia: Accounting Standard, Corporate Governance and Industrial Democracy' (2004) The Association of Industrial Relations Academics of Australia and New Zealand conference held at the University of Newcastle in 2004; Thomas, S.B. 'Unpaid Superannuation Entitlements: A Matter of Trust?' (2002) 30 *Australian Business Law Review* 423.

264 *Employment Rights Act 1996* (UK) s189.

265 Report of the Review Committee *Insolvency Law and Practice* Cmnd 8558 (1982), 'Cork Report'.

266 Ibid. para 1433.

267 Ibid. para 1440.

The Review Committee preparing the Cork Report heard that these subrogated claims should be reduced to unsecured status.[268]

It is conceded that to remove the employee priorities in the insolvency legislation would not impose a loss on employees, as they are protected by the *Employment Rights Act 1996* (UK) and the NIF.[269] However, to abolish the employee priority and the subrogation that goes with it would impose a loss on the NIF. Of course, the result would be to allow 'considerable sums for other unsecured creditors'.[270] Such a result may result in more efficiency, since the Crown as operators of the NIF are 'likely to be a lower cost risk bearer than … other unsecured creditors'.[271] However, it is unfair on the British taxpayer to contribute to a corporate insolvency and one in which they have had no direct involvement.[272]

In the United Kingdom, the subrogation right can in any event be defeated by insolvency practitioners reducing the pool of assets deemed subject to the floating charge.[273] Another criticism is that the NIF can affect the outcomes of a corporate rescue and sale of the ongoing business because insolvency practitioners look to dismiss employees to make NIF claims.[274]

The justification made for the NIF to enjoy the same priority as employees is that the employees enjoy it, so why not those standing in their shoes? However, it seems easier to cast aside the sympathy that exists for employees when talking of a fund that is administered and funded in part by the government. Milman has asked 'why the providers of labour should be treated more favourably than the providers of capital'.[275] Whilst the answer is not simple, such a line of argument could be supported when considering whether to maintain the fund's priority.

The same advantages exist under the NIF that occur in Australia under GEERS. The 'NIF [means] entitlements are guaranteed as opposed to preferred' (the priority status).[276] Payments are made 'in full (up to the statutory limit) even if the employer has no funds' and the employee is 'spared the delays' of waiting for

268 Ibid. para 1435.

269 Finch, V. *Corporate Insolvency Law Perspectives and Principles* (2002) 436.

270 Ibid.

271 Ibid.

272 Ibid.

273 Milman, D. 'Subrogation Claims on Insolvency' [2000] *Insolvency Lawyer* 130, 131.

274 Finch, V. *Corporate Insolvency Law Perspectives and Principles* (2002) 562–564. This could also have been true of GEERS from 2001–2005 when it did allow companies in voluntary administration to use the scheme. However this was highlighted in *Commonwealth of Australia v Rocklea Spinning Mills Pty Ltd* (*Rec and Mgr Apptd*) [2005] FCA 902 (1 July 2005) mentioned above and since 1 November 2005 voluntary administrations are not covered by the scheme.

275 Milman, D. 'Insolvency Reform' [2001] *Insolvency Lawyer* 153.

276 Finch, V. Corporate Insolvency Law Perspectives and Principles (2002) 555.

the 'insolvency processes to run their full course'.[277] Employees do though have to go to a tribunal to establish their redundancy claims.[278]

So while there is little court involvement and administration is conducted by the civil service, the major difference is in the legislative backing the NIF enjoys over Australia's administratively implemented GEERS.

The Future of GEERS and its Priority

The government's behaviour as a priority creditor has been observed by the ANOA Report. The Department seeks advice from the insolvency practitioner about the likelihood of recovery, that is the payment of their priority and they write a follow up letter two to three months later if nothing is heard. The auditors record that the current approach to recovery is consistent with the administration of GEERS being perceived as 'complementary to pre-existing insolvency processes'[279] – that is, the payment to priority creditors under the Act and the treatment of subrogated parties. The Department is reported as stating that: 'the Commonwealth can do no more than await the outcome of the winding up of the affairs of the insolvent company'.[280]

The audit office appears happy to accept that the current insolvency framework is 'largely left to run its course and the process is assumed to provide the appropriate amounts to the Commonwealth in due course should there be a realization of assets'.[281] With respect, the auditors are right – this priority creditor should not expect any different treatment and hence the Department must play by the rules and leave the liquidation process as it exists now.

Finally, the Government auditors in discussions with the professional body, the Insolvency Practitioners Association of Australia (now Insolvency Practitioners Association 'IPA'), revealed that insolvency practitioners have felt less pressure to pursue debtors.[282] The auditors rightly observe that employees are replaced with the government through GEERS and question why the pressure is diminished. They hypothesize (and are probably correct to acknowledge) that when employees were waiting to be paid they had a 'strong personal interest' and so they pursued the insolvency practitioner.[283] The auditors concluded that the Department needed to become an active creditor and pursue the insolvency practitioner about the very same matter of when to expect payment of the priority debt.[284]

277 Ibid.

278 Morgan, R. 'Insolvency and the Rights of Employees' [1981] *Legal Action* 21.

279 Ibid. para 7.14.

280 Ibid.

281 Ibid.

282 Ibid. para 7.16.

283 Ibid.

284 Ibid.

GEERS will continue for the foreseeable future. In 2005 there were changes to the operational arrangements to restrict its application to liquidations and bankruptcy and not extend to companies under voluntary administration (Australia's corporate rescue provisions). This change served to reduce the Federal Government's exposure in some instances where the company recovers from its financial woe; but many companies proceed down this path and still finish up being liquidated, so that GEERS would still apply, albeit a little later in the company's life.

GEERS, in its short history, has become a most important ally to the statutory employees' priorities. However its administrative nature makes it a target for easy manipulation by the Australian Federal Government. In late 2006 a Labour Government was elected and various members had been active in promoting a stronger legislative base for employees' rights upon insolvency. It is possible that changes to the scheme will be effected during the term of this new government.

Conclusion

The employee statutory priority has a long history and before long will have the distinction of two hundred years' service. It is a priority that can be easily justified. One factor that would suggest it will be a feature of the legislative landscape for many years to come is the importance it now plays for the Federal Government, who will want to be subrogated to this priority when there is an asset distribution of the insolvent company.

Chapter 6

Government Debt and Taxation as a Statutory Priority

When a company is wound up not all debt will be met from the realization of the company's assets and, as discussed in Chapters 4 and 5, the *Corporations Act 2001* (Cth) in Australia has chosen some creditors to be legitimately favoured for payment by the liquidator. Taxation and other money owed to governments might be expected as a statutory priority – the government has law-making power and so can readily give itself priority. One could expect either insolvency statutes or taxation statutes to contemplate what is to happen to unpaid taxes or other government debts when a company experiences insolvency. In Australia, however, the operation of a federation between the States and Commonwealth complicated that expectation. Later, the fiscal need for more distributions to be made to unsecured creditors expedited a removal of the government's priority.

The statutory priority of the Commonwealth to receive a priority payment in corporate insolvencies was eventually abolished from 1 November 1979,[1] apart from tax instalment deductions and withholding tax.[2] These latter amounts were still a priority until 1 June 1993. The Crown's right to priority in bankruptcy had previously been removed from 4 March 1968.[3]

The chapter concludes that Australian legislators acted with foresight in this 'early' removal of the tax priority. The United Kingdom has only recently followed the Australian example, a decade later. The governments of numerous other countries have likewise removed their tax priority status in recent years.

The 1993 changes to corporate law with regard to corporate insolvency priorities meant that the Australian Taxation Office (ATO) completely lost its status as a priority creditor.[4] It was seen at the time as an essential reform because a voluntary administration system was being introduced and this system would have a better chance of success if the tax office could not scuttle the arrangement by grabbing a casualty company's outstanding tax liability'.[5] The idea of a corporate reconstruction envisaged by the voluntary administration legislation (as introduced by Part 5.3A of the then *Corporations Law*) might have been 'stymied by an

1 *Taxation Debts (Abolition of Crown Priority) 1980* (Cth).

2 *Income Tax Assessment Act 1936* (Cth) ss221YU, 221P.

3 *Income Tax Assessment Act 1966* (Cth) s17.

4 *Insolvency (Tax Priorities) Legislation Amendment Act 1993* (Cth).

5 Boreham, T. 'Tax Office loses its place in the Creditor queue', *Business Review Weekly* (Sydney), 11 December 1992, 86.

impatient tax office'.[6] For these reasons changes were made to the tax legislation which enhanced the collection of unremitted Pay As You Earn (PAYE) tax. The ATO was given the power to estimate tax owing (which allowed quicker recovery) and to collect a company's tax debts from its directors.

Prior to 1993 when tax was a priority but not in the corporations statute, companies were meant to remit monthly amounts collected on behalf of their employees. However when these companies experienced cash flow problems they 'stretched' the payments to the ATO by effectively using the remittance money as a source of cheap finance or for emergency working capital.[7] When the ATO failed to maintain tight collection procedures it became a prominent creditor after the company collapsed. It was said that the ATO was less vigilant on collection because of its statutory priority.[8] This was disputed by the ATO, who claimed they had 'never depended' on the priority as a means of collection because they were 'lucky to get 10 cents in the dollar in an insolvency situation'.[9]

Other benefits of removing the tax priority include the end of the fighting of a fictitious battle between secured creditors and the tax office which saw both parties trying to create 'ever more divisive methods of getting on top' in the race to satisfy the outstanding debt.[10]

At present, Australian tax law ensures that company directors must arrange for their companies to make payments of tax debts to avoid personal liability[11] and the government has given the taxing authorities powers to estimate taxes in an attempt, inter alia, to reduce unpaid taxes should insolvency occur.

History of Crown and Tax Priorities

The Imperial Statutes

In 1844, s23 of the very first British Act dedicated to company winding up, known as *An Act for Facilitating the Winding up the Affairs of Joint Stock Companies unable to meet their Pecuniary Engagements* outlined that an earlier Act[12] that

---

6 Ibid. 87 quoting Ernst and Young, Chartered Accountants' partner John Gibbons.

7 Op.cit, 86.

8 Ibid.

9 Op.cit, n.5, Tim Boreham, at 87 quoting Margaret Oates, Director of ATO's debt collection program.

10 Ibid. 87 quoting Michael Jones, an insolvency practitioner.

11 See e.g., *Income Tax Assessment Act 1936* (Cth) s221F (except s221F(12), s221G (except s221G(4A), s221YHDC(2), s221YHZD(1) or (1A); *Taxation Administration Act 1953* (Cth) ss8Y, 255–5, 255–40.

12 An Act for the more speedy and effectual Recovery of Debts due to His Majesty, His Heirs and Successors, in right of the Crown of the United Kingdom of Great Britain and Ireland, and for the better Administration of Justice within the same 1801 (UK) 41 Geo 3 c 90.

had been passed for the more speedy and effectual recovery of Crown debts 'shall extend to Decrees and Orders made by Chancery in any proceeding under this Act'.[13] While not giving a priority, it indicated the special place the Crown held in the collection of debt.

The British *Joint Stock Companies Act 1856* and the *Companies Act* in 1862 did not expressly mention the Crown (and by implication taxes) as being entitled to any special distribution upon the insolvency of the company, despite these being the Acts that gave the first corporate insolvency priorities to administration expenses.[14] However, *Re Henley and Co*[15] in 1878 provided the first authority that the Crown was entitled to be paid out of assets of an insolvent company in priority to all other creditors.[16] This was at the time when the *Companies Act 1862* was silent on Crown priorities and the *Income Tax Act 1842* expressly provided for the Crown to recover all duties and to distrain upon any of the debtor's chattels for the arrears of tax.[17] Other cases during the 1880s supported the judgement of James LJ, Brett LJ and Cotton LJ in *Re Henley and Co.*[18]

The *Preferential Payments in Bankruptcy Act 1888* (UK) provided in s1 that

> [I]n the distribution of the property of a bankrupt, and in the distribution of the assets of any company being wound-up under the *Companies Act*, 1862, and the Acts amending the same, there shall be paid in priority to all other debts–
>
> (a) All parochial or other local rates due from the bankrupt or the company at the date of the receiving order, or as the case may be, the commencement of the winding-up, and having become due and payable within twelve months next before that time, and all assessed taxes, land tax, property and income tax assessed on the bankrupt or the company up to the 5th day of April next before the date of the receiving order, or as the case may be, the commencement of the winding-up, and not exceeding in the whole one year's assessment …

Priority for taxes, therefore, was given the highest ranking and there was a cap of one year's assessment. In *Re HJ Webb and Co*,[19] it was held that with the passing of the 1888 Act, the earlier authority for Crown priority (*Re Henley and*

13 *Winding up Act 1844* (UK), s23.

14 See Chapter 2 above.

15 (1878) 9 Ch D 469.

16 See generally, *Re Bonham; Ex parte Postmaster General* (1879) 10 Ch D 595; *Re Oriental Bank Corporation* (1884) 28 Ch D 643; *West London Commercial Bank* (1888) 38 Ch D 364; *Exchange Bank of Canada v R* (1886) 11 App Cas 157.

17 *Income Tax Act 1842* (UK) s1.

18 (1878) 9 Ch D 469; See also *Re Bonham; Ex parte Postmaster General* (1879) 10 Ch D 595; *Re Oriental Bank Corporation* (1884) 28 Ch D 643; *West London Commercial Bank* (1888) 38 Ch D 364; *Exchange Bank of Canada v R* (1886) 11 App Cas 157.

19 *Re H J Webb and Co* [1922] 2 Ch 369.

Co) ceased to be directly applicable. The Crown's right to a priority was abrogated by the *Companies (Consolidation) Act 1908* (UK).[20]

By 1923, in England, the Crown debt priority in the winding up of a company had been removed by the court's construction of the impact of the *Judicature Act* and various Companies Acts such as the *Companies Act 1862* and the *Companies Consolidation Act 1908*, although the tax priority remained. In the British *Companies Act 1929* the tax priority provision was repeated verbatim from the earlier *Preferential Payments in Bankruptcy Act 1888*, as quoted above.

Australian Colonial Legislation

As shown in Chapters 2, 4 and 5, Australian corporate legislation dates back to colonial times and priorities for administrative expenses and employees' wages upon insolvency are found in such statutes from 1860. However, the priorities section in these early statutes[21] remained silent on such matters as tax debts. For example, as we have seen in Chapter 5, the *Companies Act 1892* in South Australia provided in s151 for employees' wages of up to £25 to have priority upon insolvency, but no mention was made of tax debts. The Crown was not bound by this Act.[22] Despite this, the prerogative of the Crown to require payment of debts owing to it in priority to the claims of creditors in equal degree was not taken away.[23]

As with other insolvency priorities granted by statute, the history of such Australian treatment is rooted in the British statutes and so the *Preferential Payments in Bankruptcy Act 1888* was influential.

Australian colonial laws for taxation were introduced gradually during the nineteenth century. In South Australia, the colonial founders touted that it would be a place of 'few or no taxes to pay'.[24] For a while, this was the case as government expenditure was met from the funds raised through land sales. Despite this the South Australian colony became the first to introduce income tax, land tax and probate and succession duties in 1876. The first comprehensive income tax in Australia was levied under the *Taxation Act 1884* (SA). Other colonies followed suit in the 1890s[25] and, while companies were contemplated as taxpayers (for example, in the *Income Tax Act 1894* (Tas) ten pence in the pound was levied on

20 *Companies (Consolidation) Act 1908* (UK).

21 See e.g., *Insolvent Act 1860* (SA) s145.

22 *Re Commonwealth Agricultural Service Engineers Ltd* [1928] SASR 342.

23 *Re Millingen's Ltd* [1934] SASR 72, 82 (Murray CJ).

24 Howell, P.A. 'Constitutional and Political Development 1857–1890' in Jaensch, D. (ed.), *The Flinders History of South Australia, Political History* (1986) 172.

25 Driesen, I.V. and Fayle, R. 'History of Income Tax in Australia' in Rick Krever (ed.), *Australian Taxation: Principles and Practice* (1987) 28.

the incomes of companies), their insolvency and the resultant failure to pay taxes was not a feature of this colonial legislation.

Post Federation

In the first 30 years after Federation there were few company statute amendments. The *Companies Act 1915* (Vic) and the *Companies Act 1920* (Tas) did not mention the Crown or government rates and taxes. As outlined in Chapter 2, the Commonwealth enacted the *Bankruptcy Act 1924* (Cth), which did give an express priority to 'municipal, other local rates and land tax and income tax of up to one year's assessment'[26] against a bankrupt's estate.

The 1930s

As depicted in Chapter 2, a number of States around 1930 drafted new companies legislation[27] and included, for the first time, a priority for tax.

In Queensland, s273 of the *Companies Act 1931* provided that 'nothing in this Act shall prejudice the right of the Crown to be paid the debts of the Crown in priority of all other debts in the winding up of a company'.[28] However, it excluded from the priority 'any corporate body representing the Crown actually engaged in trading and carrying on business in competition with any trade or business carried on by private enterprise'.[29] This provision was inserted to achieve two outcomes: the binding of the Crown to an Act of Parliament needed express or clear implication that it was intended to be bound;[30] and to overrule cases that had interpreted the debts owed to government businesses as Crown priority.[31]

The *Companies Act 1931* (Qld) did not directly mention taxes or rates, but did attempt to import the rules of bankruptcy. Section 272 provided that these rules would apply with regard to priorities of creditors[32] and so the *Bankruptcy Act 1924* (Cth) and its mention of taxes and rates, as described above, applied.

In contrast, South Australia made express mention of the taxation priority. Section 279(1) of the *Companies Act 1934* (SA), provided that, subject to some subrogation issues, 'in a winding-up there shall paid in priority to all other debts

26 *Bankruptcy Act* (Cth) s84.

27 *Companies Act 1931* (Qld); *Companies Act 1934* (SA); *Companies Act 1936* (NSW); and *Companies Act 1938* (Vic). The latter Act was before the parliament for a number of years before eventually being enacted.

28 *Companies Act 1931* (Qld) s273.

29 *Companies Act 1931* (Qld) s273.

30 *Re Bonham; Ex parte Postmaster-General* (1879) 10 Ch D 595.

31 *Re Peterson Ltd* [1927] Q St R 134, QWN 25.

32 *Re Keep, McPherson Ltd* (1931) 48 NSW WN 180.

after costs, liquidator's remuneration, and expenses of or incurred in the winding-up … [employees' priorities then] … (d) all assessed land tax and income tax assessed prior to the relevant date and having become due and payable within the preceding twelve month, but not exceeding in the whole one year's assessment'.[33] New South Wales gave similar treatment in their legislation that followed two years later.[34]

There were three possible reasons for the inclusion of a tax priority. Firstly, the legislative changes were following recent amendments to British companies' legislation,[35] which had expressly mentioned tax debts in its list of priorities.[36] Secondly, the South Australian parliament (and the NSW parliament) were guided by the Commonwealth's *Bankruptcy Act 1924*.[37] Thirdly, the Constitution had given the Commonwealth a general power of taxation and the *Income Tax Assessment Act 1915* (Cth) had been 'enacted to provide additional revenue for Australian involvement in World War I'.[38] With companies being a popular choice of business structure, they became a substantial proportion of taxpayers.

From 1961–1990

In the early 1960s, the States agreed to attempt greater uniformity of corporate legislation. The account in Chapter 2 has already described this as essentially identical legislation in each State. Collectively, the Companies Acts of the States were known as the *Uniform Companies Act*. Section 292 of the Act, known in South Australia as *Companies Act 1962* (SA), gave priority to taxes. The section read:

> (1) subject to the provisions of this Act, in a winding up there shall be paid in priority to all other unsecured debts–
>
> … (e) fifthly, the amount of all municipal or other local rates due from the company at the relevant date and having become due and payable within the twelve months next preceding that date, the amount of all land tax and income tax assessed under any Act or Act of the Commonwealth before the relevant date and not exceeding in the whole one year's assessment.

33 *Companies Act 1934* (SA) s279(1).

34 *Companies Act 1936* (NSW) s297(1)(d).

35 *Companies Act 1929* (UK).

36 Other jurisdictions have followed the English companies legislation and still have an expressed priority for tax. See e.g., *Companies Act 1965* (Malaysia) s292; *Companies Act 1967* (Singapore) s328.

37 *Bankruptcy Act 1924* (Cth).

38 Lehmann, G. and Coleman, C. *Taxation Law in Australia* (2nd ed. 1991) 7.

These Companies Acts were still State Acts and so the *Income Tax Assessment Act 1936* (Cth) referred solely to the order of insolvency priorities found in the *Bankruptcy Act 1966* (Cth), another Commonwealth Act.[39]

As State Acts, the *Uniform Companies Acts* could provide for the taxation priority but the law of a State cannot take from the Commonwealth its right to first priority for payment. Only a Commonwealth Act or an agreement by the Commonwealth could change the Commonwealth's order of priority.[40]

The new *Bankruptcy Act* (Cth) in 1966 gave a priority for income tax to the extent of one year's assessment.[41] The priority was granted for claims not exceeding in the whole the amount of one year's assessment, so it may have been an assessment in respect of any one year where more than one assessment was outstanding, and not necessarily in respect of the year immediately preceding the bankruptcy.[42] The priority was for tax actually assessed prior to the bankruptcy. Tax 'in excess of one year's assessment and … tax on income of the debtor derived to the date of bankruptcy but not assessed' was treated as ordinary unsecured debt.[43] These interpretations from the *Bankruptcy Act 1966* (Cth) wording were carried over into the liquidator's understanding of the priority that was detailed in the *Uniform Companies Acts*.

Section 217 of the *Uniform Companies Acts* stated that the provisions of the Act relating to priority of debts, inter alia, should bind the Crown. As these were State Acts the effect of this was that the Crown in right of a State waived its normal right of first priority in the payment of debts.

Later, s441 of the *Companies Code*, which was the main Commonwealth-State cooperative corporate legislation operating in Australia between 1981–1990, provided for tax priority payments. Section 441 provided:

> Subject to the following provisions of this Subdivision, in the winding up of a company the following debts shall be paid in priority to all other debts: … (h) eighth –
>
> (i) all amounts of rates, being rates that are, or are in the nature of, municipal or other local rates (other than rates imposed by an Act of the Commonwealth or a law of the Australian Capital Territory) that were due and payable at the relevant date and the liability for which accrued within the 12 months that next preceded that date;

39 *Income Tax Assessment Act 1936* (Cth) s221.
40 Mason, H. and O'Hair, J.S. *Australian Company Law* (2nd ed. 1973) 351.
41 *Bankruptcy Act 1966* (Cth) s109.
42 *Deputy Commissioner of Taxation v Stranger* (1934) 50 CLR 468.
43 Hayek, E.J. *Principles of Bankruptcy in Australia* (2nd ed. 1967) 74.

(ii) all amounts of income tax that were assessed under any act or Act of any other State or law of a Territory other than the Australian Capital Territory before the relevant date, not exceeding in the whole one year's assessment;

(iii) all amounts of land tax that were assessed under any Act or Act of any other State or law of a Territory other than the Australian Capital Territory before the relevant date, not exceeding in the whole one year's assessment;

(iv) all amounts of pay-roll tax (other than pay-roll tax imposed by an Act of the Commonwealth) that were due and payable at the relevant date;

During the period 1981–1990, the *Income Tax Assessment Act 1936* (Cth) continued to provide an order of priority for tax due in the winding up of a company and it referred to the order of priority in the *Bankruptcy Act 1966* (Cth). Again there was no mention in the income tax legislation of company legislation and the corporate insolvency priorities, as they were State based. Hence, there was a need for the abovementioned company legislation provisions. In s221 of the *Income Tax Assessment Act* 1936 (Cth), which was the section that dealt with tax due (not PAYE deductions or withholding tax deductions), the Commonwealth accepted payment after the costs of the winding up and employees' wages. A different arrangement existed in ss221P and 221YU,[44] which dealt with PAYE deductions not yet paid to the Commissioner and withholding tax deductions not yet paid to the Commissioner. In those sections, the priority was expressed as an absolute one, over all other debts.[45]

The *Crown Debts (Priority) Act 1981* (Cth) came into operation in July 1982 and this short Act provided that the Crown in right of the Commonwealth would be subject to State and Territory laws with respect to priority. Section 3 provided that

> [N]otwithstanding any prerogative right or privilege of the Crown in right of the Commonwealth, the Crown in right of the Commonwealth is subject to any provision of a law of a State or Territory – (a) relating to the order in which debts or liabilities of a body (whether corporate or unincorporate) are to be paid or discharged; (b) relating to the avoidance of preferences received by creditors of a body (whether corporate or unincorporate).

Section 4 excused ss 221P, 221YHJ or 221YU of the *Income Tax Assessment Act 1936* (Cth) from the operation of this Act and the Companies legislation.

44 *Income Tax Assessment Act 1936* (Cth) ss221P, 221YU.

45 Mason, H. and O'Hair, J.S. *Australian Company Law* (2nd ed. 1973) 351.

The Influential Reports that Recommended Removal

There were two reports which fashioned the removal of the government and taxation priorities.

Missen Report

In 1978 the Senate Standing Committee on Constitutional and Legal Affairs recommended the total abolition of all Crown priorities.[46] This was contained in a report titled *Priority of Crown Debts* and known as the Missen Report after the Chair of the Committee, Senator Tony Missen. As a result of this Report the *Crown Debts (Priority) Act 1981* (Cth) was enacted.

ALRC No 45 'Harmer Report'

As mentioned in Chapter 1, the Australian Law Reform Commission's Harmer Report in 1988 canvassed tax priorities. It recommended the removal of the tax priority and the main justifications for the removal were that:

> at the time, the ATO could allow taxation debts to accumulate without prejudicing its position and this might disadvantage other unsecured creditors who may not know that the group tax is owed;
>
> as the situation stood, the ATO had no incentive to recover payment in the normal commercial manner;
>
> in the late 1980s, these taxation debts were relatively insignificant from the point of view of total government receipts, but might be critical to a particular creditor;
>
> the abolition would not be significant in terms of total revenue;
>
> the ATO 'should obtain no greater priority than … [any other] person claiming in respect of debts misappropriated by an agent' (the agent being the insolvent company); and
>
> there would be a reduction in litigation.[47]

---

46 Australia, *Priority of Crown Debts,* Senate Standing Committee on Constitutional and Legal Affairs (Missen Report) (Canberra, 1978).

47 ALRC, *General Insolvency Inquiry*, Report No 45 (1988) ('Harmer Report') para 735.

Public policy issues suggest that there is a clear 'public interest in ensuring' that taxes are collected 'in an efficient manner and that government revenue' is not jeopardized.[48] Balanced with this is a 'strong community view',[49] according to submissions to the Harmer Report, that the ATO's priority should be abolished and so the Report recommended this course of action.[50]

There had been no priority for unpaid income tax since 1980, when the *Crown Debts (Priority) Act 1981* (Cth) abolished it as a priority debt. 'Notwithstanding [that], until 1993 the Commonwealth did retain some priority in relation to some tax liability'.[51] Eventually, the Federal Government took up the Harmer Report recommendation and Parliament enacted the *Insolvency (Tax Priorities) Legislation Amendment Act* 1993 (Cth).

An Infamous Section

Section 221P of the *Income Tax Assessment Act 1936* (Cth)[52] provided that

> Where an employer makes a deduction for the purposes of this Division [the Division requiring employers to deduct tax] … from the salary or wages paid to an employee and refuses or fails to deal with the amount so deducted in the manner required by this Division [the Division prescribes how it shall be remitted] … he shall be liable, and where his property has become vested in, or where the control of his property has passed to, a trustee, the trustee shall be liable, to pay the amount to the Commissioner.

The court in *Barnes*[53] established that s221P applied whether the defaulting employer remained in control of the whole of their property or the whole of that property had vested in or passed under the control of a 'trustee', including a receiver.

48 Ibid. para 737.

49 Ibid. para 738.

50 Ibid. para 741.

51 Keay, A. *McPherson The Law of Company Liquidation* (4th ed. 1999) 604. The author is referring to *Income Tax Assessment Act 1936* (Cth) s221P.

52 A number of helpful articles have tried to explain the intricacies of this provision: see e.g., Coleman, C.F. 'The Commissioner of Taxation's Advantage Over Other Creditors on Insolvency', paper presented to ALTA 46th Annual Conference,12 July 1991, UWA; Coleman, C. 'The Commissioner's Advantage' (1992) 26/6 Taxation In Australia 318; Sutherland, G. and Lee, B. 'Secured Creditors v Federal Commissioner of Taxation Priorities under s221P of the Income Tax Assessment Act' (1985) 17/5 *Commercial Law Association Newsletter* 87; Brealey, D.T. 'Section 221P of the Income Tax Assessment Act; A Garrotte for the Secured Creditor?' (1987) 5 *Companies and Securities Law Journal* 12.

53 *Commissioner of Taxation v Barnes* (1975) 133 CLR 483 ('*Barnes' case*').

Then, in *Smith and Judge v Deputy Commissioner of Taxation*,[54] Brinsden J in the Western Australian Supreme Court held that a secured creditor could not avoid the section by simply electing not to appoint a receiver and allowing a liquidator to administer in insolvency. In such cases the liquidator, having the necessary control pursuant to his or her appointment, took subject to the Commissioner's priority.

The principles by which s221P applied were complex and the position in the mid 1980s was 'far from settled' as secured creditors devised new techniques in an attempt to avoid the Commissioner's priority.[55] Most of the litigation arose from the interpretation of the phrase 'control' of the company's property. *Barnes'* case[56] held that the 'control' must be over all the company's property, subject to any assets specifically charged, otherwise control did not pass to the trustee. For liquidations it was a little clearer as the appointment of a liquidator meant control of the property passed to the liquidator and if a specific asset was subject to a charge then the liquidator gained control of the company's equitable interest in that asset (in the sense used in *Barnes'* case).[57]

Section 221P[58] was said to have few friends and many critics.[59] Justice Menzies in *Card*'s case[60] said the section was 'an incredibly ill-drawn section'.[61] Justice Brinsden in *Smith and Judge*[62] said the extent of the operation of the section remained 'a matter of considerable uncertainty and the section clearly calls for amendment'.[63] Justice Gibbs in *Barnes'* case[64] said the section 'presents considerable difficulties of construction'.[65]

The effect of s221P was to make the liquidator liable to pay out of the property that passed under their control the amount of any tax deductions from the salary or wages of an employee to the Commissioner of Taxation. These were amounts that had not been made in the statutorily prescribed manner by the company. Section 221P(2) made this amount payable in priority to all other debt, whether preferential, secured or unsecured, but this was qualified by s221P(3)[66] to the extent

---

54 78 ATC 4561.

55 Sutherland, G. and Lee, B. 'Secured Creditors v Federal Commissioner of Taxation Priorities under s221P of the Income Tax Assessment Act' (1985) 17/5 *Commercial Law Association Newsletter* 87, 90.

56 (1975) 133 CLR 483, 499.

57 Op.cit. at 89.

58 *Income Tax Assessment Act 1936* (Cth) s221P.

59 Sutherland, G. and Lee, B. 'Secured Creditors v Federal Commissioner of Taxation Priorities under s.221P of the Income Tax Assessment Act' (1985) 17/5 *Commercial Law Association Newsletter* 87, 91.

60 *Commissioner of Taxation v Card* (1963) 109 CLR 177 ('*Card's case*').

61 Ibid. 194.

62 78 ATC 4561.

63 *Smith and Judge v Deputy Commissioner of Taxation* 78 ATC 4561, 4565.

64 (1975) 133 CLR 483.

65 Ibid. 498.

66 *Income Tax Assessment Act1936* (Cth) s 221P(3).

of permitting prior payment of the costs and expenses of winding up where these were payable in priority to all other debts in the winding up. Since, by virtue of s556(1)(a) of the Corporations Law (now the *Corporations Act*), the expenses of winding up were payable as a priority, it followed that the effect of s221P(3) was to relegate any amount due under s221P to the status of second priority in winding up. However, such a high priority meant that, in most estates, the Commissioner received what was owed or, if not, at least more than any other creditors.

As a trade off for abolishing any tax priority, a regime for dealing with unremitted group tax deductions was introduced in 1993 at the same time as the abolition of the priority and it is contained in Division 8 of the *Income Tax Assessment Act* 1936 (Cth). The Division empowers the Commissioner of Taxation to begin recovery proceedings much sooner than was permitted previously. Division 9 of the *Income Tax Assessment Act* 1936 (Cth) applies specifically to companies and has the potential of imposing penalties on company directors. As a consequence of the operation of ss222AOB and 222APB, duties are imposed on directors to cause their company either to comply with payment obligations, enter into a payment agreement, appoint an administrator under Part 5.3A of the *Corporations Act 2001*(Cth) or initiate the winding up process.

In 1993 when the abolition of the tax priority took place, the statutory order of priorities was laid down by s556 of the Corporations Law. It was essentially State legislation and was therefore subject to the overriding force of any valid Commonwealth legislation dealing with the same subject matter; where two such enactments are inconsistent the latter will, by virtue of s109 of the Commonwealth Constitution,[67] prevail and the former will be to that extent invalid. However there were few instances of Commonwealth legislation dealing with the matter of priorities in winding up, the only examples being ss221, 221YHJ, 221YHZD and 221YU of the *Income Tax Assessment Act 1936* (Cth). These provisions, which dealt with the priority of unremitted group tax (from the salaries and wages of employees), withholding tax on dividends or interest, unremitted deductions from prescribed payments tax and unremitted deductions from natural resource or royalty payment, respectively, were in similar form. In light of this, it is convenient to focus only on s221P.

The Harmer Report indicated that the submissions that the ALRC had received in relation to tax priority favoured abolition,[68] and it concluded that there was 'a strong community view' supporting abolition.[69] Eventually, the Federal

67 Australian Constitution s109.

68 Harmer Report, para 738, fn 47. These submissions included those by the Small Business Corporation of SA, G. McDonald, IPAA, ICAA and ASA, Australian Finance Conference, Australian Bankers Association, N.J. Pocock, D. Nelthorpe, Queensland Law Society, Corporate Affairs Commissioner (WA). Copies of all these submissions held by the writer.

69 Harmer Report, para 738.

Government took up the recommendation and Parliament enacted the *Insolvency (Tax Priorities) Legislation Amendment Act 1993* (Cth).

As a result of this Act there are now very limited claims by the Commissioner of Taxation. Under ss221P, 221YHJ, 221YHZD and 221YU of the *Income Tax Assessment Act 1936* (Cth), neither the Commissioner nor any Crown instrumentality is entitled to a special priority in liquidation.

As a postscript to the infamous s221P, it is interesting to note a recent case that questioned the absolute removal of tax as an insolvency priority. In *Deputy Commissioner of Taxation v Dexcam Australia Pty Ltd (in liq)*,[70] the Deputy Commissioner of Taxation (DCT) had been a creditor in Dexcam's Deed of Company Arrangement (DOCA) and had participated in the deed including submitting proofs of debt. The DCT had submitted amended proofs of debt which took into account the purported application of the Prescribed Payments Scheme credits and interest under s221YHG of the *Income Tax Assessment Act 1936* (Cth) and s13(1) of the *Taxation (Interest on Overpayments and Early Payments) Act 1983* (Cth). Dexcam went into liquidation in January 1998 after the DOCA was terminated. As discussed above, the *Insolvency (Tax Priorities) Legislation Amendment Act 1993* (Cth) abolished the priority enjoyed by the Commonwealth conferred by ss221P, 221YHJ, 221YHZD and 221YU of the *Income Tax Assessment Act* 1936 (Cth). The purpose of the Act was to abolish debts due to the Crown in the right of the Commonwealth and made specific reference to the above four sections. Justice Finn in *Dexcam*[71] observed that there was nothing in the language of the legislation to suggest a legislative purpose beyond those four sections. This left s221YHG which was not expressly subject to the abolition. It was a provision that required the Commissioner to apply various tax credits in payments of other tax or designated debts of the person otherwise entitled to those credits.

To determine whether the absolute removal of the Commissioner's priority has been successful is problematic, and the recent decision in *Deputy Commissioner of Taxation v Dexcam Australia Pty Ltd (in liq)*,[72] supports such a position. A staff member at the ATO expressed the view that their department would not have agreed to a removal if it was not going to be beneficial and they have not called for its re-introduction.[73]

One of the justifications for the removal of the Commissioner's taxation priority was to facilitate a larger distribution from the insolvent company's

70 *Deputy Commissioner of Taxation v Dexcam Australia Pty Ltd (in liq)* [2003] FCAFC 148 (2003) 21 ACLC 1370.

71 *Deputy Commissioner of Taxation v Dexcam Australia Pty Ltd (in liq)* [2003] FCAFC 148, para 52 (2003) 21 ACLC 1370, 1383.

72 *Deputy Commissioner of Taxation v Dexcam Australia Pty Ltd (in liq)* [2003] FCAFC 148 (2003) 21 ACLC 1370.

73 Interview with Paul Kenny, Policy Adviser, ATO (Adelaide, 14 September, 2004).

estate to unsecured creditors.[74] Whether this has been achieved is unknown. The Commissioner's published statistics before 1993 were limited to amounts of money outstanding by companies. This would have included solvent and insolvent companies and so it is not possible to identify the amount owed by insolvent companies. Then because of the lack of statistics from the former Australian Securities Commission and its predecessors no amount distributed to unsecured creditors from insolvent company administration can be identified prior to 1993. Essentially there are no figures to compare.

Another of the reasons for the removal of the taxation priority was the value to the Government in promoting the fact that they were willing to move downward in the list of distribution. While this presented the government of the day in a good light, sceptics could argue that the secured creditors continue to take much of the insolvent company's assets. Therefore, the removal did not have the impact of promoting those lower down the distribution list, such as priority and unsecured creditors, so that they would receive a dividend.

Present Treatment of Taxation

Division 9 of the *Income Tax Assessment Act* 1936 (Cth) applies specifically to companies and has the potential of imposing penalties on company directors. As a consequence of the operation of ss222AOB and 222APB of the *Income Tax Assessment Act* 1936 (Cth), duties are imposed on directors to cause their company either to comply with payment obligations, enter into a payment agreement, or appoint an administrator under Part 5.3A of the *Corporations Act 2001* (Cth) to initiate the winding up process.
According to Keay

> [I]t should be noted that the taxation authorities still have ways of, in effect, obtaining a priority. Where a person owed money to a company and was served with a notice issued under s 36 of the *Sales Tax Assessment Act 1930* (Cth)[75] or s218 of the *Income Tax Assessment Act 1936* (Cth), he or she is required to pay the amount owing to the Commissioner of Taxation, instead of the company, in payment of sales tax or income tax payable by the company.[76]

These 'provisions confer a statutory charge upon the Commissioner as soon as the notices are served on the third party. From that moment, the debts cease to be assets available to a liquidator of the company in the winding up'.[77]

---

74 Harmer Report, para 737.

75 This Act has been replaced by the Goods and Services Tax legislation and has limited application.

76 Keay, A. *McPherson The Law of Company Liquidation* (4th ed. 1999) 605.

77 Ibid.

The Legislators' Viewpoint

It is helpful, in light of what has transpired since 1993, to review the parliamentary debates that preceded the removal of tax priorities. The debates ranged over a number of areas such as whether the new legislation removing tax as a priority would be good for employees, and whether it would contribute to making the voluntary administration system work. Also there was concern whether it would overcome 'credit apathy' in the ATO towards these taxpayers.

The Senate's Justifications for Removal

In 1993, Senator McMullan introduced the Insolvency (Tax Priorities) Legislation Amendment Bill into the Senate.[78] In his second reading speech, he said the new legislation was abolishing the existing priority of the Commissioner of Taxation for debts in relation to certain unremitted amounts.[79] The changes meant that the Commissioner would be able to recover the unremitted amounts more quickly through an estimation process and it would encourage company directors to face emerging financial problems as soon as possible.[80]

Prior to this legislation the Commissioner's taxation priority applied to amounts deducted by employers from the salary or wages of their employees, and deductions of a similar nature, where those deductions were not paid to the Commissioner. The new legislation resulted in debts due to the Commissioner because of a failure to remit amounts deducted being treated in a similar manner to debts payable to other unsecured creditors.[81]

Senator McMullan remarked that the removal of the Commissioner's taxation priority was essential to the smooth operation of the scheme of voluntary administration to be introduced under new insolvency provisions of the Corporations Law in June 1993.[82] He added that '[A]ny loss of revenue from abolishing the priority will be offset by the revenue recovered under the new recovery regime.'[83] And he went on to point out to the Senate that 'the revenue recovered belongs to employees or payees and has been deducted but not remitted to the Commissioner as required by law'.[84]

Senator Watson, during debate in the Senate, suggested that there were three limbs to this Bill.[85] The first limb sought to ensure that employees' entitlements

78 Australia, Senate, *Debates*, 19 May 1993, 879 (Senator Robert McMullan).
79 Ibid.
80 Ibid.
81 Ibid. 880.
82 Ibid.
83 Ibid.
84 Ibid.
85 Australia, Senate, *Debates*, 26 May 1993, 1296 (Senator J.O.W. Watson).

and the rights of unsecured creditors, which might otherwise have been lost, would be protected. He described this as a 'good measure' and continued;

> This is a change that is sustainable for the pragmatic reason that the Consolidated Revenue is better able to sustain a reduction of the proceeds from an insolvency administration than employees or unsecured creditors might be. The pain caused to employees who have been left with nothing after the collapse of their employer and to unsecured creditors who have had to write off huge losses because of the failure of a major debtor should not be underestimated.[86]

Unfortunately though, with hindsight, this was not the effect. The media reports during 1999 and 2000 of the failure in the system to meet employee entitlements demonstrated that the changes of 1993 did not alleviate the 'pain'.[87]

Senator Watson's second limb was that the abolition of the priority would remove what may have been a cause of the new voluntary administration scheme 'falling into a heap almost immediately upon its introduction'.[88]

Perhaps the removal of the tax priority contributed to what is generally acknowledged by practitioners and academics as the success of the voluntary administration scheme.[89] However there has been no research to establish such a link.

Senator Watson's third limb was that the legislation would provide for a more effective way of collecting unremitted amounts held by entities on behalf of the Commissioner, by way of a new estimates procedure.[90] It would also provide a means to force company directors to confront insolvency problems before being tempted to use deducted amounts as 'emergency working capital'.[91]

Again, no research has been carried out on whether there is now a more effective collection of tax. Indeed the more recent reported experiences of employees missing out on entitlements suggest that unscrupulous directors are continuing to use employee entitlements as 'emergency working capital'.[92]

---

86 Ibid.

87 For example, the losses of entitlements for employees at Cobar Mines, National Textiles and later the Ansett failure. See e.g., Chapter 5 above; See also, Dodson, L. and Martin, C. 'Howard Bails out Workers' *Australian Financial Review* (Sydney), 9 February 2000, 14; Callus, R. 'Employees' entitlements up in the Air' *Canberra Times* (Canberra), 17 September 2001, 11.

88 Australia, Senate, *Debates*, 26 May 1993, 1296 (Senator J.O.W. Watson).

89 For example Philip Crutchfield in the foreword to Anderson, C. and Morrison, D. *Crutchfield's Corporate Voluntary Administration* (3rd ed. 2003) expresses the view that the 'perceived' success has been noted by UK legislators.

90 Australia, Senate, *Debates*, 26 May 1993, 1296 (Senator J.O.W. Watson).

91 Ibid.

92 Behaviour like using tax deductions from employees is hard to prove and failures like Oakdale Mines and National Textiles had satisfactory resolutions to their much publicised collapses and so avoided such scrutiny.

Senator Kernot, then leader of the Australian Democrats, supported the new legislation. She observed that the new legislation was designed to protect the revenue[93] and that the reason for the abolition was probably industrial in nature. She spoke of the existence of some vigorous complaints from various unions about the unfair nature of the priority as it previously stood.[94] She went on to cite examples from the building and textile industry as major instances where workers had not been paid directly, and nor had their deductions been paid to the ATO.[95] In light of this, she said that the legislative measure was 'fair to employees and other creditors'.[96]

Senator Kernot showed clarity in her understanding of what the legislation was attempting to achieve. In supporting the move to make directors remit the amounts of tax to the ATO, she observed that the principle was quite simple.[97] In her view at no time was the tax ever the property of the directors; it was the income of the employee and it was claimed by the government as a prepayment of an employee's tax liability for the year.[98] If the directors did not fulfil the duty to remit the money to the ATO they were, in her opinion, 'committing theft'.[99] These may seem strong words, suggesting that the company and its directors are thieves, yet some seven years later in 2000 legislation was passed making some director behaviour relating to deprivation of employee entitlements subject to criminal consequences.[100]

Senator Kernot's contribution to the debate focused on employees and rejected the request to delay the legislation put forward by the Liberal Opposition, stating that the Senate should not 'hold up the rightful place of workers in the line of creditors'.[101] She was uninterested in delay and the request to give more time for those looking to discuss directors' penalties. As she observed; 'there is one easy way for directors to avoid the problem and that is to remit the taxation as they are supposed to'. She went on with her 'theft' theme: '[I]f they do not remit moneys that they have withheld as tax, they are committing theft and theft involves penalties'.[102]

The Bill passed the Senate without more debate.

93 Australia, Senate, *Debates*, 26 May 1993, 1297 (Senator Cheryl Kernot).
94 Ibid.
95 Ibid.
96 Ibid.
97 Ibid. 1298.
98 Ibid.
99 Ibid.
100 *Corporations Law Amendment (Employee Entitlements) Act 2000* (Cth).
101 Australia, Senate, *Debates*, 26 May 1993, 1298 (Senator Cheryl Kernot).
102 Ibid.

The House of Representatives Debate

In the House of Representatives, Mr Rocher explained the need for new legislation in these terms:

> [A]s the situation now stands these arrangements can cause considerable hardship for employees as a result of an insolvency because the ATO's priority means that there is little or nothing left for employees and other creditors following the payment of these outstanding taxes.[103]

He concentrated on the position that the ATO would be in post-legislation, noting that it would be on an equal footing with other creditors, as might be expected.[104]

He offered this justification for the change to the legislation:

> [W]hile the unpaid funds which are the subject of this Bill are not assets of the company, there is always the temptation for companies to make use of deductions on behalf of employees as emergency working capital which can be ultimately disastrous for the employees.[105]

Mr Swan expressed the opinion that it is simply a false economy to put the Commissioner of Taxation ahead of employees and other small businesses in terms of insolvency. In his analysis the insolvent company has two choices: to enter a voluntary administration or a wind up voluntarily and regardless of which path is chosen it should mean 'that the company does not continue … to accumulate huge debts to the Taxation Office, thereby prolonging and creating an even bigger problem for itself and for its employees'.[106]

Mr Rocher was prepared to support the legislation because one of the many problems he saw with the existing arrangements was that the size of the debts owed to the ATO had been allowed to grow to ridiculous proportions.[107] He suggested this was because the ATO was too slow to recoup the money that it was owed by the insolvent entity. Under the existing legislation in 1993, the ATO had no incentive to take quick and decisive action in these cases because its priority under the existing arrangements guaranteed that it would get its money regardless

103 Australia, House of Representatives, *Debates*, 27 May 1993, 1125 (Mr Rocher MHR – Curtin).

104 Ibid. 1126.

105 Ibid. 1127.

106 Australia, House of Representatives, *Debates*, 27 May 1993, 1131 (Mr Swan MHR – Lilley).

107 Australia, House of Representatives, *Debates*, 27 May 1993, 1127 (Mr Rocher MHR – Curtin).

of the consequences that might have for other creditors and, most importantly, employees.[108]

Mr Bevis[109] noted that:

> [R]egrettably, employers faced with a liquidity problem have in some cases found the need or the desire to hold onto that money and not remit it to the Tax Office. Equally regrettably, it would appear that for some time the Tax Office has not been particularly efficient in its perusal, policing and collection of that money [110]

He concluded that employers who decide to solve their short-term liquidity problems by dipping into the employees' pocket, which is effectively what they do when they hold onto that group tax, should face the force of the law.[111] Mr Bevis said '[I]t is not their money, never was, never will be and should not be held by them on behalf of the employees out of the employees' income. It should be seen fairly and squarely in that light'.[112] He finished his contribution to the debate by acknowledging that they are deductions from employees' wages and employers should never use them for any purpose other than payment of tax. Employers who did otherwise were not only breaking the law but also breaching the confidence and trust of their employees.[113]

Mr Rocher also saw the crucial benefit for the voluntary administration system of the change to the legislation.[114] He told the House that creditors would not agree to use the voluntary administration procedure if the only or principal beneficiary for such an arrangement was the ATO because of its priority under the existing arrangements.[115] The ATO needed to be put on an equal footing with other creditors to permit some entities to trade out of difficulty and do so effectively.[116]

The Lower House heard that the new legislation would afford employees a greater measure of protection than was available under current arrangements.

Mr Swan for one was convinced that employees would have much improved prospects of being paid their outstanding wages and for that reason alone he saw

108 Ibid.

109 Australia, House of Representatives, *Debates*, 27 May 1993, 1134 (Mr Bevis MHR – Brisbane).

110 Ibid.

111 Ibid.

112 Ibid.

113 Ibid. 1135.

114 Australia, House of Representatives, *Debates*, 27 May 1993, 1127 (Mr Rocher MHR – Curtin).

115 Ibid.

116 Ibid.

the legislation as 'an historic reform ... [it] gives workers and others a better go'.[117]

Parliament was told during the debate in 1993 that most sectors of the community and legal profession supported the change to remove the tax priority. Mr Swan suggested 'it is pretty hard to find many people who have a bad word to say about [the removal of the priority]. Let us say goodbye and good riddance to the old legislation and welcome the new legislation as a very substantial reforming achievement'.[118]

Mr Williams[119] told the Parliament that there were very good reasons for the abolition of the priority. Firstly, he said the priority assures that the Commissioner receives payment and consequently that the Commissioner is under no pressure to recover unremitted taxes in the normal commercial manner.[120] Secondly, Mr Williams believed that by allowing taxation debts to accumulate without any real risk, the Commissioner might seriously disadvantage other secured creditors. Mr Williams understood that under the law as it stood then the Commissioner could decide to let an employer continue trading even though group tax was owing, and other creditors [such as small traders and employees] who would not be privy to this information and might ultimately be disadvantaged if the business later went into liquidation.[121]

Mr Cadman[122] bemoaned that the Commissioner of Taxation has got into the queue ahead of those with claims for the first payment of wages and salaries. He commented that

> workers' rights have been denied, as have the rights of a whole range of people whether they be suppliers, people leasing property, landlords or others who come together when there is difficulty in the company.[123]

He, too, was optimistic that the legislation would remedy the situation for more than just employees. He noted that employees and other creditors, particularly small business people and subcontractors, are in the same position as employees when firms go under. He hoped that the Government's initiatives in removing the

117 Australia, House of Representatives, *Debates*, 27 May 1993, 1130 (Mr Swan MHR – Lilley).

118 Australia, House of Representatives, *Debates*, 27 May 1993, 1130 (Mr Swan MHR – Lilley).

119 Australia, House of Representatives, *Debates*, 27 May 1993, 1131 (Mr Williams MHR – Tangney).

120 Ibid. 1132.

121 Ibid.

122 Australia, House of Representatives, *Debates*, 27 May 1993, 1136 (Mr Cadman MHR – Mitchell).

123 Ibid.

tax priority would give these employees and other creditors a greater opportunity to recoup their outstanding claims.[124]

The final Government speaker in the debate was Mr Bevis, who would later play a major role in the changes to the employees' priority in the late 1990s. During the debate he stated that the prime beneficiaries of the removal of the tax priority were likely to be the former employees of those firms that faced insolvency.[125] Mr Bevis believed that the legislation would ensure that in future employees would have greater access to their entitlements in the event of the firms for which they worked becoming insolvent.[126]

Mr. Bevis claimed that

> [I]n the past it has been a sad fact that, with the priority claim the Commissioner of Taxation has on those moneys, those employees left without a job and little resources to support themselves found themselves unable to get their wages, long service leave and other entitlements to which they were due.[127]

Arguably, this situation did not change until 2000, with the implementation of the Employee Entitlements Support Scheme (EESS).[128]

Significantly Mr Williams,[129] representing the Liberal opposition, conceded that the taxation debts of insolvents are insignificant in terms of total government receipts.[130] He even conceded that 'the amount foregone by a private creditor may be the difference between the creditor surviving or failing'.[131] He summarized that 'if one wants to put that in terms of looking after workers, employees, and looking after small businessmen [sic], we (the Liberal Opposition) agree wholeheartedly with that proposition'.[132] This was a major shift from the early 1980s when the Liberal Party in government were called upon to support an amendment to the Crown Debts (Priority) Bill that would have achieved a very similar outcome.[133]

124 Ibid.

125 Australia, House of Representatives, *Debates*, 27 May 1993, 1134 (Mr Bevis MHR – Brisbane).

126 Ibid.

127 Australia, House of Representatives, *Debates*, 27 May 1993, 1134 (Mr Bevis MHR – Brisbane).

128 See Chapter 5 above.

129 Australia, House of Representatives, *Debates*, 27 May 1993, 1132 (Mr Williams MHR – Tangney).

130 Ibid.

131 Ibid.

132 Ibid.

133 Australia, House of Representatives, *Debates*, 13 May 1993, 2345 (Mr Brown MHR– Parramatta); 2347 (Mr Moore MHR – Ryan); Senate, *Debates*, 28 May 1981, 2291 – 2293 (Senator Tate).

Synopsis of Debates

In summary, the concerns during 1993 were the slow debt recovery by the ATO, the wish to make corporate rescue legislation work, and to assist employees to be paid wages and other entitlements owing from failed corporate employers. With the benefit of hindsight a review of these concerns can conclude that the corporate rescue legislation has been a tremendous success, but it would not be possible to attribute this to the removal of the tax priority. The assistance that the removal provided for employees was probably minimal. Since 2000, the Federal Government has needed to introduce two administrative schemes (EESS[134] and GEERS[135]) to pay employee entitlements. This suggests that the issue of recovering such entitlements was still a major problem seven years after the removal of essentially all tax priorities. Whether the debt recovery of the ATO has been speeded up by removing the tax priority is debatable and hard to ascertain from available public records.[136]

Comparative Aspects

Governments around the world have been removing their priorities for taxation and other debts. The most appropriate jurisdictions to make comparisons with the abovementioned Australian treatment are the United States of America, the United Kingdom and Canada. As the International Bar Association[137] has asked members from a number of countries to report the priorities it is worthwhile to take at least a superficial look at the responses in civil and other common law countries.

United States of America[138]

There are significant parallels to the debate in the United States as to the possible removal of a tax priority. Although the motivation in the United States was not

134 Employee Entitlements Support Scheme; See Chapter 5 above.

135 General Employee Entitlements and Redundancy Scheme; See Chapter 5 above.

136 Duns, J. and Glover, J. 'The Taxation Priority: Australian Experience and International Comparisons' (Paper presented at the INSOL Academics Meeting, Cape Town, South Africa 1 April 2004) 20. This paper quotes the writer and appears to support the conclusion presented herein. The Duns and Glover paper is now published (2005) 14 (3) *International Insolvency Review* 171.

137 Committee J, International Bar Association, *Taskforce Report on Priority Claims in Insolvency Administration* (1993).

138 Significant literature on the topic includes Plumb, W.T. 'The Tax Recommendations of the Commission on the Bankruptcy Laws – Priority and Dischargeability of Tax Claims' (1974) 59 *Cornell Law Review* 991; Morgan, B.K. 'Should the Sovereign be Paid First? A Comparative International Analysis of the Priority of Tax Claims in Bankruptcy' (2000)

necessarily to change the law of corporate rescue, the idea of corporate rescue certainly hovered in the background.[139]

In the 1960s Congress was of the opinion that as a revenue item the loss to the government through unpaid tax from insolvent companies was slight and more good could be achieved through the removal of the government priority.

In 1967, Harold Marsh, who later became Chairman of the Bankruptcy Commission in the United States, asked 'does the traditional rule which has granted priority to all tax claims, at least over all general non-priority creditors, rest upon anything more than a naked assertion of power based upon the fact that this particular creditor happens to be writing the rules of distribution?'[140] Such a question can be asked of any government that maintains a government priority.

Marsh was a significant agitator for change in the 1960s and 1970s.[141] In 1972, while chair of the Bankruptcy Commission, he proposed a radical change to United States public policy with the abolishing all tax liens and priorities on the grounds that the amount realized was insignificant in light of the total revenues.[142] The minutes of the Bankruptcy Commission record that the Justice and Treasury Departments spent far more money attempting to collect the government debt by using the priority and lien provisions than was ever realized.[143]

In 1975 the Tax Division of the Justice's Department opposed legislative attempts to send the tax priority to a lower position. They reasoned that if such

---

74 *American Bankruptcy Law Journal* 461; McCoid, J.C. 'Statutory Liens in Bankruptcy' (1994) 68 *American Bankruptcy Law Journal* 269; Williams, J.F. and Ogier, T.M. 'A Collision of Policy' (1999) 50 *South Carolina Law Review* 313; Feibelman, A. 'Federal Bankruptcy Law and State Sovereign Immunity' (2003) 81 *Texas Law Review* 1381; Shanker, M.G. 'The Worthier Creditors (and a Cheer for the King)' (1976) 1 *Canadian Business Law Journal* 340; Arner, M.R. 'The Worthier Creditors (and a Cheer for the King) – Revisited' (1979) 53 *American Bankruptcy Law Journal* 389; Dunham, D. and Shimkus, A. 'Tax Claims in Bankruptcy' (1993) 67 *American Bankruptcy Law Journal* 343; Mann, R.J. 'Bankruptcy and the Entitlements of the Government: Whose Money is it Anyway?' (1995) *New York University Law Review* 993.

139 There were a number of significant events in the debate on tax priorities, including Stanley, D.T. and Girth, M. *Bankruptcy Problems Process Reform* prepared for the Brookings Institute and know as the *Brookings Report* in 1971, the Bankruptcy Commission hearings in 1972 and the ensuing report in 1974, *Report of the Commission on the Bankruptcy Laws of the United States* (1973), the Commission Bill (HR 31, S 236) and the Judges' Bill (HR 32, S 235) that formed part of the Bankruptcy Reform Act hearings. A fuller treatment is provided by Carruthers, B.G. and Halliday, T.C. *Rescuing Business: The Making of Corporate Bankruptcy Law in England and the United States* (1998) 215–222.

140 Marsh, H. 'Triumph or Tragedy? The Bankruptcy Act Amendments of 1966' (1967) 42 *Washington Law Review* 681, 729.

141 Ibid. Harold Marsh, 'Triumph or Tragedy?' and his role as Chairman of the Bankruptcy Commission 1972.

142 Report of the Commission on the Bankruptcy Laws of the United States H R Doc No 93–137, 93d Cong, 1st sess. (1973) Part II 4–606.

143 Minutes of the Bankruptcy Commission, 11–12 September 1972, 23.

proposals were implemented they would have a serious and detrimental effect on the enforcement of the tax laws and on corporate debtor attitudes to insolvency. Such a move would 'destroy the tax debtor's incentive to satisfy his tax obligations and encourages the use of tax money to finance failing businesses'.[144] They claimed that it would also have a substantial impact on the confidence of the public in the fairness of the tax collection system. The Tax Division also argued that a change would create new incentives for creditors to put the debtor into an insolvent administration and thus increase their potential distributions. It seemed to escape them that these distributions are creditors' money anyhow.

A quite unusual hypothesis put by the United States government in the 1970s was that on sociological premises there is a need in modern society to rely on a culture of taxation compliance.[145] Their argument was that the tax priority should not be surrendered because governments themselves depend upon certain 'institutional moralities, which are bases of legitimation, and without which they could not function'.[146] They were arguing that to lose the tax priority would be to put at risk the whole collection of taxes and would change peoples' attitude toward paying tax.

The Bankruptcy Commission in 1970 was not successful in removing the priority, but did achieve the introduction of time limits. The Bankruptcy Code currently grants a statutory priority to a wide variety of Federal, State and local tax claims. The categories of tax claims entitled to priority in a corporate bankruptcy Chapter 7 (liquidations) or Chapter 11 (reorganizations) case are '(1) income or gross receipts tax (three years), (2) property tax (one year), (3) taxes required to be collected or withheld (no [time limit]), (4) employment tax on wages, salaries, commissions (three years), (5) excise tax (three years), (6) customs duties (one year) and (7) penalties for the [above]'.[147] The tax priority sits below priorities for both administrative expense and employee entitlements' priorities.[148]

The United Kingdom Tax Priority

The early history of the tax priority in the United Kingdom has already been mentioned in the chapter. By the 1990s the British government could not maintain

144 Bankruptcy Reform Act Hearings on Senate 235 and Senate 236, 782 (Scott Crampton, Tax Division Justice Department, United States of America).

145 Arner, M.R. 'The Worthier Creditors (and a Cheer for the King) – Revisited' (1979) 53 *American Bankruptcy Law Journal* 389, 303.

146 Carruthers, B.G. and Halliday, T.C. *Rescuing Business: The Making of Corporate Bankruptcy Law in England and the United States* (1998) 241.

147 Morgan, B. 'Should the Sovereign be Paid First? A Comparative International Analysis of the Priority for Tax Claims in Bankruptcy' (2000) 74 *American Bankruptcy Law Journal* 461, 488.

148 *Bankruptcy Code* 11 USC 507 (a) (8) (A), (B), (C), (D), (E), (F) and (G).

the tax priority because it could not get 'any sympathy from the private sector over its long delays in collecting back-taxes'.[149] This 'rank inefficiency merely confirmed to private creditors that the government needed stronger incentives to keep abreast of taxpayer delinquency'.[150] This type of credit slackness was a luxury that unsecured creditors could not afford and so it was not surprising that as a group they had no sympathy for the government priority.

Furthermore there was not a direct link that was obvious to creditors that a government, in missing out on taxes, would not produce expenditure on health or education or defence. This meant that the British government and its tax authority had few, if any, allies when it recommended the tax priority should continue in 1985. In effect, the government was pitted against every other creditor or stakeholder, including consumer groups, professionals, the finance industry and major business groups.[151]

The opponents of a tax priority used many strong arguments. One was the principle of equity.[152] It seemed unfair that the government with all its powers of coercion should get priority as a creditor. The government had an enviable position of being able to write their own rules and grant itself strong claims amongst limited estates. This led to a strong call to reform because of this perceived unfairness. It was 'somewhat to the government's surprise' that it 'discovered how unfair most [opponents] judged the taxman's special advantages'.[153]

Next is the argument that the removal of the tax priority would assist in the drive to rescue companies. Rescuing business had become an important feature of insolvency law and practice. Many creditors could appreciate that a tax debt in one company would represent 'a minute proportion of revenue to the government' yet could be 'a major amount of revenue for small creditors, mostly small businesses'.[154] Therefore for those companies it was an obvious reform to remove the tax priority.[155]

The 'professions [in the United Kingdom] played a critical role ...' in the removal of the tax priority.[156] 'They knew the history and theory of bankruptcy law and could construe its contemporary relevance in convincing ways'.[157] Once the professionals called for change they were seen to have 'convincing authority [as

149 Carruthers, B.G. and Halliday, T.C. *Rescuing Business: The Making of Corporate Bankruptcy Law in England and the United States* (1998) 223 and 240.

150 Ibid. 240.

151 Ibid.

152 Ibid. 227.

153 Ibid. 223.

154 Ibid.

155 Ibid. 242.

156 Ibid. 242–3.

157 Ibid.

to] how things worked in practice', particularly in producing evidence of creditors missing out because of the priority claimed by government.[158]

Removal of the United Kingdom's Tax Priority

In 1982, the Cork Committee[159] began with the presumption that all priorities should be abolished. Priorities worked against principles of equity and harmed the weakest creditors, and the existing priorities diverted resources from company reorganizations.[160] This was particularly true of government priorities.

Carruthers and Halliday[161] express it this way:

> Taxes are equivalent to the property rights of the state … [and] … the mechanisms of fiscal extraction … become critically important in the capacity of the state to carry out one of its most basic functions. Its capacity to capture lost or delayed revenues should not have been impaired in the area of bankruptcy law for the state was not only the most powerful of creditors, but the ultimate arbiter of the rules by which all creditors played. *As a referee, it could enhance its capacity as a player*. [emphasis added].

This priority position represented not just a fiscal asset to the government, but a political liability as well.[162]

Eventually, s251 of the *Enterprise Act 2002* (UK) removed the Crown priorities with respect to Inland Revenue and customs and excise and social security contributions previously found in Schedule 6 of the *Insolvency Act 1986* (UK). The Act basically abolishes Crown preference. An earlier White Paper[163] had committed the government to abolish the Crown's preferential status and to ensure the benefit went to unsecured creditors of companies that have floating charges. Prior to the change, in force since 2003, the Crown could claim its debts from an insolvent company ahead of secured creditors who held floating charges. Obviously, they would also claim before unsecured creditors. The priority debts were previously in ss386 and 387 and schedule 6 of the *Insolvency Act 1986* (UK)

---

158 Ibid.

159 Insolvency Law and Practice, Report of the Review Committee (Chairman Sir Kenneth Cork), HMSO London 1982, para 1397.

160 Ibid.

161 Carruthers, B.G. and Halliday, T.C. *Rescuing Business: The Making of Corporate Bankruptcy Law in England and the United States* (1998) 240.

162 Ibid.

163 The White Paper Productivity and Enterprise: Insolvency A Second Chance is available on <http://www.insolvency.gov.uk/compwp.htp>.

and so included debts due to the Inland Revenue for 12 months prior to the relevant date and social security contributions for the 12 months prior to the relevant date.

What remains in the *Insolvency Act* 1986 (UK) is priority status for contributions to occupational pension schemes (superannuation), remuneration of employees for the relevant period and levies on coal and steel production under the European Coal and Steel Community Treaty.

The *Enterprise Act* 2002 (UK) also removed the Secretary of State's priority under the *Employment Rights Act 1996* (UK) and so the Crown will no longer be paid in priority to other preferential claims by former employees.

Of course, as expected the Secretary of State remains a preferential creditor in the subrogation sense when payments have been made from the National Insurance Fund to cover all or part of any employees' preferential claims.

Earlier in the chapter the Australian parliamentary debates were presented to provide an understanding of the reasons why government and taxation priorities have been eliminated or maintained. Certainly the modern narrative is one of removal and the British parliamentary debates below continue the story.

The Secretary of State for Trade and Industry, Ms Hewitt,[164] in the second reading debates in the Commons informed the House that 'the bill will abolish the Crown's preferential rights to recover unpaid taxes ahead of other creditors. That too will bring real benefits to unsecured creditors'.[165] She said the changes would ensure that money would not flow 'from the coffers of the creditors into the coffers of the Treasury'. She indicated that up to £110 million[166] would be made available for distribution to all creditors in Britain following the changes.[167]

Mr Burrow,[168] in welcoming the removal of Crown preferential status, said it was crucial legislation, not only to many employees in companies that currently lost out because the Crown took the first cut of any resources left in insolvency, but to many other small businesses that were dependent as creditors on the business that were going into liquidation. He said that, if the Crown had not been a preferential creditor, some failed companies in his constituency might well have received enough from businesses that went into liquidation to enable them to survive, instead of finding that the scale of loss incurred was just enough to push them into liquidation too.[169]

164 England, House of Commons, *Debates*, 10 April 2002, 53 (Ms Hewitt – Secretary of State for Trade and Industry).

165 Ibid.

166 When this figure was mentioned in the House of Lords, Lord Sainsbury said it was 115 million pounds! England, House of Lords, *Debates*, 2 July 2002, 143.

167 England, House of Commons, *Debates*, 10 April 2002, 53 (Ms Hewitt – Secretary of State for Trade and Industry).

168 England, House of Commons, *Debates*, 10 April 2002, 68 (Mr Burrow – South Ribble).

169 Ibid.

As recounted above in the Australian parliamentary debates in 1993, the same concerns for employees were a major factor in the decision to remove the tax priority.

Dr Cable[170] said the government should proceed with caution on removing the Crown's prerogative, because if the Inland Revenue continued to operate in the same way, regarding itself more or less as driven by a need to get at assets before other creditors, the same problems would arise.[171]

Mr Page[172] supported this, suggesting that parliament must take care to discover whether the actions of the Crown would precipitate a more rigorous collection method, which might in turn cause businesses to have to close much sooner.[173]

Mr Ross Cranston,[174] also a well known commercial law academic, said that it was 'altruistic of the government to abolish it [the priority]' and 'magnanimous behaviour'.[175]

There are similarities between these excerpts and the debate held in the Australian federal parliament ten years earlier. The inclusion of the provisions to remove the priority was part of a much larger reform contained in the *Enterprise Act 2002* (UK) and this paralleled Australia's reform in 1993 when major changes to insolvency were introduced in the *Corporate Law Reform Act 1992* (Cth), including the new Part 5.3A on voluntary administrations.

Other Countries

Historically, most countries have 'granted favored treatment to [government] claims in the event of a taxpayer's insolvency'.[176] Committees and commissions set up to investigate and review this treatment 'over the last forty years have recommended uniformly that tax priorities be limited or abolished'.[177] Legislators have 'responded favourably to these recommendations'.[178] It is possible to gain support for Australia's position (and other jurisdictions who have removed the priority) from a superficial comparison of the countries who responded to the

170 England, House of Commons, *Debates*, 10 April 2002, 68 (Dr Cable – Twickenham).

171 Ibid.

172 England, House of Commons, *Debates*, 10 April 2002, 68 (Mr Page – South west Hertfordshire).

173 Ibid.

174 England, House of Commons, *Debates*, 10 April 2002, 97 (Mr Cranston – Dudley).

175 Ibid.

176 Morgan, B. 'Should the Sovereign be Paid First? A Comparative International Analysis of the Priority for Tax Claims in Bankruptcy' (2000) 74 *American Bankruptcy Law Journal* 461, 462.

177 Ibid. 467.

178 Ibid.

request for information by the Taskforce Report on Priority Claims in Insolvency Administration of the International Bar Association in 1993. The data from the Report indicates that where tax remained a priority it was usually situated behind the administration costs and employee expense priorities.

The following paragraphs present a 'postcard' comparison of the recent position of the tax priority in a number of countries. The information has been compiled from work by Morgan, who in 2000 compared the US, France, Mexico, England, NZ, Canada, Australia and Germany. It has been complemented by submissions to the Taskforce Report on Priority Claims in Insolvency Administration of the International Bar Association compiled in 1993.

In Canada, the municipal taxes levied within two years immediately preceding the insolvency, and to the extent that these do not form a lien or charge, enjoy a priority after administration expenses. Where insolvents have deducted income tax from money owed to employees, this is deemed to be held in trust and forms part of the estate. The Crown is said to have a super priority with respect to these amounts.[179]

In the Czech Republic, taxes, dues, duties and social security contributions limited to three years preceding the insolvency enjoy a priority, but after administration expenses and employees.[180] In Poland, taxes and other public dues for the period of two years preceding the insolvency are given a priority after administration expenses.[181]

In Scandinavia, both Denmark and Finland have no priority for tax. Finland removed the special status for tax claims in January 1993.[182] In Sweden all taxes are included in a category of creditors with general security and these are paid pro rata.[183] Administrative expenses and employee debts are also in this group.

In the Republic of Ireland the tax priority is listed before employees and after administration expenses.[184] It includes local property taxes for twelve months prior to the date of liquidation and a limit of one year's tax in respect of capital gains tax, corporations tax, income tax and value added tax.

In Germany there are 'no priority claims under the [Insolvenzordnung]'.[185] The fiscal authorities in the past were provided with a priority, but these along with numerous others were removed in 1999. In France the General Tax Code provides

179 Submission to the Taskforce Report on Priority Claims in Insolvency Administration, Committee J, International Bar Association. Copy of the submission held by the writer.

180 Ibid.

181 Ibid.

182 Ibid.

183 Formansrattslagen (1970, 9790) An Order of Priority.

184 Ibid.

185 Morgan, B. 'Should the Sovereign be Paid First? A Comparative International Analysis of the Priority for Tax Claims in Bankruptcy' (2000) 74 *American Bankruptcy Law Journal* 461, 491.

a priority to the government over other creditors with regard to the proceeds of movable property. Direct taxes such as income and gross receipts taxes are limited in their priority to four years.[186]

Under the Italian Civil Code there is a priority for taxes on immovable property and movable property taxes. These are paid after administration expenses and employees' claims.[187] In Spain the Code of Commerce provides for privileged creditors, after a group known as singularly privileged creditors that includes employees.[188] Amongst privileged creditors and ranked after administrative expenses are Treasury amounts in relation to any taxes or duties.[189]

In Central America, the Mexican Ley de Concursos Mercantiles provides that 'all tax claims shall be paid after secured claims, "singularly privileged" claims and administrative [expenses]'.[190] In Bermuda the priority for government taxes is ranked before employees.[191]

In New Zealand there is no priority for income taxes or capital gains taxes. The New Zealand Law Commission's Advisory Report to the Ministry of Commerce on Priority Debts in the Distribution of Insolvent Estates recommended repealing the separate priority for PAYE deductions, priority for GST, custom duties, levies under the *Fisheries Act 1983* and debts under the *Radiocommunications Act 1989*.[192] The last two priorities do not feature in current New Zealand corporate insolvency law but the remaining priorities continue even though the position on employee priorities have recently changed.

Conclusion

This chapter looks back on the special treatment government debt, but particularly tax, has received when insolvency has occurred to a corporate taxpayer. While in one sense it is unnecessary to debate the justification for such priority treatment, given its abolition, it does serve an historical interest in Australia. The removal of the government debt and tax priorities reveals that Australian legislators acted with foresight during the period from 1970 through until 1993. Countries such as

186 Ibid. 495.

187 Submission to the Taskforce Report on Priority Claims in Insolvency Administration, Committee J, International Bar Association. Copy of the submission held by the writer.

188 Ibid.

189 Ibid.

190 Morgan, B. 'Should the Sovereign be Paid First? A Comparative International Analysis of the Priority for Tax Claims in Bankruptcy' (2000) 74 *American Bankruptcy Law Journal* 461, 496.

191 Submission to the Taskforce Report on Priority Claims in Insolvency Administration, Committee J, International Bar Association. Copy of the submission held by the writer.

192 See Morgan, op.cit, at 482.

the United Kingdom, Germany and New Zealand have since followed Australia's lead. The chapter demonstrates that some statutory priorities will have a 'use by' date and legislators need to make changes to reflect contemporary times.

Unfortunately, it is not possible to ascertain whether the removal of all government priority, particularly taxation, has meant more distribution from the assets of an insolvent company to unsecured creditors or even other priority creditors. The Australian political debate in the late 1990s on employee entitlements would have been even more complex had the government still been holding onto the taxation or other priorities. If the tax priority had not been removed in 1993 it would almost certainly have been sacrificed by the Federal Government in 2000 in an attempt to placate those in the Australian community who were calling for a fairer distribution of an insolvent company's assets.

Chapter 7
Can a New Statutory Priority for Environmental Expenses be Justified?

From Chapter 6 and other earlier chapters, it is obvious that there is a worldwide trend to reduce or do more than maintain existing statutory priorities,[1] the so-called exceptions to *pari passu*.[2] If the Cork Committee had been legislators these statutory priorities would have been abolished altogether in the United Kingdom from the early 1980s.[3] Other major Reports have concluded that some priorities should be removed.[4]

This chapter performs a complete reversal to the reductionist trend and contemplates environmental costs as a candidate for a new statutory priority in insolvency. In doing so, it considers the reasons that are used to justify the addition of a new priority to the statute.

In the United States of America, where both insolvency laws and environmental laws demand compliance by the insolvent company, there have been calls for one of the statutes to have precedence.[5] While the problem of which statute has

---

1 Recently, there was the removal of the statutory priority given to tax under the United Kingdom's insolvency legislation. This has been outlined in Chapter 6. As seen in that chapter the United States of America imposed restrictions on the tax priority after the Bankruptcy Commission, *Report of the Commission on the Bankruptcy Laws of the United States* HR Doc no 93 – 197 (1973) 'Bankruptcy Commission Report' 216.

2 For example, Crown debts as a priority were removed in Australia in 1968 and the Tax priority in 1993 as described in Chapter 6 above. Tax priorities were abolished in Denmark in 1969, in Austria in 1982, and in Canada in 1992. The Cork Committee in the United Kingdom in 1982 expressed the view that 'there is widespread demand for a significant reduction, and even a complete elimination, of the categories of debts which are accorded priority in an insolvency'. Report of the Review Committee *Insolvency Law and Practice* Cmnd 8558 (1982) 'Cork Report' para 1397.

3 Cork Report para 1398.

4 The New Zealand inquiry *Priority Debts in the Distribution of Insolvent Estates an Advisory Report to Ministry of Commerce* (1999) recommended abolishing Motor Vehicle Dealers Institute Inc priority, recommendation no 250. See also Advisory Committee on Bankruptcy and Insolvency, Canada, *Proposed Bankruptcy Act Amendments Report of the Advisory Committee on Bankruptcy and Insolvency* (1986) 'Colter Report' 10–11.

5 There is a plethora of academic writings on the topic: see e.g., Blackham, L. 'The Unstoppable Force Hits the Immovable Wall: Should Environmental Cleanup Liability be discharged in Bankruptcy' (1992) 25 *Creighton Law Review* 1357; Baker, D. 'Bankruptcy: The Last Environmental Loophole?' (1993) 34 *South Texas Law Review* 379; Rice, T.

precedence has not to date been identified in Australia and some other jurisdictions as a problem, there is still some justification for introducing environmental costs as a new priority.[6] The solution mooted by this chapter is to recommend that the environmental costs become a priority in insolvency statutes.

Environmental liability can result in high monetary penalties and costs which can effectively make a corporation insolvent. These costs are incurred to clean up after significant incidents of pollution. Remediation of contaminated land has gained prominence as established industry moves out of long standing sites, leaving land not suited for residential or other non-industrial development. Remediation has also become important as residential expansion into the urban fringes of cities required the redevelopment of former agricultural land, some of which has been polluted by practices such as stock dipping and chemical usage. One extreme example is the redevelopment of former petrol stations, as they were constructed with underground storage tanks that were known to leak into the surrounding soil.[7] Once incurred, the clean up costs are a debt to be recognized in any liquidation.

However, if these penalties and costs are given a statutory priority *vis-à-vis* other claims on the insolvent estate, there is a potential for a clash of interests. The secured creditor demands to be fully informed of challenges to their position and preferably wants this information before extending credit. The unsecured creditors, who often receive little or nothing in the distribution of the estate because of the other priorities, are going to be interested in, if not annoyed by, any new preferential environmental claims. Others who presently enjoy a priority, such as employees, are also going to be protective of their position in the distribution and oppose any move that would push them down the hierarchy, particularly when they are already at risk of receiving little or nothing.[8]

'Bankruptcy and the Resolvable Clash' (1993) 29 *Tulsa Law Journal* 221; Parker, D.E. 'Environmental Claims in Bankruptcy: It's a Question of Priorities' (1995) 32 *San Diego Law Review* 221; Hill, H. 'Bankruptcy v Environmental Protection: A Case Study in Normative Conflict' (1998) 16 *Canadian Journal of Law and Jurisprudence* 245.

6 Keay, A. and de Prez, P. 'Insolvency and Environmental Principles: A Case Study in a Conflict of Public Interests' (2001) *Environmental Law Review* 90, 91 describe it as an issue which is in its infancy in the United Kingdom and much of the Commonwealth.

7 Brennan, M. 'Contaminated sites' (1995) *Australian Company Secretary* 371. Brennan stated that in the early 1970s there were about 20,000 operating service stations and the Service Station Association estimated that by 2000 there would be only 6,500 stations still in operation. Sneddon, M. 'Liability for Insolvent Polluters' (1997) 5 *Insolvency Law Journal* 65, stated that there were 'conservatively estimated to be at least 1000 contaminated sites' in Victoria in 1997. He suggested that the costs of undertaking simple tests to determine whether a site was contaminated could cost approximately $40,000 for a relatively small site. The costs of 'capping' then could be $1m and the full scale remediation $10m.

8 See Holding, P. 'Who bears the risk? Protecting Employee Entitlement Upon Insolvency' (1995) 69 *Law Institute Journal* 789; Symes, C.F. *Deserving the Law's Sympathy* (unpublished LLM thesis, University of Adelaide, 1996); Australia, House of Representatives, *Debates*, 27 May 1993, 1125–1126 (Mr Rocher – Curtin).

The Australian Position

In Australia, environmental legislation is both Commonwealth and State based.[9] Under legislation such as the *Environmental Offences and Penalties Act 1989* in New South Wales and the *Environment Protection Act 1970* in Victoria, restoration compensation orders may be made and there is potential liability to pay damages. It is a principle known as 'polluter pays'[10] and it is implemented in a variety of ways, such as the requirement of financial assurances and the recovery of cleanup costs as a judgment debt.[11] However, Australia's corporate insolvency statute, the *Corporations Act 2001* (Cth),[12] makes no mention of environmental claims.

The evolution of corporate insolvency law, as outlined in Chapter 2, would at no time have contemplated the possibilities of environmental protection or the application of environmental cleanup debts in the efficacious winding up of companies. Nevertheless, Chapter 5 of the *Corporations Act 2001* (Cth) could readily be expanded to include such involuntary creditors as the government agency that has borne the cost of repairing damage to the environment caused by the [now] insolvent corporation.[13] For example, a new subsection in s556 of the *Corporations Act 2001* (Cth) could address this problem using a provision drafted like this:

> Amounts due in respect of repairing damage to the environment or to reimburse expenditure authorized under applicable law.

'Environment' would then need to be defined to assist with statutory interpretation. Several statutes in Australia already provide such a definition.[14]

9 The States have legislation that allows for clean up of contaminated land, remediation orders; *Environment Protection Act* (Qld) 1994, *Environment Protection Act* (SA) 1993; for a general discuusion see Bates, G.M. *Environmental Law in Australia* (5th ed. 2002) chapters 3 and 15.

10 The first official definition of the polluter pays principle derived from the Recommendations of the Organisation for Economic Cooperation and Development from 1972–1975, and was used by the House of Lords Select Committee on EC, *The Polluter Pays Principle* (10th Report) HL 131, session 1982–1983.

11 *Environment Protection Act 1970* (Vic) s65A.

12 *Corporations Act 2001* (Cth) s556.

13 See e.g., *In Canada Panamericana De Bienes Y Servicios S A v Northern Badger Oil and Gas Ltd (1991) 5 WWR 577*; Cantlie, S. 'When Worlds Collide: Environmental Regulation in Conflict with Bankruptcy Legislation' (1992) 21 *Canadian Business Law Journal* 190; Sneddon, M. 'Liability for Insolvent Polluters' (1997) 5 *Insolvency Law Journal* 65.

14 See e.g., *Environment Protection (Impact of Proposals) Act 1974* (Cth) s3 that defines environment to 'include all aspects of the surroundings of man, whether affecting him as an individual or in his social groupings'; or the *Environment Protection Act 1970* (Vic) s4 that refers to 'physical factors of the surroundings of human beings including land,

There could be a time limit imposed. For example a provision could be drafted so that:

> Amounts that were due and payable in respect of repairing damage to the environment or to reimburse expenditure authorised under applicable law at the relevant date and the liability for which accrued within 12 months that next preceded that date.

The clean up powers contained in the state legislation allow the Environmental Protection Authority (or equivalent government agency) to remove, disperse, destroy or abate the pollution.[15] There is also power to order a range of other persons to undertake the relevant clean up tasks and these persons include the occupier or the person who has caused the pollution.[16]

Another possibility is to bring environmental costs within the existing administrative expenses priority. Administrative expenses were analysed in Chapter 4 above. Under s556(1) of the Australian *Corporations Act 2001* (Cth), administrative expenses are entitled to first priority of payment if they were incurred as part of the actual and necessary costs of preserving and realizing the estate.[17] The rationale given by the Harmer Report for the administrative costs priority was 'that creditors have a community of interest in having a common agent to maximise a fund for distribution to them'.[18] Environmental expenses, such as where a government agency has actually expended money to cleanup an insolvent corporation's land, could likewise be considered as 'administrative

---

water, atmosphere, climate, sound, odours, tastes ... the social factor of aesthetics ... the biological factors of animals and plants'. The *Environmental Protection Council Act 1972* (SA) s3 defines environment as 'any matter or thing that determines or affects the condition or influences under which any animate thing lives or exists in the State'.

15 See e.g., *Environment Protection Act 1993* (SA) where the Environmental Protection Authority can issue to a person who has caused environmental harm by contravention of the Act or a repealed environmental law to take specified action within a specified period to make good any resulting environmental damage. This clean-up order must be in writing and served. It must specify the contravention alleged to have caused the environmental harm and it may require action to be taken to prevent or mitigate further harm. It is an offence to fail to comply with a clean-up order. Brunton, N. 'The South Australian Environment Protection Act 1993' (1995) 12 *Environment and Planning Law Journal* 3. Uniform legislation can be found in *Environmental Management and Pollution Control Act 1994* (Tas) and *Environment Protection Act* 1994 (Qld).

16 Mfodwo, K. 'Remediation and Compensation After Hazardous Waste Incidents: Recent Developments Affecting Companies and Financial Institutions in Victoria' (1991) 8 *Environment and Planning Law Journal* 211.

17 Tomasic, R. and Whitford, K. *Australian Insolvency and Bankruptcy Law* (2nd ed. 1997) 359.

18 Australian Law Reform Commission, *General Insolvency Inquiry*, Report No 45 'Harmer Report' (1988) para 717.

expenses' and, therefore, a government agency could become a priority creditor.[19] This could occur where the contaminated land owned by the company was cleaned up prior to the liquidator being able to sell and undertaken during the period of liquidation. The *Corporations Act 2001* (Cth) does not distinguish environmental claims and expenses from other administrative claims and expenses as the administrative expense priority can include a wide range of matters. The term 'expenses incurred in the winding up' was described by Maugham J as not 'a term of art'[20] and so he could 'see no reason why it should not include any expenses which the liquidator might be compelled to pay in respect of his acts in the course of a proper liquidation'.[21]

There is little debate that, after the commencement date of insolvency, there could be occasions where fixing environmental harm would be part of 'preserving and realizing the estate'. This should make them an administrative expense. However, the largest environmental expenditures could be expected to arise from pre-commencement date environmental claims and these are presently treated as a general unsecured claim.

Although environmental clean-up may be of benefit to society, it may not 'preserve or benefit' the estate. Given that one of the main policies driving insolvency law is the maximization of distribution of estate assets to creditors,[22] it is uncertain whether the courts would decide in favour of the common good for society over the company's creditors. It is submitted that to achieve clarity in the legislation the legislators should incorporate a new sub paragraph into the insolvency priorities provision, s556(1) *Corporations Act 2001* (Cth), as described above. An environmental expense priority could operate in the future in the same way as the abolished crown and tax priorities under previous corporate insolvency law. Unsecured creditors will complain because there are many occasions when they are left with little or no dividend from the estate and so to include another priority ahead of their opportunity to be paid would further diminish their likelihood of a dividend. As some small compensation, the environmental priority could be limited to a monetary maximum.

---

19 Mfodwo, K. 'Lender Liability for Environmental Impairment and Remediation in New South Wales: Issues Problems and Prospects' (1991) 8 *Environment and Planning Law Journal* 108, 120.

20 *Re Beni-Felkai Mining Co* [1934] 1 Ch 406, 419.

21 Ibid.

22 This draws on the vision of corporate insolvency law known as creditor wealth maximization promoted by Jackson, T. *The Logic and Limits of Bankruptcy* (1986) and Baird, D.G, and Jackson, T. 'Corporate Reorganisations and the Treatment of Diverse Ownership Interest: A Comment on Adequate Protection of Secured Creditors in Bankruptcy' (1984) 51 *University of Chicago Law Review* 97. There is some discussion of this 'policy' in Chapter 3 above.

Comparative Approaches

United States of America

The United States of America has devoted a great deal of attention to the crossroads of these two fields of law, insolvency and environmental law. The *Comprehensive Environmental Response, Compensation and Liability Act* of 1980 (known as CERCLA) demonstrated Congress' intention that the costs of cleaning up hazardous waste should be assessed against those responsible for creating that waste and that is essentially the private enterprise. This creates a direct conflict with the policy under the *Bankruptcy Code*,[23] where a debtor shall have a fresh start. The *Bankruptcy Code* allows for statutory priorities and one of these is for certain 'allowed unsecured claims of governmental units'.[24] However, this is a priority only for enumerated claims of taxes and customs duties and not compensatory government claims such as reimbursement for cleanup costs undertaken by a government agency.

The problem of environment clean up costs has become a major issue when contemplated in insolvency. Cleanup liabilities can become 'gargantuan' and take up most or all of the assets available for creditors.[25]

Treating environmental costs as administrative expenses has not been the position universally adopted in the United States.[26] Some United States courts have held that, since these claims arise pre-petition, they should be treated as unsecured claims,[27] while other courts have held that, to the extent that the claim represents a claim for reimbursement for money expended post-petition, it should be classified as an administrative expense,[28] because it is preserving the estate.[29] One solution

23 *Bankruptcy Reform Act* of 1978 amended 11 USC 101–1330 (1988).

24 11 USC 507 (a) (7).

25 Clarr, G.E. 'The Case for a Bankruptcy Code Priority for Environmental Clean up Claims' (1992) 18 *William Mitchell Law Review* 29, 52.

26 *Windolph Trust v Leitch (re Kent Holland Die Casting and Plating Inc)* 125 B R 493 (Bankr W D Mich. 1991).

27 *Burlington N R R v Dant and Russell Inc (re Dank and Russell Inc)* 853 F 2d 700, 708-709 (9th Cir 1988); *Walsh v West Virginia (re Security Gas and Oil Inc)* 70 BR 786, 795 (Bankr N D Cal 1987); *Re Peerless Plating Co* 70 B R 943. 948 (Bankr W D Mich 1987); *Re Pierce Coal and Constr Inc* 65 BR 521, 530 (Bankr N D W Va 1986).

28 *United States v LTV Steel Co (re Chateaugay Corp)* 944 F 2d 997, 1009 – 10 (2d Cir 1991); *Lancaster v Tennessee (re Wall Tube and Metal Products Co)* 831 F 2d 118, 121 – 23 (6th Cir 1987); *Re Stevens* 68 B R 774, 783 (D Me 1987); *Re T P Long Chem Inc* 45 B R 278, 286 (Bankr N D Ohio 1985); Mirsky, A.E., Conway, R.J. and Humphrey, G.G. 'The Interface Between Bankruptcy and Environmental Laws' (1991) 46 *Business Lawyer* 626, 654.

29 *Borden Inc v Wells-Fargo Business Credit (in re Smith-Douglass Inc)* 856 F 2d 12, 17 (4th Cir. 1988); *United States v LTV Steel Co (re Chateaugay Corp)* 944 F 2d 997, 1009 – 10 (2d Cir 1991).

is to grant the administrative priority for post-petition costs incurred in satisfying a pre-petition environmental claim only if the expenditure is necessary to protect the public from immediate danger from the environmental harm.[30] The National Bankruptcy Conference in the United States has developed a rule for granting administrative expense status to environmental claims along this line. The United States *Bankruptcy Code* does not distinguish environmental claims from other claims.[31]

United Kingdom

There is no express mention of environmental expenses in the *Insolvency Act 1986* (UK), although it is expected that liquidators will be confronted more and more with environmental problems as they wind up companies.[32] In such cases, the liquidator may find the land owned by the company is unsaleable because it is so polluted. Here lies a dilemma: the liquidators are given the power to disclaim onerous property, that is, to be able to walk away from this troublesome asset; but if there are strong cleanup laws, then who will bear the responsibility to clean the land of its contamination? At present, liquidators in the United Kingdom are advised to disclaim polluted land as soon as possible so as to avoid any claim that they have allowed an environmental problem to worsen.[33]

The decision in *Re Mineral Resources Ltd*[34] established that environmental agencies could not claim because this would undermine the public policy of making the polluter pay. This is justified by arguing that to give an environmental agency creditor status would mean other creditors would be the ones paying. This can be rebutted in part by claiming the 'polluter pays' principle in the United Kingdom has been interpreted as having no application where a company cannot pay.[35]

English judges who have had to choose between insolvency law and the environment have favoured the environment. Justice Neuberger in *Re Mineral Resources Ltd*[36] said that in the absence of strong factors to the contrary the interest in protecting the environment should take precedence over the interest in a fair and orderly winding up of companies.[37]

---

30 Parker, D.E. 'Environmental Claims in Bankruptcy: It's a Question of Priorities' (1995) 32 *San Diego Law Review* 221, 284.

31 Ibid. 254.

32 Keay, A. *McPherson The Law of Company Liquidation* (UK edition) (2002) 488.

33 Ibid.

34 *Re Mineral Resources Ltd* [1999] 1 All ER 746.

35 *Re Celtic Extraction* [1999] 2 BCLC 555.

36 *Re Mineral Resources Ltd* [1999] 1 All ER 746.

37 *Re Mineral Resources Ltd* [1999] 1 All ER 746, 757.

New Zealand

In New Zealand, the 1999 Law Commission inquiry received no submissions suggesting environmental costs should have priority status and so the Commission took the view there was no compelling need for such a priority.[38]

The New Zealand High Court, when confronted with the choice between insolvency law's right of a liquidator to disclaim or the environment under legislation that controlled the disposal of property, nevertheless chose the environment in *Tubbs v Futurity Investments and Buchanans Foundry Ltd.*[39]

Canada[40]

In Canada, federal legislation characterizes the costs of cleaning up environmental damage as a debt owing to the Crown.[41] Federal legislation also ranks creditors in corporate insolvency[42] and the Crown's claims for environmental damage rank, along with all other Crown debts, as unsecured creditors.[43] In some Canadian provinces attempts have been made to have environmental expenses treated as taxes and therefore obtain an insolvency priority. In Alberta[44] and Ontario[45] the legislatures have enacted environmental statutes that provide for clean up costs to be added to the assessment roll as a tax against land and collected in the same manner as taxes.

The courts in Canada tend to favour environmental principles over insolvency law.[46] It has been observed that when it comes to social policies involved in

38 New Zealand Law Commission, Priority Debts in the Distribution of Insolvent Estates An Advisory Report to Ministry of Commerce (1999) para 210–211.

39 *Tubbs v Futurity Investments and Buchanans Foundry Ltd* [1998] 1 NZLR 471.

40 There is a text dedicated to the topic in Canada: Klimek, J. *Insolvency and Environment Liability* (1994).

41 *Canadian Environment Protection Act* RSC 1985 c 16 (4th Supp) ss39, 60, 77 and 130; *Fisheries Act* RSC 1985 c F–14 s42; *Arctic Waters Pollution Prevention Act* RSC 1985 c A-12 s6.

42 *Bankruptcy and Insolvency Act* s136 sets out the scheme of distribution and priority creditors.

43 *Bankruptcy and Insolvency Act* RSC 1985 cB-3 as amended by SC 1992 c 27. The removal of the status of the Crown as a priority creditor changed from 23 June 1992.

44 *Alberta Environmental Protection and Enhancement Act* SA 1992 c E-13.3 s176; *Weed Control Act* RSA 1980 c W-6 s 27.

45 *Environmental Protection Act* (Ontario) RSO 1990 c E19 s154.

46 *In Canada Panamericana De Bienes Y Survicious S A v Northern Badger Oil and Gas Ltd.* (1991) 5 WWR 577; *Canada Trust v Bulora Corporation Ltd* (1980) 34 CBR (NS) 145, affrmd 39 CBR (NS) 152 (Ont CA); Tay, D.C. 'The Emerging Priority of Environmental Orders in Canadian Insolvency Situations' (1992) 5 *Journal of International Banking Law* 202.

environmental cleanup, irrespective of whether the statutes give authority the courts play a part in shaping the law.[47]

Justification

Any attempt to treat creditors differently, by way of exceptions to the *pari passu* principle, necessitates a clear justification. Any move by the legislators or the judiciary to embrace the principle of protecting the environment in insolvency law will be heavily scrutinized.[48]

From an insolvency perspective, an environment priority is more aligned to the application of communitarian thinking than the creditors' bargain model, as discussed above in Chapter 3. The creditor's bargain model requires the government to undertake the role of creditor and this is a less obvious application when the clean-up debt is incurred as a result of a non-compliance with statute. The communitarian perspective would support the grant of an environmental priority, given the benefit the entire community receives in having less polluted sites. Cleaning up a contaminated site will benefit the new occupier and their community, as well as those using it in the future.

As with the priority for wages and entitlements, it could be argued that the environment deserves the law's sympathy and should be rewarded with such a priority.[49] The environment shares a similar position to employees, in that it cannot bargain with the corporation or work into the expense or claim a premium to cover the likelihood of an unpaid debt due to insolvency. Government agencies that undertake remediation and incur environmental cleanup costs are involuntary creditors.

The cleanup of hazardous wastes is necessary and will be expected to receive emotive support from the public. However, the contest is not directly between the public and the company's creditors but whether government is to receive a priority over other unsecured creditors. The creditors are fault-free with regard to this expense.

The culpability of the pollution is with the company and yet in an insolvency where the government agency has cleaned up, it is the taxpayer who is indirectly bearing the cost. In light of such circumstances and with governments routinely paying for clean-ups, we may see funds available for such activities depleting

---

47 Tay, D.C. 'Environmental Liability and the Insolvency Professional: An Issue Whose Time has, or will surely, Come' (1994) 3 *International Insolvency Review* 60.

48 See e.g., *In Canada Panamericana De Bienes Y Survicious S A v Northern Badger Oil and Gas Ltd.* (1991) 5 WWR 577; Cantlie, S. 'When Worlds Collide: Environmental Regulation in Conflict with Bankruptcy Legislation' (1992) 21 *Canadian Business Law Journal* 190.

49 O'Donovan, J. 'Corporate Insolvency: Policies, Perspectives and Reform' (1990) 3 *Corporate and Business Law Journal* 1, 8–9.

rapidly and the government responding by refraining from cleaning up all but the worst of sites.[50] In order to prevent such an outcome a statutory priority would have to be supported by a government-initiated fund to be used in addition to available company assets.

With State and federal governments attempting to address the clean up of contaminated land, the lack of recovery from insolvent companies could compromise the environmental legislative intent. Cleanup claims are legal obligations which should be inescapable by liquidation.

Justification using Finch's Criteria

Finch, in her thought-provoking book on corporate insolvency,[51] is unexpectedly silent on matters of the environment. However, in her chapter on 'the *pari passu* principle: when everyone is equal' she considers whether the current exceptions to *pari passu* are in need of reform. In this discussion, she suggests criteria for assessing the strongest cases for a protected status or a priority. The four criteria suggested are 1) the ability to gain and use information concerning default risks, 2) the capacity to exit from excessively risk-laden arrangements, 3) the vulnerability to risks and 4) the status as a low- or high-cost bearer of risks. It is helpful to test a priority for environmental costs against her criteria to ascertain whether introducing another exception could be justified.

Finch's Criteria 1– ability to gain and use information concerning default risk If it is acknowledged that the government is going to be the one either issuing notices compelling responsible parties to clean up environmental damage or completing the clean up and looking to the company for reimbursement, then the amount of information concerning default risk will vary. Where the government merely issues a notice, it may have little or no information as to the company's ability to pay. In this way, it is similar to taxes. On the other hand, if the government cleans up and then seeks reimbursement, this may have been done in circumstances where the government has pursued the company and, when unsuccessful, has come along and done the job itself. Such circumstances might suggest to the government that the company is not in a financial position to undertake the work.

Finch's Criteria 2 – capacity to exit from excessively risk-laden arrangements The government is going to have limited capacity to exit from environmental clean up costs and these might be excessively risk-laden arrangements if they become an unpaid debt. If the government issues a notice, then they have a choice to take this no further. However, if the company fails to respond, then the government's public responsibility on environmental clean up remains unsatisfied. If the government

50 Keay, A. and de Prez, P. 'Insolvency and Environmental Principles: A Case Study in a Conflict of Public Interests' (2001) *Environmental Law Review* 90, 107.

51 Finch, V. *Corporate Insolvency Law Perspectives and Principles* (2002) 449.

moves in to clean up and then seeks reimbursement, they have little capacity to exit as their choice is either to write off the debt after having achieved a successful clean up or not to complete the job and fail in their public responsibility. Again, there are similarities with taxes as their position is as involuntary creditors.

Finch's Criteria 3 – vulnerability to risks The size of environmental clean up costs are obviously hard to determine for a particular jurisdiction. Furthermore, the incidence of insolvency changes in response to the economic climate. Despite this, there is an acknowledged problem that the environment has been degraded over the time of Western civilization and certainly from the time of the Industrial Revolution. The government is compelled to do more than adjust behaviour of its citizens: it must attempt to restore the environment. In such circumstances, therefore, it is the government that has the vulnerability of risk. The government may issue the notice for clean up but, if the company cannot afford to take the measures required, it is most likely to ignore the notice. Even if the company were to attempt to clean up, there is the likelihood of financial collapse before the job is complete. An insolvency practitioner may wish to see the task through to completion but could be expected to wind up, leaving the clean up for the new purchasers of the company's real property. Another possibility is that the liquidator would seek to walk away from the property which would also leave the clean up for someone else.[52]

If the government were to clean up and seek reimbursement, then the vulnerability of risk would increase as the very lack of response from the company could indicate insolvency. The government is very vulnerable to carrying the costs of clean up.

Finch's Criteria 4 – status as a low- or high-cost bearer of risk Environmental clean up costs are not going to be present in all insolvencies. When they do occur, the risk is essentially borne by the government. The government already has the costs of investigation and policing pollution and other environmental issues. They become a cost bearer of risk when they embark upon a clean up and hope for reimbursement. The government, as with taxation, is able to spread the costs of collection and failure to collect over the large numbers of citizens, resulting in their status as low cost bearers of risk.

52 This behavior is permitted by *Corporations Act 2001* (Cth) s568. It is in effect relieving the company of an asset that is a liability; *Re Nottingham General Cemetery Co* [1955] Ch 683. For a brief commentary see Chin, M. and Hodgson, A. 'Safety on the Site' (1994) 68 *Law Institute Journal* 1064, 1069.

Divination

A new priority for environmental clean up costs may well be justified in future insolvency statutes. The government does become an involuntary creditor upon the liquidation if they have undertaken the remediation of contaminated land. They are exposed to a potentially very large expense and this may cause them to establish a fund outside the insolvency but also use the legislative priority, mirroring in some way the existing situation for employee entitlements. Public sympathy and social concerns for a clean environment may assist the government's task of justifying a new priority to the electorate.

Conclusion

Conflicts have arisen between environmental law and insolvency law for many years in the United States of America. The potential exists for similar conflicts in Australia, the United Kingdom and many other jurisdictions. It remains to be seen whether these two laws can live together particularly if the various legislatively-created environmental protection agencies/authorities move to litigate against insolvency practitioners in control of insolvent companies. These moves could include the government seeking reimbursement expenses for clean-ups.[53] Certainly, many environmental laws contemplate liability for insolvency practitioners, albeit sometimes implicitly.[54]

Legislation in Australia allows for government agencies to undertake clean up and expect cost recovery. When the culpable company is insolvent then the debt to government remains and is presently treated on the lowest step of the priority ladder, as unsecured debt.

Corporate insolvency law remains silent on the environment, yet does provide scope for it to be included in a number of ways, including by expressing a statutory priority for clean up costs. Presently, corporate insolvency law also allows for some uncertainty, frustration and delay to become factors in potential environmental disputes. Changing the statutory priority to expressly position environmental clean up costs alongside employee entitlements could alleviate some of the present angst for liquidators and avoid a litigious future.

---

53 See e.g., *Environment Protection Act 1970* (Vic) s62.

54 Sneddon, M. 'Liability for Insolvent Polluters' (1997) 5 *Insolvency Law Journal* 65, 70; Lee, R.G. 'The Obligation to Remediate Contaminated Land – A Comparative Analysis' (1993) 10 *Environment and Planning Law Journal* 97, 102; Barrett, M. and Botten, J. 'Environmental Risk and the Insolvency Practitioner' (Paper presented at the Insolvency Practitioners' Association of Australia South Australia and Northern Territory Division, Adelaide, 11 November 1993) 3; Chin, M. and Hodgson, A. 'Safety on the Site' (1994) 68 *Law Institute Journal* 1064.

Chapter 8

Consumer Prepayments and Reward Schemes: Could these be the Next Statutory Priorities?

In corporate insolvency there are often groups that receive an unfair outcome.[1] Consumers are not singled out for any special treatment in the Australian corporate insolvency statute, the *Corporations Act 2001* (Cth). This chapter investigates whether new priorities for consumers should be considered, and, if so, whether they could be justified. In looking to justify the introduction of any consumer priority, comparisons are drawn with a number of other jurisdictions: the United Kingdom, the United States, Canada and New Zealand.[2] There is also a brief examination of how consumers are treated in specific industries where company failures have occurred.

As Chapters 4 and 5 have described, s556 of the *Corporations Act 2001* (Cth) provides for priorities for payment to certain creditors owed money by the insolvent company. While these are unsecured creditors, they are given special treatment as it has been determined by the legislature that they have special needs. Consumers who have made a prepayment for goods or services and then find the supplier business is an insolvent company have not been considered under the legislation to require such special treatment. They are merely ordinary, unsecured creditors. They wait at the end of the line for return of their money, as they are unlikely to receive the goods or services from the performance of their vendor's sales and supply contract as they had planned. This absence of priority disregards the fact that in certain industries it is common practice to pay in advance for the supply of goods or services.

Some consumers participate in reward schemes and will expect to claim their entitlements from time to time. Upon the liquidation of the companies associated with these reward schemes there is a risk that entitlements will be lost. Later in the

1 See e.g., Villiers, C. 'Employees as Creditors: A Challenge for Justice in Insolvency Law' (1999) 20 *Company Lawyer* 222; Goode, R.M. 'Is the Law Too Favourable to Secured Creditors?' (1983–4) 8 *Canadian Business Law Journal* 53.

2 International Bar Association, Committee J Bankruptcy Legislation Subcommittee, *Priority claims in insolvency administration* (1993), discuss twelve other countries: Bermuda, Bulgaria, Czech Republic, Denmark, Finland, Ireland, Italy, Norway, Poland, Romania, Spain and Sweden, and there is no mention of a priority for consumer prepayments in any of these countries. Copies of these submissions are on file with the writer.

chapter the legal status and possibility of a statutory priority for these consumers are explored.

From the outset, it is recognized there is a tendency towards reducing the number of statutory priorities.[3] In 1999 United Kingdom insolvency professionals were asked whether a new priority category for prepayment consumer creditors should be introduced and sixty per cent rejected the idea.[4] Australian insolvency professionals may give similar responses if surveyed. The rejection result would be expected to differ if researchers asked consumers whether they desired better treatment upon insolvency of a supplier.

Australian consumer legislation is mostly State-based and not completely uniform.[5] A number of specific pieces of legislation and other government-initiated regulation provide consumers with protection for a variety of financial risks. An example of this regulation relates to pre-paid funerals, as discussed later in the chapter.

The English case of *Re Kayford Ltd*[6] illustrates the problem of consumers caught up in corporate insolvency. The company, Kayford Ltd, was a mail order company that was in financial difficulties. It took moneys sent to it and held them in a special trust account. On liquidation it was held that these funds had to be returned to the consumers as the trust account did not form part of the realizable estate of the company. Justice Megarry reasoned that the consumers were 'members of the public, some of whom can ill afford to exchange their money for a claim to a dividend in the liquidation'.[7] In 2006 the Farepak administration raised similar issues.[8] Such considerations would not be in the judicial domain if the legislators were to add a consumer category to statutory priorities.

---

3 This point has been made in the previous chapter, Chapter 7. See for example, the Cork Report in the UK in 1982 that expressed the view that 'there is widespread demand for a significant reduction, and even a complete elimination, of the categories of debts which are accorded priority in an insolvency' Report of the Review Committee *Insolvency Law and Practice* Cmnd 8558 (1982) para 1397.

4 Keay, A. and Walton, P. 'Preferential Debts: An Empirical Study' (1999) *Insolvency Lawyer* 112, 116.

5 There is a Uniform Consumer Credit code but for other areas of consumer law there are individual Acts such as the Fair Trading Acts mentioned below; although some matters (notably general proscriptions on deceptive trading and unconscionable conduct) are the subject of national regulation under Part V of the *Trade Practices Act 1974* (Cth).

6 [1975] 1 WLR 279; 1 All ER 604.

7 Ibid. 282.

8 *In the matter of Farepak Food and Gifts Ltd (in administration)* and *The Insolvency Act 1986* [2006] EWHC 3272.

Australian Position

There is no mention of consumers or consumer prepayments in the *Corporations Act 2001* (Cth). Consumers, after providing money as a prepayment for goods or services to a company which later becomes insolvent, find themselves as unsecured creditors of the company. At best, they may have other means to recover their money – such as through an insurance cover or an independent special trust fund set up to address such eventualities. As part of measures aimed at consumer protection some State governments have specific 'funds' set up to 'insure' consumers.[9] Occasionally, particular industries provide similar relief. These are discussed below.

In Australia a potentially huge problem was discerned with the collapse of Ansett Airlines in 2001. The travel industry had operated for many years a form of insurance, the Travel Compensation Fund (TCF), to cover such eventualities. Upon the insolvency of Ansett this fund was accessed, along with the commercial magnanimity of the opposition carrier, Qantas, to honour tickets issued by Ansett to their customers. However, consumers involved in other financial collapses like health clubs have not been so lucky. For example, in the health club industry much of the service is sold by twelve month subscriptions. This presents real problems for the consumer who is treated as an unsecured creditor if the 'club' fails. They receive no ongoing service for the money they have pre-paid. Another example is the relatively recent failure of OneTel, a telecommunications company. 'Plans' are sold to users of mobile phones in this industry and some of these plans expect payment in advance. The failure of the telecommunications company will result in the service stopping and the consumers still being 'in credit'. Under Australian insolvency law, they too are treated as unsecured creditors. Again, when OneTel failed, commercial magnanimity (or opportunism) saw other telecommunications companies such as Optus offering to pick up customers of the failed company at special deals that incorporated the 'credit'.

Another area of consumer prepayments where the insolvency of the supplier can become troublesome is Internet trading. With the introduction of the Internet and the ever-increasing use of such means to trade, it is only a matter of time before there is a major incident of Australian (or other local) consumers losing their prepayments to a failed internet trader (who is not local). Despite the fact that businesses that offer Internet supply will often be offshore companies, some protection for Australian consumers through the *Corporations Act 2001* (Cth) may be possible by the requirement to appoint a local agent.[10] Certainly, the Act provides for some protection where a foreign company wishes to carry on business in Australia by facilitating the appointment of a local agent.

---

9 See e.g., *Travel Agents Act 1986* (SA); Funeral Funds Act 1979 (NSW).

10 See e.g., *Corporations Act 2001* (Cth) s601CF. At common law the tendency is to treat the matter of statutory priorities as determined by local law. See *Re Commonwealth Agricultural Service Engineers Ltd* [1928] SASR 342.

A History of Protection of Consumer Prepayments

Insolvency legislation has not provided for special treatment of consumer prepayments throughout its long history in Australia, or elsewhere. Consumer protection laws in Australia were developed in the early 1970s as the 'untrained consumer is no match for the businessman'.[11] However, while they addressed numerous unfair trade practices, they did not extend to giving consumers special redress upon the insolvency of the suppliers of goods and services.

A further difficulty in providing a remedy through consumer protection avenues is the legislative power over consumers. The consumer legislation is not uniform: both federal and State legislatures have legislated to varying degrees, the Commonwealth with legislation such as the *Trade Practices Act 1974* (Cth) and the States with their *Fair Trading Acts.*[12]

Harmer Report

Submissions to the Harmer Report[13] in 1988 did not show strong support for a new consumer priority in insolvency. Instead there were suggestions that consumer pre-payments should go into a separate trust fund with its own banking account.[14] This would have enabled the consumer to be paid outside of the insolvency administration and any shortfall that was unable to be met from the trust would be considered a breach of trust by the company. However, if there are few assets left then the cost of proceeding and the likelihood of an unsatisfactory return would seem to reject this alternative as viable. The Commission, in a footnote, conceded that if certain prepayments were held in trust they might be entitled to a non-statutory priority under trust law, and this would protect the interests of consumers without creating new priorities in the insolvency legislation.[15]

The Financial Counsellors Association of Victoria supported a new priority and gave evidence that:

> there is a sufficiently strong case … to justify creating a new priority. The requirement for consumer prepayments often features in the most failure prone business enterprises. Our Association believes that prepayments should be

---

11 Australia, Senate, *Debates* ,27 September 1973, 1013 (Senator L.K. Murphy QC – Attorney General).

12 *Fair Trading Act 1987* (NSW), *Fair Trading Act 1999* (Vic), *Fair Trading Act 1989* (Qld), *Fair Trading Act 1987* (SA), *Fair Trading Act 1987* (WA), *Fair Trading Act 1990* (Tas).

13 Australian Law Reform Commission, *General Insolvency Inquiry*, Report No 45 (1988) 'Harmer Report'.

14 Ibid. Submission No 156, Australian Institute of Credit Management, 8. Copy on file with the writer.

15 Ibid. fn 94.

> protected and should not be used to finance business operating costs, etc. There have been many cases in the recent past which demonstrate the need for priority status for prepayments.[16]

The only other submission listed in the Harmer Report as supporting the priority was the Department for Community Welfare from South Australia, although their submission focussed on the personal insolvency of a trader and on goods that were being held in stock.[17] The submission supported the priority repayment of money paid as a deposit, progress payment or advance payment in full for goods and services, in cases where the goods have not been supplied or the services not performed.[18] The Department rejected an idea for a priority of any expenses the consumer may have incurred in relation to these goods or services, such as the cost of having goods installed.[19]

Opposition to the idea of a consumer priority was mounted in a submission from Geoffrey McDonald of Love and Rodgers Chartered Accountants in the Harmer Report.[20] This submission suggested that the public had become more familiar with the law in general and, as a result, had changed their purchasing behaviour. McDonald believed there would be a change from the practice of paying a minimal deposit or paying for goods in whole subject to delivery.[21] This change would dramatically reduce the incidence of losses to consumers who had prepaid contracts.[22]

The Harmer Report decided that there was not a 'sufficient case regarding pre-paid consumer contracts to justify creating a new priority'.[23] As outlined above, the Commission received few submissions both for and against introducing a priority,[24] but refused to deviate from the 'fundamental principle of equal sharing' and their more general 'conclusion that the priority provisions should be limited

---

16 Ibid. Submission No 177, Financial Counsellors Association of Victoria (Inc), 8. Copy on file with the writer.

17 Ibid. Submission No 137, Department for Community Welfare (SA), 3. Copy on file with the writer.

18 Ibid. Appendix 2. Note here they were suggesting that there be an addition to the *Bankruptcy Act*'s list of priority creditors, not a change to the corporate insolvency statutory treatment.

19 Ibid.

20 Ibid. Submission No 136, G. McDonald, 17. Copy on file with the writer.

21 Ibid.

22 Ibid.

23 Ibid. para 771.

24 Ibid. Submission No 138, The Joint Submission of IPAA, ICA and ASA, 19. These bodies were against this proposal. However, their submission rejects a number of other proposals and mentions consumer prepayments only once. In rejecting a number of these ideas they then sum up by stating that they support the ALRC's rejection based on the 'philosophy of a rateable distribution amongst all creditors' despite being in favour of some priorities like administrative expenses and putting liquidator's fees and remuneration first!

rather than extended'.[25] The Harmer Report was prepared from the largest inquiry ever conducted into insolvency in Australia and these few submissions suggest it was not a major concern for most who gave evidence. The size of the problem at that time, in the late 1980s, is difficult to ascertain without empirical study. The same could be said for the current situation.

Australian Responses

Today, there may still be areas of consumer behaviour that would result in the consumer losing money following the insolvency of a corporate trader. It is difficult to generalize about the outcome of contracts that involve consumers upon the supplier's liquidation. The appointment of a liquidator does not necessarily constitute grounds for the termination of a continuing contract or a repudiation of it.[26] It will depend upon the nature and terms of the contract involved. If the contract continues then only a later repudiation will end it. If the appointment serves to discharge the contract then it will be by frustration or breach. For the consumer, this situation can mean that a continuing contract may be possible to complete by paying the balance owing on any lay-by and receiving the goods in question. This is done by the consumer dealing direct with the liquidator on behalf of the company.

However, in a situation like a prepayment for the supply of awnings which is usual given the need to make the awnings to a precise measurement, the liquidator of such a corporate supplier may not permit the work to be completed. Without completion the subsequent payment of the remainder of the contract amount by the consumer would not be required. However, in such circumstances the 'deposit' remains in the hands of the company and the consumer must prove for the amount as a debt, thus being treated as an unsecured creditor. No priority creditor status is given.

Due to the size and nature of the transaction, it is possible that the consumer has more chance of receiving goods and services completed after the appointment of a liquidator than if the work in progress was large and complicated and ordered by other larger corporate entities. The liquidator after appointment will try to calculate whether there is a financial benefit accruing to the company by completing any contracts. It is the liquidator's decision whether to complete and if he or she chooses not to complete this may result in claims for a breach of contract. Customers that have partly paid will join other unsecured creditors if there has not been a reciprocal part performance. As the CCH Australian Insolvency Management Practice text suggests:

---

25 Ibid. para 771.

26 Keay, A. *McPherson The Law of Company Liquidation* (4th ed. 1999) 235.

> [the liquidator] would be more amenable to completing the production of partially manufactured clothing in a downtown inner city location than the completion of major earthmoving contracts spread over remote areas of the State.[27]

For a consumer who has made a prepayment the type of work needed to complete the work is likely to be small and less complex.

Specific Responses by Australian State Governments

As mentioned above consumer protection laws do assist consumers faced with loss through an incomplete transaction by a failed corporate supplier. The Australian States in particular have responded by encouraging their consumer affairs departments to develop legislative and alternative resolutions responses such as those discussed below for the building industry as well as other means of regulation. For example, a state consumer affairs department may try to discuss with the liquidator the options available to consumers of a particular supplier such as a retailer who has many items held on lay-by. However, three particular areas of need have been identified since the mid 1980s. These are risks that consumers face when they make prepayments to funeral providers, travel agents and builders.

The very reason a consumer is treated as an unsecured creditor in corporate insolvency has driven States to legislate in the funeral industry. In New South Wales a *Funeral Funds Act* was enacted in 1979 and amended in 2003 by the *Funeral Funds Amendment Act*. The objects include protection of pre-payments made by consumers for funeral services[28] and this is most relevant if the contract has been made with a supplier that has now liquidated. In Queensland, the *Funeral Benefit Business Act 1982* (Qld) attempts to regulate the payments to entities in respect of prepaid funeral benefits. In Victoria, there is a *Funerals (Pre-paid Money) Act 1993* (Vic) that regulates the taking and management on money in respect of pre-paid funeral contracts. These pieces of legislation remove the prepayment from the funeral provider and require it to be invested with approved and separate trust funds that are subject to regular audit and other controls. Other States have no legislation on this issue but rely on self-regulation of these matters by voluntary codes of conduct.

In the travel industry, most Australian consumers have had protection for their travel prepayments since the late 1980s. In 1986, the New South Wales, Victorian and South Australian governments initiated a cooperative scheme for the regulation of travel agents. This scheme includes a Travel Compensation Fund

27 Taylor, T., Ferrier, I. and Hodgson, T. *CCH Australian Insolvency Management Practice* (looseleaf, 2004) 83–240.

28 *Funeral Funds Act 1979* (NSW) s3.

(TCF),[29] which provides security for monies paid in advance for travel services. The consumers are secured in the sense that those who suffer financial loss as a result of a travel agent's failure can claim against the Fund. Travel services generally involve payment of money well in advance of the services being provided. The payments can be significant and are made to persons who are not the ultimate service providers.[30] The three other States, Queensland, Tasmania and Western Australia, subsequently joined in the TCF and the Northern Territory partly joined, while not becoming a fully functioning participant.[31]

Consumers making travel prepayments bear risks arising from information asymmetry, as they have limited access to information to allow them to assess and compare the competencies and financial viability of different travel agents. With gross travel sales in Australia of $8.5 billion per annum,[32] the benefits of the TCF are obvious. However, the sustainability of the TCF has been questioned since 2000.

In a major report reviewing the regulation of travel agents, the NSW Department of Fair Trading found that consumers expect governments to regulate where prepayments are involved and governments have been even more prepared to regulate where intermediaries are involved.[33] The TCF has been a government initiated regulation without a national piece of legislation. In the period from its establishment in 1987 until 2000, there were 377 travel agency failures resulting in claims paid to consumers of over $23 million.[34] The average travel agency failure generated 48 claims totalling $75,000.[35] When conducting the review into the TCF, the Centre of International Economics ('CIE') suggested that data from the TCF indicated the rate of failure in the travel agents industry is higher than in the wider business

29 This is established under the *Travel Agents Acts* in participating states. See *Travel Agents Act* 1986 (NSW); *Travel Agents Act* 1986 (Vic); *Travel Agents Act* 1988 (Qld); *Travel Agents Act* 1985 (WA); *Travel Agents Act* 1986 (SA); *Travel Agents Act* 1987 (Tas).

30 Working Party, *Report to Ministers of Consumer Affairs (Ministerial Council on Consumer Affairs) on the National Competition Policy Review conducted by the Centre for International Economics*, National Co-operative Scheme for the Regulation of Travel Agents (2002) 14.

31 This was due to the lack of any NT legislation requiring agents to become and remain members of the TCF.

32 Working Party, *Report to Ministers of Consumer Affairs (Ministerial Council on Consumer Affairs) on the National Competition Policy Review conducted by the Centre for International Economics*, National Co-operative Scheme for the Regulation of Travel Agents (2002) 14.

33 Centre for International Economics, National Competition Policy review of the National Scheme for the Regulation of Travel Agents prepared for the Ministerial Council on Consumer Affairs (2000) 30.

34 Ibid. 45.

35 Ibid.

sector.[36] This presents a further reason for the specific regulation to protect consumers.

The CIE review canvassed various reform options to the TCF, including disbanding it altogether. The Review evaluated a 'no industry specific regulation model'. The major disadvantage to such a model was a failure to provide a mechanism for requiring travel agents to be covered by a compensation scheme to insure consumers who lose their deposits when travel agencies fail.[37] Under this option, consumers would be unable to receive timely recompense and would have to rely on more congested segments of the legal system – that is to be treated as unsecured creditors in a liquidation. In considering privatizing the compensation cover, CIE noted the existence of the International Association Travel Agents ('IATA') scheme that covers international airlines against agency collapse, agents against airline collapse, and consumers against both.[38] Based in the United States of America, the scheme is funded through a ticket levy.[39]

The third specific industry consumer protection scheme is a scheme in the building industry. It assists consumers when insolvency occurs to a domestic builder. All States have a 'builders warranty' scheme that covers both insolvency risk and quality relating to the builder's work and these are managed by private insurers. The schemes only apply to building projects where the value of the work is above a specified amount.[40] This amount varies from state to state, as does the length of the insurance and the minimum amount of cover that can be taken out. For example, in South Australia work over $12,000 requires a statutory warranty insurance cover.[41] The policy limit is $80,000 and the period is usually three months from handover until five years from the date the building was completed. In all States except Queensland the schemes are 'last resort' schemes, meaning that a claim can only be made if the builder is no longer in existence.[42]

In a recent submission to the Productivity Commission by the Builders' Collective of Australia Inc, an organization representing small and medium builders, the schemes were described as a 'cruel hoax' in consumer protection.[43] The reason for this is that the consumer must pursue the solvent builder privately through the civil courts and while claims against the insurance policy are possible when the builder is insolvent 'not one claim has been satisfied'.[44]

36 Ibid. 56.

37 Ibid. 103–108.

38 Ibid. 92.

39 Ibid.

40 See e.g., <http://www.qbe.com.au/Business/Builders-Warranty/Insurance-Cover-State/SA-South-Australia/Insurance.html> as this has a table comparing the different States and has the specified amounts.

41 See <http://www.ocba.sa.gov.au/consumeradvice/publications.html#Building_Indemnity_Insurance> accessed 1/12/05 and required by the *Building Work Contractors Act 1995* (SA).

42 Ibid.

43 <http://www.builderscollective.org.au/news/1-latest-news/49-productivity-commission-puts-pressure-on-states-over-bwi.html> accessed 1/12/05.

44 Ibid.

Despite such views, all three protections have become essential, in part due to the unsatisfactory result of leaving consumers as unsecured creditors in the liquidation of the supplier companies. One alternative for protecting consumers would be to grant a statutory priority. Although there have been just three industries identified above more may currently present problems and new developments could see the list added to in the future. The great advantage may be a comprehensive coverage of all members of society – a position that does not exist presently, due to the lack of uniform legislation on the measures taken to assist consumers in these three industries.

The other major development since the rush of consumer protection legislation in the 1970s has been the education of consumers. Government departments have been charged with educating the public on the dangers they are exposed to when dealing with unscrupulous traders. Even the media has played a role in educating consumers through avenues such as current affairs television and talkback radio. It might be expected that after the last thirty years, consumers would be less likely to trust a trader with a large deposit or prepayment. However, this is not always the case.

Comparisons with United Kingdom Consumers

The Cork Report[45] on insolvency in 1982 chronicled payments in advance for goods and services. The Cork Committee 'received many complaints that members of the public who pay in advance for goods and services have no remedy except as unsecured creditors in the event of the insolvency of the trader'.[46] The Committee recognized the problem for consumers, stating that 'they do not see themselves treated as ordinary providers of unsecured credit, though this is how they find themselves, except in those cases where special schemes have been established for their protection'.[47] The Cork Report noted that television and radio programmes and articles in the press and other media had also expressed concern that the law was unjust to members of the public who paid in advance for goods and services.[48] The Committee heard evidence that 'a considerable number of companies, dealing direct with the public, which become insolvent, have accepted or required payment prior to the delivery of the goods and services'.[49]

Despite the profiling of this problem, the Committee refused a priority treatment and specifically rejected the idea of legislation that would require all

45 Review Committee *Insolvency Law and Practice* Cmnd 8558 'Cork Report' (1982).

46 Ibid. para 1048.

47 Ibid.

48 Ibid. para 1049.

49 Ibid.

such money to be paid into special accounts having trust status.[50] In what seems a harsh treatment of consumers, the Cork Report stated:

> The customer who pays in advance for goods or services to be supplied later extends credit just as surely as the trader who supplies in advance goods or services to be paid for later. There is no essential difference. Each gives credit; and if the credit is misplaced, each should bear the loss rateably.[51]

The Cork Report also scoffed at the *Kayford* case[52] and dismissively stated 'of course, a trader is free, by taking the appropriate steps, to create a trust which will prevail in the event of … insolvency'.[53]

The Cork Report noted that one of its members expressed an opinion that a purchaser of future goods 'should not be expected to provide' for the supplier 'working capital' and recommended, inter alia, that 'payments made in advance should become trust money'.[54] Even this member did not go so far as to recommend a statutory priority.[55]

The Cork Report concluded this topic by suggesting that the principle of *pari passu* must continue to be the 'cornerstone' of any legislation and so they were not going to advocate any qualification to this principle to deal with problems such as consumer prepayments.[56]

Just two years on from the Cork Report, in 1984 the United Kingdom's Office of Fair Trading (OFT) produced a Report on *Prepayments and Insolvency*.[57] The paper found that there was no clear cut, unambiguous solution to the problem posed by prepayments in insolvency and the authors felt the most promising course of action was to pierce the veil of limited liability for company directors.[58] The authors did consider granting consumer creditors a priority in insolvency and pointed to difficulties in determining the scope of such protection.[59]

In 1984, the National Federation of Consumer Groups submitted to the Minister of Consumer Affairs a report called *Prepayments (Protecting Consumers' Deposits)*.[60] They also produced a draft Consumers' Prepayment (Protection) Bill. The Bill proposed to extend the *Kayford* principle to all prepayments received by

---

50 Ibid. para 1049, 1050.

51 Ibid. para 1052.

52 *Re Kayford Ltd* [1975] 1 WLR 279.

53 Review Committee *Insolvency Law and Practice* Cmnd 8558 (1982) para 1054.

54 Ibid. para 1053.

55 Ibid.

56 Ibid. para 1072.

57 Ogus, A.I. and Rowley, C.K. *Prepayments and Insolvency*, Office of Fair Trading Occasional Paper (1984).

58 Ibid. 34.

59 Ibid. 24–26.

60 The National Federation of Consumer Groups submission is discussed in Editorial, 'A Consumers Prepayment (Protection) Bill?' [1984] *Journal of Business Law* 105.

suppliers of goods and services. The Bill proposed that such prepayments would be impressed by a statutory trust and that the supplier be prohibited from using such prepayments as business capital or for similar purposes until the contract with the consumer was performed. The Bill also provided that the Secretary of State would have a discretion to make exceptions for areas of goods or services that had existing adequate protection. Exceptions were envisaged for the existing bonding scheme for travel agents, or insurance taken out by a supplier, or legislative protection like the Air Travel Reserve Fund, or self regulation like the Mail Order Protection Scheme.[61]

At the time the draft Bill was said to be 'worthy of consideration',[62] although it was criticized for being 'clearly insufficient' as it failed to admit exceptions for the frequent cases in which the supplier does not supply from stock but requires the prepayment in order to buy material needed for the execution of the contract.[63]

The OFT concluded that the time was not ripe for legislative action and did not adopt the proposals in the Bill. Again, the OFT were criticized because such legislative action, designed to protect consumers who have made a prepayment, was said to be unavoidable, as 'one day a widely publicized failure of a supplier'[64] would occur.

It has been suggested that about 200,000 consumers lost their consumer prepayments deposit or advance payment in 1987 in the United Kingdom.[65] At that time the size of the problem in the United Kingdom was £18 million or an average loss of £80 per consumer. In 1987, one in three adults made at least one consumer prepayment in the space of every two years.[66] Examples of the use of prepayments in the United Kingdom included outside painting, roller blinds, coach trips, holidays, air tickets, carpets and home improvements, with the last two being 'particularly bad' for consumers.[67] A number of methods of protection were espoused at the time and amongst these remedies were special insurance and separate trust accounts and suggestions that the prepayment creditor could be a priority creditor, even though there was a trend based on fairness principles to reduce the range of priority creditors.[68]

---

61 The Bill is discussed in detail in the Editorial above.

62 Ibid.

63 Ibid. 106.

64 Editorial, 'Protection of Consumers' Prepayments' [1985] *Journal of Business Law* 12. The editorial concludes 'why not shut the stable door before the horse has bolted?'

65 Samuels, A. 'Prepayments: The Lost Consumer Deposits' [1987] *Journal of Business Law* 30.

66 This could be expected to be substantially different in today's world with the increased use of credit cards and the internet.

67 Samuels, A. 'Prepayments: The Lost Consumer Deposits' [1987] *Journal of Business Law* 30.

68 Ibid. 31.

More recently, Finch has canvassed the issues for consumer prepayers in the United Kingdom.[69] She suggests that they may be geographically dispersed and this weakens their position. For example, they may not be where they can access information about the trader, to be able to assess risks and be warned against failure. She also makes the observation that 'consumer creditors may fail to see themselves as creditors at all'[70] – especially, she says, where the trader leads the consumer to think the period of prepayment is short. The *Insolvency Act 1985* (UK) and the *Enterprise Act 2002* (UK) that address other statutory priorities remain silent on a consumer priority.

Recently the Farepak case attracted considerable attention and highlighted the gaps in consumer protection.[71] The company conducted a Christmas Savings Scheme with consumers who made small contributions month by month through agents. The administration was announced in December causing a large public outcry and the administrators attempted to 'ringfence' some payments for consumers and establish a trust.

Comparisons with North American Consumers

In the United States of America, s507(a)(6) of the *Bankruptcy Reform Act 1978* (US)[72] initially granted a priority limited to $US600 (now $US2,100) to individuals who deposited money before the insolvency in connection with certain transactions for personal, family or household use, which were then not delivered or provided. [73] The transactions include the purchase, lease, or rental of property or the purchase of services. In order to reach only those persons most deserving of this special priority, there was debate regarding limiting it to favour individuals whose income was quite low.[74]

The section is designed to protect consumers in their dealings with retail merchants and these are usually deposits on merchandise that is undelivered by

---

69 Finch, V. *Corporate Insolvency Law Perspectives and Principles* (2002) 429–431.

70 Ibid. 430.

71 *In the matter of Farepak Foods and Gifts Ltd (in administration)* and *The Insolvency Act 1986* [2006] EWHC 3272.

72 *Bankruptcy Code* 11 U.S.C.S.§ 507.

73 See e.g., *In re Terra Distrib., Inc* (1992, BC DC Idaho) 148 BR 598, 20 UCCRS2d 144; *In re River Village Assocs.* (1993, BC ED Pa) 161 BR 127, 24 BCD 1400, appeal dismissed (1994, ED Pa) 1994 US Dist LEXIS 4386; *In re Elsinghorst Bros. Co* (1995, BC WD NY) 180 BR 52, 27 BCD 29; *In Re Deangelis Tangibles, Inc* (1999, BC MD Pa) 238 BR 96.

74 When introduced the priority was limited to $600 and there was a proposal for an income test of $20,000 by the Senate. This proposal was deleted.

insolvent retailers.[75] The subsection has been described as unambiguous and clear and the courts accord no weight to its legislative history.[76] The use of the term 'deposit' in the subsection is to provide a remedy for pre-purchase defaults by debtors in consumer transactions only and the appropriate definition of 'deposit' is 'putting down as pledge or partial payment'.[77]

The position of a statutory priority is not surprising given the strong advocacy by consumer groups and the subsection merely complements the extensive legislative treatment of consumer rights found in the jurisdiction.

No Priority in Canada

The *Bankruptcy and Insolvency Act 1985* does not extend a priority to any consumer matters. The most detailed Report into reform of insolvency laws, the Colter Report,[78] was completely silent on the topic of consumer prepayments while other statutory priorities for employees and the Crown featured significantly.

The only suggestion for including a consumer priority in insolvency legislation has come from the Law Reform Commission of British Columbia.[79] In 1987, the Commission discussed strategies for reform in the area of consumer prepayments and they considered recommending a statutory priority in the insolvency statute. The Commission believed that the consumer's position was 'very precarious', yet conceded that there was no way they could be fully protected from losses when a retail seller, because of insolvency, failed to deliver goods.[80] The Commission looked for ways to improve the legal position of consumers to reduce the likelihood of loss and recommended the creation of a buyers' lien.[81] They commented that a statutory priority was the most direct way of achieving an enhanced legal position for consumers and had the advantage of simplicity.[82]

Ultimately, however, the Commission rejected the idea of a consumer priority in the insolvency statute as an appropriate vehicle of reform, because of three factors. Firstly, as the insolvency statute was a federal statute they could only recommend

75 *In re Cimaglia* (1985, BC SD Fla) 50 BR 9 although other cases have dealt with services such as tuition funds in *In re Longo* (1992, BC DC Md) 144 BR 305, 5 Fourth Cir and Dist Col Bankr Ct Rep 36.

76 *United States Code Service* (2003) Annotations to § 507 under the heading 'History, Ancillary Laws and Directives', 63.

77 Ibid. *In re Heritage Village Church and Missionary Fellowship* (1991, BC DC SC) 137 BR 888, 4 Fourth Cir and Dist Col Bankr Ct Rep 531, 26 CBC2d 1093.

78 Advisory Committee on Bankruptcy and Insolvency, Canada Proposed Bankruptcy Act Amendments Report of the Advisory Committee on Bankruptcy and Insolvency 'Colter Report' (1986).

79 Law Reform Commission of British Columbia, Report on the Buyer's Lien: A New Consumer Remedy, Report No LRC 93 (1987).

80 Ibid. 4.

81 Ibid.

82 Ibid. 15.

that the provincial government make representations to the federal government on the matter.[83] Secondly, by 1987 the federal government had gone through 17 years of reform of insolvency laws with several exposure Bills but no progress, so this did not augur well for successful change for consumers.[84] Furthermore, none of the suggested reforms over those years had 'evinced any concern with consumer buyers' and the tendency for insolvency reform was towards decreasing the number and classes of priority creditors rather than increasing them.[85]

The Situation in New Zealand

In 1996, Heath reviewed a number of miscellaneous priorities including priorities for default under the *Motor Vehicles Dealers Act* 1975 (NZ) and payments for services to a company secured by a lien and commenced by stating that they were difficult to justify.[86] He concluded later that in relation to these miscellaneous priorities it was difficult to 'make out any case ... with the possible exception of lay-by sales',[87] although he offered no explanation for this view.

In 1999, the New Zealand Law Commission's Advisory Report to the Ministry of Commerce,[88] also chaired by Heath, included in a chapter on Miscellaneous Debts. Here, special mention was made of the *Lay-by Sales Act 1971*. This Act provided in s11(1) that where there was a liquidation of a seller and there were no goods or not enough goods to enable the lay-by sale to be completed, the buyer would become a priority creditor in the liquidation. The extent of the priority was the amount of payments that the buyer had made in the course of the lay-by. The Commission noted that where a company failed and there were goods the subject of a lay-by contract, these customers often sustained heavy losses.[89] Under s10(1) of the *Lay-by Sales Act 1971* if, on liquidation of the seller, the seller had goods of the kind which they had agreed to sell, whether those goods had been appropriated to the sale or not, then the buyer might pay the balance of the purchase price and obtain those goods. Such treatment alleviated the need for any sort of priority.

The Commission noted that an earlier committee – the Contracts and Commercial Law Reform Committee of New Zealand in 1969 on 'Lay-by Sales' – had stated that lay-by customers were a special class of creditors in the insolvency of the lay-

83 Ibid.

84 Ibid.

85 Ibid.

86 Heath, P. 'Preferential Payments on Bankruptcy and Liquidation in New Zealand: Are They Justifiable exceptions to the *Pari Passu* Rule?' (1996) 4 *Waikato Law Review* 24, 53.

87 Ibid.

88 New Zealand Law Commission Advisory Report to the Ministry of Commerce, *Priority Debts in the Distribution of Insolvent Estates* (1999).

89 Ibid. para 173.

by vendor.[90] This committee had expressed the view that if a priority were given it would see financiers and merchants exercising a degree of supervision over lay-by vendors and the unstable lay-by vendor would find it more difficult to raise finance or obtain credit.[91]

The New Zealand Law Commission, looking at the situation 30 years after the Contracts and Commercial Law Reform Committee of New Zealand and with 28 years of legislative experience from the *Lay-by Sales Act 1971* (NZ), stated that there were compelling reasons why the priority afforded by the Act should be continued.[92]

The Commission stated four reasons for keeping the priority. Firstly, they said prudent budgeting should be encouraged by the law and anecdotal evidence suggested that lay-by was still a popular form of purchasing goods despite the growth in the use of credit cards.[93] (This is an interesting difference to Australia, where the Rogerson Report in 1969 stated that the use of lay-by was not widespread and appeared to be declining even back then.[94]) Secondly, they recognized that those who use lay-by systems are often consumers of 'modest means' who can ill afford to lose the money.[95] Thirdly, they felt that the sums involved were 'generally modest and are unlikely to impact on dividends received by other creditors'.[96] Finally, they noted that the appropriation of goods by the vendor was typically beyond the control of the customer.[97]

The New Zealand Parliament's amendments to insolvency legislation in 2006 did not include any priorities other than the expected employee and administrative provisions.

---

90 Ibid. para 173 citing The Contracts and Commercial Law Reform Committee of New Zealand, Lay-by Sales (1969) 9.

91 Ibid.

92 Ibid. para 175, 176.

93 Ibid. para 175.

94 *Report to the Standing Committee of State and Commonwealth Attorneys-General on the Law Relating to Consumer Credit and Money Lending*, The Law School University of Adelaide (1969) (known as the Rogerson Report). See particularly chapter titled 'Miscellaneous'.

95 New Zealand Law Commission Advisory Report to the Ministry of Commerce, *Priority Debts in the Distribution of Insolvent Estates* (1999).

96 Ibid.

97 Ibid.

Justification for a Consumer Priority

While all prepayment consumers ought to have minimum protection by law, this protection can take any one of several different and alternative forms.[98] One of these could be a statutory priority for the supplier insolvency.

A Theoretical Justification

From a theoretical perspective the inclusion of a new priority could satisfy the creditors' bargain model, outlined in Chapter 3, as the priority emerges from a contractual relationship involving an identified creditor. Communitarians[99] too would be satisfied to see the *Corporations Act,* or the main corporate insolvency legislation in a jurisdiction, including consumers who, while creditors, are overlooked in a large percentage of corporate insolvency lawmaking.

The Special Nature of Consumers

It has been argued that the prepayment consumer creditor is not just another creditor, as their claims are different to those of other creditors. One commentator describes the prepayment consumer creditor as

> a layman (sic), ignorant of the law and commercial practice, with no access to information regarding creditworthiness, risking his money and not appreciating the risk ... the consumer is likely to be a small man, making a not insignificant prepayment.[100]

It was argued in 1987 that it is not right to expect the prepayment consumer to compete with public and trade creditors in a winding up.[101] This is because trade creditors can look after themselves and the debt is not likely to be personally distressing. The consumer prepayments creditor is not really a creditor, in the commercial sense, but more like a beneficiary of a trust and therefore deserving of some sort of special protection or priority.[102]

Arguments used for protecting other priority creditors like employees often criticize the company's practice of using the money for entitlements as emergency working capital, as outlined in Chapter 4. These same arguments apply to

98 See e.g., Samuels, A. 'Prepayments: The Lost Consumer Deposits' [1987] *Journal of Business Law* 30, 31.

99 See Chapter 3.

100 Samuels, A. 'Prepayments: The Lost Consumer Deposits' [1987] *Journal of Business Law* 30, 32.

101 Ibid.

102 Ibid.

consumer prepayments. Such behaviour has been considered 'morally wrong' and an 'improper business practice'.[103]

A statutory priority in the insolvency statute for consumer prepayments would be simple and overcome difficulties such as the need to keep a trust account and other record keeping. The options of establishing a trust for the prepayments or creating a statutory priority would be equally efficient and not impact greatly on post- insolvency expenses.

While every consumer prepayment needs the protection, only the unfulfilled ones need a mechanism for repayment. The statutory priority option is not an imposition on all companies and this is important because not all fail or engage in business practices that use prepayments for emergency working capital.

As analysed in the previous chapter with a new priority for the environment, the consumer priority can be tested too using the same four criteria adapted from Finch.[104]

Finch's Criteria 1 – ability to gain and use information concerning default risk Consumers have little ability to gain information about the risk they are taking with any company that requires a prepayment. Apart from requesting financial statements or credit checking, which is unlikely for consumers, there is not an easy way to facilitate the access to information. In recent times in Australia, most proprietary companies (i.e. smaller, often family or privately held companies) have been relieved from depositing an annual return with meaningful financial information to the government regulator, ASIC. Minor protection would be available from government consumer affairs departments, who can give general advice but they would not advise on the financial standing of particular trading companies. Freedom of contract principles though might suggest that consumers are always free not to contract where the prepayment aspects of the trading cause concern.

Finch's Criteria 2 – capacity to exit from excessively risk-laden arrangements The consumer may be able to exit from a trading contract with prepayments, but it may constitute a breach of contract. Contract law would probably determine that the contract is voidable if the consumer has already paid their prepayments. For the consumer the option of exit from the contract has probably expired once a liquidator is in place. The best the consumer can hope for is the completion of the contract by the liquidator. The consumer is a voluntary but unfortunate creditor.

Finch's Criteria 3 – vulnerability to risks The size of the consumer's exposure obviously varies throughout the different industries that require prepayments. For some work there is an industry standard that half the amount of the transaction will be paid in a prepayment, whereas other industries might work on just 10 percent being forwarded before work will commence. The amount of risk for the consumer

103 Ibid. 32, 33.

104 Finch, V. *Corporate Insolvency Law Perspectives and Principles* (2002) 449.

to bear is therefore different depending upon the transaction and industry. Because of the lack of uniformity across jurisdictions in Australia, the vulnerability will also differ depending upon the State the consumer resides in. Furthermore, the incidence of insolvency is greater in some industries that require prepayments than others. This is highlighted by the fact that some States have chosen to legislate to give specific protection while others States show much less interest. An insolvency practitioner may seek to complete the contracts and then the consumer achieves a satisfactory outcome, but then other liquidators may choose not to go to such lengths.

The consumer will be vulnerable to risks that they do not understand or are even aware of, as they make their prepayment after being exposed to the marketing and information asymmetry of the supplier. This is particularly likely where they are told that this is the way the corporate supplier, and all others in that particular industry, do business.

Finch's Criteria 4 – status as a low- or high-cost bearer of risk Consumer prepayments are not going to be present in all insolvencies and consumers come in all shapes and sizes, from the very wealthy to the very poor. When a consumer prepayment is lost through corporate insolvency, the risk is essentially borne by the individual consumers. Individually, they become a low cost bearer of risk because they will generally have other financial means, independent of this contract, and this may be the only contract that they have entered and for which they have not received satisfactory performance. They still hope for reimbursement but for them to fail to receive anything from this contract, and its prepayment, is unlikely to be critical to their financial position. Despite the fact that the consumer might be in the position to bear of loss of say $1,000 for awnings that they never receive due to a supplier's liquidation, it is undesirable for consumers to be burdened with a position of a low cost bearer of risk. The pensioner who has had to save up to order those awnings bears what they perceive as a high cost if they lose the prepayments and receive no awnings and then have to start saving all over again.

Divination

Based on Finch's criteria, there is some justification for a new priority to be granted in favour of some consumer creditors. However, the need is not immediate and further investigation, perhaps by way of collecting empirical data, may be needed to add to the justification.

If consumers were to be given a priority in the *Corporations Act 2001* (Cth), a new subsection could be added to s556(1) that read:

> next, if at commencement date there were amounts due in the nature of consumer prepayments such as lay-bys, advance payments or deposits and there has been no performance of the related contract, these amounts.

If such a measure were to eventuate and a consumer priority was added to the *Corporations Act 2001* (Cth) s556(1) it would surely hold a position after the existing priorities of administrative expenses and employee entitlements.

Loyalty Schemes

Related to the topic of consumers and corporate insolvency are the relatively new phenomena of loyalty points, reward schemes and frequent flyers. Could they be the new area for a statutory priority?

Frequent flyer and other such schemes attempt to reward customer loyalty. In effect a consumer is rewarded in points that can be redeemed for goods and services, mainly airline flights, by maintaining loyalty to a particular supplier. Most programmes have rigid terms and conditions which protect the supplier. The method and /or time of taking up or spending frequent flyer/ reward points are subject to the supplier's terms and conditions. Frequent flyer points have been described as 'incapable of being accurately valued and even if this were not so, the supplier's terms and conditions prohibit this conversion'.[105] Recently, there has been trading in points and, while the possibility of purchasing points from other consumers has been discouraged, some suppliers have commenced selling points that are not earned through purchases. For most consumers the frequent flyer points bestow an entitlement to certain rewards at the sole discretion of the supplier and cannot be transferred from one supplier to another and cannot be redeemed for cash. This makes them unique if the supplier is liquidated.

The Legal Status of Loyalty Schemes

From a legal point of view frequent flyer schemes have created some interesting law. In Australia, there has been litigation on the question of whether they are assessable under the *Income Tax Assessment Act 1936* (Cth) as 'income' or a 'benefit'.[106] The Federal Court has held they were not income for such purposes and, upon the facts before the court, they were not a 'benefit' as the employer did not know that the employee was receiving the benefit.[107] In Australia, there have been other cases involving their treatment in matrimonial property settlements, their inclusion in the definition of 'remuneration' under industrial law[108] and trade practices disputes (predominantly misleading and deceptive conduct claims) over

105 Farey, J. Member, Consumer, Trader and Tenancy Tribunal (NSW) in *Ling v American Express International* [2003] NSWCTTT 249 (10 March 2003).

106 *J L Payne v Commissioner of Taxation* Nos NG 461 of 1995 and NG 239 of 1995 Fed No 347/96, 94 ATC 4191.

107 Ibid. 4193.

108 *Jackson and National Aboriginal Islander Skills Development Association Inc* NSWIRComm 118 (24 April 2003).

the transfer of points[109] and the unavailability of the points for a consumer in the United States of America due to Ansett's collapse.[110]

With the failure of Ansett in 2001, there was an enormous amount of public discussion in Australia regarding the fate of loyalty 'credits' that were earned by consumers (customers) of the airline. With Ansett's liquidation in 2002 the 'credits' entitling free flights or upgrades were lost. The topic is of some legal interest because frequent flyer points are not purchased but given as a reward for choosing this particular supplier. The recipients of these entitlements are not really 'creditors' as they have no debt owed apart from an entitlement to redeem their 'credits' when the airline is flying. Many consumers even acquire them from air travel booked and paid for by their employer.

Ansett Frequent Flyers and Insolvency

The Ansett airline failure shows just how such schemes can impact in insolvency. Ansett had 2.7 million frequent flyer 'members' who had accumulated unused frequent flyer points.[111] When the insolvency administrators were working upon the Part 5.3A procedures (Australia's corporate rescue legislation) and attempting to put together a rescue package they included the frequent flyers in their deliberations. The administrators were required to hold the second statutory meeting (the meeting that determines the future of the company) and so notice of this meeting had to go to 'as many of the creditors of the company as is reasonably practicable'.[112] Notice was required to be given by delivering it personally or by sending it prepaid post or fax or DX (Document Exchange).[113] Compliance with these provisions posed administrative difficulties and considerable expense for the administrators. Ansett's financial position involved assets of $850 million and liabilities of $1.8 billion–2.0 billion.[114] The cost of sending this notice and the required documentation to creditors was estimated at $28 million.[115] Even if the

---

109 *Ling v American Express International* [2003] NSWCTTT 249 (10 March 2003).

110 *Zilka v Westpac Banking Corporation* [2002] NSWCTTT 527 (20 September 2002).

111 *Business Review Weekly* reported in October 2001 that 'more than four million Ansett Global Rewards members have probably lost all their points' and they also said that 'Ansett customers are furious that their points are now worthless'. Ross, E. 'Flyblown Rewards' 23(5) *Business Review Weekly* October 4–10 2001, 34.

112 Corporations Act 2001 (Cth) s439A(3).

113 Corporations Regulations 5.6.12(2).

114 In a book on the fall of Ansett, *Ansett the Collapse* (2002) the authors Geoff Eastdown and Peter Wilms have included an appendix listing Ansett's major creditors as at 4 March 2002. The first entry reads 'Golden Wings members, trade suppliers, frequent flyer points holders and coupon creditors 1.1b Australian dollars'.

115 Zwier, L., Merkel, D. and Buchanan, I. 'Ansett Administration Court-Approved Websites' (2002) 76(3) *Law Institute Journal* 46, 49.

administrators sent a one-page double-sided notice it would still cost nearly $1.3 million.[116] The administrators sought the Federal Court's directions. Options were given to the Federal Court such as only giving 'proper' notice to unsecured trade creditors (who had a greater right to notice) and then giving notice by way of the internet and newspaper advertisements to frequent flyers.[117]

The situation posed the question of frequent flyer points holders as creditors in the insolvency. Justice Goldberg determined that

> [A]lthough there is an issue for the administrators to resolve in relation to the value to be given to the rights of the holders of frequent flyer points as creditors, I do not regard that as a relevant consideration to take into account in determining the manner in which notice of the second meeting should be given to creditors. Nor do I regard the manner in which the holders of frequent flyer points acquired their points, or can use them, as a relevant consideration on this application. Once the administrators make the decision (as they have done) to treat the holders of frequent flyer points as creditors for the purpose of the second meeting, those holders are to be treated in the same way as other creditors in relation to the manner in which they are to be given notice of the second meeting.[118]

So without giving real direction of whether frequent flyers were creditors for insolvency purposes, Goldberg J treated them in that vein because the administrators had already done so. It was resolved that newspaper advertisements and the internet web page could be used to satisfy the notice provisions in question.

The Growing Importance of Frequent Flyers as Creditors in Insolvency

There is a threshold issue of whether frequent flyers really are creditors.[119] If they are creditors, then their need for a statutory priority can be explored. Firstly, the difficulty in valuing frequent flyer points is acknowledged. Next, should they be given any priority treatment in the legislation due to their 'consumer' standing? Many who acquire these points do so when travelling for business purposes on flights paid for by their employer and so are not really consumers in the same way as an individual consumer who may spend personal funds on prepaying for curtains only to find the supplier in insolvency.[120] On the other hand, courts have decided that the frequent flyer membership is a contract and the use of the points

116 Ibid.

117 *In the matter of Ansett Australia Ltd and Mentha* [2002] FCA 2 (7 January 2002).

118 *In the matter of Ansett Australia Ltd and Mentha* [2002] FCA 2 (7 January 2002) 9.

119 See Symes, C. 'Lessons on Loyalty Schemes in Insolvency' (2003) 4 (3) *Insolvency Law Bulletin* 33.

120 In taxation law it has been determined that the tickets that result from cashing in the points are not 'income' for Australian tax purposes.

results from a personal contractual entitlement with the individual who earned them.[121] Such considerations are likely to feature in future litigation.

Many present marketing strategies encompass loyalty schemes, some that involve large retailers (e.g. Flybuys at Target), large banks (e.g. at Citibank) and tourism operators, and this way of doing business is likely to continue. Airlines are frequently the purveyor of the frequent flyer points and the deliverer of the rewards from loyalty schemes. Now consider that in March 2002 *Business Review Weekly* reported that 'the world's 523 airlines lost a combined $US10 billion during 2001'[122] and as airline insolvencies occur there is frequent flyer disappointment. In Australia, Qantas has been joined by Virgin Blue as airlines offering frequent flyer points. The size of the potential problem can be represented by Qantas, who, in 2005, had 4.1 million frequent flyers[123] all that are exposed to a risk of loss should the airline fail.

Corporate failure of the company that offers such schemes may occur and it would have a really large impact on the community who lost entitlements. It would be a popular electoral move for the Federal Government to introduce protection in the form of a statutory priority so that if such a circumstance were to arise the community would be protected. Such a legislative move would cost governments nothing, would be simple to implement and would not upset nor impose costs on the business community. Whether it could be justified remains uncertain.

Conclusion

Consumers could be given priority treatment for 'lost' prepayments under insolvency legislation. Furthermore, legislation could clarify the position of loyalty schemes in insolvency and points-holders could become priority creditors now that it has been established that they are creditors.[124] As a piece of social legislation it may lack support from some sections of the community, however, because of the mix of private and business expenditure that is used to accumulate the points.

Legislation could clarify the position of frequent flyer holders and other points-holders in loyalty schemes upon a company's insolvency. At present upon liquidation all loyalty scheme participants lose their points. As identified already in this chapter, often it is information that is crucial for the protection of

121 *Payne v Commissioner of Taxation* Nos NG 461 of 1995 and NG 239 of 1995 Fed No 347/96.

122 Holloway, N. and Wherry, R. 'Troubled Airlines may have to Fly United', 24(2) *Business Review Weekly*, 21–27 March 2002, 38.

123 A current figure quoted in Innes, S. 'Frequent Flyers Demand an Upgrade', *The Advertiser* (Adelaide), 19 February 2005, 54.

124 It is possible that this interpretation by the Federal Court in *Ansett* as reported above could be tested in the future.

consumers.[125] Lack of information on frequent flyer schemes for consumers has been criticized.[126] Information is going to be crucial if the consumers are going to be able to scrape out any benefit from the liquidated supplier.

Consumer prepayments have various protections through State legislation and regulation and self-regulation. Some consumer prepayments have no protection upon a supplier's insolvency and so further consideration could be given to a new statutory priority.

---

125 The website <www.frequentflyer.com.au> assisted consumers during the Ansett downfall. They reported that Ansett Global Reward members (the frequent flyer scheme) were being discouraged from registering as creditors. They encouraged members to register and ignore the consultant on the Ansett help line who would 'probably tell you that you cannot register'. The advice was to request a proof of debt form, complete it and lodge it as soon as possible.

126 For example, in Canada, *Democracy Watch* said 'With airlines offering an increasingly broad array of inter-airline partnership and frequent flyer deals, consumers often lack the information needed to take advantage of these deals … consumers are largely unorganized … and … few consumer groups exist to represent the consumer interest and provide information to consumers'. Democracy Watch, 'Creation of Watchdog Groups to Monitor Canadian Banks, Cable TV and Telephone Companies, and Airlines', Democracy Watch On-line 26 August 2003, <www.dwatch.ca/camp/actcub.htm>.

Chapter 9
Musing on Other Possibilities for Statutory Priorities

To complete the narrative of exploring the justifications and history of statutory priorities, it is important to consider what other statutory priorities have had consideration in the past or could be expected to feature in future legislation dealing with the distribution of corporate assets in an insolvency. In presenting 'other' priorities, the chapter canvasses their justification using the criteria used in the previous two chapters and the possible theoretical viewpoints highlighted in Chapter 3.

From time to time, new ideas enter into the debate on what should exist as a statutory priority in corporate insolvency. For example, small businesses as unsecured trade creditors in insolvency will argue that they receive poor treatment and should receive greater assistance from the statute.[1] Certainly, lobby groups representing small business interests agitate this way. Likewise, any person caught up in insolvency of a company may express the desire to be considered for priority treatment. These possibilities are discussed below.

From the outset in this exercise in augury, it is acknowledged that new priorities are unpopular.[2] For example, 97 percent of insolvency practitioners responding to a survey in the United Kingdom indicated they would not advocate the introduction of any other new class of priority creditors.[3]

In Australia, the Harmer Report[4] only discussed one new priority and that was protection for pre paid consumer contracts,[5] as discussed in Chapter 8. As outlined, the Commission considered that there was an insufficient case to justify

1 See e.g., Goode, R.M. 'Is the Law Too Favourable to Secured Creditors?' (1983–4) 8 *Canadian Business Law Journal* 53.

2 As already suggested in Chapter 8 above. See e.g., Garrido, J.M. 'The Distributional Question in Insolvency: Comparative Aspects' (1995) 4 *International Insolvency Review* 25, 53.

3 Keay, A. and Walton, P. 'Preferential Debts: An Empirical Study' [1999] *Insolvency Lawyer* 112, 116.

4 Australian Law Reform Commission, *General Insolvency Inquiry*, Report No 45 (1988), 'Harmer Report' para 769.

5 See also New Zealand, Heath, P. 'Preferential Payments on Bankruptcy and Liquidations in New Zealand: Are They Justifiable Exceptions to the *Pari Passu* Rule (1996) 4 *Waikato Law Review* 24, who includes 'lay-by sales' in discussion of miscellaneous priorities, ibid. 53.

the introduction of this as a new priority.[6] Other new priorities did not feature either in the submissions or in the final report.

This chapter ponders the position of small businesses, franchisees, tort victims, primary producers, landlords, essential service providers, international creditors, and indigenous corporations as possible recipients of future statutory priorities in corporate insolvency. It is necessarily superficial in its treatment of their possibilities.

Each is set out in a separate discussion section.

Small Business

Governments in Australia and other countries often assert that there is a need to support and grow small businesses. Yet the fact remains that small businesses appear in great numbers in the insolvency statistics. For example, in the United Kingdom, 88.5 percent of companies subject to formal insolvency have a turnover of less than £5 million.[7] In Australia, the figures are difficult to identify; in one investigation in 1985, it was found that 54.8 percent of all companies entering liquidation were small businesses.[8]

Small businesses dominate the unsecured credit provided to corporate Australia and so could be expected to receive little as unsecured creditors in the denouement of corporate insolvency proceedings. This has led to a number of commentators questioning the plight of unsecured creditors.[9]

The definition of a 'small' business has been the subject of some debate. For corporate insolvency law purposes, it would be appropriate to use the 'small proprietary limited' company definition as used in the *Corporations Act 2001* (Cth) and extend it to partnerships, individuals and other small trading vehicles. Section 45A of the *Corporations Act 2001* (Cth) defines a proprietary company as 'small' if the company satisfies two of the following three criteria: less than 50 equivalent full time employees, less than 12.5 million in assets and less than 25 million in turnover. Such a definition could be used in any statutory priority.

---

6 Australian Law Reform Commission, *General Insolvency Inquiry*, Report No 45 (1988) para 771.

7 White Paper *Productivity and Enterprise Insolvency: A Second Chance* <http://www.insolvency.gov.uk/compwp.htm>.

8 Peacock, R.W. 'The Financial Effects of the Legal Failure of Proprietary Companies' (1985) 8 *Accounting Forum* 25. This finding confirmed Peacock's earlier work; Peacock, R.W. 'Small Business Mortality: Legal Failures in South Australia' (Forum Series No 8, School of Accountancy, South Australian Institute of Technology, 1984).

9 See e.g., Bebchuk, L.A. and Fried, J.M. 'The Uneasy Case for the Priority of Secured Claims in Bankruptcy' (1996) 105 *Yale Law Review* 857; Goode, R.M. 'Is the Law Too Favourable to Secured Creditors?' (1983–4) 8 *Canadian Business Law Journal* 53; Klotz, R.A. 'Protection of Unpaid Suppliers under the New Bankruptcy and Insolvency Act' (1993) 21 *Canadian Business Law Journal* 161.

One of the most well known cases to company lawyers in the common law countries is *Salomon v Salomon and Co Ltd.*[10] The facts of the case illustrate how small business can expose itself in insolvency. The court held that Salomon had good security in his lending to the 'one man' company he was controlling: that is, the company was separate from its shareholders. The outcome of the decision would have been tough on the company's suppliers such as the small businesses that might have supplied the leather for the company's shoemaking, as they would have been left to be paid as unsecured creditors after Mr Salomon. While giving the leather suppliers a priority might not have resulted in a greater dividends because the secured creditors, like Mr Salomon, still would have outranked them, it does illustrate there are a number of persons dealing with the company who lack economic power and, indeed, legal knowledge. Many of these persons will be the small businesses that supply the company on credit. Certainly, the use of secured credit and the recognition of floating charges affected unsecured creditors greatly and, so as described in Chapter 2, legislation like the *Preferential Payments in Bankruptcy Act 1897* (UK) was needed to give certain unsecured creditors special treatment. Small business has never featured for such favourable attention. In fact small business has been on the losing end as others have gained priority creditor status and taken priority payments from assets that might have been available for all unsecured creditors if no scheme of statutory priority existed.

It should be recognized that small business is an effective lobby group in the corporate world in modern times. In 1982, the United Kingdom contemplated a 10 percent fund that would have seen 10 percent of the net realizable assets made available to ordinary unsecured creditors.[11] While attractive to small businesses, the proposal met with considerable opposition from vested interests. In 1984, a White Paper reprehended the idea and the result was that the idea was 'consigned ... to the shelf to gather dust'.[12] Eventually, in 2003, the *Enterprise Act 2002* (UK) provided for an amount to be siphoned off from the recovery by the floating chargeholder and earmarked for unsecured creditors.[13] In part, this is a reflection of what is possible for small business – a statutory priority would give special treatment as well.

One British proposal put forward in 1991,[14] and building upon the 10 percent fund idea, suggested that 'sympathetic treatment could be afforded to (both trade and consumer) creditors [who were] owed small sums', for example below £750 which equated to the minimum debt for a winding up petition.[15] The proposal,

10 *Salomon v Salomon and Co Ltd* [1897] AC 22.

11 Review Committee, *Insolvency Law and Practice* Cmnd 8558 (1982), 'Cork Report' para 1538–1549.

12 Milman, D. 'Ten Per Cent Fund' [1999] *Insolvency Lawyer* 47

13 *Enterprise Act 2002* (UK) s252.

14 Milman, D. 'Priority Rights in Corporate Insolvency' in Clarke, A. (ed.), *Current Issues in Insolvency Law* (1991) 78.

15 Ibid.

which focused on the size of the debt and not the size of the creditor, would have provided 'less attractive rates of return being offered to the balance of the debt over and above' the £750.[16] This proposal could be worked up into a statutory priority where any unsecured debt of a specified maximum could be paid in priority. The disadvantage is the inefficiency in having an insolvency practitioner spend time extracting small debts for special treatment. Another disadvantage with such a proposal is that it is difficult to correlate the size of the loan (the credit extended by the creditor) with the vulnerability of the creditor.[17]

Finch explores the possibility of special treatment for small businesses in her analysis of 're-thinking *pari passu*'.[18] Although branding them traders, she assesses the small business along with all other traders, recognizing that they bear risk and they are not in a position to adjust (credit) rates.[19] They are left therefore to carry the burden of extending credit to companies that become insolvent.

Justification for Small Businesses

As outlined in Chapters 7 and 8, Finch[20] proposes four criteria to justify a priority (hereafter the Finch criteria). These criteria can be applied to small businesses as potential priority creditors.

Finch's Criteria 1 – ability to gain and use information concerning default risk Small businesses will not gain and use information concerning default risk because the time scales to which they work tend to be too short, the costs of information are too high, or relevant data may be unavailable.

Finch's Criteria 2 – capacity to exit from excessively risk-laden arrangements Small businesses may have a capacity to exit from arrangements, but they will be unlikely to detect the excessively risk-laden debtors. They are unlikely to have such established credit control or the ready availability of a substitute market. Their performance of the supply contract will probably have been completed and it will be the debtor's performance that is outstanding.

Finch's Criteria 3 – vulnerability to risks Small businesses tend not to be totally dependent upon the viability of one debtor who they then later find is insolvent. They would tend to have a large number of customers and if one becomes insolvent they are less exposed than the few traders who are involved in the supply of goods or services to one main customer.

16 Ibid.
17 Finch, V. 'Is *Pari Passu* Passé?' [2000] *Insolvency Lawyer* 194, 209.
18 Ibid. 206.
19 Ibid.
20 Finch, V. *Corporate Insolvency Law Perspectives and Principles* (2002) 449.

Finch's Criteria 4 – status as a low- or high-cost bearer of risk Some small businesses might be more energetic at their debt collection and so do not need the protection when just one of their customers fails. They may be wise enough to spread risks and ensure that they do not have a narrow customer base.

Despite this analysis it cannot be assumed that small business creditors are necessarily less well-informed, expert or strongly positioned to negotiate than large creditors.[21] It is easy to imagine a local small business having local knowledge that informs them of one of their debtors facing financial troubles and the small business reacting by reducing their credit exposure and converting to cash-only transactions. This may depend on the particular market or organizational set up involved, the relevant regulatory regime or even the state of the economy.

Divination on Small Businesses

The divination for this group is that there are just too many small businesses in corporate insolvency to extend a priority. The occurrence of a small business as an unsecured creditor will be consistently very high in corporate insolvency and there is not a strong case to justify the introduction of a statutory priority.

Franchisees

One group of creditors generally falling into the 'small business' category would be franchisees. A franchise involves a business, the franchisee, being permitted to use a well-known business name, and receiving advice and assistance, in return for money and/or purchasing stock-in-trade from, or at the direction of a franchisor.[22] A franchise agreement should contain terms and conditions relating to termination as well as many other aspects, although it is unlikely to specify the consequences upon the insolvency of a franchisor. Franchisees often borrow money to enter these contracts and if the franchisor fails shortly thereafter then their 'up-front' payment will deliver little and they are left to claim as an unsecured creditor.

Statistics suggest franchises have been embraced in Australia, with over 700 different franchise systems and around 50,000 franchisees with an industry turnover in excess of $82 billion.[23]

Ansett's airline failure in Australia also caused loss to travel agents as franchisees under a franchise business known as Traveland.[24] Once the product

21 Finch, V. 'Is *Pari Passu* Passé?' [2000] *Insolvency Lawyer* 194, 209.

22 Definition taken from Hardy Ivamy, E.R. *Mozley & Whiteley's Law Dictionary* (10th ed. 1988).

23 Figures appearing in Latimer, P. *2004 Australian Business Law* (23rd ed. 2004) 713.

24 The writer is indebted to Jenny Buchan of the University of New South Wales School of Business Law and Taxation who drew my attention to the plight of franchisees under Ansett.

was gone, in this case airline travel with Ansett, then their franchisees (over 200 in all) were very exposed. Some franchisees 'rebadged' themselves by joining other franchises or travel agency businesses but others lingered and closed down.[25] They merely enjoyed unsecured creditor status in the liquidation. Many would have borrowed to enter the franchise (including mortgaging personal property) to make the 'up front' payment to join the franchise and some could have been with the franchise for only a few months.

A franchisee's ability to manage the risk of their failed franchisor is negligible and their access to information of the franchisor is likely to be minimal. Yet their vulnerability to risk is high despite them choosing this form of business structure to assist them in being successful in starting a new business; despite trying to be risk adverse they may experience the very opposite. Their ability to spread the risk is also hampered by their type of business structure, as they are contracted to purchase exclusively from the franchisor.

It is possible that a series of large franchisors failing could spark media interest and lead to lobbying to change the position of these franchisees. They have many similarities with, and are as vulnerable as employees.

Justification for Franchisees

Finch's Criteria 1 – ability to gain and use information concerning default risk Franchisees in Australia are assisted in some measures by the Franchising Code of Conduct.[26] The Code requires franchisors to give franchisees a disclosure document before entering into the franchise agreement and yearly thereafter. This document must disclose amongst other things the business experience of the

25 There were about 300 travel agencies in Traveland in early 2001. 150 of the former Traveland franchisees moved into another franchise Jetset Travelworld when paid $A225,000 in December 2001. Traveland was a wholly owned subsidiary of Ansett and went into voluntary administration on 12 September 2001. Travelworld unsuccessfully bid $A3.6 million for Traveland in October 2001. The successful bidder Internova was subsequently placed into liquidation. Financial Options Group Inc entered a sale agreement to buy Traveland in December but failed to meet the sale agreement and then they liquidated. It was then that Travelworld had 150 of the former Traveland franchisees convert to it. Australian Stock Exchange Announcements 04/03/02 and Australian Associated Press *Financial News* wire 10/04/02. *Business Review Weekly* (Sydney) 14 March 2002 reported that 'The 300-store Traveland franchise network was sold to Travelworld in December and the 120 wholly owned stores closed'. However, many Traveland franchisees had deserted the group before the sale; Australian Stock Exchange Announcements 04/03/02. *The Advertiser* (Adelaide) on 8 June 2002 reported that United Travel Agents Group had launched Travelscene, a franchise 'taken up by 50 former Traveland agencies mainly in New South Wales and Queensland'.

26 The Franchising Code of Conduct was released by the Federal Government in 1998 and is legally enforceable as it has effect pursuant to s51AE of the *Trade Practices Act 1974* (Cth).

franchisor, present or past litigation and details of specified events that may have occurred in the last three financial years. Such treatment gives the franchisee some limited ability to gauge the risks of the franchisor's insolvency.

Finch's Criteria 2 – capacity to exit from excessively risk-laden arrangements Again, in Australia, the Franchising Code of Conduct allows for franchisees to be able to terminate before the agreement expires and provided there is no breach by the franchisee.[27] However, it may be that the franchisee only realizes that they want to exit when it is too late and the franchisor has gone into liquidation. It is imperative that, as a franchise is a contract based business entity, the terms and conditions of termination are clearly set out.

Finch's Criteria 3 – vulnerability to risk Most franchises are commenced with an upfront payment and this franchise fee is meant to cover a host of property and intellectual property matters. If a franchisor goes into liquidation without continuing to provide the promised property or intellectual property then the franchisee will have difficulty acquiring a replacement. For example, the upfront fee may include a fee for ongoing training and this is lost if the franchise collapses due to franchisor liquidation.

Finch's Criteria 4 – status as a low- or high-cost bearer of risk A franchisee does not have any ability to spread the risk that they adopt when entering the franchise agreement. The freedom of contract principle will work to suggest that they happily accepted the restrictions within the franchise agreement. They were, after all, free to enter the contract and take the risks. They were a voluntary creditor. While the liquidation of the franchisee is likely to be discussed, the same discussion is unlikely to be had regarding the franchisor. Assuming the franchise business is up and running before a liquidation of the franchisor, then the franchisee probably is a low-cost bearer of risk in the sense that they can move into a rival franchise. In their business the loss of the franchise fee is one of many business expenses.

Divination for Franchises

It is worth investigating whether franchisees should become recipients of a statutory priority, as the franchise method of doing business involves large numbers of individuals who risk significant life savings, redundancy payouts and domestic mortgages to enter into these franchise agreements. However, there has been increased protection from other methods, such as trade practices law, and there is not an overwhelming case that justifies the introduction of a statutory priority.

27 Trade Practices (Industry Codes – Franchising) Regulations 1998 (Cth) cl 22.

Tort Victims

There is a potential that a liquidated company will owe money to persons who have suffered as the result of a tort committed by the company. A judgment ordering the company to pay may be still outstanding upon the company entering into liquidation. The tort victim is considered an unsecured creditor. It could be expected that the occurrence of tort creditors in insolvency is infrequent, but there is some scholarship[28] that reports that company directors have been targeted as the more convenient defendant due to a greater chance of recovery than if the victim pursued the financially stressed corporation. This suggests that unpaid amounts to tort creditors may be a significant issue.

Companies are subject to liability for an enormous range of torts. Companies nearing insolvency may be more careless than the financially robust company in addressing matters such as repairs to poorly maintained plant and equipment or other property that has the potential to cause personal injury. Furthermore, they may forego compliance with occupational health and safety standards or be more reckless in matters that result in defamation actions. Victims of these torts may be successful in obtaining a judgment for such wrongdoing and then find that the unsuccessful corporate defendant is now insolvent and they stand to be paid *pari passu* with other unsecured creditors, and only after the secured creditors and priority creditors have been satisfied. Their plight would be improved by granting a statutory priority.[29]

Insurance will play an important role in any tort litigation. Most companies could be expected to have insurance cover for many torts such as negligence. Occasionally though, they will not have sufficient insurance cover, or they may not be in the position to obtain cover from insurance companies for particular torts. It is likely that there would be a strong correlation between those companies who are underinsured or who fail to obtain cover and those who are financially stressed.

There is little support for a statutory priority to be considered in Australia or elsewhere. It has been acknowledged by one commentator that tort creditors are

28 See e.g., Farrar, J. 'The Personal Liability of Directors for Corporate Torts' (1997) 9 *Bond Law Review* 102; Leebron, D.W. 'Limited Liability, Tort Victims, and Creditors' (1991) *Columbia Law Review* 1565. See e.g., *Trevor Ivory Ltd v Anderson* [1992] 2 NZLR 517, *Williams v Natural Life Health Food Ltd and Mistlin* [1998] 1 WLR 830.

29 Spain introduced tort creditor priority in 1995 Propuesta de Anteproyecto de Ley Concursal Art. 125 in Garrido, J.M. 'Some Reflections on the EU Bankruptcy Convention and its Implications for Secured and Preferential Creditors' (1998) 7 *International Insolvency Review* 79, 93 fn 45. International Bar Association Committee J Bankruptcy Legislation Subcommittee, *Priority claims in insolvency administration* (1993) shows that no country who responded to the survey on priorities grant priority to torts. The Bulgarian Decree in Article 78 includes mention of 'tortious acts' but then follows mention of claims for wages and for compensation of damages caused by [such acts] so appears to be linked to employment and probably refers to workers compensation.

'in real need of protection, especially in comparison with contractual creditors'[30] and that this protection 'is an underdeveloped area, due to the lack of power and organization of these creditors'.[31] Of course, providing protection for tort victims to recover their damages need not be limited to giving them a statutory priority. Other alternatives to the company paying, such as making directors personally liable (or concurrently liable) for the corporate tort, have been a trend since the last part of the twentieth century.[32]

Justification for Tort Victims

As employed above in this chapter and Chapters 7 and 8, Finch's criteria in rethinking *pari passu* allows some exploration of the justification for a priority for vulnerable parties like torts victims.[33]

Finch's Criteria 1 – ability to gain and use information concerning default risk When considering a notion of fairness for statutory priorities 'it can be argued that it is wrong to burden creditors with risks that they were in no position to recognize, have notice of, calculate, bargain for or protect themselves against'.[34] Tort victims are the classic involuntary creditors who do not have the ability to gain or use information concerning default risk. They do not get to choose their tortfeasor.

Finch's Criteria 2 – capacity to exit from excessively risk-laden arrangements There is no capacity to exit from excessively risk-laden arrangements for torts creditors. They suffer the damage and receive judgment in their favour and it is not within their capabilities to choose to exit from the court order. Of course, they could

30 Garrido, J.M. 'The Distributional Question in Insolvency: Comparative Aspects' (1995) 4 *International Insolvency Review* 25, 49.

31 Ibid.

32 See generally, Fridman, G.H.L. 'Personal Tort Liability of Company Directors' (1992) 5 *Canterbury Law Review* 41; Wishart, D. 'The Personal Liability of Directors in Tort' (1992) 10 *Company & Securities Law Journal* 363; Farrar, J. 'The Personal Liability of Directors for Corporate Torts' (1997) 9 *Bond Law Review* 102; Borrowdale, A. 'Directors Liability in Tort' (1999) *New Zealand Law Journal* 51; Grantham, R. and Rickett, C. 'Directors' Tortious' Liability: Contract, Torts or Company Law?' (1999) 62 *Modern Law Review* 133; Reynolds, F. 'Personal Liability of Company Directors in Tort' (2003) 33 *Hong Kong Law Journal* 51; Anderson, H. 'The Theory of the Corporation and its Relevance to Directors' Tortious Liability to Creditors' (2004) paper presented to Corporate Law Teachers Association National Conference, ANU Canberra, February 2004; (2004) 16 *Australian Journal of Corporate Law* 73.

33 Finch, V. *Corporate Insolvency Law Perspectives and Principles* (2002) chapter 13 summarized at 449.

34 Finch, V. and Worthington, S. 'The *Pari Passu* Principle and Ranking Restitutionary Claims' in Rose, F. (ed.), *Restitution and Insolvency* (2000) 6.

choose not to pursue the tortfeasor if they believed they stood to gain little due to a lack of insurance or other factors. However, once judgment is given they are a creditor until paid, regardless of their efforts.

Finch's Criteria 3 – vulnerability to risks The torts creditor may be vulnerable in the sense that they need the debt to be paid, particularly if, as an example, it is to compensate future medical expenses. Whether the torts creditor has a low capacity to absorb losses (which really means spreading the risk of not being paid) will usually be determined by the victim's circumstances. Tort victims 'do not merit especially high levels of protection in insolvency because they are unlikely to be highly vulnerable to instances of default'.[35]

Finch's Criteria 4 – status as a low- or high-cost bearer of risk Torts creditors are 'not usually extremely high-cost risk bearers'[36] as they are likely to have other sources of income, funds and products and so the risks will be spread by such diversification.

Perhaps a new priority for torts victims could extend only to part of the payment expected from the judgment. That is, an extensive priority may be too unpalatable for unsecured creditors who already have merely a minor chance of receiving some distribution of company assets. A partial priority could be implemented where the judgment was for a substantial amount and remained unpaid upon the company's insolvency. Governments would need to decide the proportion to be paid. This would add complexity and time to the liquidation. To make such a scheme marginally palatable to the public and unsecured creditors (and any possible members in a voluntary winding up) a minimum percentage of the judgment such as 20 percent may be required.

To grant a priority to tort victims could allow legislators to discriminate between different classes of tort victims. As in Chapter 2, where the history of priorities shows a different treatment in the statutory provisions for clerks and servant to labourers and workmen, legislators could choose for example negligence victims to have more of the statutory priority than those who were defamed. Such an approach may be justified upon the ground that many defamation victims are persons of substantial independent financial means. As an alternative, legislators could be influenced by social welfare arguments to prefer only those victims who were considered low income earners.

Divination of Tort Creditors

The number of tort creditors present in liquidations is completely unknown and it is hard to envisage recommendations for them to receive a statutory priority without more evidence of a problem. Even then, as mentioned above, there are

35 Ibid. 429.

36 Ibid.

other ways of dealing with the non-payment of tort victims. The law of statutory priorities may recognize that there is a wider constituency to be considered on corporate insolvency in the future and it could encompass the tort victim who has suffered at the hands of the now insolvent company. Development could occur in the development of theoretical perspectives that move beyond the creditors bargain model to encompass involuntary creditors like torts victims. A final hurdle is that the victim is not currently thought of as a 'creditor'.

Primary Producers

Australia, like so many countries, does not prescribe a statutory priority for rural creditors such as farmers and other primary producers.[37] However, there is some history of legislators contemplating this path. As described in Chapter 2, in the 1930s legislation controlling companies was introduced into Australian States repealing earlier colonial laws[38] and South Australia contemplated adding grain producers to the list of priority debts. The attempt, that was defeated narrowly,[39] was to grant a priority for all amounts due or accruing due to any person in respect of grain delivered to a grain merchant company. South Australia in the 1930s was a large producer of wheat and other grain.[40]

Such an attempt at special treatment was justified on the basis that farmers worked throughout the year and then delivered their only harvest to recipients, the grain merchants. They were financially dependent upon the payment(s) from these recipients and should these recipients fail then the individual was affected as well as the State, as such an outcome would have meant many of the State's farmers faced financial ruin. A failed rural sector would have been extremely serious because of the rural based economy of the day. Since that time, the States of Australia have moved from being primary producers to having predominantly secondary (manufacturing) economies and in more recent times, being predominantly

37 This priority has attracted little academic comment. Garrido suggests that the need for this priority in the United States was debatable and in his words 'it deprives the system of its sense': Garrido, J.M. 'The Distributional Question in Insolvency: Comparative Aspects' (1995) 4 *International Insolvency Review* 25, 48.

38 As described in Chapter 2 a number of Australian States in the 1930s drafted new companies legislation – New South Wales in 1936, Victoria in 1938, Queensland in 1931, South Australia 1934 and they included, for the first time, a priority for tax.

39 The motion was lost 19:16 in South Australia, House of Assembly, *Debates*, 31 October 1934, 168.

40 There is some similarity with United States and Canadian priorities law where specific local nuances see people like fishermen and foresters having special treatment. There are also producer's liens in some States. See Bratton, D. 'The California Agricultural Producer's Lien, Processing Company Insolvencies, and Federal Bankruptcy Law: An Evaluation and Alternative Methods of Protecting Farmers' (1985) 36 *Hastings Law Journal* 609.

oriented towards the tertiary or services sector. Despite this, primary production and mining are still massive contributors to the Australian economy.

Since 1979, in the United States of America, s507(a)(5) of the *Bankruptcy Code* has given a priority for grain producers and fishermen for credits against a debtor who operates a storage facility.[41] There is a quantitative limit of US$4,650.[42] The priority operates for producers to the extent that they do not recover the full amount for their grain under other procedures.[43] The balance owing beyond the limit is treated as an unsecured debt.[44] Being seen as a consumer remedy it does not apply to corporate farmers and is available for grain and the proceeds of grain.[45]

Currently, in Australia grain storage facilities are operated by or under the strict control of government owned enterprises, with payments to producers tied to specific regimes. For example, a barley farmer sells to the Australian Barley Board and is paid in three instalments such as upon delivery, then at the end of the month following delivery and finally an outstanding balance several months later. Such a payment regime and the fact that it is a government owned enterprise appears to make any special treatment in insolvency unnecessary. Payments could be considered to be 'guaranteed' by the government.

Australia's fishing and aquacultural industry does not rely so heavily on seasonal factors and is quite different from the traditional methods of fishing where fishers spent many months at sea before returning with their catch. Fishers in the past with their entire season's catch would have been at risk of not being paid and would have remained as unsecured creditors in a purchaser's insolvency. The aquacultural developments, and modern fishing practices where boats are unloaded frequently, suggest that there is less need to 'protect' this industry as the fishers are not so dependent on the purchaser's solvency as they were in the past.

Wine Growers

One industry that could warrant consideration by the government to assist by granting a special priority is Australia's large and growing wine industry. Recently, there have emerged large wine producers in the market and they typically obtain their grapes from small wine growers. The development of the large wine producer has been helped along by a series of mergers over the last 10 years. The industry still includes large numbers of small wineries and even greater numbers of winegrowers. Winegrowers are increasing each year as more arable land is

---

41 For a detailed discussion see 'Counsel's Corner: Farmer Priority in Bankrupt Warehouses – Yellow Light for Country Banks' (1982) 99 *Banking Law Journal* 964.

42 Initially this amount was US$2,000 until 1994, then US$4,000, and from 1998–2001 it was US$4,300.

43 11 USCS §557.

44 *In re Esbon Grain Co* (1985, BC DC Kan) 55 BR 308, 13 CBC2d 1328, affd. (1987, DC Kan) 72 BR 528.

45 *In re Hawkins* (1992, BC DC Idaho) 144 BR 481.

turned over to vineyards. Wine growers are paid by the wine producers in a partial payment arrangement. Large wine producers exert economic pressure over small winegrowers who grow most of their produce for sale. This pressure takes many forms and can be reflected in installment payments made subsequent to the grape deliveries.

The financial collapse of large wine producers would have significant impact upon the small winegrowers, although their loss would probably be confined to one vintage.[46] Rather than the winegrowers being left as unsecured creditors, legislators could grant a statutory priority and limit it both in relation to a set amount and to a particular vintage. Such an outcome is not so fanciful if winegrowers were to agitate or lobby for such a change.[47]

Justification for Primary Producers

Finch's Criteria 1 – ability to gain and use information concerning default risk The primary producer probably has informal methods available to gain information about the buyer/recipient of their produce. There may be other available markets where the produce can be sold. Winegrowers may suffer from information asymmetry when contracting with large wine producers.

Finch's Criteria 2 – capacity to exit from excessively risk-laden arrangements Small primary producers, like many small businesses, will have entered arrangements which can be laden with risk for them due to economic pressure and inequality of bargaining power. The capacity to exit from excessively risk-laden arrangements for a primary producer may be extremely limited if they have perishable produce. Only if the produce can be sold elsewhere can they mitigate their loss.

Finch's Criteria 3 – vulnerability to risks Primary producers are vulnerable because they may rely substantially upon the payment for their catch or harvest for their yearly financial income. The market may be such that they can reasonably only sell to one merchant and so they are vulnerable to the insolvency risks of that merchant. Avoiding this risk may be extremely costly if, for instance, the harvest has to be delivered interstate or overseas to avoid the local merchant.

Finch's Criteria 4 – status as a low- or high-cost bearer of risk There is real potential for primary producers to be high-cost bearers of risk. There is little opportunity for them to spread the risk as they may have only one debtor owing

46 There have been a few substantial wine producers fail in recent years in Australia. An example is Norman's Wines in South Australia and growers had been paid prior to the insolvency and then had to fight preference claims by the liquidator. Personal interview with solicitors for the liquidator, Johnson Winter Slattery, 28 February 2005.

47 Wine industry lobbying was experienced during debates over the introduction of the GST.

them money and that is the insolvent merchant who has contracted to buy their yearly harvest.

Divination of Primary Producers

Governments can do a lot more economically for deserving primary industries such as in areas of tax relief and incentives and these may be considered better options than altering corporate insolvency legislation to grant a new priority. Certainly, a major corporate failure of a primary industry merchant could expose the vulnerability of a particular creditor group[48] within the primary industry sector of the economy. Such a failure could enliven a debate to consider primary producers as priority creditors.

Landlords

Landlords have had a long history of special treatment in the priorities section of insolvency legislation and they have been strong political lobbyists. However, landlords no longer receive a first charge over the goods or other effects that they distrain or the sale proceeds of such property.

Landlords featured in insolvency statutes from colonial days and this was mainly in a separate section dedicated to distress being made available but limited to a certain period. For example the *Insolvent Act 1860* (SA) provided different limits for the distress and the limit for distress was a year's rent when the tenement was let by the year.[49] The section was positioned immediately before the section on the statutory priority for wages. Subsequent legislation in the colony adopted the same path.

A change for landlords occurred following the *Preferential Payments in Bankruptcy Act 1888* (UK) in s1(4) which provided that:

---

48 In Australia the vulnerability of employees of insolvent companies has been heavily manipulated by the media leading to changes in their treatment. See Riley, J. 'Lessons from Ansett – Locating the Employees' Voice in Corporate Enterprise' (2002) 27 *Alternative Law Journal* 112.

49 *Insolvent Act 1860* (SA) s144 provided:

No distress for rent, made and levied upon goods and effects of any insolvent, shall be available where the tenement is let by the week, for more than four weeks' rent, or for more than the rent accruing due in two terms of payment where the tenement is let for any other term less than a year, nor for more than a year's rent where the tenement is let by the year, unless the said goods and effects shall have been *bona fide* sold under such distress, previous to the filing of the petition for adjudication of insolvency; but the landlord, or person to whom the rent shall be due, shall be allowed to come in as a creditor for the overplus of the rent due, for which the distress shall not be available.

> In the event of a landlord or other person distraining or having distrained on any goods or effects of any bankrupt or a company being wound up within three months next before the date of the receiving order or the winding up order respectively, the debts to which priority is given by this section shall be a first charge or the goods or effects distrained on, or the proceeds of the sale thereof:

Provided, that in respect of any money paid under any such charge the landlord or other person shall have the same rights of priority as the person to whom such payment is made.

This legislation began the application of an express statutory priority for landlords to companies.

Australian legislation followed this provision and, taking the South Australian *Companies Act 1934* in s279(6)[50] as an example, the wording was identical to the *Preferential Payments in Bankruptcy Act 1888* (UK) provision.

The *Uniform Companies Act* that applied in Australia in 1961,[51] omitted any express priority for landlords and no corporate insolvency legislation since has attempted to reinstall it. Of course, as outlined in Chapter 4, administrative expenses can include an amount for rent incurred after the appointment of the liquidator.

Justification for Landlords

Again, it is appropriate to ascertain if any justification exists to reintroduce a priority for landlords and this is explored using the Finch criteria already applied to other possibilities above.

Finch's Criteria 1 – ability to gain and use information concerning default risk Landlords are generally in a strong position to gain and use information concerning default risk. They will usually have access to credit references before entering the contract with a corporate entity, have the opportunity to take personal guarantees for corporate rent arrears and work in a market where they can choose who to do business with. The rent arrears will usually be 'managed' so that large amounts are not permitted to accumulate and a tenant company would find themselves locked out of the premises if they were in serious default of rent payments.

---

50 *Companies Act 1934* (SA) s279(6) provided that in the event of a landlord or other person distraining or having distrained on any goods or effects of the company within three months before the relevant date, the priority debts should be a first charge on the goods or effects so distrained or on the proceeds of their sale.

51 As described in Chapter 2 all States tried for uniform companies' legislation. See e.g., *Companies Act 1962* (SA).

Finch's Criteria 2 – capacity to exit from excessively risk-laden arrangements Landlords generally have capacity to exit from a lease and, in most cases, it would not be excessively risk-laden for the landlord but quite the opposite. In times of high interest rates, on the other hand, perhaps it could be argued that landlords are highly geared and would rely very heavily on collecting rental income and a tenant's failure would be risk-laden with little capacity to exit.

Finch's Criteria 3 – vulnerability to risks The landlord is vulnerable in the sense that they may suffer some loss of rent or damage to property, but the risks are usually well covered by the contractual arrangements and the access to many legal remedies including eviction and lock-out. Landlords are likely to have many tenants and the failure of one should not severely affect their income.

Finch's Criteria 4 – status as a low- or high-cost bearer of risk As a creditor in a corporate insolvency, a landlord would be considered an extremely low-cost bearer of risk. They will have a relatively small sum outstanding given their other remedies even before default and they are likely to have exercised these to their benefit.

Divination of Landlords

The statutory priority for landlords belongs to another era and there is essentially no justification for them to receive special treatment in this way. So many other legal and business practices are in the landlord's favour that the priority does not need to be revived.

Essential Services

Liquidators upon appointment need to ensure that essential services such as telephone, electricity and gas continue to be supplied and that such suppliers are notified of the appointment. The post-appointment supply is given a statutory priority as part of the administration expenses.[52] However, for the pre-appointment supply, the suppliers of gas, electricity, water and telecommunications are frequently among the creditors of an insolvent company. They represent the essential services

52 CCH, *Australian Insolvency Management Practice*, Vol. 2 (at 26.10.91) 92–316 in a sample letter referred to as a 'Letter to suppliers of essential suppliers' suggests the administrator include a paragraph advising 'The amounts incurred for such supply will be regarded as liquidators' costs and expenses and will be paid on normal credit terms from the assets of the company in priority to the claims of creditors existing at the date of the liquidation'. The following 'suggested' paragraph advises 'You will rank as an unsecured creditor for supply up to the date of liquidation, entitled to prove against the estate'.

and their accounts enjoy no statutory priority in the Australian *Corporations Act 2001* (Cth); instead, they are treated as unsecured creditors.

During most of the twentieth century, governments were sole providers of these necessary resources or services essential to operating a business. Due to the government's monopoly, it could ensure that its accounts be paid in priority to others during the company's life. Utilities frequently took advantage of their critical position by insisting that all their debts be paid in full by the insolvent company if the utility were to continue the service.[53] By using 'their dominant market positions to compel the payment of debts' they could threaten 'to cut off a supply unless arrears were paid in full or payment was personally guaranteed by the liquidator'.[54]

The Cork Report[55] expressed no sympathy for 'powerful utilities that impeded companies' rescue and muscled aside weaker creditors'[56] with Sir Kenneth Cork,[57] the Chairman, calling it 'blackmail'.[58] Evidence from groups appearing before the Review Committee supported the Report's rejection of any special treatment that would favour the utilities.[59] A number of the groups called upon the Review Committee to remove the de facto priorities unofficially enforced by the utilities.[60]

The Cork Report proposed to treat the insolvent or reorganizing company as a new customer with an unencumbered right to receive the utility services.[61] As a 'new customer', the insolvent estate would be under no obligation to pay the existing debts of the 'old customer' and thus could not be threatened to any great effect by the utility.[62]

53 Carruthers, B.G. and Halliday, T.C. *Rescuing Business The Making of Corporate Bankruptcy Law in England and the United States* (1998) 234–235.

54 Finch, V. *Corporate Insolvency Law Perspectives and Principles* (2002) 425.

55 Review Committee, *Insolvency Law and Practice* Cmnd 8558 (1982) 'Cork Report' para 1451–1462.

56 Carruthers, B.G. and Halliday, T.C. *Rescuing Business The Making of Corporate Bankruptcy Law in England and the United States* (1998) 235.

57 Cork, before he was chair of the Insolvency Committee in the UK, had personal experience of utilities threatening and cutting off gas supplies to the detriment of his task as a receiver. Interview recorded in Carruthers, B.G. and Halliday, T.C. *Rescuing Business The Making of Corporate Bankruptcy Law in England and the United States* (1998) 235.

58 Ibid. 236.

59 Carruthers, B.G. and Halliday, T.C. *Rescuing Business The Making of Corporate Bankruptcy Law in England and the United States* (1998) 235 fn 81 suggests submission to Review Committee by Association of British Chambers of Commerce, Public Records Office, 28 June 1997 and the Consultative Committee of Accountancy Bodies, Public Record Office, April 1978.

60 Ibid.

61 Review Committee, *Insolvency Law and Practice* Cmnd 8558 (1982) para 1462.

62 Ibid.

Section 233 of the *Insolvency Act 1986* (UK) now prohibits the practice of paying essential suppliers to enable continuing supply. The supplier may require the liquidator 'to undertake personal responsibility for payment of any new supply but may not make the availability of a new supply, conditional on receiving payment or security for the old supply'.[63]

In Australia, s600F of the *Corporations Act 2001* (Cth) is to similar effect. Subsection (1) provides:

> [Past debt not ground to refuse request for essential services] If:
>
> (a) a relevant authority of an eligible company requests, or authorises someone else to request, a person or authority (the supplier) to supply an essential service to the company in Australia; and
>
> (b) the company owes an amount to the supplier in respect of the supply of the essential service before the effective day;
>
> the supplier must not:
>
> (c) refuse to comply with the request for the reason only that the amount is owing; or
>
> (d) make it a condition of the supply of the essential service pursuant to the request that the amount is to be paid.

The legislation then goes on to define 'effective day', 'eligible company', 'essential service' and 'relevant authority' in *Corporations Act* (Cth) 2001 s600F(2).

The section places a limitation on the rights of suppliers of essential services to insist on payment for previous services as a condition of supply.

The Harmer Report labeled these creditors as ones that 'hold a de facto priority'.[64] There was recognition that private suppliers of goods could 'be in the same position' but it was the statutory monopolies that were the 'subject of most complaint'.[65] With strong support from five submissions,[66] the Harmer Report took

63 Finch, V. *Corporate Insolvency Law Perspectives and Principles* (2002) 425.

64 Australian Law Reform Commission, *General Insolvency Inquiry*, Report No 45 (1988) para 756.

65 Ibid.

66 Australian Law Reform Commission, *General Insolvency Inquiry*, Report No 45 (1988) Submission No 131, Foster, N. Submission No 138 IPAA, ICAA and ASA, 18; Submission No 150 Keenan, P. 14; Submission No 136 McDonald, G. 17 and Submission No 183 Privacy Committee (NSW). Copies of all submissions held by the writer.

an identical course to the Cork Report and recommended that a supplier shall not make it a condition of supply that outstanding charges be paid.

Since white settlement in Australia, the essential services were provided by government owned enterprises or instrumentalities but now the privatization of many of these services is almost complete. There are presently more suppliers and more customer choice. The Cork Report's description of 'blackmail' in the past is not so relevant today as there is more than one essential service provider for most services so there is a choice to comply with a supplier's demands or choose a different supplier. For example, with many telecommunications carriers present in the Australian market, if a liquidator was refused service by one, they could simply engage another provider. With privatization of essential services, there are more players but, occasionally, the delivery of the service is split. This could mean there is only one company providing the delivery of gas supplies whereas other gas maintenance is carried out by a government instrumentality in a monopoly position. Regardless, the legislation now outlaws the demand of 'no payment, no supply'.

Justification for Essential Service Providers

The justification of an essential service provider priority can be considered using Finch's criteria as employed above.

Finch's Criteria 1 – ability to gain and use information concerning default risk Essential service providers have some ability to gain and use information concerning default risk. With some of the essential service providers, the risk of some customers defaulting may become very obvious through their debtor payment history. Providers will suffer somewhat from the sheer size of the market contributing to a lack of helpful personal information due to the extensive coverage and the expectation that all customers should be supplied the service despite poor payment histories.

Finch's Criteria 2 – capacity to exit from excessively risk-laden arrangements It would be unlikely that an essential service provider would be in an excessively risk-laden arrangement with a corporate customer and so the need to exit should not be a consideration. The supply contract will have been drawn by the provider's lawyers and should favour them rather than expose them to excessive risk.

Finch's Criteria 3– vulnerability to risks Essential service providers are vulnerable to risks of non-payment as they have certain government imposed requirements to provide the service. They may be required to operate in a market where there is no choice of supply and they then will be supplying to corporate businesses that collapse. On the other hand, they do have a freedom of contract when there is no monopoly market and could refuse to supply thus avoiding the risk of dealing with an insolvent company.

Finch's Criteria 4 – status as a low- or high-cost bearer of risk Essential service providers in the past did not really get to choose who they would supply. They were low cost bearers of risk because of their monopoly. For example, the supply of electricity, from a government owned supplier, would be connected to a building and if that building were rented to a company then the company would become a new customer of the supplier regardless of their financial standing. Then if the company failed the supplier would be faced with a bad debt for unpaid 'essential' services. The provider was an 'involuntary, non adjusting creditor',[67] although there was some relief as they could adjust prices for supply to cover such occurrences and this would spread the cost of that essential service to all customers, which meant everybody connected to that service. Such an impact was unfair on all non-defaulting users, but an economic reality. Present day essential service providers still enjoy the position of low-cost bearers of risk and have greater choice in their customer lists and hence their debtors.

Divination of Essential Services

The legislation has remedied the mischief of forcing the company in liquidation to pay outstanding amounts as a prerequisite for ongoing supply. There is less justification for making the essential service providers the next priority creditors for their outstanding pre-appointment debts now that they are not as 'involuntary' as in the past.

International Creditors

It would be a brave government who would attempt to legislate to change statutory priorities to give special treatment to international creditors in preference to local ones. Of course it is possible, but the outcry from local creditors would be substantial. Such a legislative move would enrage local creditors who would remind the government of their suffrage. Accepting creditors from beyond their borders into local insolvency procedures has been difficult enough for some jurisdictions.[68] It would seem unlikely that international creditors would be granted a priority, particularly in light of the discussions in earlier chapters about the difficulties for existing local priority creditors in achieving payment.

---

67 This is terminology used by Finch, V. *Corporate Insolvency Law Perspectives and Principles* (2002) 427.

68 Garrido, J.M. 'Some Reflections on the EU Bankruptcy Convention and its Implications for Secured and Preferential Creditors' (1998) 7 *International Insolvency Review* 79, 90.

Countries who have trading blocks may contemplate a priority for creditors in those jurisdictions. For example, a number of years ago Australia and New Zealand signed a Closer Economic Relations agreement and, as an expression of this, each government could legislate to give a statutory priority to creditors from the others' country. The five jurisdictions in the Nordic countries (or even the European Union) could make similar legislative moves.[69] In these days of Model Laws[70] and harmonization,[71] it seems, however, the climate is definitely wrong to even contemplate selecting the debts of businesses in allied countries to give a statutory priority.

Justification for International Creditors

Again, it is technically possible to put international creditors to the test formed by Finch for granting statutory priorities although it is making a large generalization to attempt to describe who may comprise these 'international creditors'.[72]

Finch's Criteria 1 – ability to gain and use information concerning default risk The international creditors would have marginally less ability to gain and use information concerning default risk than local creditors. This is due to the typically greater ability of local creditors to access information about the financial viability of the debtor from informal avenues.

Finch's Criteria 2 – capacity to exit from excessively risk-laden arrangements The international creditor, in finding itself in an excessively risk laden arrangement, could expect to exit in similar circumstances to all other unsecured creditors. The international creditor could adjust their international business methods to use letters of credit that would eliminate most of the risk.

Finch's Criteria 3 – vulnerability to risks The international creditor, like the local creditor, can choose the risk as they are voluntary creditors. Their vulnerability arises from their possible lack of familiarity with local conditions and the use of local agents could assist them more efficiently than a statutory priority.

---

69 There is a Nordic Bankruptcy Convention that facilitates matters relevant to cross-border insolvency between Sweden, Finland, Norway, Denmark and Iceland.

70 The Model Law on Cross Border Insolvency is published in Official Records of the General Assembly, Fifty-second Session, Supplement No 17 (A/52/17, annex I) (UNCITRAL Yearbook, Vol. XXVIII: 1997, Part 3). See <http://www.uncitral.org/uncitral/en/uncitral_texts/insolvency/1997Model.html3> accessed on 1/12/05.

71 The United Nations Commission on International Trade Law (UNCITRAL) was established by the United Nations to 'further promote the progressive harmonisation and unification of the law of international trade'.

72 Finch,V. *Corporate Insolvency Law Perspectives and Principles* (2002) 449.

Finch's Criteria 4 – status as a low- or high-cost bearer of risk International creditors are low-cost bearers of risk as they will usually have other debtors and can spread the risks of unpaid international debts across other local and international customers.

Divination of International Creditors

The entire international business and trade scene would have to change dramatically for any proposal for granting a statutory priority to international creditors to gain credence.

Indigenous Corporations in Australia

Australia has developed significant statutory regulation of indigenous affairs since the 1970s and one piece of legislation that is a corporate regulatory vinculum is the *Aboriginal Councils and Associations Act 1976* (Cth) ('*ACA Act*'). This Act directly adopts the provisions of the *Corporations Act 2001* (Cth) on insolvency. There are over 3,000 associations incorporated under the *ACA Act*[73] and so this Act is the most visible vehicle for the incorporation of indigenous bodies. The *ACA Act*, when enacted was intended to

> recognise cultural differences between Aboriginal and non-Aboriginal societies and enable Aboriginal communities to develop legally recognisable bodies which reflect their own culture and do not require them to subjugate this culture to overriding Western European legal concepts.[74]

However, there is criticism that the Act and its administration has moved too much towards the *Corporations Act*. In any event, s67 of the *ACA Act* states that the provisions of the *Corporations Act* relating to the winding up of companies registered under the *ACA Act* apply so far as they are capable of application. The section also provides that a reference to a company in provisions of the *Corporations Act* shall be read as a reference to an Incorporated Aboriginal Association. Therefore, s556 of the *Corporations Act 2001* (Cth) applies the statutory priorities to the liquidation of aboriginal corporations.

---

73 Registrar of Aboriginal Corporations, *Annual Report 2001–2002*. See <http://www.orac.gov.au/about_ORIC/publications.aspx#1>.

74 Australia, House of Representatives, *Debates*, 3 June 1976 (Ian Viner, Minister for Aboriginal Affairs) 2946.

Unfortunately, Aboriginal corporations have a history of financial failure.[75] It may be that a future Federal Government could seek to assist their viability by granting them a statutory priority when they find themselves as an unsecured creditor in another company's liquidation.

Like many small businesses, indigenous businesses often struggle to find start-up capital and the cash flow to survive the early years. Additionally, there are cultural hurdles to operating the business in a Western way. Governments, particularly the Federal Government, have made capital available for the commencement of commercial projects, and the recipients use the *ACA Act* to incorporate. To grant a statutory priority could indirectly assist the government to recover their 'investment' of this start-up capital.

From a theoretical viewpoint, the granting of a statutory priority for indigenous corporations would suggest a social justice motivation perhaps more akin to the communitarian approach briefly described in Chapter 3, while still maintaining the crucial creditor/debtor bargain of the contractual model in place at present.

Justification of Indigenous Corporations

To test the justification for a new statutory priority the Finch criteria are, yet again, pressed into service.

Finch's Criteria 1 – ability to gain and use information concerning default risk Indigenous corporations as creditors are likely to receive no different access to information provided to any other corporate debtor and so their ability to gain and use information concerning default risk should be no better than other unsecured creditors. Most of these corporations are going to be located in remote Australia and so the ability to gain information about risk may be slightly worse than those in more urban locations. Arguably though, there is no great advantage in operating even across the road from a liquidated company if, as a creditor, you cannot change your exposure because future default may not be obvious.

Finch's Criteria 2 – capacity to exit from excessively risk-laden arrangements Aboriginal corporations are likely to have no different capacity to exit from excessively risk-laden arrangements than any other unsecured creditor. They cannot be considered an involuntary creditor and they undertake the risk of extending credit by choice.

Finch's Criteria 3 – vulnerability to risk The aboriginal corporation is vulnerable to the risks of extending credit but no more so than other creditors. They may be vulnerable in the sense that they are often remote and may lack the choice of

75 See e.g., Annual Report of the Registrar of Aboriginal Corporations <http://www.orac.gov.au/about_ORIC/publications.aspx#1> and <www.democrats.org.au/speeches/?speeches-id=294&display=1>.

whom to do business with and this may result in them having to extend credit to debtors that, in a more ideal situation, they would decline. However, this is a problem for all remote businesses. Contractual freedom will still exist and so the aboriginal corporation will have choice in the parties they contract with and take on as credit risks. Aboriginal corporations can be seen as unsophisticated and lacking in business acumen and this may be a consideration for government in their decision to grant a statutory priority as one aspect of providing special protection.

Finch's Criteria 4 – status as a low- or high-cost bearer of risk Aboriginal corporations could be expected to be low-cost bearers of risk in that their business operations will be spread across many transactions with many debtors and so the failure of one will mean just the loss of the amounts exposed to that one debtor, albeit that this could be a substantial sum.

Divination of Indigenous Corporations

Government and private assistance will be needed to assist indigenous corporations for the foreseeable future and a statutory priority for debts owed to them should not be considered without significant change in the justifications mentioned above. While the *ACA Act* continues to operate it should continue to apply s556 of the *Corporations Act 2001* (Cth) to maintain a consistent approach to statutory priorities for both indigenous and non-indigenous corporations.

Conclusion

This chapter has taken the licence to contemplate both likely and unlikely new priorities. This has essentially involved an exploration of various types of contract and debts. As signalled in Chapter 1, it is the legislators, using the statute, who could choose to assist any of the creditors and give them a better of chance of receiving something from the distribution. Such legislative change may come after the politicians yield to the most powerful pressure groups.

This chapter has mused over a government's choice to grant a priority to a group of creditors such as all small business creditors, franchisees, international creditors, indigenous corporation creditors, or a particular industry group like fishers or other primary producers. Other groups such as high tech industry creditors could also at some point appear on the legislator's radar because of a particular policy direction or mounting agitation.

Specialist statutory priorities could be considered in the future. For example, if Australia and other parts of the world experienced an extreme failure of the banking system, perhaps on a scale of even greater magnitude than the Great Depression, bank depositors would stand to lose significant amounts. It is conceivable that, in a government's attempt to re-establish confidence in the banking system and encourage corporate investment a separate priority could be created to expressly rank bank deposits as a priority debt in the insolvency of a bank.

One final specialist priority that may be required in the future is the corporate fine. Corporations are exposed to fines as the most appropriate penalty for breaches of the criminal law. Some corporate offenders will experience insolvency, and when they are being wound up they will have unpaid fines. These are presently treated as unsecured debts and receive no priority. In Chapter 6, the removal of the priority for Crown and government debts was outlined and corporate fines arguably share in the lack of justification for any special treatment. A further reason for continuing their present ordinary unsecured creditor status is that the company that committed the 'crime' is not continuing and payment of this fine before payment of the other company creditors means that they would, in effect, share in this penalty by receiving less than if the fine remained unpaid. A case could be made for such fines to be given a deferred status. Despite all this, governments are often elected on a platform of improving 'law and order' and then are publicly criticized when 'white collar' crime and corporate crime are highlighted by the media. When companies are liquidated and the non-payment of their fines is identified, this can lead to public criticism and one possible government response would be to amend the statutory priorities.

Political pragmatism will determine what other priorities join the insolvency statute books after the strong pressure group lobbying[76] and the testing for justification conducted in this chapter suggests none of the categories identified is ripe just yet to be added in Australia or other similar Western countries.

76 Garrido, J.M. 'Some Reflections on the EU Bankruptcy Convention and its Implications for Secured and Preferential Creditors' (1998) 7 *International Insolvency Review* 79, 90.

Chapter 10

The Justification of Statutory Priorities as a Keystone to Further Research and Action

The above chapters have sought to justify keeping statutory priorities in corporate insolvency legislation. By using doctrinal research to explain the existing statutory priorities the chapters point to a conclusion that it is clearly expedient to maintain the present treatment of administrative expenses and employee creditors. The later chapters have presented possible developments in Australian statutory priorities, by using comparisons with other jurisdictions, and by reference to judicial and academic comment. Additionally, some attempt has been made to reflect the various voices of the community.

With the earlier chapters setting the foundation, it is possible to envisage the future for statutory priorities. This chapter explores that possibility and makes recommendations both for the maintenance of existing priorities for administrative expenses and employees and for the introduction of some new priorities in the future.

There are other methods of exploring the justification of statutory priorities, one of which involves conducting empirical research. Two approaches to collecting empirical data seem appropriate for statutory priorities, namely collecting information from liquidators' reports or conducting surveys of users such as insolvency practitioners. Empirical information gleaned from either of these sources would further reveal the impact of insolvency's statutory treatment of priority creditors. Although both approaches were beyond the scope of the present research they present as the next obvious step and a preamble to such work is discussed later in the chapter.

Recalling History and Perspectives

From Chapter 2's mapping of the history of statutory priorities it is readily apparent that Australian and other common law legislatures over the last 175 years have spent little time in debate on this topic. Australian parliaments have generally accepted and applied without question what the English parliament of the day decided. Certainly in colonial Australia what Westminster implemented was considered sufficient. It was only when the opportunity arose to remove the tax priority from insolvency distributions that Australian companies' legislation showed evidence of independence. Further research beckons on the development of a wider history of corporate insolvency law in Australia and England, but again that has been beyond the scope of this text.

In Chapter 3, it was argued that the creditors' bargain model (together with the associated concept of contractarianism) has been the most influential perspective in Australian corporate insolvency law generally, albeit that locally it is an underdeveloped and rarely discussed paradigm. It is also paramount throughout the common law world. Statutory priorities have likewise been governed and shaped by the creditors' bargain model and the perspectives offered by contractarianism. Despite these influences, future scholarship may see further debate on other evolving perspectives. As Chapter 3 identified, these perspectives are scarcely mentioned nor understood at present in the Australian setting. The chapter raised communitarianism as the most appropriate contender for a future vision of Australian corporate insolvency law, particularly when discerning statutory priority features.

In reviewing the history of the topic and the various perspectives associated with it, it is mere conjecture as to how the law of statutory priorities might have been developed had there been an 'unshackling' of corporate insolvency from the companies legislation as occurred in the United Kingdom in 1986 with the *Insolvency Act 1986*. It is possible that a separate, independent insolvency statute in Australia might result in fresh thought and new priorities.[1] But while corporate insolvency law remains tied within the much larger *Corporations Act 2001* (Cth), little change, particularly on the radical side, can be expected.

Recommendations

Chapters 4 through to 9 above have presented various statutory priorities in detail. Chapter 4 described the administrative expenses priority and Chapter 5 the treatment of employee entitlements. Chapter 6 presented the tax priority and its history to date. Chapters 7, 8, and 9 drew attention to other priorities that are yet to be recognized. However amongst all this detail one must remember that statutory priorities are the domain of the legislature and so any future contemplation of removing, adjusting, adding or merely exercising a monitoring role over them must be carried out by the parliament. In keeping with the traditional outcomes when a review of an area of law has been completed, the following are recommendations which specifically address the present legal position. As previously mentioned, little radical reform can be expected, particularly within the present *Corporations Act 2001* (Cth) or its equivalent in comparable jurisdictions.

1 Keay, A.R. 'The Unity of Insolvency Legislation: Time for a Re-think?' (1997) 7 *Insolvency Law Journal* 4.

Recommendation – Administration Expenses – Liquidator's Remuneration

Liquidators' remuneration should continue to enjoy a statutory priority under the heading of administrative expenses, but include a measure of a performance-based incentive or be based upon a fixed fee.

Discussion

Liquidators must receive a priority, as they could not be expected to perform professional duties with the uncertainty of being paid, particularly as their engagement is to a business structure that is already in a position of being unable to pay its debts. However, there is little incentive for them to maximize distributions to priority and unsecured creditors when they occupy a superior position. If a company has few assets these will be consumed in liquidators' fees and administration expenses, leaving nothing for employee creditors, other priority creditors and the unsecured creditors.

Recommendation – Administration Expenses – Audit Fees

Complete disclosure should be made to a committee of creditors or a corporate regulator like ASIC as to any relationship between the auditor and the insolvency practitioner before any priority payment is made for audit fees as part of the expenses of the administration.

Discussion

Certain audit fees are given statutory priority under *Corporations Act 2001* (Cth) s556(1)(db), and these fees will be incurred by the company for the audit of the liquidator's accounts. The audit is required by s539. Invariably, there is a close connection between insolvency professionals and audit professionals. The auditors will be accountants and are likely to have a close relationship due to the same accounting firm offering both professional services, auditing and insolvency, or holding reversible appointments in a number of companies where they are auditor for one and liquidator for another. Again the opportunity exists for collusion to a degree where the accountants (as auditors or as liquidators) get paid and the remainder of priority and unsecured creditors miss out. Requiring disclosure and appropriate reporting could alleviate the risk of collusion by empowering the committee of creditors or ASIC to monitor audit payments as part of the expenses of administration.

Recommendation – Income Thresholds For Employees

There should be an inquiry into the feasibility of a progressive qualification system to be applied to employee priorities that would favour lower income employees.

Discussion

A regularly reviewed progressive qualification system of statutory priorities for employees could give lower income employees a greater chance of qualifying for a distribution. While the General Employee Entitlements and Redundancy Scheme (GEERS) currently ensures all of the employee's wages are paid, along with most other entitlements, the employee statutory priority remains an issue for the Federal Government by reason of subrogation. With GEERS in operation, there are maximum annual wage limits on entitlements such that even lower income employees can miss out. It is possible for long serving employees to miss out on their entitlements if they have extensive redundancy pay entitlements, beyond the maximum covered by GEERS. Additionally, with GEERS being a purely administrative scheme with no legislative backing, the government can remove all or part of it at any time, exposing employees to their former position. This former position was merely a statutory priority but with an uncertainty about ever being paid, as the company might not have had sufficient assets to enable a distribution.

A regularly reviewed progressive qualification system of employee priority could follow similar lines to the assessment of income tax. Lower income employees are treated more favourably in relation to income tax rates in Australia using a progressive scale and a similar qualification system for priorities could be introduced. Implementing a similar system would allow lower paid employees to receive their entitlements before those receiving more executive style remuneration packages. Current industrial practices that encourage workplace agreements present opportunities for higher income employees to negotiate high redundancy amounts. A progressive qualification system for employees would result in overcoming unfair treatment created by workplace agreements when the company's assets are proportionally divided between the entire workforce in an insolvency.

Recommendation – Employees – GEERS

The Australian Federal Government legislate to put GEERS on a statutory footing, so as to provide certainty to the Australian workforce regarding employee priorities.

Discussion

The present situation sees the government operating GEERS and paying a large percentage of employee priorities with the intention of it being subrogated. In time it will become obvious to the Federal Government that their expectation of recovering funds expended from GEERS may well be unfulfilled. Many companies will fall short of having assets available to cover these subrogated amounts and the Federal Government will recoup very little. An administrative scheme is easily removed and if this happened, employees would be left relying on their statutory priority for payment. It would be seen as further protection for employees if the Federal Government legislated for GEERS.

Recommendations – 'Excluded Employees'

The category of 'excluded employees' as used in s556 of the *Corporations Act* 2001 (Cth) should be redefined to allow for some directors and their families to qualify for the employee priority without being subject to the statutory imposed maximum.

or as an alternative

The statutory maximum for excluded employees should be reviewed, with consideration being given to its complete removal.

Discussion

Some family members of directors are presently disadvantaged because they are classified as excluded employees and only entitled to a priority of $A1500. These members may have no knowledge or input into the company, but because of their relationship to the managing director, for example, they may have been pressured not to take long service leave or annual leave. This results in their entitlements being large, yet with the application of ss556(1) and (2) a substantial part of their entitlements will be treated as if they are an unsecured creditor. Therefore they may have been treated differently by the company's management, and possibly unfavourably, yet the legislation assumes a favourable treatment and consequently imposes a restriction on their employee priority. Excluded employees should be given the opportunity to present evidence that demonstrates grounds upon which the statutory limit should not apply.

Recommendation – Taxation

The present treatment of tax upon insolvency be maintained.

Discussion

There is little point in returning to a priority for tax or any other State or Federal Government debt. The present treatment of company directors' liability under the *Income Tax Assessment Act 1936* (Cth) ensures that directors attend to the company's tax obligations and it appears to be working efficiently.

Recommendation – A Priority for Environment Clean-up Costs

The Australian Federal Government should investigate the introduction of an environmental status audit during the liquidation of all companies. If the report indicated that expenditure was required to clean up contaminated land or similar work, then this expenditure should be granted an express statutory priority.

Discussion

Many problems of an environmental kind can be identified in the sale of land. In a liquidation these become the concerns of the liquidator. Additional expenses can be incurred in cleaning up contaminated land or repairing other environmental damage. However, there is no incentive to address these problems if the purchaser is willing to accept the problems. To encourage good environmental practice, companies should be aware that a compulsory environmental audit report will be undertaken upon liquidation so there is no incentive to allow deterioration as the company enters financial difficulties. Governments should be encouraged to set up a fund to facilitate the clean up of land where the company cannot meet its obligations due to insolvency. A statutory priority would assist to meet environmental expenses, especially if these were commenced pre-appointment. Expenses post appointment would qualify as administration expenses and already enjoy a priority.

Recommendation – Consumer Prepayments

A new priority should be added to the *Corporations Act 2001* (Cth) that recognizes domestic consumers who have made a prepayment for goods and services which they are no longer going to receive.

Discussion

Continuous monitoring by ASIC and State Consumer Affairs offices should continue to identify 'risk' industries and companies that obtain prepayment for goods or services which they cannot deliver due to insolvency. Special purpose funds should be set up to protect domestic consumers. Some industries, such as travel agencies, already have this type of arrangement. Additionally, there should be a priority so that other prepayments, not supported by an industry wide fund, could be refunded.

Recommendation – Loyalty Schemes

The Federal Government should monitor the development of loyalty schemes and their impact on occurrences of corporate insolvency.

Discussion

If Government monitoring in the future showed that loyalty schemes impose increased problems for individual consumers, such as the loss of extensive amounts of 'rewards', then they should consider legislating to grant a statutory priority.

Empirical Testing of Statutory Priorities

The corporate insolvency system has evolved based on the basis of limited empirical data. This is despite arguments that empirical data distinguishes what actually happens or exists from what is a hypothetical reality. It is rare for studies to be conducted on corporate insolvency in Australia. Even in other parts of the world, such as the United States of America, there are only a small number of studies and given the population and the number of companies, the empirical information that is gathered is scant. The literature featuring empirical results is growing, but very slowly.

Future applied research involving empirical data gained from the public record would help to answer quantitative questions in the debate on statutory priorities, such as accurate financial outcomes for all present priority creditors. This research could also indicate the amounts foregone by each group of creditors.

The hypotheses (empirically-tested statements) that might be contemplated in the future for statutory priorities include that:

1. voluntary liquidation affords greater distributions for priority creditors than court appointed liquidations;
2. amounts of unmet employee entitlements are higher than all other priority claims;
3. there is a positive statistical relationship between unmet employee entitlements and unmet administration expenses.

Exploring such hypotheses should achieve the empirical research objectives of measuring the size of unmet priority claims and assist the justification for maintaining priorities. One method of exploration for such hypotheses is the use of a liquidator's report form that is required by statute to be completed for each liquidation.

Use of a Liquidators' Report Form

In Australia section 539(1) of the *Corporations Act 2001* (Cth) provides for the lodging by the liquidator of six-monthly accounts in a prescribed form, Form 524, verified by a statement in writing. In the past under the *Companies Act 1961* (NSW) s281(1) (and the equivalent in each State under the Uniform Companies Acts), this statement was done by affidavit.

This statement and Form 524 cannot be avoided by arguments that to complete them would involve too much expense. In *Re Metropolitan Bank Ltd (in liq)*[2] the Victorian Supreme Court in 1900 refused to accept an argument by a liquidator that complying with the rules to conduct an audit and make a return under the *Companies Act 1896* (Vic) would be a great expense and a waste of time. Today's forms should still be treated with such respect.

Form 524 provides for the particulars of receipts and payments. It also requires particulars of dividends declared in respect of unsecured and priority creditors for the six-month period covered by the statement. The statement requires details of the liquidator's investments and the realization of any investments. The prescribed form provides particulars of the rate per share of the return of assets in specie and/or cash to contributories. As these forms are six-monthly they require the liquidator to make an assessment of the current progress of the winding up.

Within one month of ceasing to act as liquidator, the liquidator must lodge with the ASIC a final account using Form 524.

Difficulties with Using Form 524 in Research

Form 524 appears to be considered by the regulator, ASIC, as containing information relevant to the company it describes, but this is not used in policy formation. The regulator peruses the individual picture of the insolvent state of the company but no reports exist that summarize the forms over, say, a year. Such inadequate use was indirectly highlighted during the late 1990s debate over the size of the unpaid employee entitlements owed by insolvent employers. ASIC was unable to supply the appropriate Federal Government Minister with a detailed picture of the rate at which employees missed out on their priority.[3] Other organizations such as the Australian Council of Trade Unions (ACTU) and

2 Re Metropolitan Bank Ltd. (in liq) (1900) 25 VLR 697, 698.

3 ASIC were unable to supply Peter Reith MHR when Minister for Employment, Workplace Relations and Small Business with required information (1998). From a personal interview with ASIC staff in Adelaide regional office 4 May 2000.

the Insolvency Practitioners Association of Australia (IPAA)[4] conducted their own sample in an attempt to support their version of the problem. Both attempts were very minimal research projects, though neither attempted to use data from Form 524.

The use of Form 524 in research is limited because it cannot be checked without great effort. The potential audit of the Form could be conducted through approaching liquidators directly and asking them to retrieve archived files and then matching up the information therein with the Form.

Another difficulty is that the Form is subject to some misunderstanding by liquidators and regulators and ASIC has agreed it is not a good form.[5]

As data from Form 524 is considered secondary data from an empirical viewpoint, it will almost always be gathered faster and at a lower cost than primary data.[6] While secondary data has invariably been collected for another purpose (here the purposes of monitoring liquidations carried out by ASIC), it may be outdated and may not exactly meet the needs of the research. Nevertheless secondary sources often prove to be of great value in exploratory research.

Another weakness acknowledged in using secondary data is that the user has no control over the accuracy.[7] This would be true of the Form 524, although there would be some justification in believing that following scrutiny by ASIC it should reflect a great deal of accuracy. Research based upon data from Government enjoys greater acceptance because of the integrity of these sources.[8] As the objective would be 'fact-finding' regarding the position of priority creditors, this is a typical objective for research based on secondary data, that is, the accumulation of descriptive information.[9]

4 The Insolvency Practitioners Association of Australia, Submission Regarding the Protection of Employee Entitlements in the Event of Employer Insolvency, 18 November 1999 to Ministerial Discussion Paper issued by Peter Reith MHR speaks of a limited survey of 13 member firms. Copy of submission held by the writer.

5 The writer has been informed of this through discussions with the Insolvency Policy branch of ASIC.

6 Zikmund, W.G. *Business Research Methods* (4th ed. 1994) 116.

7 Ibid. 117, 124.

8 Ibid.

9 Ibid. 118.

Benefits of Using Form 524s

One great benefit is that it is a statutory form. This will generally mean that the form has been the subject of careful drafting from the parliamentary drafters. Furthermore, professional bodies and individual professionals, such as insolvency practitioners, may have been consulted before the implementation of such a form, although no evidence is available in this particular case to support these expectations. A statutory form has a great benefit as a research tool in that there are formal sanctions available for non-compliance. Such an outcome will mean that the data should be full and complete from each liquidation, subject to the enforcement undertaken by ASIC.

Form 524 is a form that is filled out for all liquidations. This provides for the most complete picture as is possible. Court-appointed and creditors' voluntary liquidations will be expected to involve insolvent companies and both require a Form 524 to be lodged every six months.

A major factor in choosing to use Form 524 for empirical research would be its large cost benefit over the use of other methods. Form 524 is cheap to access in that it is a form available on the public record after its lodgment with ASIC.

When considering an empirical research model for statutory priorities it would be important to ascertain what data already existed that might permit research questions to be appropriately and adequately addressed. The use of ASIC data in the guise of a Form 524 is not ideal, although the same could be said for other models such as using liquidators' files, as accessing these would be inconvenient, less effective and costly.

Data from Form 524s as secondary data may be used as the sole basis for a research study. Retrospective research often requires the use of past published data and the use of the data from Form 524 would be different from its original use by ASIC. The data is usually more quickly available than primary data, for instance by asking the liquidators in person to provide data on priority creditors from their files, and much less organization is required to obtain the data from ASIC. Furthermore, the data exists in considerable quantity and contains information that is fairly easy for a Government agency with legal backing to collect. Obtaining the equivalent data without such factors is very difficult for the lone researcher. Such is the case when contemplating empirical research of statutory priorities.

Survey of Insolvency Professionals

A second method of exploring the hypotheses mentioned above could involve the use a survey of insolvency professionals. Insolvency professionals can be a useful source of information on the role of statutory priorities. Response rates might be very low if insolvency professionals were simply asked to contribute quantifiable data such as what percentage of priority creditors were paid in their last five insolvency administrations. Instead a survey in the form of a questionnaire could be sent to a statistically significant sample, say 100 practitioners. A similar survey was undertaken in the United Kingdom by Keay and Walton in 1998. Replicating the research in Australia and other common law jurisdictions would be most worthwhile.

Keay and Walton argue that the current analysis of the legal position on preferential debts is incomplete as '[I]t does not tell us what is actually happening in practice; only an empirical study can do that'.[10] They found that determining what empirical data should be obtained on statutory priorities was 'not an easy task'.[11] They suggest the only technically correct way of determining whether the regime should be abolished or not would be to collect data during the course of two time periods, one when the regime was in force and one where it was not and then compare the results.[12] They acknowledge though that this is not practical.[13]

Keay and Walton prepared a questionnaire addressing issues pertinent to the UK regime and how it impacted on relevant aspects of insolvency law. They then sent it to licensed insolvency practitioners in England and Wales, who they claimed were 'the persons who would have the most information concerning the operation of the regime in practice'.[14] The questionnaire was sent in mid-1998 to 225 practitioners and 77 responded – a response rate of approximately 34 percent.[15]

It is problematical to ask busy practitioners to complete questionnaires because of the time commitment taken to complete them. Keay and Walton comment that to elicit as many responses as possible they kept the questionnaire 'relatively short'. The Keay and Walton questionnaire went to three pages and was divided into three main parts. It was drafted in such a way as to be completed as quickly as possible by the practitioner. The three parts were divided into: 'A' where responses were sought in order to gauge whether respondents felt that the regime precipitated problems; 'B' where the researchers sought estimates of the fate of funds payable by liquidators; and 'C' which canvassed the views of practitioners on the abolition or alteration of rights for preferential creditors.[16]

An Australian survey was conducted in late 2001 of insolvency practitioners to consider the impact of insolvency on employees.[17] This survey was designed to

---

10 Keay, A. and Walton, P. 'Preferential Debts: An Empirical Study' [1999] *Insolvency Lawyer* 112, 114.

11 Ibid.

12 Ibid.

13 Ibid.

14 Ibid.

15 Ibid.

16 Ibid.

17 David Noakes (with PhD supervisor Geof Stapledon as co-investigator) conducted the survey and it was published as Noakes, D. 'Measuring the Impact of Strategic Insolvency on Employees' (2003) 11 *Insolvency Law Journal* 91. Another study was conducted by the National Centre for Social and Economic Modelling and KPMG Consulting, *Alternative Models for an Australian Employee's Entitlement Support Scheme* (Report to the NSW Department of Industrial Relations, The Queensland Department of Employment, Training

capture information about the loss of employee entitlements, as well as to examine recent reforms and the viability of alternatives for future reform in the area of employees and corporate insolvency. This survey was not designed to cover the topic of statutory priorities but merely one facet, that of employees.

A more extensive future survey of Australian insolvency practitioners, perhaps based on the Keay and Walton model, could provide feedback about statutory priorities that would corroborate any empirical research based on ASIC data and provide additional information on statutory priorities. The survey research, using a structured questionnaire, might ask Australian insolvency practitioners such questions as:

1. Over the last 5 years how many court appointed liquidations have you conducted that resulted in a full distribution to priority creditors?
2. Has GEERS satisfied all employees' wages and entitlements in the liquidations you have undertaken?
3. Are 'excluded employees' precluded from entitlements in many liquidations and if so to what extent?
4. Do you believe that a different form of wage earner protection fund or insurance scheme would be useful to your administration of employees' wages and entitlements?
5. Has the removal of the tax priority since 1993 assisted in more money being available to meet priority debts?
6. Has your recent practice revealed circumstances of others that you feel should be granted a priority?

Undertaking such a survey would be appropriate and timely at the present time now that GEERS has been subject to further refinement. As previously mentioned, it would be a logical follow up from the research presented in this thesis.

Conclusion

While this work has explored Australian statutory priorities and has attempted to be theoretically informed, methodologically sound, narrowly focused and argued from a specific position it has also used comparative elements. While conceding there is no settled theory of corporate insolvency law, there has been ready acceptance of the perspective of a creditors' bargain model being applied in Australia and elsewhere. Broader perspectives have been briefly discussed and support given to a vision of communitarianism, especially when the analysis is conducted on statutory priorities. Given the infancy of corporate insolvency scholarship in Australia the foregoing chapters have relied upon legally based doctrinal analysis,

and Industrial Relations and the Victorian Department of State and Regional Development, March 2001.

while acknowledging that other methods lend themselves towards further inquiry of statutory priorities, as briefly mentioned in this chapter.

If corporate insolvency is the 'destroyer and spoliator' and such a 'drastic remedy', as some are apt to say,[18] then the statutory priorities that presently exist do serve to repair and remedy some creditors. Those claimants that do not as yet hold priority status, but could be contemplated as the subject of future priorities, would also be rendered some greater financial assistance by obtaining a favourable statutory priority treatment.

The non-compliance with the fundamental principle of *pari passu* in the distribution of the insolvent estate is due to the provision of statutory priorities. However, as demonstrated above, there is persuasive justification for Australian law to maintain the present s556(1) of the *Corporations Act 2001* (Cth). Future legislators are unlikely to remove the administration expenses and despite alternative systems that protect employees' wages and entitlements these are unlikely to lose the extra protection of a statutory priority.

The presence of statutory priorities in corporate insolvency legislation contributes in achieving one of the fundamental aims and objectives of insolvency law, that of providing an orderly processing of insolvency claims after some measured assessment and realization of available assets. Such an outcome must be maintained. The rich legal materials used in the preceding chapters that have been drawn from other jurisdictions such as the United Kingdom, Canada, New Zealand and the United States, demonstrate just how vital the priorities have become.

In conclusion the existing statutory priorities are justified. They appear to work satisfactorily and should continue to feature in the relevant statute. Despite this, some minor changes are recommended in this chapter. Concepts of fairness and equity in corporate insolvency distributions could be better served by the implementation of the priority recommendations contained within this chapter to deserving claimants. However as the law must choose who is to be paid from a limited supply of funds in the insolvent estate, insolvency law can never satisfy all creditors.

18 Wood, P.H. *Principles of International Insolvency* (1995) 1-1; Flessner, A. 'Philosophies in Business Bankruptcy Law: An International Overview' in Ziegel, J.S. (ed.), *Current Developments in International and Comparative Corporate Insolvency Law* (1994) 19.

Bibliography

Journal Articles

Anderson, Hamish, 'Receivership Preferential Creditors: Prior Floating Charges, Trading Receipts, Work in Progress and Allocation of Fees and Expenses' (1995) 15 *Company Lawyer* 195

Anderson, Helen, 'The Theory of the Corporation and its Relevance to Directors' Tortious Liability to Creditors' (2004) 16 *Australian Journal of Corporate Law* 73

Arjuran, Kris, 'Locus Standi of Employees in Companies Winding Up' (1993) 11 *Corporate and Securities Law Journal* 141

Armour, John, 'The Chequered History of the Floating Charge' (2004) 13 *Griffith Law Review* 25

Arner, Michael R, 'The Worthier Creditors (and a Cheer for the King) – Revisited' (1979) 53 *American Bankruptcy Law Journal* 389

Baird, Douglas G and Jackson, Thomas, 'Corporate Reorganisation and the Treatment of Diverse Ownership Interests: A Comment on Adequate Protection of Secured Creditors in Bankruptcy' (1984) 51 *University of Chicago Law Review* 97

Baird, Douglas G, 'A World Without Bankruptcy' (1987) 50 *Law and Contemporary Problems* 173

Baird, Douglas G, 'Loss Distribution, Forum Shopping, and Bankruptcy: A Reply to Warren' (1987) 54 *University of Chicago Law Review* 815

Baker, Debra L, 'Bankruptcy: The Last Environmental Loophole?' (1993) 34 *South Texas Law Review* 379

Bebchuk, Lucian A and Fried, Jesse M, 'The Uneasy Case for the Priority of Secured Claims in Bankruptcy' (1996) 105 *Yale Law Journal* 857

Ben-Dror, Yoav, 'An Empirical Study of Distribution Rules under California Corporations Code s500: Are Creditors Adequately Protected?' (1983) 16 *University of California Davis Law Review* 375

Bennett, John Michael, 'Historical Trends in Australian Law Reform' (1969–1970) 9 *University of Western Australia Law Review* 211

Benveniste, Ivor, 'Receiverships and the Protection of Unsecured Creditors' (1985) 6 *The Company Lawyer* 161

Black, Julia, 'Critical Reflections on Regulation' (2002) 27 *Australian Journal of Legal Philosophy* 1

Blackham, L, 'The Unstoppable Force Hits the Immovable Wall: Should Environmental Cleanup Liability be Discharged in Bankruptcy' (1992) 25 *Creighton Law Review* 1357

Blewett, Estelle, 'Employees, Unlawful Termination and the Insolvency Practitioner' (1996) *Australian Accountant* 48

Boreham, Tim, 'Tax Office Loses Its Place in the Creditor Queue' (1992) *Business Review Weekly* (11 December 1992) 86

Borrowdale, Andrew 'Directors Liability in Tort' [1999] *New Zealand Law Journal* 51

Bratton, Daniel, 'The California Agricultural Producers' Lien, Processing Company Insolvencies, and Federal Bankruptcy Law: An Evaluation and Alternative Methods of Protecting Farmers' (1985) 36 *Hasting Law Journal* 609

Brealey, Daniel T, 'Section 221P of the Income Tax Assessment Act, A Garrote for the Secured Creditors' (1987) 5 *Company and Securities Law Journal* 12.

Brennan, Gerard, 'Commercial Law and Morality' (1989) 17 *Melbourne University Law Review* 100

Brennan, Mark, 'Contaminated Sites' (1995) *Australian Company Secretary* 371

Broderick, Matthew, 'Extending the Liability for Insolvent Trading' (2001) 19 *Company and Securities Law Journal* 58

Bronstein, Arturo S, 'Wage Guarantee Funds in Belgium, Spain and France' (1986) 3–4 *Social Labour Bulletin* 481

Bronstein, Arturo S, 'The Protection of Workers' Claims in the Event of the Insolvency of their Employer' (1987) 126 *International Labour Review* 715

Brough, Michelle, 'Costs and Expenses Incurred by an Administrator in the Preservation or Maintenance of Assets' (1995) 11 *Insolvency Law and Practice* 103

Brown, Murray, 'The Priority of the Expenses and Remuneration of an Administrator or Provisional Liquidator in the Winding Up of a Company' (1998) 9 *Journal of Banking and Finance Law and Practice* 126

Brunton, Nicholas, 'The South Australian Environmental Protection Act 1993' (1995) 12 *Environmental and Planning Law Journal* 3

Buckley, Francis H, 'The Bankruptcy Priority Puzzle' (1986) 72 *Virginia Law Review* 1393

Cantlie, Susan, 'When Worlds Collide: Environmental Regulation in Conflict with Bankruptcy Legislation' (1992) 21 *Canadian Business Law Journal* 190

Chartrand, Rupert H, 'Labour and Insolvency in the 1990s' (1994–5) 24 *Canadian Business Law Journal* 193

Cheffins, Brain R, 'Using Theory to Study law: A Company Law Perspective' (1999) 58 *Cambridge Law Journal* 197

Chin, Michael and Hodgson, Anne, 'Safety on the Site' (1994) 68 *Law Institute Journal* 1064

Clarr, Gary E, 'The Case for a Bankruptcy Code Priority for Environmental Cleanup Claims' (1992) 18 *William Mitchell Law Review* 29

Close, A L, 'The British Columbia Buyer's Lien – A New Consumer Remedy' (1995) 25 *Canadian Business Law Journal* 127

Cole, James S, 'The "Carve out" from Liens and Priorities to Guarantee Professional Fees in Chapter 11' (1993) 4 *Detroit College of Law Review* 1499

Coleman, Cynthia F, 'Insolvency: The Commissioner's Advantage' (1992) 26 *Taxation in Australia* 318

Collins, Hugh, 'Transfer of Undertakings and Insolvency' (1990) 19 *Industrial Law Journal* 144

Cuming, Ronald C C, 'Canadian Bankruptcy Law: A Secured Creditor's Heaven' (1994–5) 24 *Canadian Business Law Journal* 17

Darvas, Paula, 'Employees and Insolvency: A Public Policy Approach' (1999) 17 *Company and Securities Law Journal* 103

Davies, Paul and Freedland, Mark, 'The Effects of Receiverships upon Employees of Companies' (1980) 9 *Industrial Law Journal* 95

Davies, Paul 'Employee Claims in Insolvency: Corporate Rescues and Preferential Claims' (1994) 23 *Industrial Law Journal* 141

Davis, Kevin, 'Priority of Crown Claims in Insolvency: Royal Bank of Canada v Sparrow Electric Corp and its Aftermath' 29 *Canadian Business Law Journal* 145

Delaney, Kevin J, 'Power, Intercorporate Networks, and "Strategic Bankruptcy"' (1989) 23 *Law and Society Review* 643

Drabkin, Murray, Moorman, James W, Kirsch, Laurence S, 'Bankruptcy and the Cleanup of Hazardous Waste: Caveat Creditor' (1985) 15 *Environmental Law Reporter* 10168

Dunham, Darrell and Shimkus, Alex, 'Tax Claims in Bankruptcy' (1993) 67 *American Bankruptcy Law Journal* 343

Duthie, Leigh, 'The Priority of Retrenchment Payments in a Liquidation or Receivership' (1992) 20 *Australian Business Law Review* 378

Editorial, 'A Consumers' Prepayment (Protection) Bill?' [1984] *Journal of Business Law* 106

Editorial, 'Protection of Consumers' Prepayments' [1985] *Journal of Business Law* 12

Eisenberg, Theodore, 'Differing Perceptions of Attorney Fees in Bankruptcy Cases' (1994) 72 *Washington University Law Quarterly* 979

Epling, Richard L, 'Environmental Liens in Bankruptcy' (1988) 44 *The Business Lawyer* 85

Farrar, John H, 'The Reform of Insolvency Law – 3' (1984) *Journal of Business Law* 424

Farrar, John, 'The Personal Liability of Directors for Corporate Torts' (1997) 9 *Bond Law Review* 102

Feilbelman, Adam, 'Federal Bankruptcy Law and State Sovereign Immunity' (2003) 81 *Texas Law Review* 1381

Finch, Vanessa, 'The Measures of Insolvency Law' (1997) 17 *Oxford Journal of Legal Studies* 227

Finch, Vanessa, 'Security, Insolvency and Risk: Who Pays the Price?' (1999) 62 *Modern Law Review* 633

Finch, Vanessa, 'Is *Pari Passu* Passé?' [2000] *Insolvency Lawyer* 194

Fletcher, Ian F, 'The Genesis of Modern Insolvency Law – An Odyssey of Law Reform' [1987] *Journal of Business Law* 365

Fridman, Gerald Henry Louis, 'Personal Tort Liability of Company Directors' (1992) 5 *Canterbury Law Review* 41

Frost-Drury, Greg, Greinke, Amanda and Shailer, Andrew, 'Financial Differences between Administrations and Liquidations' (1998) 6 *Insolvency Law Journal* 153

Garrido, José M, 'The Distributional Question in Insolvency: Comparative Aspects' (1995) 4 *International Insolvency Review* 25

Garrido, José M, 'Some Reflections on the EU Bankruptcy Convention and its Implications for Secured and Preferential Creditors' (1998) 7 *International Insolvency Review* 79

Gleig, D Bruce, 'Unpaid Wages in Bankruptcy' (1987) 21 *University of British Columbia Law Review* 61

Goode, Royston M, 'The Death of Insolvency' (1980) 1 *The Company Lawyer* 123

Goode, Royston M, 'Is the Law Too Favourable to Secured Creditors?' (1983–4) 8 *Canadian Business Law Journal* 53

Grantham, Ross and Rickett, Charles, 'Directors' "Tortious" Liability: Contract, Torts or Company Law?' (1999) 62 *Modern Law Review* 133

Gronow, Michael, 'Insolvent Corporate Groups and Their Employees: The Case For Further Reform' (2003) 21 *Companies and Securities Law Journal* 188

Gross, Karen, 'Taking Community Interests Into Account in Bankruptcy' (1996) 72 *Washington University Law Quarterly* 1031

Ham, C Keith, 'Bankruptcy – Secured Creditors Issuing Petition – Effect on Preferred and Unsecured Creditors: Bank of Montreal v Scott Road Enterprises Limited' (1990) 69 *Canadian Bar Review* 315

Hammond, Celia, 'Are Receivers and Administrators Liable for the Wages of Company Employees Retained After Their Appointment?' (1997) 5 *Insolvency Law Journal* 136

Hammond, Celia, 'The Relationship of Administrators to Company Employees: Issues Arising under Part 5.3A of the Corporations Law' (1999) 7 *Insolvency Law Journal* 74

Heath, Paul, 'Preferential Payments on Bankruptcy and Liquidations in New Zealand: Are they Justifiable Exceptions to the *Pari Passu* Rule?' (1996) 4 *Waikato Law Review* 24

Heidt, Kathryn R, 'The Automatic Stay in Environmental Bankruptcies' (1993) 67 *American Bankruptcy Law Journal* 69

Herbert, Michael J, and Pacitti, Domenic E, 'Down and Out in Richmond Virginia: The Distribution of Assets in Chapter 7 Bankruptcy Proceedings Closed during 1984–1987' (1988) 22 *University of Richmond Law Review* 303

Hill, Jennifer, 'At the Frontiers of Labour Law and Corporate Law: Enterprise Bargaining, Corporations and Employees' (1995) 23 *Federal Law Review* 204

Hill, H Hamner, 'Bankruptcy v Environmental Protection: A Case Study in Normative Conflict' (1998) 16 *Canadian Journal of Law and Jurisprudence* 245

Ho, Look Chan, 'On *Pari Passu*, Equality and Hotchpot in Cross Border Insolvency' [2003] *Lloyd's Maritime Commercial Law Quarterly* 95

Holding, Peter, 'Who Bears the Risk? Protecting Employee Entitlements Upon Insolvency' (1995) 69 *Law Institute Journal* 789

Holloway, Nigel and Wherry, Rob, 'Troubled Airlines May Have to Fly United' 24(2) *Business Review Weekly* 21–27 March 2002, 38

Innes, Stuart, 'Frequent Flyers Demand an Upgrade' *The Advertiser* 19 February 2002, 54

Jackson, Thomas H, 'Bankruptcy, Non-Bankruptcy Entitlements, and the Creditors' Bargain' (1982) 91 *Yale Law Journal* 857

Jensen-Cocklin, Susan, 'Do Confimed Chapter 11 Plans Consummate? The Results of a Study and Analysis of the Law' (1992) 97 *Commercial Law Journal* 297

Johannsen, Linda, 'United States v Whizco, Inc: A Further Refinement of the Conflict Between Bankruptcy Discharge and Environmental Cleanup Obligations' (1990) 20 *Environmental Law* 207

Kahn, Phillipe J, 'Bankruptcy Versus Environmental Protection: Discharging Future CERCLA Liability in Chapter 11' (1993) 14 *Cardozo Law Review* 2000

Kang, Justin, 'Section 221P – Alive and Well in Voluntary Administrations' (1994) September *Commercial Law Association* 12

Keating, Daniel, 'The Fruits of Labor: Worker Priorities in Bankruptcy' (1993) 35 *Arizona Law Journal* 905

Keay, Andrew, 'The Unity of Insolvency Legislation: Time for a Re-think?' (1999) 7 *Insolvency Law Journal* 4

Keay, Andrew, 'Balancing Interests in Bankruptcy Law' (2000) *Common Law World Review* 206

Keay, Andrew, 'Insolvency Law: A Matter of Public Interest' (2001) 51 *Northern Ireland Legal Quarterly* 509

Keay, Andrew, Boraine, Andre and Burdette, David, 'Preferential Debts in Corporate Insolvency: A Comparative Study' (2001) *International Insolvency Review* 167

Keay, Andrew and de Prez, P, 'Insolvency and Environmental Principles: A Case Study in a Conflict of Public Interests' (2001) 3 *Environmental Law Review* 90

Keay, Andrew and Walton, Peter, 'Preferential Debts: An Empirical Study' (1999) *Insolvency Lawyer* 112

Keay, Andrew, and Walton, Peter, 'The Preferential Debts Regime in Liquidation Law: In The Public Interest?' (1999) 3 *Company Financial and Insolvency Law Review* 84

Kinsey, Samantha, 'A Triumph for Labour over Capital: Employee Entitlements in Insolvency in the Wake of the Ansett Collapse' (2002) 10 *Insolvency Law Journal* 132

Kloss, Diana M and Milman, David, 'The Rights of Employees on Corporate Insolvency' (1982) *The Conveyancer* 99

Klotz, Robert A, 'Protection of Unpaid Suppliers Under the New Bankruptcy and Insolvency Act' (1993) 21 *Canadian Business Law Journal* 161

Korobkin, Donald R, 'Rehabilitating Values: A Jurisprudence of Bankruptcy' (1991) 91 *Columbia Law Review* 717

Korobkin, Donald R, 'The Role of Normative Theory in Bankruptcy Debates' (1996) 82 *Iowa Law Review* 75

Lackey, Paul B, 'An Empirical Survey and Proposed Bankruptcy Code Section Concerning the Propriety of Bidding Incentives in a Bankruptcy Sale of Assets' (1993) 93 *Columbia Law Review* 720

Lawlor, James N, 'Toxic Tug of War: Environmental Cleanup Costs, Bankruptcy and the Administrative Expense Priority – Is It A Collision of Conflicting Policies or Just Plain Confusion?' (1991) 21 *Seton Hall Law Review* 832

Lee, Robert G, 'The Obligation to Remediate Contaminated Land – A Comparative Analysis' (1993) 10 *Environment and Planning Law Journal* 97

Leebron, David W, 'Limited Liability, Tort Victims, and Creditors' (1991) 91 *Columbia Law Review* 1565

Lightman, Justice, 'Office Holders' Charges: Cost Control and Transparency' [1998] 19 *Company Lawyer* 72

Lightman, Justice, 'The Challenge Ahead: Address to the Insolvency Lawyers' Association' (1996) *Journal of Business Law* 113

Lockett, Laurel E, 'Environmental Liability Enforcement and the Bankruptcy Act of 1978:A Study of H.R.2767, The "Superlien" Provision' (1984) 19 *Real Property, Probate and Trust Journal* 859

LoPucki, Lynn M, 'The Systems Approach to Law' (1997) 82 *Cornell Law Review* 479

Lynch, J J, 'Lay-by Sales: The Case for Further Reform' (1988) 18 *Victoria University Wellington Law Review* 181

Lynch, Paul, 'Drafting a Deed of Company Arrangement' (1995) 3 *Insolvency Law Journal* 115

Mann, Ronald J, 'Bankruptcy and the Entitlements of the Government: Whose Money is it Anyway?' (1995) 70 *New York University Law Review* 993

Marsh, Harold, 'Triumph or Tragedy? The Bankruptcy Act Amendments of 1966' (1967) 42 *Washington Law Review* 681

McCoid, J, 'Statutory Liens in Bankruptcy' (1994) 58 *American Bankruptcy Law Journal* 269

McIntyre, Lisa J, 'A Sociological Perspective on Bankruptcy' (1989) 65 *Indiana Law Journal* 123

McQuade, Paul, 'A Receiver's, Liquidator's and Provisional Liquidator's Claim to a Lien or Charge for Remuneration and Expenses' (1993) 1 *Insolvency Law Journal* 199

McQueen, Rob, 'Why High Court Judges Make Poor Historians: The Corporations Act Case and Early Attempts to Establish a National System of company Regulation in Australia' (1990) 19 *Federal Law Review* 245

McQueen, Rob, 'Limited Liability Company Legislation – The Australian Experience' (1991) 1 *Australian Journal of Corporate Law* 22

McQueen, Rob, 'An Examination of Australia Corporate Law and Regulation 1901–1961' (1992) 15 *University of New South Wales Law Journal* 1

McQueen, Rob, 'Company Law as Imperialism' (1995) 5 *Australian Journal of Corporate Law* 1

Meyerowitz, Steven A, 'Bankruptcy and the Environment' [1986] *The Amicus Journal* 9

Mfodwo, Kwame, 'Remediation and Compensation After Hazardous Waste Incidents: Recent Developments Affecting Companies and Financial Institutions in Victoria' (1991) 8 *Environment and Planning Law Journal* 211

Mfodwo, Kwame, 'Lender Liability for Environmental Impairment and Remediation in New South Wales in New South Wales: Issues Problems and Prospects' (1991) 8 *Environmental and Planning Law Journal* 108

Millon, David, 'Communitarians, Contractarians, and the Crisis in Corporate Law' (1993) 50 *Washington & Lee Law Review* 1373

Milman, David, 'Ten Per Cent Fund' editorial [1999] *Insolvency Lawyer* 47

Milman, David, 'The Liquidation Expense Principle' [2000] *Insolvency Lawyer* 126

Mirsky, Arlene E, Conway, Richard J, Humphrey, Geralyn G, 'The Interface Between Bankruptcy and Environmental Laws' (1991) 46 *The Business Lawyer* 626

Mitchell, Lawrence E, 'The Fairness Rights of Corporate Bondholders' (1990) 65 *New York University Law Review* 1165

Mokal, Rizwaan Jameel, 'Priority as Pathology: The Pari Passu Myth' (2001) 60 *Cambridge Law Journal* 581

Mokal, Rizwaan Jameel, 'The Authentic Consent Model: Contractarianism, Creditors' Bargain and Corporate Liquidation' (2001) 21 *Legal Studies* 400

Mokal, Rizwaan Jameel, 'On Fairness and Efficiency' (2003) 66 *Modern Law Review* 452

Morgan, Barbra K, 'Should the Sovereign Be Paid First? A Comparative International Analysis of the Priority of Tax Claims in Bankruptcy' (2000) 74 *American Bankruptcy Law Journal* 461

Morgan, Richard, 'Insolvency and the Rights of Employees' (1989) *Legal Action* 21

Morrow, Paul, 'Tax Priorities Legislation: Dynamite for Directors' (1993) December *Commercial Law Association* 19

Murray, Michael, 'Commonwealth Subrogation to Employee Entitlements' 1 (5) *Insolvency Law Bulletin* (2000) 78

Nejat seyhun, H, and Bradley, Michael, 'Corporate Bankruptcy and Insider Trading' (1997) 70 (2) *Journal of Business* 189

Noakes David, 'Reform to the Law of Corporate Groups in Australia to Protect Employees' (2000) 34 *University of British Columbia Law Review* 239

Noakes David, 'Corporate Groups and the Duties of Directors: Protecting the Employee or the Insolvent Employer?' (2001) 29 *Australian Business Law Review* 124

Noakes, David, 'Measuring the Impact of Strategic Insolvency on Employees' (2003) 11 *Insolvency Law Journal* 91

O'Donovan, James, 'Corporate Insolvency: Policies, Perspectives and Reform' (1990) 3 *Corporate and Business Law Journal* 1

O'Donovan, James, 'The Administrator's Priority and Statutory Lien in a Winding Up' (1994) 12 *Company and Securities Law Journal* 382

O'Donovan, James, 'Employees, Voluntary Administrations and Deeds of Company Arrangement' (1994) 12 *Corporate and Securities Law Journal* 457

O'Donovan, James, 'The Harmer Reforms: Arranged Marriages and Extended Honeymoons' (1995) 8 *Corporate and Business Law Journal* 101

Paige, Richard B, 'In Re Quanta Resources Corp.: Bankruptcy Policy v Environmental Interests; A Polluted Judicial Theory' (1985) 59 *American Bankruptcy Law Journal* 357

Painter, Christopher M E, 'Tort Creditor Priority in the Secured Credit System: Asbestos Times, The Worst of Times' (1984) 36 *Stanford Law Review* 1045

Palans, Lloyd A, 'Comments on Eisenberg Differing Perceptions of Attorney Fees in Bankruptcy Cases' (1994) 72 *Washington University Law Quarterly* 997

Parker, Deborah E, 'Environmental Claims in Bankruptcy: It's a Question of Priorities' (1995) 32 *San Diego Law Review* 221

Patel, Niranjan, 'Employee Creditors' Rights in Collective Proceedings: A Comparative Perspective' (1979) 3 *Comparative Law Yearbook* 52

Peacock, Rolfe W, 'The Financial Effects of the Legal Failure of Proprietary Companies'(1985) 8 *Accounting Forum* 25

Phillips, Victoria and Healy, Christopher, 'Environmental Considerations for Insolvency Practitioners: Part 2 – Investigating Environmental Problems' (1993) 8 *Insolvency Law and Practice* 117

Phillips, Victoria, 'Environmental Considerations for Insolvency Practitioners: Part 3 – Dealing with Contaminated Land' (1993) 8 *Insolvency Law and Practice* 153

Plumb, William T, 'The Tax Recommendations on the Bankruptcy Laws – Priority and Dischargeability of Tax Claims' (1974) 59 *Cornell Law Review* 991

Pollard, David, 'Adopted Employees in Insolvency – Orphans No More' (1995) 24 *Industrial Law Journal* 141

Price, Andrew, 'Tort Creditor Superpriority and Other Proposed Solutions to Corporate Limited Liability and the Problem of Externalities' (1995) 2 *George Mason University Law Review* 439

Quinn, Margaret, 'Remuneration' (1999) 9(1) *New Directions in Bankruptcy* 14 and 9(3) *New Directions in Bankruptcy* 14

Ramsay, Ian, 'Corporate Law in the Age of Statutes' (1992) 14 *Sydney Law Review* 474

Reynolds, Francis, 'Personal Liability of Company Directors in Tort' (2003) 33 *Hong Kong Law Journal* 51

Reynolds, Michael, 'The Corporations Law Amendment (Employee Entitlements) Act 2000 (Cth): To What Extent Will It Save Employee Entitlements' (2001) 1 *Queensland University of Technology Law Journal* 134

Rice, T, 'Bankruptcy and the Resolvable Clash' (1993) 29 *Tulsa Law Journal* 221

Riley, Joellen, 'Lessons from Ansett – Locating the Employee's Voice in Corporate Enterprise' (2002) 27 *Alternative Law Journal* 112

Riley, Joellen, 'Bargaining for Security: Lessons for Employees from the World of Corporate Finance' (2002) 44 *Journal of Industrial Relations* 491

Riley, Joellen, 'Protection of Employment Entitlements: A Legal Perspective (2003) 29 *Australian Bulletin of Labour* 31

Robinson, Dominic, 'Remuneration of Corporate Insolvency Practitioners' (2000) 8 *Insolvency Law Journal* 20

Ross, Emily, 'Flyblown Rewards' 23(5) *Business Review Weekly* October 4–10 2001, 34

Routledge, James, 'An Exploratory Empirical Analysis of Part 5.3A of the Corporations Law (Voluntary Administrations)' (1998) 16 *Company and Securities Law Journal* 4

Samuels, Alec, 'Prepayments: The Lost Consumer Deposits' [1987] *Journal of Business Law* 30

Schrag, J, and Ratner, B C, 'Caveat Emptor Empty Coffer: The Bankruptcy Has Nothing To Offer' (1972) 72 *Columbia Law Review* 1147

Shandro, Sandy and Osborne, Liz, 'Insolvency Practitioner Fees in the UK' (2004) Fourth Quarter *INSOL World* 6

Shanker, Morris G, 'The Worthier Creditors (and a Cheer for the King)' (1976) 1 *Canadian Business Law Journal* 340

Schwartz, Alan, 'Security Interests and Bankruptcy Priorities: A Review of Current Theories' (1981) 10 *Journal of Legal Studies* 1

Sneddon, Michael, 'Liability for Insolvent Polluters' (1997) 5 *Insolvency Law Journal* 65

Sturgess, James, 'Insolvency and Employee Claims' (2000) (September) 74 *Law Institute Journal* 81

Sutherland, Geoff, and Lee, Bret, 'Secured Creditors v Federal Commissioner of Taxation Priorities under s221P of the Income Tax Assessment Act' (1985) 17/5 *Commercial Law Association Newsletter* 87

Symes, Christopher F, 'The Protection of Wages When Insolvency Strikes' (1997) 5 *Insolvency Law Journal* 196

Symes, Christopher F, 'Do Not Dismiss the Employee as a Statutory Priority Creditor in Corporate Insolvency' (1998) 26 *Australian Business Law Review* 450

Symes, Christopher F, 'The Dawn of Green Corporate Insolvency Law: Environmental Accountability Creeping Over the Horizon' (1998) 9 *Australian Journal of Corporate Law* 64

Symes, Christopher F, 'It Would Be "Bettaform" To Give A Priority: Irving v. Construction Industry Long Service Leave Board' (1998) 10 *Corporate and Business Law Journal* 101

Symes, Christopher F, 'Insuring wage robbers' (1998) 23 *Alternative Law Journal* 198

Symes, Christopher F, 'Brassed Off – Australian Version' (1999) 24 *Alternative Law Journal* 190

Symes, Christopher F, 'Remuneration, Rent and "Requisite" Costs: The 3 R's of Insolvency's Administrative Expense Priority' (2000) 11 *Australian Journal of Corporate Law* 149

Symes, Christopher F, 'Worker's Entitlements: The Government's Options' (2000) 25 *Alternative Law Journal* 14

Symes, Christopher F, 'Workers' Entitlements: Probation Period Over' (2001) 26 *Alternative Law Journal* 298

Symes, Christopher F, 'Will There Ever be a Successful Prosecution of Part 5.8A?'(2002) 3 (1) *Insolvency Law Bulletin* 17

Symes, Christopher F, 'The $44 Question – To Make Tax Installment Deductions or Not? *Deputy Commissioner of Taxation v Applied Design Development Pty Ltd (in liq)*' [2002] FCA 205; (2002) 2 (9) *Insolvency Law Bulletin* 156

Symes, Christopher F, 'Employee Entitlements – a Performance Review for GEERS' (2003) 3 (7) *Insolvency Law Bulletin* 128

Symes, Christopher F, 'Are Directors (and their Families) Treated Too Harshly Under Insolvency Entitlements Law? (2003) 3 (8) *Insolvency Law Bulletin* 137

Symes, Christopher F, 'Subrogation in Insolvency' (2003) 3 (9) *Insolvency Law Bulletin* 153

Symes, Christopher F, 'Lessons on Loyalty Schemes in Insolvency' (2003) 4(3) *Insolvency Law Bulletin* 33

Symes, Christopher F, 'Reminiscing the Taxation Priorities in Insolvency' (2005) 1(2) *Journal of the Australasian Tax Teachers Association* 435

Symposium, 'Paying the Piper; Rethinking Professional Compensation in Bankruptcy' (1993) *1 American Bankruptcy Institute Law Review* 231

Tay, Derrick C, 'The Emerging Priority of Environmental Orders in Canadian Insolvency Situations' (1992) 7 *Journal of International Banking Law* 202

Tay, Derrick C, 'Environmental Liability and the Insolvency Professional: An Issue Whose Time Has, Or Will Surely, Come' (1994) 3 *International Insolvency Review* 60

Tiller, E. Allan, 'Personal Liability of Trustees and Receivers in Bankruptcy' (1979) 53 *American Bankruptcy Law Journal* 75

Unattributed, 'Counsels' Corner: Farmer Priority in Bankrupt Warehouses – Yellow Light for Country Banks' (1982) 99 *Banking Law Journal* 964

Van Wezel Stone, K, 'Policing Employment Contracts within the Nexus-of-Contracts Firm' (1993) 43 *University of Toronto Law Journal* 353

Villiers, Charlotte, 'Employees as Creditor: A Challenge for Justice in Insolvency Law' (1999) 20 *Company Lawyer* 222

Walczyk, Leonard, 'An Overview of Taxation Issues in Bankruptcy' (2001) 151 *New Jersey Lawyer* 17

Wallace, P, 'Ferris Revisited – SIP9 updated' (1998) 10(4) *Australian Insolvency Journal* 36

Warren, Elizabeth, 'Bankruptcy Policy' (1987) 54 *University of Chicago Law Review* 775

Weisberg, Robert, 'Commercial Morality, the Merchant Character, and the History of the Voidable Preference' (1986) 39 *Stanford Law Review* 3

Wheatley, Derek, 'Greener than Green?' (1991) 141 *New Law Journal* 208

Williams, Jack F, and Ogier, Tamara M, 'A Collision of Policy: A Chapter 13 and Taxes' (1999) 50 *South Carolina Law Review* 313

Wishart, David, 'The Personal Liability of Directors in Tort' (1992) 10 *Company and Securities Law Journal* 363

Wolfe, Alan, 'The Modern Corporation: Private Agent or Public Actor?' (1993) 50 *Washington & Lee Law Review* 1673

Wood, Philip R, 'Principles of International Insolvency (Part 1)' (1995) 4 *International Insolvency Review* 94

Zatzman, Debbie, 'The Unpaid Employee as Creditor: Case Comment on Homeplan Realty' (1980) 6 *Dalhousie Law Journal* 148

Ziegel, Jacob S, 'The Travails of Bill C-12' (1983–4) 8 *Canadian Business Law Journal* 374

Ziegel, Jacob S, 'Preferences and Priorities in Insolvency Laws: Is There a Solution?' (1995) 39 *St Louis University Law Journal* 793

Zwier, Leon, Merkel, Dany and Buchanan, Ian, 'Ansett Administration Court-Approved Websites' 76(3) *Law Institute Journal* 46

Books

Ames, N., *An Evaluation of the US Trustee Pilot Program for Bankruptcy Administration: Findings and Recommendations* (US Department of Justice, Cambridge Mass. 1983) (Abt Associates Consultants Study).

Anderson, C. and Morrison, D., *Crutchfield's Corporate Voluntary Administration* (3rd ed. 2003).

Austin, R.P. and Ramsay, I.M., *Ford's Principles of Corporations Law* (12th ed. 2005).

Cantlie, S.J., 'Preferred Priority in Bankruptcy' in Ziegel, J.S. (ed.), *Current Developments in International and Comparative Insolvency Law* (1994) 413.

Carruthers, B.G. and Halliday, T.C., *Rescuing Business The Making of Corporate Bankruptcy Law in England and the United States* (1998).

Clarke, A., (ed.), *Current Issues in Insolvency Law* (1991).

Corkery, J. and Lessing, J.P.G., (eds), *Corporate Insolvency Law* (1995).

Creighton B. and Stewart, A., *Labour Law* (4th ed. 2005).

Davis, R., 'The Environmental Wave' in *Construction Insolvency* (1991) 383.

Eastdown, G. and Wilms, P., *Ansett the Collapse* (2002).

Finch, V. and Worthington, S., 'The *Pari Passu* Principle and Ranking Restitutionary Claims' in Rose, F. (ed.), *Restitution and Insolvency* (2000).

Finch, V., *Corporate Insolvency Law Perspectives and Principles* (2002).

Flessner, A., 'Philosophies of Business Bankruptcy Law: An International Overview' in Ziegel, J.S. (ed.), *Current Developments in International and Comparative Corporate Insolvency Law* (1994).

Ford, H.A., Austin, R.P., and Ramsay, I.M., *Ford's Principles of Corporations Law* (10th ed. 2001) and (11th ed. 2003).

Goode, R.M., *Principles of Corporate Insolvency Law* (2nd ed. 1997) esp Ch 5.

Gough, W.J., *Gough on Company Charges* (2nd ed. 1996) esp Ch 39.

Gower, *Modern Company Law* (2nd ed. 1957).

Gross, K., *Failure and Forgiveness; Rebalancing the Bankruptcy System* (1997) esp Ch 4 and 9.

Hardy, A.E., *Crown Priorities in Insolvency* (1986).

Harmer, R., 'Employee Creditors and Corporations' in McCallum, R., McCarry, G. and Ronfeldt, P. (eds), *Employment Security* (1994).

Hayek, E.J., *Principles of Bankruptcy in Australia* (2nd ed. 1967).

Howell, P.A., 'Constitutional and Political Development 1857–1890' Jaensch, D. (ed.), *The Flinders History of South Australia, Political History* (1986).

Jackson, T.H., *The Logic and Limits of Bankruptcy Law* (1986).

Jaensch, D., *The Flinders History of South Australia Political History* (1986).

Keay, A.R., *Insolvency: Personal and Corporate Law and Practice* (3rd ed. 1998).

Keay, A.R., *McPherson The Law of Company Liquidation* (4th ed. 1999).

Kenny P., *Taxation Law* (2004).

Kilpi, J., *The Ethics of Bankruptcy* (1998).

King, L.P., *Collier on Bankruptcy* (15th ed. 1987).

Klimek, J., *Insolvency and Environmental Liability* (1994).

Latimer, P., *2004 Australian Business Law* (23rd ed. 2004).

Lehmann, G. and Coleman, C., *Taxation Law in Australia* (2nd ed. 1991).

Leonard, E.B., *Guide to Commercial Insolvency in Canada* (1988) esp Ch 6.

Lester, V.M., *Victorian Insolvency* (1995).
Lipton, P. and Herzberg, A., *Understanding Company Law* (12th ed. 2004).
Mason, H.H. and O'Hair, J.S., *Australian Company Law* (2nd ed. 1973).
Millon, D., 'Communitarianism in Corporate Law: Foundations and Law Reform Strategies' in Mitchell, L.E. (ed.), *Progressive Corporate Law* (1995).
Milman, D., 'Priority Rights on Corporate Insolvency' in Clarke, A. (ed.), *Current Issues in Insolvency Law* (1991).
Parsons, G.T.E. and Ratford, W.F., *Tolley's Employees' Rights in Receiverships and Liquidations* (1979) esp Ch 9.
Picarda, H., *The Law Relating to Receivers, Managers and Administrators* (2nd ed. 1990).
Pilcher, N.G., Uther, A.H., and Baldock, W.J., *The Australian Companies Act Reconciled and Annotated* (1937).
Pollard, D., *Tolley's Employment and Pension Rights in Corporate Insolvency* (1994).
Rose, D., *Lewis' Australian Bankruptcy Law* (11th ed. 1999).
Ryan, M., *The Last Resort: A Study of Consumer Bankrupts* (1995).
Sharrock, R., Van Der Linde, K. and Smith, A., *Hockly's Insolvency Law* (7th ed. 2002).
Stanley, D.T., and Girth, M., *Bankruptcy Problem, Process, Reform* (1971).
Sullivan, T., Warren, E. and Westbrook, J.L., *As We Forgive Our Debtors* (1989).
Tam, H., *Communitarianism a New Agenda for Politics and Citizenship* (1997).
Tomasic, R., *Australian Corporate Insolvency Law* (1993).
Tomasic, R. and Whitford, K., *Australian Insolvency and Bankruptcy Law* (2nd ed. 1997).
Trebilcock, M., and Katz, J., 'The Law and Economics of Corporate Insolvency: A North American Perspective' in Rickett, C. (ed.), *Essays in Corporate Restructuring and Insolvency* (1996).
Vanden Driesen, I., and Fayle, R., 'History of Income Tax in Australia' in Krever, R. (ed.), *Australian Taxation: Principles and Practice* (1987).
Wishart, D., *Company Law in Context* (1994).
Wood, P.R., *Principles of International Insolvency* (1995).

Looseleaf Services

CCH, *Australian Corporations and Securities Law Reporter*, Butterworths, *Australian Corporations Law Principles and Practices Vol. 2.*
CCH, *Australian Insolvency Management Practice.*
Lamer, F.L., *Priority of Crown Claims in Insolvency* (1996).

Conference Papers

Banks, G., 'The Good, The Bad and the Ugly: Economic Perspectives on Regulation in Australia' (Address to Conference of Economists, Business Symposium, Canberra, 2 October 2003).

Barrett, M. and Botten, J., 'Environmental Risk and the Insolvency Practitioner' (Paper presented at the Insolvency Practitioners' Association of Australia South Australia and Northern Territory Division, Adelaide, 11 November 1993).

Bennetts, K.J., 'The Future of Bankruptcy – Developing Our Bankruptcy Law' (Paper presented at the Australian Bankruptcy Congress, ITSA, Sydney, 19 March 1996).

Coleman, C.F., 'The Commissioner of Taxation's Advantage Over Other Creditors on Insolvency' (Paper presented to the Australasian Law Teachers Conference 46th Annual Conference, University of Western Australia, 12 July 1991).

Cunningham, A., 'The Effect of Different Insolvency Administrations on the Contract of Employment' (Paper presented to the Insolvency and Reconstruction Committee, Business Law Section Law Council of Australia, Sydney, 19–21 October 1995) 123.

Darvas, P., 'Employees and Voluntary Administration: A Survey of the Issues (Speech delivered to the Commercial Law Association, Canberra, April 1999).

Duns, J. and Glover, J., 'The Taxation Priority: Australian Experience and International Comparisons' (Paper presented to the INSOL Academics Meeting, Cape Town, South Africa, 2 April 2004).

Manthorpe, M., 'The Employee Entitlements Support Scheme' (Paper presented to the SA & NT Insolvency Practitioners' Association Australia, Adelaide, 18 November 2000).

Noakes, D., 'Creating Constellations: Interdisciplinary Conversations on Law, Public Policy and Society' (Paper presented to conference held at University of British Columbia, Vancouver, May 1999).

Riley, J., 'Unravelling National Textiles; A Labour Lawyer's Perspective on a Company Collapse' (Paper presented to the 2000 Australian Law Teachers Association National Conference, Canberra, July 2000).

Symes, C., 'Observing the Dawn Of The Greening Of Australia's Corporate Insolvency Law: Environmental Accountability Slowly Creeping Over The Horizon' (Paper presented to the Corporate Law Teachers National Conference and included in Proceedings, Flinders University, Adelaide, February 1998).

Symes, C., 'Preferential Debts are Always Controversial and Need Justifications even for the Colonial Beneficiaries of Australia, Malaysia and Singapore' (Paper presented to the Corporate Law Teachers National Conference Proceedings, Monash University, Melbourne, February 1999).

Symes, C., 'Researching the Favourites: Statutory Priorities in Insolvency' (Paper presented to the INSOL Pacific '99 Academics Session, Auckland, February 1999).

Symes, C., 'Attacking Restructured Corporations to Protect Workers Entitlements' (Paper presented to the Australian Society of Labor Lawyers 20th National Conference, Adelaide, October 1999).

Symes, C., 'Remuneration, Rent and "Requisite" Costs: The 3 R's of Insolvency's Administrative Expense Priority' (Paper presented to the Corporate Law Teachers National Conference, University of Wollongong, Wollongong, February 2000).

Symes, C., 'Employee Entitlements; Understanding the Issues' (Address delivered at the Breakfast Seminar of the Industrial Relations Society of South Australia, Adelaide, April, 2001).

Symes, C., 'Employee Entitlements Australia's Ongoing Debate' (Paper presented to the LawFest Conference of the South Australian Law Society, Adelaide, August 2002).

Symes, C., 'Consumers and Corporate Insolvency Priorities' (Paper presented to the Flinders University, School of Law Staff Seminar Series, May 2003).

Symes, C., 'Reminiscing the Taxation Priority' (Paper presented to the 16th Annual Australasian Tax Teachers' Association Conference, Flinders University, Adelaide, January 2004).

Symes, C., 'Environmental and Other "New" Priorities' (Paper presented to the INSOL Academics Group Meeting Cape Town, April 2004).

Symes, C., 'Colonial Corporate Insolvency: [Not] a Lot to be Said' (Paper presented to the Flinders University, School of Law, Staff Seminar, October 2005).

Tyler, E.L.G., 'Has the Judge Gone Too Far? Le Pichon J and Office-Holders Remuneration' (Paper presented at the INSOL Pacific 1999 Conference Academics Forum, Auckland, New Zealand, February 1999).

Young, M., 'Protecting Workers During Receivership, Liquidation and Transmission Of Business' (Paper presented to the Unions and the Law Seminar, Trades Hall, Melbourne, 25 February 1991) 63.

Websites

Justice Ferris' Working Party on the Remuneration of Office Holders <www.open.gov.uk/lcd/civil/ferrisfr.htm>.

<www.homesite.com.au/insurance/insurance_for_building/builders_warranty>.

<www.pc.gov.au/study/building/subs/sub0039.pdf>.

<www.med.govt.nz/ri/insolvency/review/consultation/priority/priority/02.html>.

Creation of Citizen Watchdog Groups to Monitor Canadian Corporations (for individual investors), Banks, Cable TV and Telephone Companies, and Airlines.

<www.dwatch.ca/camp/actcub.htm>.

Government and Law Reform Committee Reports

Advisory Committee on Bankruptcy and Insolvency, Canada Proposed Bankruptcy Act Amendments Report of the Advisory Committee on Bankruptcy and Insolvency (Report of the. Advisory Committee on Bankruptcy and Insolvency, January 1986), Chair Prof Gary F. C. Colter. Known as "Colter Report".

Australian Law Reform Commission, General Insolvency Inquiry (Report No 45, AGPS, Canberra, 1988) Chair Ronald W Harmer. Known as 'Harmer Inquiry' and 'Harmer Report'.

Australian Law Reform Commission, Insolvency: The Regular Payment of Debt (Report No 6, AGPS, Canberra, 1977).

Australian Law Reform Commission, Debt Recovery and Insolvency (Report No 36, AGPS, Canberra, 1987).

Australian Law Reform Commission, Legal Risk in International Transactions (Report No 80, AGPS, Canberra, 1996).

Centre for International Economics, National Competition Policy Review of the National Scheme for the Regulation of Travel Agents, prepared for the Ministerial Council on Consumer Affairs (2000).

Director General of Fair Trading, The Protection of Consumer Prepayments (1986).

International Bar Association Committee J Bankruptcy Legislation Subcommittee, Task Force on Priority Claims in Insolvency Administration (Report to International Bar Association, New Orleans, 1993).

Law Reform Committee of British Columbia, Report on the Crown as Creditor: Priorities and Privileges (Report No LRC 57, Vancouver, October 1982).

Law Reform Commission of British Columbia, Report on the Buyers' Lien: A New Consumer Remedy (Report No LRC 93, Vancouver, 1987).

New Zealand Law Commission, Priority Debts in the Distribution of Insolvent Estates, An Advisory Report to Ministry of Commerce (1999).

Office of Fair Trading, Anthony I Ogus and Charles K Rowley, Prepayments and Insolvency An Occasional Paper prepared for the Office of Fair Trading (OFT, London, 1984).

Registrar of the Aboriginal Corporations Annual Report 2001–2002.

Report of the Review Committee, Insolvency Law and Practice (Review Committee, HMSO, London, June 1982) Chair Sir Kenneth Cork. Known as "Cork Report" Cmnd 8558.

Scottish Law Commission, Bankruptcy and Related Aspects of Insolvency and Liquidation, Report No 68 (1982).

The Contracts and Commercial Law Reform Committee of New Zealand, Lay-by Sales (1969).

The Law School University of Adelaide, Report to the Standing Committee of State and Commonwealth Attorneys General on the Law Relating to Consumer Credit and Money Lending (1969).

Working Party, Report to Ministers of Consumer Affairs (Ministerial Council on Consumer Affairs) on the National Competition Policy Review conducted by the Centre for International Economics, National Co-operative Scheme for the Regulation of Travel Agents (2002).

Government Publications

Australian Government Publishing Service, Explanatory Memorandum for the Corporate Law Reform Act 1992 Commonwealth.

Professional Publications

International Bar Association, Committee J, Bankruptcy Legislation Subcommittee, *Priority Claims in Insolvency Administration* (1993).

Unpublished Work

Bergmann, K.S., 'Bankruptcy, Limited Liability and CERCLA: Closing the Loophole and Parting the Veil' (2004) *University of Maryland School of Law Accepted and Working Research Paper Series No 2004-02.*

Index